Agglomeration Economics

A National Bureau
of Economic Research
Conference Report

Agglomeration Economics

Edited by **Edward L. Glaeser**

The University of Chicago Press

Chicago and London

EDWARD L. GLAESER is the Fred and Eleanor Glimp Professor of Economics at Harvard University, where he also serves as director of the Taubman Center for State and Local Government and director of the Rappaport Institute for Greater Boston. He is a research associate and director of the Urban Economics working group at the National Bureau of Economic Research.

The University of Chicago Press, Chicago 60637
The University of Chicago Press, Ltd., London

Printed and bound by CPI Group (UK) Ltd, Croydon, CR0 4YY

19 18 17 16 15 14 13 12 11 10   1 2 3 4 5
ISBN-13: 978-0-226-29789-7 (cloth)
ISBN-10: 0-226-29789-6 (cloth)

Library of Congress Cataloging-in-Publication Data

Agglomeration economics / edited by Edward L. Glaeser.
p. cm. — (National Bureau of Economic Research conference report)
Includes proceedings of the National Bureau of Economic Research conference, held in 2007.
Includes bibliographical references and index.
ISBN-13: 978-0-226-29789-7 (alk. paper)
ISBN-10: 0-226-29789-6 (alk. paper)
1. Industrial clusters—Congresses. 2. Industrial location—Congresses. 3. Business networks—Congresses. 4. Regional economics—Congresses. 5. Space in economics—Congresses. I. Glaeser, Edward L. (Edward Ludwig), 1967– II. Series: National Bureau of Economic Research conference report.
HC79.D5A33 2010
338.8'7—dc22

2009025777

♾ The paper used in this publication meets the minimum requirements of the American National Standard for Information Sciences—Permanence of Paper for Printed Library Materials, ANSI Z39.48-1992.

Relation of the Directors to the Work and Publications of the National Bureau of Economic Research

1. The object of the NBER is to ascertain and present to the economics profession, and to the public more generally, important economic facts and their interpretation in a scientific manner without policy recommendations. The Board of Directors is charged with the responsibility of ensuring that the work of the NBER is carried on in strict conformity with this object.

2. The President shall establish an internal review process to ensure that book manuscripts proposed for publication DO NOT contain policy recommendations. This shall apply both to the proceedings of conferences and to manuscripts by a single author or by one or more co-authors but shall not apply to authors of comments at NBER conferences who are not NBER affiliates.

3. No book manuscript reporting research shall be published by the NBER until the President has sent to each member of the Board a notice that a manuscript is recommended for publication and that in the President's opinion it is suitable for publication in accordance with the above principles of the NBER. Such notification will include a table of contents and an abstract or summary of the manuscript's content, a list of contributors if applicable, and a response form for use by Directors who desire a copy of the manuscript for review. Each manuscript shall contain a summary drawing attention to the nature and treatment of the problem studied and the main conclusions reached.

4. No volume shall be published until forty-five days have elapsed from the above notification of intention to publish it. During this period a copy shall be sent to any Director requesting it, and if any Director objects to publication on the grounds that the manuscript contains policy recommendations, the objection will be presented to the author(s) or editor(s). In case of dispute, all members of the Board shall be notified, and the President shall appoint an ad hoc committee of the Board to decide the matter; thirty days additional shall be granted for this purpose.

5. The President shall present annually to the Board a report describing the internal manuscript review process, any objections made by Directors before publication or by anyone after publication, any disputes about such matters, and how they were handled.

6. Publications of the NBER issued for informational purposes concerning the work of the Bureau, or issued to inform the public of the activities at the Bureau, including but not limited to the NBER Digest and Reporter, shall be consistent with the object stated in paragraph 1. They shall contain a specific disclaimer noting that they have not passed through the review procedures required in this resolution. The Executive Committee of the Board is charged with the review of all such publications from time to time.

7. NBER working papers and manuscripts distributed on the Bureau's web site are not deemed to be publications for the purpose of this resolution, but they shall be consistent with the object stated in paragraph 1. Working papers shall contain a specific disclaimer noting that they have not passed through the review procedures required in this resolution. The NBER's web site shall contain a similar disclaimer. The President shall establish an internal review process to ensure that the working papers and the web site do not contain policy recommendations, and shall report annually to the Board on this process and any concerns raised in connection with it.

8. Unless otherwise determined by the Board or exempted by the terms of paragraphs 6 and 7, a copy of this resolution shall be printed in each NBER publication as described in paragraph 2 above.

Contents

Acknowledgments

This book was funded by both the National Bureau of Economic Research and the Taubman Center for State and Local Government. We are grateful to Martin Feldstein for his unflinching support of the urban working group. The Taubman Center support is the result of the generosity of A. Alfred Taubman, a man who knows much about cities and the magic of agglomeration.

The staff at the National Bureau were, as usual, unfailingly excellent. Carl Beck and the conference department arranged the two meetings that led to this book. Helena Fitz-Patrick shepherded the volume through the production process, and at the Taubman Center, Erin Dea did a terrific job organizing the editorial process.

Introduction

Edward L. Glaeser

Agglomeration economies are the benefits that come when firms and people locate near one another together in cities and industrial clusters. These benefits all ultimately come from transport costs savings: the only real difference between a nearby firm and one across the continent is that it is easier to connect with a neighbor. Of course, transportation costs must be interpreted broadly, and they include the difficulties in exchanging goods, people, and ideas. The connection between agglomeration economies and transport costs would seem to suggest that agglomerations should become less important, as transportation and communication costs have fallen. Yet, a central paradox of our time is that in cities, industrial agglomerations remain remarkably vital, despite ever easier movement of goods and knowledge across space.

Declining transport costs have facilitated trade between China, India, and the rest of the world, but within those countries, development has centered in urban areas. Across the world, urbanization continues to increase, and the United Nations reports that by the end of 2008, one-half of the world will live in cities.[1] Indeed, megacities have become the gateways between those developing countries and the developed world. Within the richer nations of the West, many cities, like New York and London, have experienced remarkable comebacks since the dire days of the 1970s. Wages, population, and especially housing prices in many dense centers have experienced robust growth. Indices of industrial agglomeration show only a slight decrease in concentration over the last thirty years (Dumais, Ellison, and Glaeser

Edward L. Glaeser is the Fred and Eleanor Glimp Professor of Economics at Harvard University, and a research associate and director of the Urban Economics working group at the National Bureau of Economic Research.

1. http://www.un.org/esa/population/meetings/EGM_PopDist/EGM_PopDist_Report.pdf.

2002). If transport costs are so low, then why has the urge to agglomerate remained so strong?

This volume collects eleven chapters on the economics of agglomeration. They cover far-ranging topics, from the productivity of hospitals to the location of fast food joints, yet they are all joined by a common goal of seeking to understand why economic activity clusters together. Making sense of this clustering is the crucial step in understanding the present and future economics of place. All of these chapters approach agglomeration economies from different angles, but taken together, the volume is meant to provide a sample of cutting-edge work on the economics of agglomeration.

While the chapters in the volume are far ranging, they focus on the agglomeration of people within countries. Researchers such as Paul Krugman, Tony Venables, and Gordon Hanson have produced much knowledge about the links between agglomeration and international trade. Other research has focused on agglomeration economies within specific manufacturing industries in an attempt to understand why some cities specialize in specific sectors. There is also nothing here on agglomeration economies in the developing world. While these topics are extremely important, the limited space available in one volume precluded their inclusion here.

Measuring Agglomeration: Prices, Wages, Quantities

Urban economists infer urban success from high local wages, robust real estate prices, and growth in the number of people within an area. If a place is doing well, then employers should be willing to pay more for workers in that area, people should be willing to pay more for access to that place, and more people should move to that area. The first three chapters in the volume separately consider these three different measures of local economic well-being.

Over the last forty-five years, the spatial equilibrium has been the primary tool for urban and regional economists trying to make sense of cities. The logic of the spatial equilibrium is that since people can move freely within a nation, they must be indifferent between different locales. This indifference implies that high wages must be offset by high prices or low amenities; otherwise, people would flock to high-wage areas. High housing prices reflect high wages, high amenities, or both.

However, the spatial equilibrium concept only gives us one-half of the labor market equilibrium that determines area wages. The other half is labor demand—the willingness of firms to pay for their workers. So, while high wages must reflect something bad about an area, like high prices or poor amenities, high wages must also reflect something good about an area that makes firms willing to tolerate a high cost of labor. Firms wouldn't continue to locate to New York City or the San Francisco Bay region unless those areas were productive enough to offset the cost of expensive workers.

Neoclassical economics tells us that wages reflect the marginal product of labor. In a standard Cobb-Douglas formulation of the producer's problem, where most capital is mobile, the high marginal product of labor in a given area must either reflect a high productivity level or an abundance of nontraded capital inputs to production. Wages, therefore, can be interpreted as telling us about the core determinants of urban productivity, and high wages in an area are usually interpreted as meaning that the area is unusually productive.

One of the facts that supports the existence of agglomeration economies is the strong relationship between density and high wages. This fact is mirrored in the strong relationship between area density and per capita gross metropolitan product (GMP) shown in figure 1. This fact is quite statistically robust, but the causal chain in the relationship is difficult to infer. Does the density-productivity relationship mean that the dense places become more productive or that productive places attract more people? The need to tease out the direction of causality in this relationship motivates the first chapter in this volume, on agglomeration in France, written by Pierre-Philippe Combes, Gilles Duranton, Laurent Gobillon, and Sébastien Roux.

Their chapter looks at the connection between density and both wages and total factor productivity in France. They start by confirming the existence of a strong, robust relationship between density and both wages and productivity in France. This fact parallels the well-known density-productivity relationship in the United States (Ciccone and Hall 1996). They then consider two challenges in interpreting this fact as evidence for agglomeration economies. One possibility is that dense places are more productive because they attract more skilled workers. Glaeser and Mare (2001) find little evi-

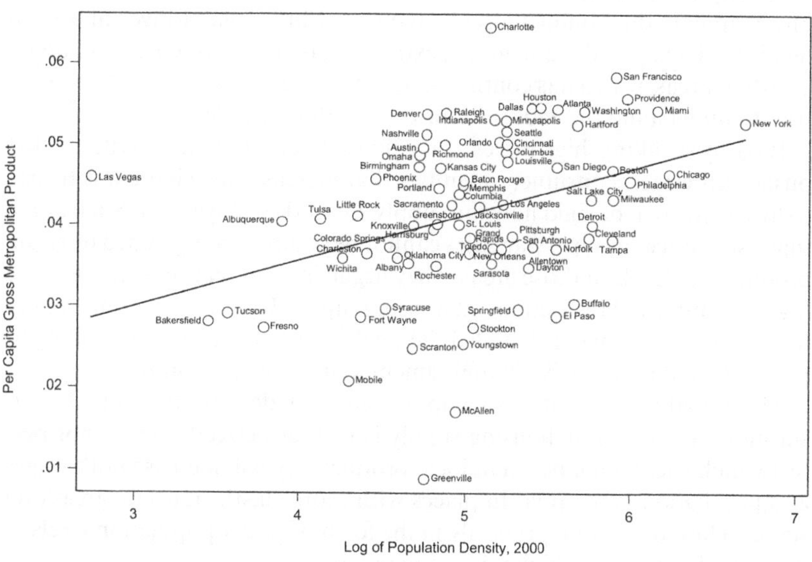

Fig. 1 Area density and per capita GMP

dence that this is the case in U.S. cities, but the selection of the skilled into cities seems to be much stronger in France. They use an individual fixed effects approach and find that allowing for individual fixed effects reduces the estimated impact of density on wages by about one-third.

Their second contribution is to use a wide range of historical and geological instruments for current density levels. Population patterns in France are remarkably permanent. The density of districts in France today is highly correlated with density 170 years ago and with basic features of the soil. Their instrumental variables estimates are generally quite close to estimates found using ordinary least squares. As long as we believe that these instruments are not independently correlated with productivity today, then this provides evidence for strong agglomeration economies. If readers doubt that this orthogonality condition holds, then their results at least provide a striking set of facts about the correlation between geology and prosperity.

Real estate prices provide a second means of assessing the success of an area. One sign that agglomeration has been doing well over the last twenty-five years is that housing prices have risen more dramatically in dense metropolitan areas. Figure 2 shows the 0.42 percent correlation between density in 1980 and price growth between 1980 and 2006 (calculated using the Office of Federal Housing Enterprise Oversight repeat sales index). The spatial equilibrium framework suggests that this fact can either mean that dense places have become more pleasant over time or that dense places have become more productive.

But the growth in housing prices has not been uniformly experienced across all metropolitan areas. Some places, like San Francisco and New York City, have been christened "superstar cities" by the authors of the second chapter in this volume: Joseph Gyourko, Christopher Mayer, and Todd Sinai. Their chapter documents the extraordinary price growth of a small set of urban areas, which has continued decade by decade since 1940, and then tries to understand the causes for price growth in these areas.

Broadly speaking, high prices in a region can reflect economic vitality that pushes up wages, consumer amenities that increase the willingness to pay to live in an area, or rigid housing supply. Gyourko, Mayer, and Sinai argue that rising prices in superstar cities cannot be completely explained by rising productivity levels in those areas. They argue instead that these places have high amenities and restrictions on housing supply. Rising levels of inequality in the country as a whole have led the wealthiest Americans to be willing to pay more and more to live in high-amenity areas of the country.

The growth of population or employment provides a third means of measuring local success. If housing supply is neither perfectly elastic nor perfectly inelastic, then a boom in local productivity will increase both wages and population in an area. In places with more elastic housing, area-level success should show up primarily in the form of larger population levels—not in higher wages or higher housing prices.

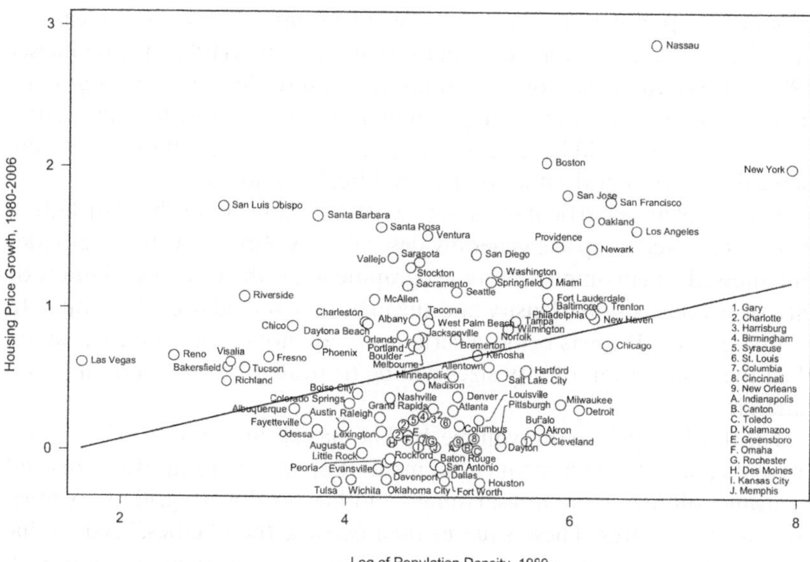

Fig. 2 Population density and housing price growth

The concentration of people and industries has long been seen by economists as evidence for the existence of agglomeration economies. After all, why would so many people suffer the inconvenience of crowding into the island of Manhattan if there weren't also advantages from being close to so much economic activity? However, there is a debate about interpreting the concentration of people and firms, just as there is about interpreting the connection between density and productivity. People and firms might be clustering because of some innate advantage possessed by a particular spot of earth, not just because of agglomeration economies. Indeed, in the nineteenth century, some of Manhattan's mass appeal may well have reflected the natural advantages bestowed by its remarkable port.

Today, it is harder to believe that industrial and urban clusters reflect natural advantage rather than agglomeration economies. The statistical work that has tried to assess the importance of natural advantage to geographic concentration finds that only about one-quarter of industrial concentration can be explained by observable sources of natural advantage (Ellison and Glaeser 1999). But all of the work measuring the clustering of population has tended to measure agglomerations based on political boundaries. These political boundaries are often drawn around existing agglomerations, and this creates an inherent bias in using political borders.

If political boundaries are drawn in a way that reflects existing population patterns, then we might think that we observe agglomerations of activity, even when there is no innate tendency for clustering. Even a random distribution of population across space will be lumpy. While some measures of industrial concentration correct for that lumpiness (Ellison and Glaeser 1997), standard corrections for lumpiness can do little if the geographic units are drawn around the lumps. In many cases, the statistical properties of spatial areas would be far easier to understand if geographic areas were defined by a fixed grid rather than by political boundaries.

This problem is particularly severe when thinking about the distribution of city sizes across space, generally described by Zipf's law. If larger cities are allowed to encompass more geographic area, then the distribution of city sizes reflects both density and the arbitrary boundaries that adjust to fit that density. If areas below a certain size are not considered cities at all, then the distribution of city sizes will be truncated below a certain population level.

The third chapter in this volume, by Thomas Holmes and Sanghoon Lee, presents a new take on the measurement of spatial concentration. Instead of using political boundaries, Holmes and Lee lay down a grid of six-mile-by-six-mile squares. These squares then become their "cities," geographic areas that are truly random. While they focus on using their grid approach to revisit the topic of Zipf's law, this type of approach could be valuable in many other settings. For example, it would be useful to measure industrial concentration using their thirty-six mile squares instead of counties or to look at population growth regressions using their natural geographic areas instead of counties or political cities.

Holmes and Lee have a number of striking findings. Cities and metropolitan areas follow a Zipf distribution, where there is always a greater density of smaller cities. However, the left tail of the distribution of squares looks much more bell-shaped and normal. For example, there are about twice as many squares with two people than there are with one person. In low-density areas, the political definitions of units seem to be driving the received wisdom about the size distribution of cities.

In high-density areas, Holmes and Lee find a kink in the distribution of population around 50,000 people. Above that point, the number of really populous places falls much more radically than Zipf's law suggests. While Zipf's law suggests that the coefficient between rank and population size is 1, they find a coefficient of 2 among their high-density squares, which means that rank rises more quickly than population.

Gabaix (1999) connects Zipf's law with Gibrat's law. He finds that if places grow proportionally, then the distribution of place populations should follow Zipf's law. Since Holmes and Lee find that their squares do not follow Zipf's law, we shouldn't be surprised that they also find that Gibrat's law fails for their thirty-six mile squares. They find that growth rates are much lower among places that start with more people, which perhaps explains the absence of ultra-high population areas. Their results can be taken to suggest that some form of congestion sets in at ultra-high densities.

The Sources of Agglomeration: The Costs of Moving People

Understanding agglomeration economies requires us to move beyond measuring the overall extent of agglomeration as revealed by housing prices, productivity, and population concentration. We must also understand the exact mechanisms that make it more productive to cluster. While all agglomeration economies can be understood as consequences of reduced transport costs, the nature of the agglomeration economy will depend on what transport costs are being reduced. For example, the classic Krugman (1991) model of agglomeration emphasized agglomeration benefits that come from reducing the costs of moving goods over space. When an input supplier locates next to a final goods producer, these firms become more productive by saving the costs of shipping the input.

None of the chapters in this volume focus on agglomeration economies that come from reducing the costs of moving goods over space, perhaps because researchers have reached a consensus that such agglomeration economies are now relatively second order. A century or more ago, when shipping goods was expensive, cities like Chicago and New York formed around ports and rail yards. Over the twentieth century, the cost of moving goods declined enormously, and few modern agglomerations seem built on the easy movement of physical output. Today, the bulk of urban growth, at least in the United States, appears to be in far-flung places that seem to have little advantage in the shipment of goods. There is some evidence that manufacturing firms still cluster near suppliers and customers, but even this clustering seems relatively weak (Dumais, Ellison, and Glaeser 2002).

While the costs of moving goods may have declined dramatically, the cost of moving people is still high. After all, time is a major input into human travel, and the value of time continues to rise as people become more productive. Even if changes in transportation technology make it possible to locate goods production anywhere in the world, there will still be an advantage from clusters that minimize the costs of moving people across space. This volume has three chapters that look at different types of agglomeration economies that come from reducing the costs of moving people.

Chapter 4 by Henry Overman and Diego Puga examines labor market pooling—an idea whose pedigree stretches back to Alfred Marshall. The basic concept is that if there are many employers within an area, then workers can change employers without changing residences. Job hopping creates advantages if workers don't know where they will be most productive or if the productivity of different firms changes over time. Labor market pooling allows labor to be more efficiently allocated following productivity shocks, because workers can leave firms that have become less productive and move to employers that have become relatively more productive.

Krugman (1991) provided a simple and elegant model of labor market pooling that illustrates its basic mechanism. Overman and Puga's model extends the Krugman model to multiple sectors and multiple locations. This extension is important because it generates predictions about which types of firms will colocate with one another and what types of colocation will generate the biggest benefits. A key result is that the agglomeration benefits are biggest when the sectors have shocks that are heterogeneous so that their shocks are particularly uncorrelated. This result, of course, requires that the sectors are still similar enough so that workers can move across them.

To test this implication empirically, Overman and Puga look across sectors within the United Kingdom. They calculate a measure of the benefits of labor market pooling by estimating the extent to which different plants within a sector seem to have idiosyncratic employment shocks. Presumably, workers can always move across plants within an industrial sector, and sectors with more plant-level employment variation would seem to be sectors with more shocks to plant-level productivity. They find that sectors with more plant-level employment shocks are more geographically concentrated. While one can reasonably worry whether greater geographic concentration within a sector is partially responsible for greater plant-level variation in employment, that reverse causality should also be seen as a prediction of a labor market pooling model. This chapter is one of the few papers that attempt to test this important, century-old idea.

The next two chapters examine a simpler agglomeration mechanism that still stems from the benefits that come from reducing transport costs for people. Service industries can almost be defined as sectors that require person-to-person delivery. While this statement may be too strong, there is no doubt that services involve a lot more face-to-face contact than manufacturing. As a result, when service industries cluster near customers, they reduce the travel costs, either for their customers or for their workers. The continuing importance of transport costs for people may explain why services have remained urbanized, even as manufacturing has fled to lower-density settings.

Chapter 5 by Jed Kolko provides a sweeping view of agglomeration and urbanization in the service sector. Services are less agglomerated but more urbanized than manufacturing. City streets are a good setting for services, because they enable service providers to readily link with large numbers of their diverse customers. The higher transport costs involved in face-to-face delivery tie services to dense urban areas. Across services, Kolko finds a positive relationship between urbanization and concentration. The services that are most likely to benefit from connections to diverse urban populations are also most likely to concentrate. Perhaps these are the sectors with the highest transport costs.

Across service industries, human capital strongly predicts urbanization. As chapter 10 by Glaeser and Ponzetto emphasizes, cities seem to be particularly important for the transmission of ideas. Selling services directly to consumers also predicts location in big cities, while intensive use of natural resources is negatively associated with urbanization. The use of specialized occupations is positively associated with both urbanization and agglomeration, perhaps because the benefits of labor market pooling are higher for such specialized workers who cannot readily just take up another task.

Kolko also studies coagglomeration—the tendency of industries to colocate with other industries. He finds a strong tendency of service industries to locate near their suppliers and customers. This result contrasts with the much weaker links between customers and suppliers found in manufacturing (Dumais, Ellison, and Glaeser 2002). Since the costs of delivering services are much higher than the costs of delivering goods, it is reassuring that location patterns seem aimed at reducing those costs.

Chapter 6 by Waldfogel continues the examination of the impact of transport costs, but it focuses on retail establishments. Since these establishments require visits by customers, we would expect them to be located near those customers. Waldfogel finds a strong pattern where retail establishment sectors locate near demographic groups that regularly buy from that sector. Stores catering to the well educated locate near the well educated. While the basic effect may be unsurprising, the measured magnitude of the tendency to locate near likely buyers is remarkably strong.

Waldfogel then suggests that the locational tendency of retail shops provides an added benefit to demographic clustering. If a family is more likely to have access to stores that meet its needs if it locates near similar families, then this provides a good reason for neighborhood homogeneity. This mechanism is a consumption-related agglomeration effect, where locating near similar people increases one's ability to shop efficiently.

The Sources of Agglomeration: Knowledge Spillovers

Many recent papers on agglomeration economies have followed Marshall and Jane Jacobs and have emphasized the role that cities can play in speeding the flow of ideas. The core idea at the center of information-based agglomeration economies is that all of our knowledge builds on things that we learn from people around us. The central premise is that the presence of knowledgeable neighbors enables an apprentice steelworker to learn his craft, but it also makes a biotechnology researcher more innovative. The interaction of smart people in urban areas both enhances the development of person-specific human capital and increases the rate at which new ideas are formed.

In chapter 7, Katherine Baicker and Amitabh Chandra look at the diffusion of high-quality health care in hospitals. They argue that there are a number of low-cost procedures that significantly improve health outcomes and that those procedures should be used universally. When hospitals fail to use these procedures, Baicker and Chandra argue that the hospital is being less productive. One significant contribution of this chapter is to show the diversity in this productivity measure across space. In many cases, the hospitals that have high quality, using their metric, are not the same hospitals that spend more per patient.

Baicker and Chandra illustrate the remarkable heterogeneity across metropolitan areas in hospital productivity, which seems comparable to the diversity in productivity overall. However, in the case of Baicker and Chandra's measures, higher productivity doesn't require any more physical capital but just enough human capital to use these low-cost, high-value procedures. They find that areas with more nongovernment doctors and a higher overall skill base are more likely to deliver higher-quality health care, which again supports the view that local human capital matters for productivity.

They also specifically test a learning model by regressing the quality of a hospital on the lagged quality of that hospital's geographic neighbors and the hospital's own lagged quality level. Hospitals that are surrounded by higher-quality hospitals tend to improve in quality. One interpretation of these results is that doctors in one hospital learn how to practice better medicine by interacting with doctors in nearby hospitals. If this is the case, then the flow of ideas across people in metropolitan areas is actually saving lives.

Chapter 8 by William Kerr looks at intellectual connections among inventors. His chapter shows that American patents are increasingly being given to inventors with non-European last names. Patents are also increasingly geographically concentrated. Kerr connects these two facts and shows that the increasing geographic concentration of inventive activity is associated with the tendency of ethnic inventors to cluster in a few metropolitan areas. This clustering of ethnic inventors can explain a significant amount of the increased clustering of patents.

Why do ethnic inventors cluster in a small number of geographic areas? One possibility is that these inventors are intellectually linked, and geographic proximity allows those links to flourish. An alternative explanation is that different immigrant groups cluster in different cities to enjoy consumption-related advantages, such as access to religious organizations or relevant consumer goods, or just to friends with a similar background. Hopefully, future work will sort out the different explanations of the remarkable concentration of ethnic inventors.

Chapter 9 by Stuart Rosenthal and William Strange offers a third approach to invention and entrepreneurship in urban areas. Almost fifty years ago, Ben Chinitz (1961) argued that one of the reasons why New York was more dynamic than Pittsburgh was that New York had abundant small enterprises, while Pittsburgh was concentrated in a few large businesses. Abundant small enterprises facilitated a culture of entrepreneurship, because those smaller firms needed independent input providers who could also provide inputs for other start-ups. Likewise, more small firms might mean more independent customers, and these could provide a ready market for start-ups.

If small firms are less able to protect their ideas, then new innovations might spread more easily in places with lots of little employers.

Rosenthal and Strange find that the amount of new establishment formation in an area is tightly linked to the number of small firms. Employment in big firms doesn't predict these start-ups. Employment in small firms does. Their research is done at the census tract level, so they are looking at very small geographic areas, and within these areas, there seems to be a strong tendency of new firms to locate where there are already many small establishments.

The penultimate chapter in the volume is more of a theoretical chapter on the interaction between intellectual spillovers and communication and transportation costs. I began this introduction with the seeming paradox that many cities are more vital than ever, despite the fact that declining transportation and communication costs would seem to be making proximity obsolete. Chapter 10 by Edward Glaeser and Giacomo Ponzetto tries to make sense of those two facts.

The model assumes that there are three sectors in the economy: an innovative sector that produces new ideas, a manufacturing sector that makes goods, and a sector that directly uses natural resources (like farming). All three sectors receive advantages from urban areas, and all three sectors use land. The sectors are ordered so that the innovative sector receives the biggest benefits from urban location because of idea spillovers, and the natural resource sector gets the least out of being in a city. The natural resource sector, however, uses the most land, and the innovative sector needs the least. This ordering means that the innovative sector is always urbanized, and under some conditions, it is the manufacturing sector that will be on the margin between urban and nonurban locations.

The authors model an increase in communication and transportation costs as improving the productivity in the nonurban area, relative to the city, in all three sectors. This has the effect of moving the manufacturing sector out of the city and also of making the manufacturing sector more productive. As manufacturing becomes more productive, the returns to ideas increases, and this increases the size of the innovative sector in the city. In one version of the model, improvements in transportation and communication costs cause the decline of cities that specialize in manufacturing, like Detroit, and the rise of cities that specialize in innovation, like New York.

This model does appear to fit some of the recent facts about urban change. In the 1960s, almost all cities specialized in manufacturing. The ability to produce goods more cheaply outside of cities caused almost all of those places to do poorly in the 1970s. However, since then, cities with abundant human capital that specialized in innovation have done exceedingly well. In many cases, these places are coming up with new ideas that will then be produced in low-cost areas throughout the world. This chapter suggests that globalization seems likely to be good for cities that continue to specialize in the production of innovation, but it will continue to mean decline for manufacturing areas.

A Congestion Cost: Pollution and Cities

Density is not without its costs. Not only is land more expensive in urban areas, but congestion, pollution, and social problems often accompany the crowding of people into cities. The last chapter in this volume, by Matthew Kahn, reviews these costs of urban density and their trends over time.

Kahn presents an intensive look at commute times by distance to the city center. He distinguishes between big and small metropolitan areas, and he compares the years 1980 and 2000. In most metropolitan areas, commute times rise monotonically with distance to the city center, but in the largest metropolitan areas (New York, Los Angeles, Chicago), there is a nonmonotonic relationship between distance to the city center and commute times. In those largest areas, people who are far from the city center aren't commuting downtown at all. In all areas at all distances from the city center, commute times have been rising. Higher levels of congestion mean that the speed of travel has slowed significantly. Those speeds are slowest in big metropolitan areas, and this congestion is one of the big costs of living in a large metropolitan area.

While commuting costs are rising, the pollution problems of big cities appear to have been falling over the last twenty-five years. Kahn links this decline to the exodus of manufacturing from big cities, but cleaner big-city air also reflects the rise of catalytic converters and the lower levels of car emissions. Crime rates have also been falling in big cities over the past twelve years. While big cities bore the brunt of the national crime increase between 1960 and 1975, big cities have also seen the biggest drops in crime rates since their peak in the early 1990s. One possible explanation for this phenomenon is that big cities, like New York, have experienced the greatest improvements in policing quality.

Overall, Kahn's chapter suggests a mixed picture. Congestion is getting worse, but pollution and crime are getting better. One possible interpretation of these facts is that new technologies, whether used by automobile manufacturers or police departments, have been more effective in fighting pollution and crime than in reducing congestion.

Agglomeration Economies and Public Policy

None of the chapters offer any specific public policy proposals, but research on agglomeration economies should be of interest to both local and national policymakers. For example, if concentrations of skilled workers increase local productivity or growth, then attracting or educating more skilled workers may appeal to local politicians interested in boosting incomes or city populations. If agglomeration economies mean that cities become wealthier once they reach a certain scale, then city planners might want to permit enough housing to expand to that scale.

The existence of agglomeration economies can imply different things for local and national policymakers. For example, if moving skilled people from New York to Detroit makes Detroit richer, then it is easy to imagine that Detroit policymakers would find policies that achieved that goal attractive. It is, however, harder to imagine that national policymakers, or policymakers representing New York, would see an advantage in redistributing talent between these two cities.

In general, the existence of agglomeration economies does not itself give guidance about optimal regional policy. For example, advocates of London's Crossrail system emphasized that increasing commuter access to the city would bring in more workers who might generate agglomeration economies. However, those workers would presumably be coming from somewhere else. Any gains to London might be offset by reductions in agglomeration economies elsewhere. The existence of agglomeration economies does not itself suggest moving people from less-dense to denser areas, because as long as people remain in the less-dense areas, their productivity will fall with the move.

Questions of regional policy often require more than just a general sense that agglomeration economies exist. Instead, policymakers would presumably be interested in whether agglomeration economies are stronger in some areas than others. In particular, the agglomeration economy case for policies like Crossrail that enhance larger cities often rests on the existence of nonlinearities, such that agglomeration economies get stronger as cities grow. Despite the century or so of research on agglomeration economies, we are still far from having reliable estimates of such nonlinearities.

Directions for Future Research

The measurement of such nonlinearities is only one of the pressing topics for future research in this area. The chapters in this volume point to two major lines of research. One area, suggested by the Combes, Duranton, Gobillon, and Roux chapter, is to focus on providing better estimates of overall agglomeration effects. After all, these overall effects are a necessary parameter in many policy puzzles. However, estimating these effects will requires solving a thorny identification problem.

The basic problem with estimating agglomeration effects on productivity is that population density is not itself exogenous. People move to places that are more productive. To solve this problem, researchers need sources of variation that are unrelated to productivity. Some amenities or quirks of housing supply might provide tools for estimating the impact of increasing population on productivity. Historical population levels are somewhat more difficult to use, because they are correlated both with historic productivity and with productivity-enhancing investments made over time.

The second line of research on agglomeration economies is to focus on particular industries or elements in overall agglomeration effects. In this volume, the chapters by Baicker and Chandra, Kahn, and Kolko all illustrate this approach. The disadvantage with this approach is that it will not tell us about overall agglomeration effects, and overall effects may be an important component of policy discussion. The advantage is that these more focused studies allow for better identification. As usual, there is a trade-off between the size of the question and the precision of the answer.

More focused studies offer more precision, because it is possible to believe that the outcome variables do not directly determine the level of population or employment concentration. For example, productivity certainly attracts population, which makes it hard to use the cross-sectional relationship between density and productivity to assess agglomeration effects. More specific outcomes, like local traffic congestion, are less likely to drive population patterns, and as a result, the identification problems are less difficult.

This volume is meant to give a sample of the exciting work that is being done to understand the mysteries of agglomeration. Big cities are more productive for many reasons, but they also have their costs. Indeed, if they didn't, then everyone would live in one. These chapters are by no means the last word on agglomeration economies, but they do illustrate the wide range of exciting work that is being done by economists in this area.

References

Chinitz, B. 1961. Contrasts in agglomeration: New York and Pittsburgh. *American Economic Review* 51 (2): 279–89.

Ciccone, A., and R. E. Hall. 1996. Productivity and the density of economic activity. *American Economic Review* 86 (1): 54–70.

Dumais, G., G. Ellison, and E. Glaeser. 2002. Geographic concentration as a dynamic process. *Review of Economics and Statistics* 84 (2): 193–204.

Ellison, G., and E. Glaeser. 1997. Geographic concentration in U.S. manufacturing industries: A dartboard approach. *Journal of Political Economy* 105 (5): 889–927.

———. 1999. The geographic concentration of industry: Does natural advantage explain agglomeration? *American Economic Review* 89 (2): 311–16.

Gabaix, X. 1999. Zipf's law and the growth of cities. *American Economic Review* 89 (2): 129–32.

Krugman, P. 1991. *Geography and trade.* Cambridge, MA: MIT Press.

Mare, C., and E. Glaeser. 2001. Cities and skills. *Journal of Labor Economics* 19 (2): 316–42.

1

Estimating Agglomeration Economies with History, Geology, and Worker Effects

Pierre-Philippe Combes, Gilles Duranton, Laurent Gobillon, and Sébastien Roux

1.1 Introduction

Productivity and wages are higher in larger cities and denser areas. This fact was first noted by Adam Smith (1776) and Alfred Marshall (1890) and has been confirmed by the modern empirical literature on this topic (see Rosenthal and Strange [2004] for a review). The measured elasticity of local productivity with respect to employment density is typically between 0.04 and 0.10. We confirm this on French data. Panel A of figure 1.1 plots mean log wages against employment density over 1976 to 1996 for 306 French employment areas. The measured density elasticity of wages is 0.05. Panel B of figure 1.1 conducts a similar exercise using log of total factor productivity (TFP) for the same 306 employment areas over 1994 to 2002. The measured density elasticity of TFP is 0.04.

To draw inference from figure 1.1, two fundamental identification prob-

Pierre-Philippe Combes is a CNRS research professor at GREQAM, University of Aix-Marseille, and a fellow at the Centre for Economic Policy Research (CEPR). Gilles Duranton is professor of economics at the University of Toronto, where he holds the Noranda Chair in Economics and International Trade. He is also a fellow at the CEPR. Laurent Gobillon is a researcher at the Institut National d'Études Démographiques (French Institute of Demographics), an associate researcher at CREST, Paris, and at the Paris School of Economics—INRA, and a research affiliate of the CEPR. Sébastien Roux is a researcher at the Centre de Recherche en Économie et Statistique (CREST) and an associate researcher at the Paris School of Economics—INRA.

We are grateful to Alejandra Castrodad for superb research assistance with the GIS work and to France Guérin-Pace for providing us with historical data for French municipalities. Thanks also to Jason Faberman, Megan MacGarvie, Stuart Rosenthal, Will Strange, AEA, NARSA, and NBER conference participants, and more particularly to the editor, Ed Glaeser. Financial support from the Centre National de la Recherche Scientifique (Combes) and from the Canadian Social Science and Humanities Research Council (Duranton) is gratefully acknowledged.

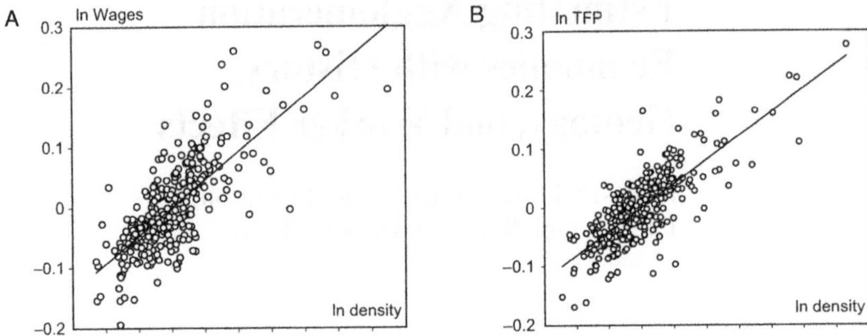

Fig. 1.1 Productivity and employment density in France: *A*, wages and employment density (306 employment areas, 1976 to 1996 average); *B*, TFP (Olley-Pakes) and employment density (306 employment areas, 1994 to 2002 average)

Source: DADS, BRN, RSI, SIREN, and authors' calculations.

Note: All variables are centered around their mean. The R^2 is 56 percent in panel A and 61 percent in panel B. See the rest of the chapter for the details of the calculations.

lems must be dealt with. First, density and measures of productivity (wage or TFP) may be simultaneously determined. This could happen because more productive places tend to attract more workers and as a result become denser. An alternative explanation, albeit equivalent from an econometric perspective, is that there may be a missing local variable that is correlated with both density and productivity. We refer to this issue as the "endogenous quantity of labor" problem. Since Ciccone and Hall (1996), a standard way to tackle this problem has been to use instrumental variables (IV).

The second major identification problem is that more productive workers may sort into denser areas. This may occur for a variety of reasons. For instance, skilled workers may have a stronger preference for high density, perhaps because density leads to better cultural amenities. Alternatively, the productivity benefits of high density may be stronger for skilled workers. These explanations suggest that it is not only density that we expect to be simultaneously determined with productivity but also the characteristics of the local workforce. To make matters worse, we expect characteristics that are not usually observed by the statistician, such as ambition or work discipline, to matter and to be spatially unevenly distributed. For instance, French university professors may have similar observable characteristics everywhere, but a disproportionate fraction of the better ones are working in or around Paris. We refer to this problem as the "endogenous quality of labor" problem. Since Glaeser and Maré (2001), a standard way to tackle this problem has been to use the longitudinal dimension of the data.

One may also be concerned that density affects productivity in a myriad of ways, directly and indirectly (see Duranton and Puga [2004] for a review). Denser markets allow for a more efficient *sharing* of indivisible facilities (e.g., local infrastructure), risks, and the gains from variety and specialization. Next, denser markets also allow for a better *matching* between employers and employees, buyers and suppliers, partners in joint projects, or entrepreneurs and financiers. This can occur through both a higher probability of finding a match and a better quality of matches when they occur. Finally, denser markets can facilitate *learning* about new technologies, market evolutions, or new forms of organization. Some of these mechanisms (e.g., matching) may have instantaneous effects, while others (e.g., learning) may take time to materialize.[1]

Our chapter addresses the issues of endogenous quantity and endogenous quality of labor. We do not attempt to distinguish between the different channels through which density could affect productivity and only aim at estimating a total net effect of density on wages. To deal with the endogenous quantity of labor problem, we take an IV approach, using both history and geology as sources of exogenous variation for population. To deal with the endogenous quantity of labor problem, we proceed as in Combes, Duranton, and Gobillon (2008) and use the longitudinal dimension of extremely rich wage data. We impose individual fixed effects and local time-varying fixed effects in a wage regression. This allows us to separate local from individual effects and to reconstruct some local wages net of individual observed and unobserved effects. Note that both approaches are necessary to identify the effect of density on productivity. Neither approach on its own would be sufficient.

Our main results are the following. The raw elasticity of mean wages to density is slightly below 0.05. Controlling only for the endogenous quantity of labor bias lowers this estimate to around 0.04. Historical and geological instruments lead to roughly the same answer. Controlling only for the endogenous quality of labor bias yields an even lower density elasticity of 0.033. Controlling for both source of biases leads to a coefficient of 0.027. When we also control for the fact that agglomeration economies spill over the spatial units boundaries, our preferred estimate for the elasticity of wages to local density stands at 0.02. These results are broadly confirmed when we use an alternative measure of productivity, TFP, rather than wages.

We draw a number of conclusions from this work. First, even though we control for two major sources of bias, we still find evidence of small but significant agglomeration effects. Second, the sorting of workers across places is a quantitatively more important issue than their indiscriminate agglomeration in highly productive locations. Third, the importance of unobserved labor quality implies that wages should be favored over TFP and other productivity measures, since wage data are our main hope to deal with unobserved worker characteristics.

The rest of this chapter is as follows. Section 1.2 provides a simple model of productivity and wages in cities and discusses the two main estimation issues. Section 1.3 presents the wage data and our approach to the endog-

1. Even if the overall effect is positive, there may also be many negative effects of density on productivity due to crowding or congestion.

enous quality of labor bias. Section 1.4 presents our instruments and discusses the details of our instrumentation strategy. Our results for wages are presented in section 1.5, while those for productivity follow in section 1.6. Finally, section 1.7 concludes.

1.2 Identification Issues when Estimating Agglomeration Effects

We consider a simple theoretical model of the relationship between local characteristics and wages or productivity. Take a competitive firm i operating under constant returns to scale. Its output y_i depends on the amounts of capital k_i and labor l_i it uses and its total factor productivity A_i:

$$y_i = A_i k_i^{\alpha} l_i^{1-\alpha}. \tag{1}$$

If all firms face the same interest rate r, the first-order conditions for profit maximization imply that the wage *rate* is given by:

$$w_i = (1-\alpha)\left(\frac{\alpha}{r}\right)^{\alpha/(1-\alpha)} A_i^{1/(1-\alpha)}. \tag{2}$$

Taking logs directly leads to

$$\ln w_i = \text{Constant} + \frac{1}{1-\alpha}\ln A_i. \tag{3}$$

The whole focus of the agglomeration literature, then, is on how the local characteristics of area a where firm i is located determine productivity. We assume that TFP depends on a vector of local characteristics X_a and (observed and unobserved) firm characteristics μ_i:

$$\ln A_i = X_{a(i)}\varphi + \mu_i. \tag{4}$$

Inserting into equation (3) implies:

$$\ln w_i = \text{Constant} + \frac{1}{1-\alpha}(X_{a(i)}\varphi + \mu_i). \tag{5}$$

This equation can in principle be estimated using wage data and local characteristics. An alternative strategy is to insert equation (4) into equation (1), take logs, and estimate:

$$\ln y_i = \alpha \ln k_i + (1-\alpha)\ln l_i + X_{a(i)}\varphi + \mu_i. \tag{6}$$

Hence, both wage- and firm-level (TFP) data can be used to estimate the coefficients of interest in the vector φ or $\varphi/(1-\alpha)$.[2] The first identification problem when estimating equation (5) or (6) is that the effect of local characteristics, $X_{a(i)}$, on wages and productivity may not be causal (endogenous

2. Combes, Mayer, and Thisse (2008, chapter 11) provide a more complete model of local productivity and a precise discussion of a number of issues, including those that relate to the prices of factors, intermediates, and final output.

quantity of labor bias). In other words, unobserved local determinants of firm productivity that are part of the error term μ_i may well be correlated with $X_{a(i)}$. Second, local characteristics of workers that are not observed and therefore not included in $X_{a(i)}$ may not be comparable across areas (endogenous quality of labor bias). Again, this creates some correlation between μ_i and $X_{a(i)}$.[3]

To provide further justification for equations (5) and (6) and to clarify some issues regarding endogenous quantity of labor bias, we note that the literature on the microfoundations of agglomeration (e.g., Duranton and Puga 2004) typically leads to equilibria, where the wage in area a, w_a, depends on a local productivity shifter, B_a, and the local workforce, N_a:

$$w_a = B_a N_a^{\delta}. \tag{7}$$

This equation is consistent with equation (5) when agglomeration effects are such that $A_i^{1/(1-\alpha)} = B_a N_a^{\delta} e^{\mu_i}$. The variable B_a can be viewed as a short-hand for all variables other than N_a in X_a. With $\delta > 0$, individual wages increase with N_a. If N_a is exogenously determined, it can be part of the vector of local characteristics X_a, and δ can be appropriately estimated with ordinary least squares (OLS). Following Roback (1982) and subsequent literature, we may assume instead that workers choose their city of residence. This choice is determined through utility maximization by the difference between the wage and the local cost of living:

$$U_a = w_a - C_a N_a^{\lambda}. \tag{8}$$

In any city, the cost of living increases with the city workforce and depends on other characteristics such as amenities, which have utility costs (and benefits). A spatial equilibrium equalizes utility across cities.

Assuming $\lambda > \delta$ and normalizing equilibrium utility to zero, the above yields:

$$N_a = \left(\frac{B_a}{C_a}\right)^{1/(\lambda - \delta)} \quad \text{and} \quad w_a = B_a^{\lambda/(\lambda-\delta)} C_a^{-\delta/(\lambda-\delta)} \tag{9}$$

At one extreme, if there are no differences in productivity across cities other than those due to population difference (i.e., $B_a = B$) and only costs vary, the OLS coefficient on log workforce, when regressed against log wage, will be (appropriately) δ. In the opposite case where costs are the same everywhere ($C_a = C$) and only productivity varies, the regression will estimate instead λ. In the general case where both costs and productivity vary, the estimated coefficient on log workforce will be between δ and λ.[4] The intuition

3. In addition, when estimating equation (6), factors might be endogenous as well. This issue is discussed in section 1.6.

4. Using the results from equation (9), it is easy to show that the estimated coefficient for log workforce will be: $[\lambda \text{Var}(\ln B_a) + \delta \text{Var}(\ln C_a) - (\delta + \lambda)\text{Cov}(\ln B_a, \ln C_a)]/[\text{Var}(\ln B_a) + \text{Var}(\ln C_a) - \text{Cov}(\ln B_a, \ln C_a)]$. With zero covariance between B_a and C_a and equal variance, this reduces to $(\delta + \lambda)/2$.

for that result is that if the variation in local workforce comes solely from local costs, it is exogenous, and the proper coefficient is estimated. If instead the workforce is determined by the variation in productivity, wages in equilibrium only reflect the extent to which local costs increase with the size of the workforce. We need to keep this point in mind for our estimation strategy.

This problem actually goes deeper than that. Our model considers only two factors of production—labour and physical capital—the latter of which is mobile and its price can reasonably be taken to be constant everywhere. Then, the term associated with its price r enters the constant and raises no further problem. However, land may also enter as a factor of production. Unlike for capital, the price of land varies across areas. Following again Roback (1982), we expect better consumption amenities to draw in more population and imply higher land prices. Firms will thus use less land. In turn, this lowers the marginal product of labor when land and labor are imperfect substitutes in the production function (as might be expected). Put differently, nonproduction variables may affect both population patterns and may be capitalized into wages. To deal with this problem, we could attempt to control for local variables that directly affect consumer utility and thus land prices. However, our range of controls is limited, and we are reluctant to use a broad range of local amenities, since many of them are likely to be simultaneously determined with wages.

Faced with reverse causality and missing variables that potentially affect both wages and the density of employment, our strategy is to rely on instrumental variables.[5] Hence, we are asking our instrument to deal with both the reverse-causality problem and the missing-variable issue highlighted here.[6]

Turning to the endogenous quality of labor bias, note that the quantity derived in equation (2) and used throughout the model is a wage rate per

5. Alternative approaches may include focusing on groups of workers for which there is an element of exogeneity in their location decision. One could think, for instance, of spouses of military personnel. However, such groups are likely to be very specific. Another alternative may be to look at "natural experiments" that led to large-scale population and employment changes. Such experiments are very interesting to explore a number of issues. For instance, Davis and Weinstein (2008) estimate the effects of the U.S. bombing of Japanese cities during World War II on their specialization to provide some evidence about multiple equilibria. Redding and Sturm (2008) use the division of Germany after World War II to look at the effects of market potential. However, such natural experiments are not of much relevance to study productivity, since the source of any such large-scale perturbation (e.g., the bombing of Japanese cities) is also likely to affect productivity directly, and there is no natural exclusion restriction.

6. The issue with instrumenting is that the number of possible instruments is small, while there are potentially dozens of (endogenous) variables that can describe a local economy. In view of this problem, our strategy is to consider parsimonious specifications with no more than one or two potentially endogenous variables. The drawback is that the exclusion restriction for the instruments (i.e., lack of correlation between the instruments and the error) is more difficult to satisfy than with a greater number of controls. Despite this, we think that a more demanding exclusion restriction is preferable to the addition of inappropriate and possibly endogenous controls.

efficiency unit of labor. Even if we are willing to set aside the issue that different types of labor should be viewed as different factors of production, not all workers supply the same number of efficiency units of labor per day. However, the data for individual workers is about their daily earnings—that is, their wage *rate* times the efficiency of their labor. For worker j employed by firm i, it is convenient to think of their earnings as being $W_j = w_{i(j)} \times s_j$, where their level of skills s_j is assumed to map directly into the efficiency of their labor. Hence, individual skills must be conditioned out from the regression to estimate equation (5) properly. Otherwise, any correlation between local characteristics and the skills of the local workforce will lead to biased estimates for agglomeration effects. Put differently, the quality of workforce in an area is likely to be endogenous. Previous work on French data (Combes, Duranton, and Gobillon 2008) leads us to be believe that this is a first-order issue.

To deal with this problem of endogenous labor quality, a number of approaches can be envisioned. The first would be to weigh the workforce by a measure of labor quality at the area level and try to instrument for labor quality just like we instrument for labor quantity. Instruments for labor quality are very scarce. The only reasonable attempt is by Moretti (2004), who uses land-grant colleges in U.S. cities to instrument for the local share of workers with higher education. In any case, this is unlikely to be enough, because we also expect unobservables such as ambition or work discipline to matter and to be spatially unevenly distributed (Bacolod, Blum, and Strange 2009).

To tackle sorting head-on, previous literature has attempted to use area characteristics at a different level of spatial aggregation. For instance, Evans, Oates, and Schwab (1992) use metropolitan characteristics to instrument for school choice, while Bayer, Ross, and Topa (2008) use location at the block level and assume an absence of sorting conditional on neighborhood choice.[7] In our data, although we know location at the municipal level, we are loathe to make any strong spatial identifying assumption of that sort. A more satisfactory alternative would be to estimate a full system of equations, modeling explicitly location choice. Unfortunately, due to both the difficulty of finding meaningful exclusion restrictions and to the complications introduced by the discrete nature of the choice among many locations, this is a difficult exercise. Dahl (2002) proposes a new approach to this problem, but this can be applied to cross-sectional data only.

The last existing approach is to use the longitudinal dimension of the data, as in Glaeser and Maré (2001), Moretti (2004), and Combes, Duranton, and

7. Opposite spatial identifying assumptions are made. In Evans, Oates, and Schwab (1992), the choice of the more aggregate area is assumed to be exogenous, while location choice at a lower spatial level is not. Bayer, Ross, and Topa (2008) assume instead that randomness prevails at the lower level of aggregation and not at the higher level of aggregation.

Gobillon (2008). This is the approach we follow. The details of our methodology are described in the next section.

1.3 Sorting and Wage Data

1.3.1 Choice of Spatial Zoning, Sectoral Aggregation, and Explanatory Variables

The choice of geographical units could in principle be of fundamental importance. With the same data, there is no reason why a partial correlation that is observed for one set of spatial units should also be observed for an alternative zoning. In particular, the shape of the chosen units may matter. However, Briant, Combes, and Lafourcade (2007) compare the results of several standard exercises in spatial economics using both official French units, which were defined for administrative or economic purposes, and arbitrarily defined ones of the same average size (i.e., squares on a map). Their main finding is that to estimate agglomeration effects, the localization of industries, and the distance decay of trade flows across areas, the *shape* of units makes no difference.

With respect to our choice of units, we opt for French employment areas ("zones d'emploi"). Continental France is fully covered by 341 employment areas, whose boundaries are defined on the basis of daily commuting patterns. Employment areas are meant to capture local labor markets, and most of them correspond to a city and its catchment area or to a metropolitan area. This choice of relatively small areas (on average 1,500 km^2) is consistent with previous findings in the agglomeration literature that agglomeration effects are in part very local (Rosenthal and Strange 2004). Nevertheless, we are aware that *different spatial scales* may matter with respect to agglomeration effects (see Briant, Combes, and Lafourcade [2007] and previous literature). We need to keep this important issue in mind when deciding on a specification.

Turning to the level of sectoral aggregation, a key question regards whether the benefits from agglomeration stem from the size of the overall local market (*urbanization economies*) or from geographic concentration at the sector level (*localization economies*). Although we want to focus on overall scale effects, sector effects cannot be discarded. Previous results for France suggest that they matter, although they are economically far less important than overall scale effects (Combes, Duranton, and Gobillon 2008). In the following, we work at the level of 114 three-digit sectors.[8]

The main explanatory variable we are interested in is employment den-

8. We view this level of aggregation as a reasonable compromise. On the one hand, we need finely defined sectors in wage regressions and for TFP estimation. On the other hand, localization economies are expected to be driven by similarities in customers, suppliers, workers, and technology, and thus take place at a fairly broad level of sectoral aggregation.

sity. It is our favorite measure of local scale. Since Ciccone and Hall (1996), density-based measures have often been used to assess overall scale effects. Their main advantage compared to alternative measures of size, such as total employment or total population, is that density-based measures are more robust to the zoning. In particular, Greater Paris is divided into a number of employment areas. The true economic scale of these Parisian employment areas is much better captured by their density than by any absolute measure of employment.

To repeat, French employment areas are relatively small and are determined by commuting patterns. On the other hand, input-output linkages may not be limited by commuting distances. Hence, we expect some agglomeration effects to take place at a scale larger than employment areas. There is by now a lot of evidence that the market potential of an area matters (Head and Mayer 2004). Thus, in some regressions, we also consider the market potential of an area that we define as the sum of the density of the other areas, weighted by the inverse distance to these areas.[9] Experimenting with other measures leads to very similar results.

1.3.2 Main Wage Data

We use an extract from the Déclarations Annuelles des Données Sociales (DADS) or the Annual Social Data Declarations database from the French statistical institute (INSEE). The DADS are collected for pension, benefits, and tax purposes. Establishments must fill a report for each of their employees every year. An observation thus corresponds to an employee-establishment-year combination. The extract we use covers all employees in manufacturing and services working in France and born in October of even-numbered years.

For each observation, we know the age, gender, and occupation at the two-digit level. Except for a small subsample, education is missing. We also know the number of days worked but not hours for all years so that we restrict ourselves to full-time employees for whom hours are set by law. For earnings, we focus on total labor costs, deflated by the French consumer price index. We refer to the real 1980 total labor cost per full working day as the wage. The data also contains basic establishment-level information such as location and three-digit sector.

The raw data contains 19,675,740 observations between 1976 and 1996 (1981, 1983, and 1990 are missing). The details of the cleaning of the data is described in Combes, Duranton, and Gobillon (2008). After selecting only full-time workers in the private sector, excluding outliers, dumping a number of industries with reporting problems, and deleting observations

9. We retain a simple specification for market potential and do not aim to derive it from a "new economic geography" model (Head and Mayer 2004). Alternative specifications for market potential are highly correlated with the one we use. See Head and Mayer (2006) for further evidence and discussion of this fact.

with coding problems, we end up with 8,826,422 observations. For reasons of computational tractability, we keep only six points in time (every four years: 1976, 1980, 1984, 1988, 1992, and 1996), leaving us with 2,664,474 observations.

Using this data, we can construct a number of variables for each year. Our main explanatory variable, employment density, can be readily calculated from the data.[10] So can market potential. For each area and sector, we also compute the number of establishments, the share of workers in professional occupations, and the share of the sector in local employment. As controls, we also use three amenities variables. These amenities variables are the share of population located on a sea shore, mountains, and lakes and waterways. These variables come from the French inventory of municipalities. We aggregate them at the level of employment areas, weighting each municipality by its population.[11] Table 1.1 reports a number of descriptive statistics for French employment areas.

1.3.3 Three Wages

The simplest way to implement equation (5) is to compute the mean wage for each area and year and take its log:

$$W^1_{at} \equiv \ln \overline{w}_{at} \equiv \ln\left(\frac{1}{N_{at}} \sum_{j\in(a,t)} w_{jt}\right), \tag{10}$$

where w_{jt} is the wage of worker j and year t, and N_{at} is the number of workers in area a and year t.

We can then use W^1_{at} as the dependent variable to be explained by local employment density and other local characteristics in equation (14). Using a simple log mean like W^1_{at} throws a number of problems. First, when using mean wages, we do nothing regarding the endogenous quality of labor bias. Second, we do not condition out sector effects.[12]

To deal with these two problems, a first solution is to use all the available observables about workers and proceed as follows. We first compute a mean wage per employment area, sector, and year:

$$\overline{w}_{ast} \equiv \frac{1}{N_{ast}} \sum_{j\in(a,s,t)} w_{jt}. \tag{11}$$

10. We keep in mind that the years are not the same for the wage and TFP regressions. For each set of regressions, the explanatory variables are constructed from the corresponding data sources.

11. Each employment area contains on average more than one hundred municipalities.

12. One further (minor) issue needs to be mentioned. We take the log of mean wages rather than the mean of log (individual) wages. When viewing local wages as an aggregate of individual wages, the log of mean wages is not the proper aggregate to consider. Mean log wages should be used instead. However, the former is easier to implement than the latter, especially for those who do not have access to microdata. In any case, this issue is empirically unimportant, since the correlation between log mean wages and mean log wages is 0.99.

Table 1.1 **Summary statistics for our main variables (averages across 306 employment areas)**

	Mean	Standard deviation
Mean wage (1976–1996, in 1980 French francs, per day)	207.9	15.8
W^1	5.3	0.074
W^2	5.2	0.070
W^3	–0.04	0.049
Employment density (workers per sq. km)	64.4	543.0
Ln employment density	2.4	1.2
Market potential (workers per sq. km)	108.1	139.9
Ln market potential	4.4	0.7
1831 Urban population density (inhabitants per sq. km)	38.2	419.8
1881 Urban population density (inhabitants per sq. km)	106.8	1232.3
Sea (average % municipalities on a coast line)	8.8	21.1
Lake (average % municipalities on a lake)	17.2	12.9
Mountain (average % municipalities on a mountain)	9.8	19.7

Source: DADS for the first eight lines, historical censuses for the next two, and 1988 municipal inventory for the last three. For sea, lake, and mountain, we have for each employment area the percentage of municipalities on a coast, with a lake, or on a mountain. We average this quantity across employment areas.

This wage can then be regressed on a number of (mean) characteristics of the workers and the local sector. More specially, we can estimate the following first-step regression:

$$\ln \overline{w}_{ast} = W^2_{at} + \gamma_s + X_{ast}\varphi + \varepsilon_{ast}. \tag{12}$$

In this equation, γ_s is a sector dummy, and X_{ast} is a set of characteristics for sector s in area a and year t and the workers employed therein. To capture sector effects, we use in X_{ast} the (log) share of local employment in sector s and the (log) number of local establishments in this sector. Also in X_{ast}, the mean individual characteristics are the age, its square, and the shares of employment in each of six skill groups.[13] In equation (12), the coefficient of interest is W^2_{at}, a fixed effect for each employment area and year. When estimating equation (12), all local sector and mean individual characteristics are centered, and the observations are weighted by the number of workers in each cell to avoid heteroscedasticity.

The coefficients W^2_{at} can, in a second step, be regressed on local employment density and other local characteristics, as stipulated by equation (5). While further details and justifications about the estimation of equation (12) are given in Combes, Duranton, and Gobillon (2008), three important

13. The shares of each skill in local sector employment capture the effects of both individual characteristics at the worker level and the interactions between workers. The two cannot be separately identified with aggregate data.

issues need to be briefly discussed. First, the approach described here first estimates local fixed effects before using them as the dependent variable in a second step. We prefer this two-step approach to its one-step counterpart for reasons made clear next.

Below, estimating equation (12) with OLS may condition out sectoral effects, but it does not take care of the possible simultaneity between mean sector wages and local sector characteristics. A high level of specialization in a certain sector may induce high wages in this sector. Alternatively, high local wages may simply be a reflection of strong local advantage, also leading to a high level of specialization. We acknowledge this concern at the sector level, but we do not deal with it. The main reason is that the coefficients for local specialization and the number of establishments, although significant, only explain a very small part of the variation in equation (12) (Combes, Duranton, and Gobillon 2008).

Finally, controlling for observable labor market characteristics including one-digit occupational categories (for lack of control for education) attenuates concerns about the endogenous quality of labor bias. However, they do not eradicate them entirely.

A more powerful way to deal with the endogenous quality of labor bias is to estimate:

$$\ln w_{jt} = W^3_{a(jt)t} + \gamma_{s(jt)} + X^1_{a(jt)s(jt)t}\varphi^1_{s(jt)} + X^2_{jt}\varphi^2 + \theta_j + \varepsilon_{jt}. \tag{13}$$

This equation is estimated at the level of individual workers and contains a worker fixed effect θ_j, which controls for all fixed individual characteristics.[14] The use of individual data also allows us to control for individual characteristics X^2_{jt} (age and its square) separately from (centered) local industry characteristics X^1_{ast}. The latter contain the share of local employment of the sector, the local number of firms in the sector, and the local share of professional workers. The coefficient of interest in equation (13) is the wage index W^3_{at} for each area and year after conditioning out sector effects, observable time-varying individual characteristics, and all fixed individual characteristics. If we ignore again the possible endogeneity of local sector characteristics, the main issue when estimating equation (13) regards the endogeneity of location or sector choices. However, because we have sector effects and time-varying local effects, W^3_{at}, problems only arise when we have spatial or sector sorting based on the worker-specific errors. In particular, there is no bias when sorting is based on the explanatory variables, *including individual, area-year, and industry fixed effects.* More concretely, there is a bias when the location decision is driven by the exact wage that the worker can get at locations in a given year, but there is no bias when workers base their location decision on the average wage of other workers in an area and

14. Equation (13) is identified from both the movers (to identify the difference between W^3_{at} and $W^3_{a't+1}$) and the stayers (to identify the difference between W^3_{at} and W^3_{at+1}).

their own characteristics (i.e., when they make their location decision on the basis of their expected wages). See Combes, Duranton, and Gobillon (2008) for further discussion.

Note that we prefer this two-step approach, which first estimates equation (12) or (13) before regressing W^2_{at} or W^3_{at} on local characteristics, to its corresponding one-step counterpart for three reasons. First, we can properly take into account correlations between area-sector variables and error terms at the area level. Second, a two-step approach allows us to account for area-specific error terms when computing the standard errors for the coefficients we estimate. Doing so is important, because Moulton (1990) shows that standard errors can be seriously biased otherwise. Accounting for area-specific errors with a one-step approach is not possible, given that workers can move across areas. Third, we can conduct a variance decomposition for the second stage.[15]

Finally, to avoid identifying out of the temporal variation, we average the three wage variables and all the explanatory variables across the six years of data we use.[16] Before turning to our results, it is interesting to note that these three local wage variables are strongly correlated with one another. The correlation between W^1 and W^2 is 0.87, the correlation between W^1 and W^3 is 0.81, and the correlation between W^2 and W^3 is 0.91. Table 1.1 reports a number of descriptive statistics for French employment areas.

1.4 Instruments

That the estimation of agglomeration economies could be plagued by simultaneity was first articulated by Moomaw (1981). To preview our IV approach, we note first that using historical variables such as long lags of population density to instrument for the size or density of local population has been standard since Ciccone and Hall's (1996) pioneering work. To the extent that (a) there is some persistence in the spatial distribution of population and (b) the local drivers of high productivity today differ from those of a long-gone past, this approach is defensible. An alternative strategy is to use the nature of soils, since geology is also expected to be an important determinant of settlement patterns. Some soils are more stable than others and thus can support a greater density of people. More fertile lands may have also attracted people in greater numbers, and so forth. To the extent that

15. It is also true that using as the dependent variable a coefficient estimated in a previous step introduces some measurement error. The procedure used in Combes, Duranton, and Gobillon (2008) to control for this problem shows that it makes no difference, because the coefficients are precisely estimated at the first step.

16. These averages are weighted by the number of workers in the area for each year to obtain a wage index for the average worker in the area over time. By contrast, our final regressions for the cross-section of employment areas assess whether denser areas make their average firm more productive. There is no longer any reason to weigh the observations (by the number of workers) in these regressions.

geology affects the distribution of population (i.e., labor supply) and does not otherwise cause productivity (i.e., labor demand) because fertile lands are no longer a relevant driver of local wealth, it can provide reasonable instruments to explain the distribution of employment. Except by Rosenthal and Strange (2008) in a slightly different context, geology has not been used to instrument for the distribution of population.

1.4.1 Description of the Instruments

Our first set of instruments is composed of historical populations from early French censuses. For twenty-six French censuses prior to our earliest year of data (1976), we know the urban population for each municipality. Among available censuses, we choose the earliest one from 1831 and another from 1881, fifty years later.[17] We also experimented with other years. Unfortunately, urban population in historical censuses is only reported above a threshold of 5,000. For 1831, there are thirty-five employment areas for which no municipality had an urban population above 5,000. A small majority of them are rural areas, while the others are densely populated employment areas with strong municipal fragmentation. We think of this as being measurement error. To minimize weak instrument problems, we drop these thirty-five employment areas.

Our second group of instruments is composed of geological variables from the European Soil Database (ESDB) compiled by the European Soil Data Centre. The data originally come as a raster data file with cells of 1 km per 1 km. We aggregated it at the level of each employment area.[18] Given that soil characteristics are usually discrete, we use the value that appears most often in each area. To take an illustrative example, the initial and transformed data for the water capacity of the subsoil are represented in figure 1.2. For a small number of densely populated employment areas in Greater Paris, the most important category is sometimes missing. When this is the case, we turn to the second-most important category. In the rare instances where the information is missing from all the pixels in an employment area, we impute the value of a neighboring area (chosen because it takes similar values for other soil characteristics). For instance, the water capacity of the subsoil in Central Paris is missing. We impute the value of its close neighbor Boulogne-Billancourt.

In total, we generate twelve variables from the ESDB.[19] The first four

17. Because they are in log, using these two variables together allows us to instrument for both past 1831 level and past growth between 1831 and 1881.

18. To aggregate the information from 1-km-by-1-km pixels to employment areas, the zonal statistics tool from ArcGIS 9 software was used. The tool uses the zones defined in the zone data set (in our case, French employment areas) and internally converts the vectors into a zone raster, which it aligns with the value raster data set for soils.

19. The ESDB (v2.0 Raster Archive) contains many more characteristics. For France, some of them, like the soil code according to the standard Food and Agricultural Organization classification, are poorly reported. A large number of characteristics also contain categories

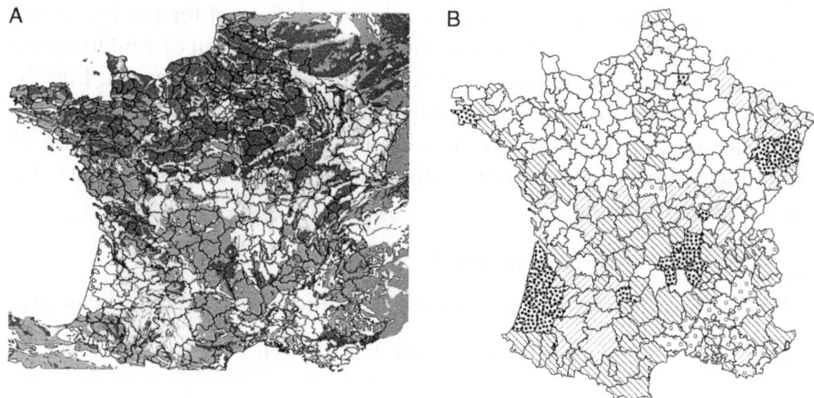

Fig. 1.2 Geological characteristics—water capacity of the subsoil: *A*, original data; *B*, transformed data

Source: European Soil Database.

Note: Panel A represents the initial raster data. Panel B represents the transformed version of the same data after imputation of the missing values for seven employment areas in Greater Paris. In panel A, the darkest shade of gray corresponds to "very high" (i.e., above 190 mm), the second-darkest shade corresponds to "high" (between 140 and 190 mm), followed by "medium" (100–140 mm), "low" (5–100 mm), and "very low" (0–5 mm). Missing values in panel A (around Paris) are in white.

describe the nature of the soils, according to the mineralogy of their subsoil (three categories) and topsoil (four categories) and the nature of the dominant parent material at a broad level of aggregation (six categories) and at a finer level (with twenty categories). More precisely, the mineralogy variables describe the presence of various minerals in the topsoil (the first layer of soil, usually 5 to 15 cm deep) and the subsoil (the intermediate layer between the topsoil and the bedrock). The dominant parent material of the soil is a description of the underlying geological material (the bedrock). Soils usually get a great deal of structure and minerals from their parent material. The more aggregate dominant parent material variable (in six categories) contains entries such as igneous rocks, glacial deposits, or sedimentary rocks. Among the latter, the detailed version of the same variable (with twenty categories) distinguishes between calcareous rocks, limestone, marl, and chalk.

The next seven geological characteristics document various characteristics of the soil, including the water capacity of the subsoil (five categories) and topsoil (three categories), depth to rock (four categories), differentiation (three categories), erodibility (five categories), carbon content (four catego-

that refer to land use (e.g., "urban" or "agriculture") and are thus not appropriate here. More generally, characteristics a priori endogenous to human activity were discarded. Finally, some characteristics such as the secondary dominant parent material struck us as anecdotal and unlikely to yield relevant instruments.

ries), and hydrogeological class (five categories). Except for the hydrogeological class, which describes the circulation and retention of underground water, the meaning of these variables is relatively straightforward. Finally, we create a measure of local terrain ruggedness by taking the mean of maximum altitudes across all pixels in an employment area minus the mean of minimum altitudes. This variable thus captures variations of altitude at a fine geographical scale.

1.4.2 Relevance of the Instruments

Following equations (5) and (6), the specifications we want to estimate are:

$$\ln W_a = \text{Constant} + X_a\varphi^W + \mu_a^W \tag{14}$$

and

$$\ln \text{TFP}_a = \text{Constant} + X_a\varphi^{\text{TFP}} + \mu_a^{\text{TFP}}, \tag{15}$$

where μ_a^W and μ_a^{TFP} are the error terms for the wage and TFP equations. The vector of the dependent variables X_a contains the three amenity variables previously discussed, (log) employment density, and sometimes market potential. These last two variables are suspected of being simultaneously determined with wages and TFP.

Estimating the effect of employment density and market potential on local wages and productivity using instrumental variables can yield unbiased estimates, provided that the instruments satisfy two conditions: relevance and exogeneity. Formally, these conditions are

$$\text{Cov}(\text{Density}_a, Z_a|.) \neq 0, \quad \text{Cov}(\text{MarketPotential}_a, Z_a|.) \neq 0, \tag{16}$$

and

$$\text{Cov}(\mu_a^X, Z_a) = 0 \quad \text{for } X = W \text{ and } X = \text{TFP, respectively}, \tag{17}$$

where Z denotes the set of instruments. We begin by discussing the ability of our instruments to predict contemporaneous employment density and market potential conditionally to the other controls.

The stability of population patterns across cities over time is a well-documented fact (see Duranton [2007] for a recent discussion). This stability is particularly strong in France (Eaton and Eckstein 1997). The raw data confirm this. Table 1.2 presents pairwise correlations between our four historical instruments and current employment density and market potential.[20] For the sake of comparison with the following geology variables, we also report the R^2s of the corresponding univariate regressions. We can see that the log urban population densities of 1831 and 1881 are good predictors

20. We use the measures of density used for our wage regressions (1976 to 1996). Our measures of density for the TFP regressions differ slightly, since they are calculated from a slightly different source and cover different years.

of current employment density. Past market potentials computed from 1831 and 1881 urban populations also predict current market potential extremely well.

Turning to geological characteristics, we expect the nature of soils and their characteristics to be fundamental drivers of population settlements. Soil characteristics arguably determine their fertility. Since each soil characteristic is described by several discrete variables, it is not meaningful to run pairwise correlations as with historical variables. Instead, table 1.3 reports the R^2 when regressing employment density and market potential against various sets of dummies for soil characteristics. The results show that some geological characteristics such as the dominant parent material or the depth to rock have good explanatory power. Other soil characteristics such as their mineralogy or their carbon content are less powerful predictors of current population patterns. Note also that soil characteristics tend to be better at explaining the variations of market potential than employment density. This is not surprising, since most soil characteristics vary relatively smoothly over

Table 1.2 **R^2s of univariate regressions and pairwise correlations: Historical versus density and market potential (1976 to 1996)**

	Ln (employment density)	Ln (market potential)
Ln (1831 density)	0.57 (0.75)	0.05 (0.24)
Ln (1881 density)	0.78 (0.88)	0.10 (0.33)
Ln (1831 market potential)	0.21 (0.46)	0.96 (0.98)
Ln (1881 market potential)	0.22 (0.47)	0.99 (0.99)

Note: 306 observations; adjusted R^2 in plain text, and pairwise correlations between parentheses.

Table 1.3 **R^2s when regressing density and market potential on soil characteristics**

	Ln (employment density)	Ln (market potential)
Subsoil mineralogy (2 dummies)	0.02	0.06
Topsoil mineralogy (3 dummies)	0.02	0.06
Dominant parent material (5 dummies)	0.11	0.31
Dominant parent material (19 dummies)	0.13	0.48
Topsoil water capacity (2 dummies)	0.03	0.23
Subsoil water capacity (3 dummies)	0.01	0.32
Depth to rock (3 dummies)	0.10	0.35
Soil differentiation (2 dummies)	0.07	0.19
Erodibility (4 dummies)	0.04	0.19
Carbon content (3 dummies)	0.04	0.04
Hydrogeological class (4 dummies)	0.01	0.04
Ruggedness	0.05	0.10

Note: Adjusted R^2s; 306 observations.

fairly large spatial scales, while variations in density are more abrupt and take place at smaller spatial scales.

While the correlations and R^2s reported in tables 1.2 and 1.3 are interesting, equation (16) makes clear that the relevance of an instrument depends on the *partial* correlation of the instrumental variables and the endogenous regressor. To assess these partial correlations, table 1.4 presents the results of OLS regressions of log density on our instrumental variables and controls. Table 1.5 reports results for a similar exercise with market potential.

Column (1) of table 1.4 examines the partial correlation between employment density and 1831 population density while conditioning out amenities (sea, lake, and mountain). Column (2) performs a similar regression using 1881 instead of 1831 population density. In both columns, the coefficient on past density is highly significant and close to unity. In columns (3) to (9), we regress contemporaneous employment density on a series of soil dummies concerning their mineralogy, dominant parent material, water capacity, carbon content, depth to rock, and soil differentiation. For lack of space, we do not report all the coefficients, but it must be noted that at least one dummy is significant at 5 percent in each regression.

The comparison of R^2s in columns (1) to (2) versus (3) to (9) immediately shows that long lags of population density explain a greater share of the variations in contemporaneous employment density than soil characteristics. To make a more formal assessment of the relevance of our instruments, we turn to the weak instrument tests developed by Stock and Yogo (2005).[21] Table 1.4 presents the relevant F-statistics. The two lagged density instruments in columns (1) and (2) have F-statistics close to 400 and 1,000, respectively. This makes them very strong in light of the critical values reported by Stock and Yogo (2005) in their tables 1 through 4. The soil instruments are weaker by comparison and fall below the critical values of Stock and Yogo (2005) with two-stage least squares (TSLS). To avoid the pitfalls of weak instruments, a number of possible strategies can be envisioned. First, it would be possible to increase the strength of some soil instruments by considering only the more relevant dummies and by dropping insignificant ones. In absence of a well-articulated theory of how soils affect economic development, we acknowledge an element of "data mining" in our use of soil characteristics. We are nonetheless reluctant to push it to such extremes. Second, we experiment next with estimation strategies that are less sensitive to weak instruments, such as limited information maximum likelihood

21. Stock and Yogo (2005) provide two tests for weak instruments. They are both based on a single F-statistic of the instrumental variables but use different thresholds. The first one tests the hypothesis that the two-stage least square (TSLS) small sample bias is small relative to the OLS endogeneity bias ("bias test"). Second, an instrument is considered strong if, from the perspective of the Wald test, its size is close to its level for all possible configurations of the IV regression ("size test"). Note that instruments may be weak in one sense but not another, and instruments may be weak in the context of TSLS but not when using limited information maximum likelihood (LIML).

Table 1.4 First stage: Density

Variable	(1)	(2)	(3)	(4)	(5)	(6)	(7)	(8)	(9)
Ln (1831 density)	0.906 (0.046)***								
Ln (1881 density)		0.924 (0.030)***							
Ruggedness			–0.710 (0.224)***						
Subsoil mineralogy	N	N	N	Y	N	N	N	N	N
Dominant parent material (6 categories)	N	N	N	N	Y	N	N	N	N
Subsoil water capacity	N	N	N	N	N	Y	N	N	N
Soil carbon content	N	N	N	N	N	N	Y	N	N
Depth to rock	N	N	N	N	N	N	N	Y	N
Soil differentiation	N	N	N	N	N	N	N	N	Y
R^2	0.58	0.78	0.07	0.07	0.17	0.06	0.10	0.15	0.11
F-test (H_0—all instruments zero)	395.7	1,018.8	10.0	5.5	9.1	1.7	6.5	12.6	12.3
Partial R^2	0.57	0.77	0.03	0.04	0.13	0.02	0.06	0.11	0.08

Note: Dependent variable: ln (employment density); 306 observations for each regression. All regressions include a constant and three amenity variables (sea, lake, and mountain). Standard errors in parentheses.

***Significant at the 1 percent level.

Table 1.5 First stage: Market potential

Variable	(1)	(2)	(3)	(4)	(5)	(6)	(7)	(8)	(9)
Ln (1831 market potential)	1.026 (0.012)***								
Ln (1881 market potential)		0.970 (0.007)***							
Ruggedness			–0.339 (0.111)***						
Subsoil mineralogy	N	N	N	Y	N	N	N	N	N
Dominant parent material (6 categories)	N	N	N	N	Y	N	N	N	N
Subsoil water capacity	N	N	N	N	N	Y	N	N	N
Soil carbon content	N	N	N	N	N	N	Y	N	N
Depth to rock	N	N	N	N	N	N	N	Y	N
Soil differentiation	N	N	N	N	N	N	N	N	Y
R^2	0.97	0.99	0.23	0.24	0.43	0.41	0.28	0.44	0.31
F-test (H_0—all instruments zero)	7,106.47	21,503.0	9.4	7.3	23.1	26.3	11.3	41.2	24.0
Partial R^2	0.96	0.99	0.03	0.05	0.28	0.26	0.10	0.29	0.14

Note: Dependent variable: ln (market potential); 306 observations for each regression. All regressions include a constant and three amenity variables (sea, lake, and mountain). Standard errors in parentheses.

***Significant at the 1 percent level.

(LIML), as advocated by Andrews and Stock (2007). Third, we repeat the same regressions with different sets of soil instruments and see how this affects the coefficient(s) of interest. Obtaining the same answer over and over again would be reassuring.

In table 1.5, we repeat the same exercise with market potential using lagged values of that variable and the same set of soil instruments as in table 1.4. Both historical and soil variables are much stronger instruments for market potential than for employment density. For historical variables, the reason is that market potential is computed as a weighted mean of employment density. As a result, this washes out much idiosyncratic variation and naturally yields higher R^2s. Put differently, soil variables are better in replicating the smooth evolution of market potential than the spikes of employment density. The facts that in column (1), the coefficient on 1831 market potential is essentially 1 and that the partial R^2 is 95 percent also indicate that we should not expect much difference between OLS and TSLS.

Because both market potential and soil characteristics vary smoothly over space, one may worry that the good explanatory power of soil characteristics may be spurious. This will be the case if some large areas with particular soil characteristics spuriously overlap with areas of particularly high or low market potential. However, a detailed reading of the coefficients on soil dummies (not reported in table 1.5) indicates that this is not the case. For instance, areas for which the dominant parent material is conditionally associated with the lowest market potential are eolian sands, molasse (sand stone), and ferruginous residual clay. Sands, which drain very fast, and ferruginous clay, a heavy soil which does not drain at all, do not lead to very fertile soils. On the other hand, the parent materials associated with a high market potential are loess, a notably fertile type of soil, and chalk, a stable and porous soil, which can be very fertile, provided it is deep enough. Similarly, a high water capacity of the subsoil is associated with a higher market potential, as could be expected.

1.4.3 Instrument Exogeneity

Equation (17) gives the second condition that must be satisfied by a valid instrument: orthogonality to the error term. Intuitively, the difficulty in inferring the effect of density and market potential on wages and TFP arises because of the possibility that a missing local characteristic or some local shocks might be driving both population location and economic outcomes. To overcome this problem, we require instruments that affect wages and TFP only through the spatial distribution of population. That is, as made clear previously, we need our instruments to affect the supply of labor but not directly productivity. We now discuss the a priori arguments for why our instruments may (or may not) satisfy this exogeneity condition.

We begin with historical variables dating back to 1831. Long-lagged values of the same variable obviously remove any simultaneity bias caused by contemporaneous local shocks. For such simultaneity to remain, we would need these shocks to have been expected in 1831 and to have determined population location at the time. This is extremely unlikely. However, endogeneity might also arise because of some missing permanent characteristic that drives both past population location and contemporaneous productivity. A number of first-nature geographic characteristics such as a coastal location may indeed explain both past population location and current economic outcomes. In our regressions, we directly control for a number of such first-nature characteristics (coast, mountain, lakes and waterways).

Hence, the validity of long population lags rests on the hypothesis that the drivers of population agglomeration in the past are not related to modern determinants of local productivity after controlling for first-nature characteristics of places. The case for this relies on the fact that the French economy in the late twentieth century is very different from what it was in 1831. First, the structure of the French economy in the late twentieth century differs a lot from that of 1831. In 1831, France was only starting its industrialization process, whereas it is deindustrializing now. Manufacturing employment was around 3 million in 1830, against more than 8 million at its peak in 1970 and less than 6 million today (Marchand and Thélot 1997). Then, agriculture employed 63 percent of the French workforce against less than 5 percent today. Since 1831, the workforce has also doubled. Second, the production techniques in agriculture, manufacturing, and much of the service industries are radically different today from what they were more than 150 years ago. With technological change, the location requirements of production have also changed considerably. For instance, the dependance of manufacturing on sources of coal and iron has disappeared. Third, the costs of shipping goods and transporting people from one location to another have declined considerably. Actually, 1831 coincides with the construction of the first French railroads. Subsequently, cars, trucks, and airplanes have further revolutionized transport. At a greater level of aggregation, trade has also become much easier because of European integration over the last fifty years. Fourth, other drivers of population location not directly related to production have changed as well. With much higher standards of living, households are arguably more willing to trade greater efficiency against good amenities (Rappaport 2007). Some previously inhospitable parts of the French territory such as its Languedocian coast in the south have been made hospitable and are now developed, and so on. Finally, since 1831, France has been successively ruled by a king, an emperor, and presidents and prime ministers from five different republics. The country also experienced a revolution in 1848, a major war with Germany in 1870, and two world wars during the twentieth century.

With so much change, a good case can indeed be made that past determinants of population location are not major drivers of current productivity. As a result, historical variables have been the instrument of choice for current population patterns since Ciccone and Hall (1996). They have been widely used by the subsequent literature.

Although the a priori case for historical instruments is powerful, nothing guarantees that it is entirely foolproof. The fact that long lags of the population variables usually pass overidentification tests and other ex post diagnostics may not constitute such a strong argument in favor of their validity. Population variables are often strongly correlated with one another so that any permanent characteristics that affect both measures of past population location and contemporaneous productivity may go unnoticed due to the weak power of overidentification tests when the instruments are very similar and thus highly correlated.

We now consider geological characteristics. The a priori case for thinking that geological characteristics are good instruments hinges first on the fact that they have been decided mostly by nature and do not result from human activity. This argument applies very strongly to a number of soil characteristics we use. For instance, soil mineralogy and their dominant parent material were determined millions of years ago. Other soil characteristics might seem more suspect in this respect. For instance, a soil's depth to rock or its carbon content might be an outcome of human activity. In the very long run, there is no doubt that human activity plays a role regarding these two characteristics. Whether recent (in geological terms) economic activity can play an important role is more doubtful (e.g., Guo and Gifford 2002). A second caveat relates to the measurement of some soil characteristics. In particular, it is hard to distinguish between a soil's intrinsic propensity to erodibility from its actual erosion (see Seybold, Herrick, and Brejda [1999]). In relation to these two worries, our wealth of soil characteristics implies that we can meaningfully compare the answers given by different soil characteristics as instruments in different regressions. We can also use overidentification tests to assess this issue more formally.

Nonetheless, that soils predate patterns of human settlement does not ensure that any soil characteristics will automatically satisfy the condition in equation (17) and be valid instruments. More specifically, we expect soil characteristics to have been a major determinant of local labor demand in the past. The main argument for the validity of geological instruments, then, is that soil quality is no longer expected to be relevant in an economy where agriculture represents less than 5 percent of employment. We also exclude agricultural activities from our data. Put differently, the case for geological characteristics relies on the fact that this important, though partial, determinant of past population location is now largely irrelevant. Hence, like with historical instruments, the a priori case for geological instruments is strong, but there is no way to be entirely sure.

It is important to note that the cases for the validity of historical and geological variables as instruments differ. Historical variables are broad determinants of current population location. Soil characteristics are narrower but more fundamental determinants of current population location. Put differently, although we expect soils to have determined history, they were not the sole determinants of population patterns in 1831. Geological characteristics also explain current patterns of employment density over and above past employment density. If one group of instruments fails, it is unlikely that the second will do so in the same way. Finally, it is also important to keep in mind that these two sets of instruments can only hope to control for the endogenous quantity of labor bias. That a higher density can lead to the sorting of better workers in these areas is not taken care of by these instruments. Put differently, we expect the endogenous quality of labor bias to remain. Moving from crude measures of wage such as W^1 to more sophisticated ones (W^2, and most of all, W^3) is designed to tackle this second issue.

1.5 Main Wage Results

Table 1.6 presents the results of three simple regressions for our three wages: W^1, the mean local wage as computed in equation (10); W^2, the wage index after conditioning out sector effects and observable individual characteristics as estimated in equation (12); and W^3, the wage index from equation (13), which also conditions out individual fixed effects. In columns (1), (2), and (3), these three wages are regressed on log employment density, controlling for three amenity variables (coast, lakes and waterways, mountain) using OLS. The measured density elasticity of mean wages is at 0.048. This is very close to previous results in the literature (Ciccone and Hall 1996; Ciccone 2002). Controlling for sector effects in column (2) implies a marginally higher estimate of 0.051 for the density elasticity and significantly improves the explanatory power of employment density. This suggests that although the local characteristics of the sector of employment matter, conditioning out sector effects does not affect our estimates of the density elasticity. Controlling also for unobserved individual characteristics yields a significantly lower elasticity of 0.033. This suggests that a good share of measured agglomeration effects are in fact attributable to the unobserved characteristics of the workforce. More specifically, workers who command a higher wage on labor market sort in denser areas.

In columns (4), (5), and (6), we perform the same regressions as in columns (1), (2), and (3), but we instrument employment density with 1831 urban population density. Compared to their corresponding OLS coefficients, the TSLS coefficients for employment density are marginally lower. The instrument is very strong, with a first-stage F- (or Cragg-Donald) statistic close to 400. In columns (6), (7), and (8), we add 1881 population density as a second instrument for employment density. The results are virtually undistinguishable from those of columns (4), (5), and (6). With two instruments, it is also possible to run Sargan tests of overidentification. They are passed

Table 1.6 **Local wages as a function of density: OLS and historical instruments**

Variable	W^1 OLS (1)	W^2 OLS (2)	W^3 OLS (3)	W^1 TSLS (4)	W^2 TSLS (5)	W^3 TSLS (6)	W^1 TSLS (7)	W^2 TSLS (8)	W^3 TSLS (9)
Ln (density)	0.048	0.051	0.033	0.040	0.042	0.026	0.040	0.044	0.027
	(0.002)***	(0.002)***	(0.001)***	(0.003)***	(0.002)***	(0.002)***	(0.003)***	(0.002)***	(0.002)***
Instruments used:									
Ln (1831 density)	—	—	—	Y	Y	Y	Y	Y	Y
Ln (1881 density)	—	—	—	—	—	—	Y	Y	Y
First-stage statistics	—	—	—	395.7	395.7	395.7	518.7	518.7	518.7
Overidentification test p-value	—	—	—	—	—	—	0.99	0.19	0.21
R^2	0.56	0.72	0.65	—	—	—	—	—	—

Note: 306 observations for each regression. All regressions include a constant and three amenity variables (sea, lake, and mountain). Standard errors in parentheses.

***Significant at the 1 percent level.

in all three cases with p-values above 10 percent. However, we can put only a limited weight on this test, because the correlation between 1881 and 1831 density is high at 0.75.

If we think of table 1.6 as our baseline, a number of findings are worth highlighting. The density elasticity of mean wages is 0.048 (column [1]). Controlling for the endogenous quality of labor bias through a fixed effect estimation reduces the size of the coefficient by about one-third to 0.033 (column [3]). Controlling for the endogenous quantity of labor bias using long historical lags as instruments reduces it by another one-fifth to 0.027 (column [9]). Hence, this table provides evidence about both the quality and quantity of labor being simultaneously determined with productivity. It also suggests that the endogenous quality of labor bias is more important than the quantity bias.

Next, table 1.7 reports results for a number of regressions, which all use geological characteristics as instruments for employment density. Following the results of table 1.4, we expect geological instruments to be on the weak side. Furthermore, table 1.5 also makes clear that geological characteristics appear to explain market potential better than employment density. Hence, we need to keep in mind that our geological instruments are correlated with a variable—market potential—that is (for the time being) missing from the regression and suspected to have an independent effect on wages. As a consequence, IV estimations that rely solely on geological characteristics may not perform very well and should be interpreted with caution.

In each of the regressions in table 1.7, we use two different soil characteristics. Except for ruggedness, because each soil characteristic is documented with a series of dummy variables, we could technically run overidentification tests while instrumenting for only one characteristic. However, such tests may not be economically meaningful, since we would end up testing for overidentification using the particular categorization of the ESDB. We experimented extensively with soil characteristics. The results we report in the table are representative of what is obtained using any combination of the soil characteristics listed in the table. With them, overidentification tests are usually passed. This is not the case with the other soil characteristics.

More precisely, in column (1) of table 1.7, we regress mean wages on density and other controls using subsoil mineralogy and ruggedness as instruments for employment density. We obtain a density elasticity of 0.042, which is consistent with what we find in table 1.6 when we use historical variables. We repeat the same regression in columns (2) and (3) using W^2 and W^3 as dependent variables. In column (3), the coefficient is slightly above its OLS counterpart rather than slightly below when using historical instruments. The difference, nonetheless, is not significant. Before going any further, note that the low first-stage statistics in columns (1) through (3) raise some questions about the strength of these geological instruments. With weak instruments, a number of authors (e.g., Stock and Yogo 2005) now argue for

Table 1.7 **Local wages as a function of density: Geological instruments**

Variable	W^1 TSLS (1)	W^2 TSLS (2)	W^3 TSLS (3)	W^3 LIML (4)	W^3 LIML (5)	W^3 LIML (6)	W^3 LIML (7)	W^3 LIML (8)
Ln (density)	0.042	0.047	0.038	0.038	0.048	0.050	0.048	0.047
	(0.010)***	(0.008)***	(0.006)***	(0.006)***	(0.005)***	(0.005)***	(0.005)***	(0.005)***
Instruments used:								
Subsoil mineralogy	Y	Y	Y	Y	Y	N	N	N
Ruggedness	Y	Y	Y	Y	N	N	N	N
Depth to rock	N	N	N	N	Y	Y	Y	N
Soil carbon content	N	N	N	N	N	Y	N	N
Topsoil water capacity	N	N	N	N	N	N	Y	Y
Dominant parent material (6 categories)	N	N	N	N	N	N	N	Y
First-stage statistics	6.2	6.2	6.2	6.2	8.3	8.2	8.1	6.8
Overidentification test p-value	0.99	0.90	0.67	0.67	0.45	0.12	0.34	0.15

Note: 306 observations for each regression. All regressions include a constant and three amenity variables (sea, lake, and mountain). Standard errors in parentheses.

***Significant at the 1 percent level.

the superiority of the LIML estimator to the TSLS estimator. Column (4) of table 1.7 reports the LIML estimate for a specification similar to column (3). The TSLS and LIML results are the same.[22]

In columns (5) to (8), we report LIML results regarding our preferred measure of wages, W^3, for further combinations of instruments. The coefficient on employment density is positive and highly significant in all cases. However, it is above its OLS counterpart rather than below, even more so than in column (4). This discrepancy between the IV results using history in table 1.6 and those using geology in table 1.7 is due to the fact that soil variables are not only correlated with the employment density but also with the market potential, which is missing. As a result, the density elasticities in table 1.7 may be biased upward. To see this, note that in column (4), the correlation between the predicted values of employment density obtained from the instrumental regression and actual density is 0.29. The correlation between predicted density and actual market potential (omitted from the regression) is nearly as high at 0.27. In column (5), the problem is even worse, since the correlation between predicted and actual density is 0.37, while the correlation between predicted density and market potential is 0.48.[23]

To explore this problem further, we now consider historical and geological instruments at the same time. Table 1.8 reports the results for a number of regressions using both 1831 density and some soil characteristics. In all cases, the instruments are strong because of the presence of 1831 density. Subsoil mineralogy (along with 1831 density) is used in columns (1) to (3) to instrument for density and explain W^1, W^2, and W^3. The results are the same as those of columns (4) to (6) of table 1.6, which use only 1831 density, while they differ more with those of columns (1) to (3) of table 1.7, which use subsoil mineralogy (together with ruggedness) but not 1831 density. This is unsurprising, given that 1831 density is a much stronger instrument. Using a generalized method of moments (GMM) IV estimation rather than TSLS in column (4) does not change anything. Using ruggedness or hydrogeological class in columns (5) to (7) also implies a similar coefficient on density. With these three soil characteristics (and 1831 density), the overidentification test is passed. For the other soil characteristics, however, this test is failed. An example is given in column (8) with topsoil water capacity. This is in line with the results of the previous table that a majority of soil characteristics do not give the same answer as 1831 density when used as instruments to estimate the density elasticity of wages.

To confirm that this problem is due to the strong correlation between soil

22. In the other regressions, the differences in the point estimates and standard errors between TSLS and LIML remain small. The differences with respect to the overidentification tests are sometimes more important. This is due to the greater power of the Anderson-Rubin test under LIML relative to the Sargan test used with TSLS.

23. This is consistent with the fact that overidentification tests are passed only for the small set of regressions reported in the table.

Table 1.8 **Local wages as a function of density: Historical and geological instruments**

Variable	W^1 TSLS (1)	W^2 TSLS (2)	W^3 TSLS (3)	W^3 GMM (4)	W^3 TSLS (5)	W^3 TSLS (6)	W^3 TSLS (7)	W^3 TSLS (8)
Ln (density)	0.040	0.042	0.027	0.027	0.027	0.027	0.027	0.027
	(0.003)***	(0.002)***	(0.002)***	(0.002)***	(0.002)***	(0.002)***	(0.002)***	(0.002)***
Instruments used:								
Ln(1831 density)	Y	Y	Y	Y	Y	Y	Y	Y
Subsoil mineralogy	Y	Y	Y	Y	N	Y	N	N
Ruggedness	N	N	N	N	Y	Y	Y	N
Hydrogeological class	N	N	N	N	N	N	Y	N
Topsoil water capacity	N	N	N	N	N	N	N	Y
First-stage statistics	138.7	138.7	138.7	116.2	208.7	108.1	69.8	76.2
Overidentification test *p*-value	0.98	0.83	0.15	0.13	0.31	0.21	0.53	0.02

Note: 306 observations for each regression. All regressions include a constant and three amenity variables (sea, lake, and mountain). Standard errors in parentheses.

***Significant at the 1 percent level.

characteristics and market potential, table 1.9 reports results for a number of regressions in which market potential is added as a control. In columns (1) to (3), our measures of wages W^1, W^2, and W^3 are regressed on density and market potential using OLS. The measured elasticity of wages with respect to market potential is between 0.01 and 0.03. It is also interesting to note that the density elasticity is slightly lower than in columns (1) to (3) of table 1.6, where market potential is omitted. In columns (4) to (9), we instrument employment density with 1831 density and a range of soil characteristics. The density elasticity is very stable at 0.02, while the market potential elasticity is also very stable at 0.034. Importantly, the overidentification tests are passed (whereas they fail without market potential as a control). More generally, the overidentification test is passed for most combinations of geological instruments and 1831 density. The main systematic failure occurs when the dominant parent material dummies are used. It should be noted that 1831 density is a much stronger instrument, and as a result, it does most of the work in generating the predicted density at the first stage. This greater strength of past density may explain the stability of the coefficients. Nonetheless, in each of the IV regressions of table 1.9, at least one soil dummy (and usually more) is significant (and usually highly so). This implies that we can run meaningful overidentification tests. The fact that their p-values are usually well above 10 percent is strongly suggestive that 1831 density and a broad range of soil characteristics all support this 0.02 estimate for the density elasticity of wages.

Finally, in table 1.10, we consider that market potential could also be endogenous. In columns (1) to (3), we use only historical instruments: 1831 and 1881 density, as well as 1831 market potential. The results for W^3 in column (3) are similar to the IV results in table 1.8. In columns (4) to (9), we use 1831 employment density in each regression with two different soils characteristics among erodibility, carbon content, subsoil water capacity, depth to rock, ruggedness, and soil differentiation. The overidentification test is always passed in the table. Although the results are not reported here, this test is also passed for all the other pairwise combinations of these characteristics (except the combination of soil differentiation and carbon content for which the test marginally fails). For our preferred concept of wage, W^3, the coefficients on density and market potential are very stable and confirm the estimates of column (3) with historical instruments and those of the previous table, where market potential is taken to be exogenous. This stability across columns (3) to (9) is interesting, because, as instruments in columns (4) to (9), geological variables and past density are not as strong as the combination of past density and past market potential. Our preferred estimate for the elasticity of wages with respect to employment density is 0.02. With respect to market potential, our preferred estimate is at 0.034.

While regressing mean wages on employment density leads to a measured

Table 1.9 **Local wages as a function of density and (exogenous) market potential: Historical and geological instruments**

Variable	W^1 OLS (1)	W^2 OLS (2)	W^3 OLS (3)	W^3 TSLS (4)	W^3 TSLS (5)	W^3 TSLS (6)	W^3 TSLS (7)	W^3 TSLS (8)	W^3 TSLS (9)
Ln (density)	0.042	0.048	0.026	0.020	0.020	0.020	0.020	0.020	0.020
	(0.003)***	(0.002)***	(0.001)***	(0.002)***	(0.002)***	(0.002)***	(0.002)***	(0.002)***	(0.002)***
Ln (market potential)	0.024	0.012	0.027	0.034	0.034	0.034	0.034	0.034	0.034
	(0.006)***	(0.004)***	(0.003)***	(0.003)***	(0.003)***	(0.003)***	(0.003)***	(0.003)***	(0.003)***
Instruments used:									
Ln (1831 density)	—	—	—	Y	Y	Y	Y	Y	Y
Subsoil mineralogy	—	—	—	Y	N	N	N	N	N
Ruggedness	—	—	—	N	Y	N	N	N	N
Subsoil water capacity	—	—	—	N	N	Y	N	N	N
Depth to rock	—	—	—	N	N	N	Y	N	N
Erodibility	—	—	—	N	N	N	N	Y	N
Soil differentiation	—	—	—	N	N	N	N	N	Y
First-stage statistics	—	—	—	128.5	191.6	80.9	96.9	77.9	130.0
Overidentification test p-value	—	—	—	0.72	0.82	0.42	0.54	0.37	0.10
R^2	0.59	0.73	0.73	—	—	—	—	—	—

Note: 306 observations for each regression. All regressions include a constant and three amenity variables (sea, lake, and mountain). Standard errors in parentheses.

***Significant at the 1 percent level.

Table 1.10 **Local wages as a function of density and (endogenous) market potential: Historical and geological instruments**

Variable	W^1 TSLS (1)	W^2 TSLS (2)	W^3 TSLS (3)	W^3 TSLS (4)	W^3 TSLS (5)	W^3 TSLS (6)	W^3 TSLS (7)	W^3 TSLS (8)	W^3 TSLS (9)
Ln (density)	0.033	0.040	0.020	0.018	0.019	0.020	0.020	0.020	0.020
	(0.003)***	(0.003)***	(0.002)***	(0.002)***	(0.002)***	(0.002)***	(0.002)***	(0.003)***	(0.002)***
Ln (market potential)	0.034	0.020	0.034	0.048	0.039	0.036	0.036	0.033	0.034
	(0.006)***	(0.005)***	(0.003)***	(0.007)***	(0.005)***	(0.005)***	(0.006)***	(0.010)***	(0.007)***
Instruments used:									
Ln (1831 density)	Y	Y	Y	Y	Y	Y	Y	Y	Y
Ln (1881 density)	Y	Y	Y	N	N	N	N	N	N
Ln (1831 market potential)	Y	Y	Y	N	N	N	N	N	N
Erodibility	N	N	N	Y	N	N	N	N	Y
Soil carbon content	N	N	N	Y	Y	N	N	N	N
Subsoil water capacity	N	N	N	N	Y	Y	N	N	N
Depth to rock	N	N	N	N	N	Y	Y	N	N
Ruggedness	N	N	N	N	N	N	Y	Y	N
Soil differentiation	N	N	N	N	N	N	N	Y	Y
First-stage statistics	298.0	298.0	298.0	8.3	17.0	23.0	19.8	8.3	10.5
Overidentification test p-value	0.57	0.36	0.67	0.62	0.19	0.36	0.54	0.11	0.14

Note: 306 observations for each regression. All regressions include a constant and three amenity variables (sea, lake, and mountain). Standard errors in parentheses.

***Significant at the 1 percent level.

elasticity of 0.05, adding further controls and correcting for the endogenous quality and quantity of labor biases bring this number down to about 0.02.

1.6 TFP

1.6.1 Firm and Establishment Data

To construct our establishment-level data, we proceed as follows. We first put together two firm-level data sets: the BRN (Bénéfices Réels Normaux) and the RSI (Régime Simplifié d'Imposition). The BRN contains the balance sheet of all firms in the traded sectors with a turnover above 730,000 euros. The RSI is the counterpart of the BRN for firms with a turnover below 730,000 euros. Although the details of the reporting differ, for our purpose, these two data sets contain essentially the same information. Their union covers nearly all French firms.

For each firm, we have a firm identifier and detailed annual information about its output and its consumption of intermediate goods and materials. This allows us to construct a reliable measure of value added. To estimate TFP (see the following), we use a measure of capital stock based on the sum of the reported book values of productive and financial assets.[24] We also experiment with TFP estimations using the cost of capital rather than assets values, following the detailed methodology developed by Boutin and Quantin (2006).

Since firms can have many establishments at many locations, we also use the SIREN data (Système d'Identification du Répertoire des ENtreprises), which is an exhaustive registry of all establishments in the traded sectors. For each establishment and year, SIREN reports both a firm and an establishment identifier, a municipality code, and total employment. Finally, note that BRN, RSI, and SIREN only report total employment and not hours worked.

To obtain information about hours, we return to the DADS, which reports them after 1993. Hence, for 1994 to 2002, we use another, this time exhaustive, DADS data set.[25] Using the individual information about hours and two-digit occupations that this source contains, we can aggregate it at the establishment level to obtain the hours for all employees and by skill group. We emphasize this because of the suspected importance of labor quality.

24. In this respect, we proceed like Syverson (2004). Nevertheless, valuing assets at their historical costs is not without problems. We minimize them by estimating TFP at the three-digit level with 114 sectors. Indeed, the capital stocks of firms within the same sector are likely to be of the same vintage when sectors are more narrowly defined. We also use year dummies. An alternative would be to deflate assets using economic criteria. However, our panel is rather short, which makes it difficult to trace the original investments. Our procedure also differs from that of Olley and Pakes (1996), who use a permanent inventory method.

25. Unfortunately, this data cannot be used for our wage regressions, because the different years have not been linked up.

To avoid estimating too many coefficients for different types of labor, we aggregate two-digit occupational categories into three groups: high-, intermediate- and low-skill workers, following the classification of Burnod and Chenu (2001).

To merge these four data sets, we extend the procedure of Aubert and Crépon (2004). At the establishment level, we first match SIREN with DADS using the establishment identifier present in both data sets. This establishment-level data set (sector and hours by skill group) is needed later to create a number of local characteristics. Next, we aggregate this establishment data set at the firm level using the firm identifier. Finally, we merge this firm data with RSI and BRN to recover firm-level information. For each firm between 1994 and 2002, we end up with its value added, the value of its assets, and total hours worked by establishment and skill group. The total number of observations for 1994 is 942,506. This number rises slowly over the period.

Finally, to avoid dealing with the complications of TFP estimation for multiestablishment firms for which capital and output are known only at the firm level, we restrict our attention to single-establishment firms to estimate TFP.[26] Because the information about very small firms tends to be noisy, we only retain firms with more than five employees.

1.6.2 Constructing Area-Year Measures of TFP

We now turn to TFP and start by constructing productivity measures for each employment area and year from TFP regressions. We estimate TFP for 114 sectors separately. For simplicity, we ignore sector subscripts for the coefficients. For firm i in a given sector, its value added va_{it} is specified as:

$$\ln \text{va}_{it} = \alpha \ln k_{it} + \beta \ln l_{it} + \sum_m \beta_m^S q_{imt} + \phi_t + \varepsilon_{it}, \tag{18}$$

where k_{it} is the capital of firm i, l_{it} is its labor (in hours), q_{imt} is the share of labor hours in skill group m, ϕ_t is a year fixed effect, and ε_{it} is an error term measuring firm TFP. The way we introduce skill shares is justified in Hellerstein, Neumark, and Troske (1999).

Three important issues are worth highlighting at this stage. First, we face the same problem as with wages regarding input quality, and more particularly, labor. Unfortunately, workers characteristics are typically scarce in firm- or establishment-level data. We use the strategy used in equation (18) based on occupational categories to control for labor quality.[27] This is obvi-

26. With multiestablishment firms, we need to impute the same residual estimated from a firm-level production function to all establishments of the same firm. This is a strong assumption that we would rather not make. In results not reported here, we nonetheless experimented with TFP estimated from multiestablishment firms.

27. An obvious way to deal with the unobserved quality of the workforce is to use fixed effects, but unfortunately, their use is often problematic with firm-level data because of the

ously a less powerful set of controls than the individual fixed effects used in the preceding wage regressions.

Second, we can hope to control for the two main factors of production—capital and labor—but not for other factors—and in particular.[28] As argued previously, the price of land is expected to affect the consumption of land and thus production while at the same time to be correlated with other local characteristics. Again, instrumenting for these local characteristics is the solution we consider here. Furthermore, output prices are unobserved and are likely to be correlated with local characteristics as well. To the extent that we think of our work as looking into the determinants of local value added rather than pure productivity, this need not bother us much here.[29]

The third issue about TFP estimation is related to the fact that input choices are expected to be endogenous. This issue has received a lot of attention in the literature (see Ackerberg, Caves, and Frazer [2006], for a recent contribution). For our purpose, this endogeneity bias matters only when it differs across areas. Our main TFP results were estimated using Olley and Pakes (OP; 1996). See appendix A for details about the OP approach. This approach allows us to recover r_{it}, an estimator of ε_{it}. We then average it within sectors, areas, and years:

$$r_{ast} \equiv \frac{1}{L_{ast}} \sum_{i \in (a,s,t)} l_{i,t} r_{i,t}, \tag{19}$$

where $L_{ast} \equiv \Sigma_{i \in (a,s,t)} l_{i,t}$ is the total number of hours worked in area a, sector s, and year t. A first measure of the local productivity of the average firm in area a and year t, denoted TFP^1_{at}, is obtained by averaging equation (19) across sectors, within areas and years, with weights equal to the number of firms:

$$\mathrm{TFP}^1_{at} \equiv \frac{1}{n_{at}} \sum_{s \in (a,t)} n_{ast} r_{ast}, \tag{20}$$

where n_{ast} and n_{at} are the total numbers of firms for area a, sector s, and year t, and for area a and year t, respectively.

This measure of TFP does not control for the local sector structure. To control for the fact that high productivity sectors may have a propensity to locate in particular areas, we regress r_{ast} on a full set of sector fixed effects, γ_s:

sluggish adjustment of capital. See Fox and Smeets (2007) for a more thorough attempt to take (observable) input quality into account when estimating TFP. Like us, they find that measures of labor quality are highly significant, but taking labor quality into account does not reduce the large dispersion of TFP across firms.

28. We also expect the functional form to matter, although we limit ourselves to simple specifications here.

29. In a different context where one is interested in distinguishing between price and productivity effects, such benign neglect may not be warranted. See, for instance, Combes et al. (2007). Note that this issue also applies to wages.

(21) $$r_{ast} = \gamma_s + \iota_{ast}.$$

This equation is estimated with weighted least squares, (WLS), where the weights are the number of establishments associated with each observation.[30] To estimate a productivity index TFP^2_{at}, we average the estimated residuals of equation (21) for each area and year:

(22) $$\text{TFP}^2_{at} \equiv \frac{1}{n_{at}} \sum_{s \in (a,t)} n_{ast} \hat{\iota}_{ast}.$$

The variable TFP^2_{at} can thus be interpreted as a productivity index net of sector effects.

We finally compute a third local productivity index, TFP^3_{at}, controlling for variables at the area and sector level, X_{ast}. For that purpose, we estimate the equation:

(23) $$r_{ast} = \text{TFP}^3_{at} + \gamma_s + X_{ast}\varphi + \varepsilon_{ast}.$$

This equation is estimated with WLS, where weights are once again the number of establishments associated with each observation. It mimics equation (12) for wages and uses the same (centered) local characteristics (same sector specialization, number of firms, share of professionals, average age, and average squared age). The main difference, however, is that these characteristics are constructed using the TFP data and not the wage data.

For comparison, we also estimate equation (18) with OLS. Denote $\hat{\varepsilon}_{it}$ the estimated residual for firm i. We then define:

(24) $$r^{\text{OLS}}_{ast} \equiv \frac{1}{L_{ast}} \sum_{i \in (a,s,t)} l_{it} \hat{\varepsilon}_{it},$$

the OLS counterpart to equation (19). It is possible to recompute our three measures of local productivity, TFP^1_{at}, TFP^2_{at}, and TFP^3_{at}, using equation (24) rather than equation (19). Next, we compare the coefficients in our main regressions using local productivity indices computed from OP and OLS.

One aspect of the simultaneity bias at the area level is that establishments may produce more and grow larger in areas where the local productivity is higher. It is possible to control for that by introducing area and year fixed effects g_{at} in equation (18):

(25) $$\ln \text{va}_{it} = \alpha \ln k_{it} + \beta \ln l_{it} + \sum_m \beta^S_m q_{imt} + \phi_t + g_{at} + \varepsilon_{it}.$$

This equation is estimated with OLS. Since this equation is estimated for each sector, the area-year fixed effects depend on the sector and can be rewritten with a sector subindex, g_{ast}. We can then define $r^{\text{FE}}_{ast} \equiv g_{ast}$, the fixed

30. These weights give more importance to sectors and areas for which a larger number of $r_{i,t}$ are considered when constructing $r_{s,a,t}$. For these area-sector-years, the sampling error on $r_{s,a,t}$ is usually smaller. Weighing should thus reduce the impact of the sampling error on the dependent variable that comes from the first-stage estimation.

effect counterpart to equations (19) and (24), and construct once again our three measures of local productivity.[31]

Finally, we average our estimates across years as we did for wages to avoid identifying out of the temporal variation.[32] Before going to our results, note that our local productivity variables are strongly correlated with one another. Using OP estimates, the correlation between TFP^1 and TFP^2 is 0.93, the correlation between TFP^1 and TFP^3 is also 0.93, and the correlation between TFP^2 and TFP^3 is 0.98. For TFP^3, the correlation between OP and OLS estimates is 0.96, the correlation between OP and fixed effects estimates is 0.91, and the correlation between OLS and fixed effects is also 0.91. Finally, the correlation between TFP^3 estimated with OP and mean wages (W^1) is 0.77.[33] This correlation rises to 0.88 after correcting wages of sector effects (W^2) or to 0.87 after correcting wages of sector and worker effects (W^3).

1.6.2 Results

Table 1.11 presents the results of three regressions for our three measures of local OP productivity: TFP^1, the mean productivity computed in equation (20); TFP^2, the local productivity controlling for sector fixed effects as estimated in equation (21); and TFP^3, the local productivity estimated in equation (23), which conditions out a broader set of sector effects. This table mirrors the wage table 1.6 for productivity. In columns (1), (2), and (3), these three measures of local productivity are regressed on log employment density controlling for amenities using OLS. The mean elasticity of TFP with respect to density is at 0.04 for mean productivity, 0.041 when taking out sector effects, and 0.047 when also controlling for the local sector structure. In columns (4), (5), and (6), we instrument employment density with 1831 urban population density. The TSLS coefficients for employment density are marginally lower than in columns (1), (2), and (3). In columns (7), (8), and (9), we add 1881 population density to instrument for contemporaneous employment density. Although the Sargan test of overidentification marginally fails in column (7) with a p-value of 7 percent, the results are very close to those of columns (4), (5), and (6).

Comparing these results to those of table 1.6 for wages, we note the following. First, instrumenting for contemporaneous employment density with deep historical lags lowers the coefficients in roughly the same proportion in both cases. This confirms our finding of a mild simultaneity bias regarding the quantity of labor. Second, controlling for sector effects in TFP^3 compared to TFP^1 raises the coefficient on employment density, just like it does when considering W^2 instead of W^1 (although the increase is slightly more

31. We also experimented with a number of alternative TFP approaches, such as GMM, cost shares, IV cost shares, Levinsohn and Petrin (2003), and so forth.

32. Like with wages, these averages are now unweighted.

33. Recall that the years over which TFP and wages are computed are not the same.

Table 1.11 **Local TFP (Olley-Pakes) as a function of density: OLS and historical instruments**

Variable	TFP^1 OLS (1)	TFP^2 OLS (2)	TFP^3 OLS (3)	TFP^1 TSLS (4)	TFP^2 TSLS (5)	TFP^3 TSLS (6)	TFP^1 TSLS (7)	TFP^2 TSLS (8)	TFP^3 TSLS (9)
Ln (density)	0.040	0.041	0.047	0.031	0.034	0.038	0.033	0.035	0.039
	(0.002)***	(0.002)***	(0.002)***	(0.003)***	(0.002)***	(0.002)***	(0.002)***	(0.002)***	(0.002)***
Instruments used:									
Ln (1831 density)	—	—	—	Y	Y	Y	Y	Y	Y
Ln (1881 density)	—	—	—	—	—	—	Y	Y	Y
First-stage statistics	—	—	—	371.4	371.4	371.4	429.1	429.1	429.1
Overidentification test p-value	—	—	—	—	—	—	0.07	0.18	0.37
R^2	0.63	0.70	0.75	—	—	—	—	—	—

Note: 306 observations for each regression. All regressions include a constant and three amenity variables (sea, lake, and mountain). Standard errors in parentheses.

***Significant at the 1 percent level.

important here).[34] A stronger effect of density after conditioning out sector effects is consistent with the notion that sectors located in less-dense areas may gain less from overall density and perhaps more from same sector specialization or another sector characteristics that are conditioned out in TFP^3.[35] Third, it is also interesting to note that when a direct comparison is possible, the density elasticities for wages tend to be above those for TFP. From the theoretical framework developed previously (and particularly equations [5] and [6]), we actually expect the coefficients on employment density to be higher for wages by a factor equal to the inverse of the labor share ($1/[1-\alpha]$). With labor coefficients typically between 0.5 and 0.75, the difference between the two sets of estimates is of the right magnitude, although a bit smaller than expected.

To assess the sensitivity of our results to the approach used to estimate TFP, we reproduce in table 1B.1 of appendix B some of the regressions of table 1.11 using alternative local productivity indices. These measures of local TFP are constructed from the OLS estimates of equation (18) and from equation (25), which computes local productivity fixed effects. When TFP is estimated with OLS instead of OP, the coefficients on density are close, though not exactly the same.[36] When TFP is estimated with local fixed effects instead of OP, we find lower coefficients on density. At this stage, our best estimate of the density elasticity of TFP is at 0.04.[37]

Turning to geological instruments, table 1.12 mirrors for TFP what table 1.7 does for wages.[38] Columns (1) to (3) use subsoil mineralogy and ruggedness to instrument for employment density using our three measures of TFP as dependent variables. The coefficients on density are higher than with historical instruments in table 1.11. Such a difference between geological

34. While TFP^1 may be taken to be the counterpart of W^1, TFP^3 corresponds to W^2. Because we cannot control for input quality well, there is no TFP concept that corresponds to W^3.

35. This higher coefficient on density with TFP^3 is also consistent with possible correlations between unobserved input quality and the local structure of production.

36. When TFP is estimated with OP, we must drop the first year of data and firms with no investment. Estimating TFP with OLS on the same sample of firms as with OP makes no difference with respect to OLS estimates of local productivity.

37. Comparing these results to Henderson (2003), the main study about agglomeration effects using TFP data in the literature, is not easy. First, Henderson (2003) uses very different U.S. data for which value added cannot be measured directly, and he focuses on five industries only. Second, he concentrates on sector effects and uses as a key independent variable the number of plants in the local industry. We focus instead on total local employment, conditioning out local industry shares (among others) in some TFP measures. Third, he estimates TFP and the effects of local characteristics in one stage using a different specification for productivity, which includes firm fixed effects. Finally, he tackles endogeneity problems using a GMM approach. Despite these differences, his findings of strong heterogeneity across industries and modest to high scale effects at the industry level are consistent with ours.

38. That is, aside from the difference in dependent variables, the regressions are exactly the same. The values taken by employment density differ very slightly because of the differences in years between the wage and TFP data and the difference in data source.

Table 1.12 **Local TFP (Olley-Pakes) as a function of density: Geological instruments**

Variable	TFP^1 TSLS (1)	TFP^2 TSLS (2)	TFP^3 TSLS (3)	TFP^3 LIML (4)	TFP^3 LIML (5)	TFP^3 LIML (6)	TFP^3 LIML (7)	TFP^3 LIML (8)
Ln (density)	0.054	0.041	0.045	0.045	0.048	0.047	0.045	0.046
	(0.009)***	(0.007)***	(0.007)***	(0.007)***	(0.005)***	(0.005)***	(0.007)***	(0.005)***
Instruments used:								
Subsoil mineralogy	Y	Y	Y	Y	Y	N	N	N
Ruggedness	Y	Y	Y	Y	N	N	N	N
Depth to rock	N	N	N	N	N	Y	N	N
Soil carbon content	N	N	N	N	N	Y	Y	N
Topsoil water capacity	N	N	N	N	N	N	Y	Y
Dominant parent material (6 categories)	N	N	N	N	Y	N	N	Y
First-stage statistics	5.5	5.5	5.5	5.5	5.9	7.4	5.2	6.0
Overidentification test p-value	0.58	0.60	0.38	0.38	0.26	0.19	0.15	0.22

Note: 306 observations for each regression. All regressions include a constant and three amenity variables (sea, lake, and mountain). Standard errors in parentheses.

***Significant at the 1 percent level.

and historical instruments is also observed with wages.[39] To repeat, it reflects the fact that geological instruments have a larger correlation with market potential than local density. The results of column (3) are confirmed in column (4), when LIML rather than TSLS is used, and in columns (5) to (8), when different sets of instruments are used. It is interesting to note that the overidentification tests are passed for the same specifications as with wages (and they also fail for the same unreported regressions).

To mirror again the analysis performed with wages, table 1B.2 of appendix B performs the regressions of table 1.8 with TFP rather than wages, using historical and geological instruments at the same time. The results are again extremely consistent with the wage results. The coefficients on employment density in table 1B.2 with both sets of instruments are the same as those that use historical instruments only in table 1.11. This near equality also holds with wages. Furthermore, overidentification tests appear to be passed or failed with the same combinations of instruments. An exception is column (8) with dominant parent material and topsoil water capacity. The test is passed with wages with a p-value of 15 percent, while it is failed with TFP (p-value of 5 percent).

In table 1B.3 of appendix B, we add market potential as the explanatory variable, just as we do with wages in table 1.9. We again use the exact same specifications as with wages. Adding market potential to the OLS specifications lowers the coefficient on employment density for TFP. The elasticity of TFP with respect to market potential is about half the density elasticity. These two results closely mirror what happens in our wage regressions when we add market potential as an explanatory variable. In the second part of table 1B.3, we instrument employment density with 1831 density and a range of soil characteristics. The coefficient on density declines by about 0.01 point to 0.033, while that on market potential increases by about the same amount to 0.027. This again is very close to what happens in the wage regressions. Interestingly, the same combinations of instruments pass the overidentification tests with both wages and TFP. The failure of the Sargan test in the last column of table 1B.3 is an exception.

Finally, in table 1.13, market potential is also assumed to be endogenous. As with wages in table 1.10, we instrument density and market potential with historical and soil variables. The main result is that instrumenting for market potential leaves its coefficient unchanged. The IV coefficient on employment density is also unchanged. This is the same outcome as with wages. In tables 1B.4 and 1B.5 of appendix B, we repeat the same exercise but use TFP indices estimated with OLS and with local fixed effects, as in equation (25). As in previous comparisons, the results for OLS and OP TFP are very close. With (local) fixed effect TFP, the density and market potential elasticities are

39. As previously, the coefficients on density are also slightly above those obtained with wages for similar regressions.

Table 1.13 **Local TFP (Olley-Pakes) as a function of density and (endogenous) market potential: Historical and geological instruments**

Variable	TFP[1] TSLS (1)	TFP[2] TSLS (2)	TFP[3] TSLS (3)	TFP[3] TSLS (4)	TFP[3] TSLS (5)	TFP[3] TSLS (6)	TFP[3] TSLS (7)	TFP[3] TSLS (8)	TFP[3] TSLS (9)
Ln (density)	0.028	0.030	0.035	0.034	0.034	0.034	0.034	0.035	
	(0.003)***	(0.002)***	(0.002)***	(0.003)***	(0.003)***	(0.003)***	(0.003)***	(0.004)***	(0.003)***
Ln (market potential)	0.025	0.027	0.026	0.021	0.023	0.021	0.022	0.024	0.018
	(0.005)***	(0.004)***	(0.004)***	(0.009)***	(0.007)***	(0.006)***	(0.008)***	(0.013)***	(0.009)***
Instruments used:									
Ln (1831 density)	Y	Y	Y	Y	Y	Y	Y	Y	Y
Ln (1881 density)	Y	Y	Y	N	N	N	N	N	N
Ln (1831 market potential)	Y	Y	Y	N	N	N	N	N	N
Erodibility	N	N	N	Y	N	N	N	N	Y
Soil carbon content	N	N	N	Y	Y	N	N	N	N
Subsoil water capacity	N	N	N	N	Y	Y	N	N	N
Depth to rock	N	N	N	N	N	Y	Y	N	N
Ruggedness	N	N	N	N	N	N	Y	Y	N
Soil differentiation	N	N	N	N	N	N	N	Y	Y
First-stage statistics	230.6	230.6	230.6	8.2	16.4	22.8	20.2	8.0	10.5
Overidentification test p-value	0.16	0.43	0.17	0.68	0.90	0.60	0.29	0.04	0.16

Note: 306 observations for each regression. All regressions include a constant and three amenity variables (sea, lake, and mountain). Standard errors in parentheses.

***Significant at the 1 percent level.

**Significant at the 5 percent level.

*Significant at the 10 percent level.

lower than with OLS and OP TFP. However, we observe the same stability in the coefficients across regressions. This suggests that the method used to estimate TFP matters with respect to the point estimates for the density and market potential elasticities (though by only 0.01). However, the choice of TFP estimation does not matter otherwise.

1.7 Conclusions

We revisit the estimation of local scale effects using large-scale French wage and TFP data. To deal with the "endogenous quantity of labor" bias (i.e., urban agglomeration is a consequence of high local productivity rather than a cause), we take an instrumental variable approach and introduce a new set of geological instruments in addition to standard historical instruments. To deal with the "endogenous quality of labor" bias (i.e., cities attract skilled workers so that the effects of skills and urban agglomeration are confounded), we take a worker fixed effect approach.

Our first series of findings relates to the endogenous quantity of labor bias. Long lags of our endogenous explanatory variables make for strong instruments. Geological characteristics are more complicated instruments to play with. Nevertheless, geological and historical instruments lead to similar answers once the regression is properly specified: the simultaneity problem between employment density and local wages/productivity is relatively small. It reduces the impact of density by around one-fifth.

Our second finding relates to the endogenous quality of labor bias. Better workers are located in more productive areas. This sorting of workers by skills (observed and unobserved) is quantitatively more important than the endogenous quantity of labor bias. In our regressions, we address sorting using the panel dimension of our wage data. The density elasticity is divided by almost 2. Applying this type of approach to TFP is problematic. We thus put more weight on our wage results than we do on our TFP results. Nonetheless, the high degree of consistency between wage and TFP results is reassuring.

We believe the priority for future work should be to develop more sophisticated approaches to deal with the sorting of workers across places. Awaiting progress on this issue, our preferred estimates for the elasticity of wages to density is at 0.02 and is around 0.035 for the density elasticity of TFP. For market potential, we find elasticities around 0.035 for wages and 0.025 for TFP. Finally, our result about the relative importance of the two biases raises an interesting question. To what extent does it reflect particular features of the French housing and labor market institutions? One may imagine that in a country like the United States with greater labor mobility and a much flatter housing supply curve (in at least part of the country), the endogenous quantity of labor bias might dominate. Further research should inform this question.

Appendix A
Implementation of Olley and Pakes (1996)

The error term in equation (18) is rewritten as $\varepsilon_{it} \equiv v_{it} + \xi_{it}$, where v_{it} is the part of the error term that influences the decision of the firm regarding its factors, and ξ_{it} is an independent noise. The crucial assumption is that capital investment, I_{it}, can be written as a function of the error term, v_{it}, and current capital: $I_{it} \equiv f_t(k_{it}, v_{it})$, with $\partial f_t / \partial_{it} > 0$. The investment function can be inverted to yield: $v_{it} = f_t^{-1}(k_{it}, I_{it})$. Equation (18) can then be rewritten as:

$$\text{(A1)} \quad \ln \text{va}_{it} = \alpha \ln k_{it} + \beta \ln l_{it} + \sum_m \beta^S_m q_{imt} + \phi_t + f_t^{-1}(k_{it}, I_{it}) + \xi_{it}.$$

This equation can be estimated in two stages. Denote $\Phi_t(k_{it}, I_{it}) \equiv f_t^{-1}(k_{it}, I_{it}) + \alpha \ln k_{it} + \phi_t$. Equation (A1) becomes:

$$\text{(A2)} \qquad \ln \text{va}_{it} = \beta \ln l_{it} + \sum_m \beta^S_m q_{imt} + \Phi_t(k_{it}, I_{it}) + \xi_{it}.$$

This equation can be estimated with OLS after approximating $\Phi_t(k_{it}, I_{it})$ with a third-order polynomial, crossing k_{it}, I_{it}, and year dummies. Its estimation allows us to recover some estimators for the labor- and skill-share coefficients ($\hat{\beta}$ and $\hat{\beta}^S_m$). It is then possible to construct $z_{it} \equiv \ln \text{va}_{it} - \hat{\beta} \ln l_{it} - \Sigma_m \hat{\beta}^S_m q_{imt}$. Furthermore, the error v_{it} is rewritten as the projection on its lag and an innovation: $v_{it} \equiv h(v_{it-1}) + \zeta_{it-1}$. Using $v_{it-1} = f_{t-1}^{-1}(k_{it-1}, I_{it-1}) = \Phi_{t-1}(k_{it-1}, I_{it-1}) - \alpha \ln k_{j,t-1} - \phi_{t-1}$, the value added equation then becomes:

$$\text{(A3)} \quad z_{it} = \alpha \ln k_{it} + \phi_t + h\,[\hat{\Phi}(k_{it-1}, I_{it-1}) - \alpha \ln k_{jt-1} - \phi_{t-1}] + \psi_{it},$$

where ψ_{it} is a random error. The function $h(.)$ is approximated by a third-order polynomial, and equation (A3) is estimated with nonlinear least squares. It allows us to recover some estimators of the capital coefficient $\hat{\alpha}$ and the year dummies $\hat{\phi}_t$. Firm TFP is then defined as $r_{it} \equiv z_{it} - \hat{\alpha} \ln k_{it} - \hat{\phi}_t$. It is an estimator of ε_{it}. For further details about the implementation procedure in stata used in our chapter, see Arnold (2005).

Although the OP method allows us to control for simultaneity, it has some drawbacks. In particular, we need to construct investment from the data: $I_{it} = k_{it} - k_{it-1}$. As a consequence, it can be computed only for firms that are present in two consecutive years. Other observations must be dropped. Furthermore, the investment equation $I_{it} = f_t(k_{it}, v_{it})$ can be inverted only if $I_{it} > 0$. Hence, we can keep only observations for which $I_{it} > 0$. This double selection may introduce a bias, for instance, if (a) there is greater "churning" (i.e., entry and exits) in denser areas and (b) age and investment affect productivity positively. Then, more establishments with a low productivity may be dropped in high-density areas. In turn, this may increase the measured difference in local productivity between areas of low and high density. Reestimating OLS TFP on the same sample of firms used for OP shows that fortunately, this is not the case on French data.

Appendix B
Further Results

Table 1B.1 **Local TFP (OLS and fixed effects) as a function of density: OLS and historical instruments**

	TFP estimated with OLS				TFP with fixed effects			
Variable	TFP^1 OLS (1)	TFP^3 OLS (2)	TFP^1 TSLS (3)	TFP^3 TSLS (4)	TFP^1 OLS (5)	TFP^3 OLS (6)	TFP^1 TSLS (7)	TFP^3 TSLS (8)
Ln (density)	0.035	0.049	0.029	0.042	0.027	0.040	0.018	0.033
	(0.002)***	(0.002)***	(0.002)***	(0.002)***	(0.002)***	(0.002)***	(0.002)***	(0.002)***
Instruments used:								
Ln (1831 density)	—	—	Y	Y	—	—	Y	Y
Ln (1881 density)	—	—	Y	Y	—	—	Y	Y
First-stage statistics	—	—	432.3	432.3	—	—	432.3	432.3
Overidentification test *p*-value	—	—	0.21	0.10	—	—	0.85	0.75
R^2	0.63	0.75	—	—	0.45	0.67	—	—

Note: 306 observations for each regression. All regressions include a constant and three amenity variables (sea, lake, and mountain). Standard errors in parentheses.

***Significant at the 1 percent level.

Table 1B.2 **Local TFP (Olley-Pakes) as a function of density: Historical and geological instruments**

Variable	TFP^1 TSLS (1)	TFP^2 TSLS (2)	TFP^3 TSLS (3)	TFP^3 TSLS (4)	TFP^3 GMM (5)	TFP^3 TSLS (6)	TFP^3 TSLS (7)	TFP^3 TSLS (8)
Ln (density)	0.031	0.034	0.038	0.038	0.039	0.039	0.039	0.038
	(0.003)***	(0.002)***	(0.002)***	(0.002)***	(0.002)***	(0.002)***	(0.002)***	(0.002)***
Instruments used:								
Ln (1831 density)	Y	Y	Y	Y	Y	Y	Y	Y
Subsoil mineralogy	Y	Y	Y	Y	N	Y	N	N
Ruggedness	N	N	N	N	Y	Y	Y	N
Hydrogeological class	N	N	N	N	N	N	Y	N
Topsoil water capacity	N	N	N	N	N	N	N	Y
First-stage statistics	129.7	129.7	129.7	103.3	194.1	100.3	64.5	125.7
Overidentification test p-value	0.14	0.56	0.78	0.66	0.14	0.46	0.33	0.05

Note: 306 observations for each regression. All regressions include a constant and three amenity variables (sea, lake, and mountain). Standard errors in parentheses.

***Significant at the 1 percent level.

Table 1B.3 **Local TFP (Olley-Pakes) as a function of density and (exogenous) market potential: Historical and geological instruments**

Variable	TFP[1] OLS (1)	TFP[2] OLS (2)	TFP[3] OLS (3)	TFP[3] TSLS (4)	TFP[3] TSLS (5)	TFP[3] TSLS (6)	TFP[3] TSLS (7)	TFP[3] TSLS (8)	TFP[3] TSLS (9)
Ln (density)	0.036	0.037	0.043	0.033	0.033	0.034	0.033	0.033	0.033
	(0.002)***	(0.002)***	(0.002)***	(0.003)***	(0.003)***	(0.003)***	(0.003)***	(0.003)***	(0.003)***
Ln (market potential)	0.017	0.019	0.017	0.027	0.027	0.027	0.028	0.027	0.028
	(0.004)***	(0.004)***	(0.004)***	(0.004)***	(0.004)***	(0.004)***	(0.004)***	(0.004)***	(0.004)***
Instruments used:									
Ln (1831 density)	—	—	—	Y	Y	Y	Y	Y	Y
Subsoil mineralogy	—	—	—	Y	N	N	N	N	N
Ruggedness	—	—	—	N	Y	N	N	N	N
Subsoil water capacity	—	—	—	N	N	Y	N	N	N
Depth to rock	—	—	—	N	N	N	Y	N	N
Erodibility	—	—	—	N	N	N	N	Y	N
Soil differentiation	—	—	—	N	N	N	N	N	Y
First-stage statistics	—	—	—	115.0	170.6	71.4	86.6	70.7	116.1
Overidentification test p-value	—	—	—	0.27	0.50	0.69	0.32	0.42	0.05
R^2	0.64	0.72	0.76	—	—	—	—	—	—

Note: 306 observations for each regression. All regressions include a constant and three amenity variables (sea, lake, and mountain). Standard errors in parentheses.

***Significant at the 1 percent level.

Table 1B.4 Local TFP (OLS) as a function of density and (endogenous) market potential: Historical and geological instruments

Variable	TFP^1 TSLS (1)	TFP^2 TSLS (2)	TFP^3 TSLS (3)	TFP^3 TSLS (4)	TFP^3 TSLS (5)	TFP^3 TSLS (6)	TFP^3 TSLS (7)	TFP^3 TSLS (8)	TFP^3 TSLS (9)
Ln (density)	0.023	0.022	0.037	0.035	0.035	0.036	0.037	0.036	0.035
	(0.002)***	(0.002)***	(0.002)***	(0.003)***	(0.003)***	(0.003)***	(0.003)***	(0.004)***	(0.003)***
Ln (market potential)	0.030	0.030	0.024	0.022	0.026	0.019	0.012	0.020	0.020
	(0.004)***	(0.004)***	(0.004)***	(0.010)**	(0.007)***	(0.007)***	(0.008)	(0.013)	(0.009)**
Instruments used:									
ln (1831 density)	Y	Y	Y	Y	Y	Y	Y	Y	Y
ln (1881 density)	Y	Y	Y	N	N	N	N	N	N
ln (1831 market potential)	Y	Y	Y	N	N	N	N	N	N
Erodibility	N	N	N	Y	N	N	N	N	Y
Soil carbon content	N	N	N	Y	Y	N	N	N	N
Subsoil water capacity	N	N	N	N	Y	Y	N	N	N
Depth to rock	N	N	N	N	N	Y	Y	N	N
Ruggedness	N	N	N	N	N	N	Y	Y	N
Soil differentiation	N	N	N	N	N	N	N	Y	Y
First-stage statistics	232.2	232.2	232.2	8.2	16.4	22.9	20.2	8.0	10.5
Overidentification test *p*-value	0.54	0.56	0.04	0.73	0.29	0.05	0.14	0.38	0.87

Note: 306 observations for each regression. All regressions include a constant and three amenity variables (sea, lake, and mountain). Standard errors in parentheses.

***Significant at the 1 percent level.

**Significant at the 5 percent level.

Table 1B.5 **Local TFP (fixed effects) as a function of density and (endogenous) market potential: Historical and geological instruments**

Variable	TFP^1 TSLS (1)	TFP^2 TSLS (2)	TFP^3 TSLS (3)	TFP^3 TSLS (4)	TFP^3 TSLS (5)	TFP^3 TSLS (6)	TFP^3 TSLS (7)	TFP^3 TSLS (8)	TFP^3 TSLS (9)
Ln (density)	0.011	0.013	0.028	0.030	0.029	0.030	0.030	0.030	0.030
	(0.002)***	(0.002)***	(0.002)***	(0.003)***	(0.003)***	(0.003)***	(0.003)***	(0.004)***	(0.003)***
Ln (market potential)	0.032	0.027	0.022	0.013	0.015	0.011	0.008	0.012	0.010
	(0.004)***	(0.004)***	(0.004)***	(0.009)	(0.007)**	(0.007)	(0.008)	(0.013)	(0.009)
Instruments used:									
Ln (1831 density)	Y	Y	Y	Y	Y	Y	Y	Y	Y
Ln (1881 density)	Y	Y	Y	N	N	N	N	N	N
Ln (1831 market potential)	Y	Y	Y	N	N	N	N	N	N
Erodibility	N	N	N	Y	N	N	N	N	Y
Soil carbon content	N	N	N	Y	Y	N	N	N	N
Subsoil water capacity	N	N	N	N	Y	Y	N	N	N
Depth to rock	N	N	N	N	N	Y	Y	N	N
Ruggedness	N	N	N	N	N	N	Y	Y	N
Soil differentiation	N	N	N	N	N	N	N	Y	Y
First-stage statistics	232.1	232.1	232.1	8.2	16.4	22.9	20.2	8.0	10.5
Overidentification test p-value	0.63	0.15	0.89	0.68	0.79	0.56	0.38	0.33	0.57

Note: 306 observations for each regression. All regressions include a constant and three amenity variables (sea, lake, and mountain). Standard errors in parentheses.

***Significant at the 1 percent level.

**Significant at the 5 percent level.

References

Ackerberg, D. A., K. Caves, and G. Frazer. 2006. Structural identification of production functions. University of California, Los Angeles, Department of Economics. Manuscript, December.

Andrews, D. W. K., and J. H. Stock. 2007. Inference with weak instruments. In *Advances in economics and econometrics, theory and applications: Ninth World Congress of the Econometric Society,* vol. 3, ed. R. Blundell, W. K. Newey, and T. Persson, ch. 6. Cambridge: Cambridge University Press.

Arnold, J. M. 2005. Productivity estimation at the plant level: A practical guide. Bocconi University, Department of Economics. Available at: http://www.jens arnold.de/prodest.pdf.

Aubert, P., and B. Crépon. 2004. La productivité des salariés âgés: Une tentative d'estimation. *Economie et Statistique* 368 (April): 65–94.

Bacolod, M., B. S. Blum, and W. C. Strange. 2009. Skills in the city. *Journal of Urban Economics* 65 (2): 136–53.

Bayer, P., S. L. Ross, and G. Topa. 2008. Place of work and place of residence: Informal hiring networks and labor market outcomes. *Journal of Political Economy* 116 (6): 1150–96.

Boutin, X., and S. Quantin. 2006. Une méthodologie d'évaluation comptable du coût du capital des entreprises françaises: 1984–2002. INSEE-DESE Working Paper no. G2006/09. Paris: National Institute of Statistics and Economic Studies, Economic Studies and National Accounts Directorate.

Briant, A., P.-P. Combes, and M. Lafourcade. 2007. Does the size and shape of geographical units jeopardize economic geography estimations? Paris-Jourdan Sciences Economiques. Manuscript, June.

Burnod, G., and A. Chenu. 2001. Employés qualifiés et non-qualifiés: Une proposition d'aménagement de la nomenclature des catégories socioprofessionnelles. *Travail et Emploi* 86 (April): 87–105.

Ciccone, A. 2002. Agglomeration effects in Europe. *European Economic Review* 46 (2): 213–27.

Ciccone, A., and R. E. Hall. 1996. Productivity and the density of economic activity. *American Economic Review* 86 (1): 54–70.

Combes, P.-P., G. Duranton, and L. Gobillon. 2008. Spatial wage disparities: Sorting matters! *Journal of Urban Economics* 63 (2): 723–42.

Combes, P.-P., G. Duranton, L. Gobillon, S. Roux, and D. Puga. 2007. The productivity advantages of large markets: Distinguishing agglomeration from firm selection. University of Toronto, Department of Economics. Manuscript, June.

Combes, P.-P., T. Mayer, and J. Thisse. 2008. *Economic geography.* Princeton, NJ: Princeton University Press.

Dahl, G. B. 2002. Mobility and the return to education: Testing a Roy model with multiple markets. *Econometrica* 70 (6): 2367–420.

Davis, D. R., and D. E. Weinstein. 2008. A search for multiple equilibria in urban industrial structure. *Journal of Regional Science* 48 (1): 29–65.

Duranton, G., and D. Puga. 2004. Micro-foundations of urban agglomeration economies. In *Handbook of regional and urban economics,* vol. 4, ed. V. Henderson and J.-F. Thisse, 2063–117. Amsterdam: North-Holland.

Eaton, J., and Z. Eckstein. 1997. Cities and growth: Theory and evidence from France and Japan. *Regional Science and Urban Economics* 27 (4/5): 443–74.

Evans, W. N., W. E. Oates, and R. M. Schwab. 1992. Measuring peer group effects: A study of teenage behavior. *Journal of Political Economy* 100 (5): 966–91.

Fox, J. T., and V. Smeets. 2007. Do input quality and structural productivity estimates drive measured differences in firm productivity? University of Chicago, Department of Economics. Manuscript, February.

Glaeser, E. L., and D.C. Maré. 2001. Cities and skills. *Journal of Labor Economics* 19 (2): 316–42.

Guo, L. B., and R. M. Gifford. 2002. Soil carbon stocks and land use change: A meta analysis. *Global Change Biology* 8 (4): 345–60.

Head, K., and T. Mayer. 2004. The empirics of agglomeration and trade. In *Handbook of regional and urban economics,* vol. 4, ed. V. Henderson and J.-F. Thisse, 2609–69. Amsterdam: North-Holland.

———. 2006. Regional wage and employment responses to market potential in the EU. *Regional Science and Urban Economics* 36 (5): 573–94.

Hellerstein, J. K., D. Neumark, and K. R. Troske. 1999. Wages, productivity, and worker characteristics: Evidence from plant-level production functions and wage equations. *Journal of Labour Economics* 17 (3): 409–46.

Henderson, J. V. 2003. Marshall's economies. *Journal of Urban Economics* 53 (1): 1–28.

Levinsohn, J., and A. Petrin. 2003. Estimating production functions using inputs to control for unobservables. *Review of Economic Studies* 70 (2): 317–42.

Marchand, O., and C. Thélot. 1997. *Le travail en France (1800–2000).* Paris: Nathan.

Marshall, A. 1890. *Principles of economics.* London: Macmillan.

Moomaw, R. L. 1981. Productivity and city size? A critique of the evidence. *Quarterly Journal of Economics* 96 (4): 675–88.

Moretti, E. 2004. Estimating the social return to higher education: Evidence from longitudinal and repeated cross-sectional data. *Journal of Econometrics* 121 (1/2): 175–212.

Moulton, B. R. 1990. An illustration of a pitfall in estimating the effects of aggregate variables on micro units. *Review of Economics and Statistics* 72 (2): 334–8.

Olley, G. S., and A. Pakes. 1996. The dynamics of productivity in the telecommunication equipment industry. *Econometrica* 64 (6): 1263–97.

Rappaport, J. 2007. Moving to nice weather. *Regional Science and Urban Economics* 37 (3): 375–98.

Redding, S. J., and D. M. Sturm. 2008. The costs of remoteness: Evidence from German division and reunification. *American Economic Review* 98 (5): 1766–97.

Roback, J. 1982. Wages, rents and the quality of life. *Journal of Political Economy* 90 (6): 1257–78.

Rosenthal, S. S., and W. C. Strange. 2004. Evidence on the nature and sources of agglomeration economies. In *Handbook of regional and urban economics,* vol. 4, ed. V. Henderson and J.-F. Thisse, 2119–71. Amsterdam: North-Holland.

———. 2008. The attenuation of human capital spillovers. *Journal of Urban Economics* 64 (2): 373–89.

Seybold, C. A., J. E. Herrick, and J. J. Brejda. 1999. Soil resilience: A fundamental component of soil quality. *Soil Science* 164 (4): 224–34.

Smith, A. 1776. *An inquiry into the nature and causes of the wealth of nations.* London: W. Strahan and T. Cadell.

Stock, J. H., and M. Yogo. 2005. Testing for weak instruments in linear IV regression. In *Identification and inference for econometric models: Essays in honor of Thomas Rothenberg,* ed. D. W. K. Andrews and J. H. Stock, 80–108. Cambridge: Cambridge University Press.

Syverson, C. 2004. Market structure and productivity: A concrete example. *Journal of Political Economy* 112 (6): 1181–222.

2

Dispersion in House Price and Income Growth across Markets
Facts and Theories

Joseph Gyourko, Christopher Mayer, and Todd Sinai

2.1 Introduction

One of the most striking patterns in the American socioeconomic landscape since World War II involves the skewness of long-run house price growth. Real house prices in metropolitan statistical areas (MSAs) such as San Francisco, Boston, and New York have appreciated at rates well above the national average over the postwar period. Indeed, this time period has witnessed two very different patterns of urban success: one pairs strong population expansion with mild house price appreciation, but the other involves very high house price growth with relatively little population growth.

This latter phenomenon is especially intriguing, because high house price growth in an MSA implies that new residents have to pay ever-increasing amounts to live there, especially relative to the MSAs with greater population growth. Of course, basic price theory tells us that consistently high prices require some limits on new supply. After all, if land were plentiful and homebuilders could supply new units whenever prices rose sufficiently above

Joseph Gyourko is the Martin Bucksbaum Professor of Real Estate and Finance and chairperson of the real estate department at the Wharton School of the University of Pennsylvania and a research associate of the National Bureau of Economic Research. Christopher Mayer is the senior vice dean and Paul Milstein Professor of Real Estate at Columbia Business School and a research associate of the National Bureau of Economic Research. Todd Sinai is associate professor of real estate at the Wharton School of the University of Pennsylvania and a research associate of the National Bureau of Economic Research.

A previous version of this chapter was written for the NBER Economics of Agglomeration conference held in Cambridge, Massachusetts, on November 30, 2007 to December 1, 2007. We appreciate the comments of Ed Glaeser and anonymous referees. Gyourko and Sinai also thank the Research Sponsors Program of the Zell/Lurie Real Estate Center at the Wharton School for financial support. Mayer thanks the Milstein Center for Real Estate at the Columbia Business School for its support.

production costs to provide them a competitive return, prices would never exceed construction cost in the long run. Others have studied supply side constraints, and there is no doubt that many localities have become expert at imposing a myriad of hurdles that raise the cost of developing new housing (Glaeser and Gyourko 2003; Glaeser, Gyourko, and Saks 2005a, 2005b; Gyourko, Saiz, and Summers 2008; Saks 2008).

While inelastic supply is necessary for above-average long-run house price growth, it is not sufficient. Some factor must drive demand for living in the high price growth MSAs so that households are willing to pay an increasing house price premium to live there. In this chapter, we consider four potential explanations that stem from recent urban research. One possibility is that the value of agglomeration is rising in some inelastically supplied cities. Another is that these cities simply have become more productive but not due to agglomeration. A third possibility is that the level of amenities in these cities has grown. And the fourth explanation is that the dispersion in house price growth arises from an increasing number of high-income families at the national level, combined with households sorting across metropolitan areas. In this case, the rich households ultimately outbid others for the scarce slots available in supply-constrained metropolitan areas. We will conclude that the evidence suggests that this sorting mechanism is at least partially responsible for the urban outcomes we see, but it also is clear that much more work is needed to pin down the relative contributions of these basic factors.

We begin in the next section by describing some basic facts about the long-run evolution of house prices over time by MSA.[1] There is considerable heterogeneity in long-run house price growth across MSAs, and those cross-MSA differences persist. We show that many MSAs that experienced high house price growth had little population growth and vice versa. Following Gyourko, Mayer, and Sinai (2006), we classify a subset of MSAs with high house price growth and low population growth as "superstar cities." These cities experienced growing demand that was capitalized into land prices rather than manifested as new construction.

In section 2.3, we use a spatial equilibrium structure developed by Glaeser and Tobio (2008) to decompose the patterns of income, population, and housing unit growth to shed light on how superstar cities differ from other cities in regard to growth in their amenities, productivity, and housing supply. This framework implies that superstar cities have much lower housing supply growth than other cities. It also shows little difference between superstars and other cities in the growth rate of amenities or productivity.

The spatial distribution of income growth is brought to bear in section 2.4 as another set of stylized facts that needs explaining. Not only do long-run income growth rates vary widely across MSAs, but those MSAs with

1. Because we use decennial census data, our empirical analysis stops before the recent housing market bust. While this cycle is very interesting for a variety of reasons, our story and analysis are much more about trends that are not dependent on short-run dynamics.

growing house prices experience more rapidly growing average incomes, as well as a right shift in the entire income distribution. This fact is not true for any high-demand MSA, only those where it is difficult to construct new housing.

In sections 2.5 and 2.6, we discuss how the various possible explanations for urban growth—growing amenities, greater productivity, agglomeration benefits, or growth in the right tail of the national income distribution—comport with the stylized facts we established earlier. Section 2.7 briefly concludes.

2.2 Stylized Facts on the Growing Dispersion in House Prices

2.2.1 House Price Growth

We use and discuss a variety of data from the U.S. decennial censuses, aggregated to the level of the metropolitan area, which corresponds to the local labor market. We use a sample of 280 such areas that had populations of at least 50,000 in 1950 and that are in the continental United States.[2] Information on the distribution of house values, family incomes, population, and the number of housing units were collected.

Since the definitions of metro areas change over time, we use one based on 1999 county boundaries to project consistent metro-area boundaries forward and backward through time.[3] Data were collected at the county level and aggregated to the metropolitan statistical area, or to the primary metropolitan statistical area (PMSA) level in the case of consolidated metropolitan statistical areas. Data for the 1970 to 2000 period are obtained from GeoLytics, which compiles long-form data from the Decennial Censuses of Housing and Population. We hand collected 1950 and 1960 data from

2. Thirty-six areas with populations under 50,000 in 1950 were excluded from our analysis because of concerns about abnormal house quality changes in markets with so few units at the start of our period of analysis. Those MSAs are: Auburn-Opelika, Barnstable, Bismarck, Boulder, Brazoria, Bryan, Casper, Cheyenne, Columbia, Corvallis, Dover, Flagstaff, Fort Collins, Fort Myers, Fort Pierce, Fort Walton Beach, Grand Junction, Iowa City, Jacksonville, Las Cruces, Lawrence, Melbourne, Missoula, Naples, Ocala, Olympia, Panama City, Pocatello, Punta Gorda, Rapid City, Redding, Rochester, Santa Fe, Victoria, Yolo, and Yuma. That said, none of our key results are materially affected by this paring of the sample. Similar concerns account for our not using data from the first Census of Housing in 1940 in the regression results reported in the following text. (All individual housing trait data from the 1940 Census were lost, so we cannot track any trait changes over time from that year.) However, we did repeat our MSA-level analysis over the 1940 to 2000 time period. While the point estimates naturally differ from those previously reported, the magnitudes, signs, and statistical significance are essentially unchanged. Finally, the New York PMSA is missing crucial house price data for 1960 and is excluded from the analysis reported in the following text. The Census did not report house value data for that year, because it did not believe it could accurately assess value for cooperative units, the preponderant unit type in Manhattan at that time.

3. We use definitions provided by the Office of Management and Budget (OMB), available at: http://www.census.gov/population/estimates/metro-city/90mfips.txt. One qualification is that in the case of New England county metropolitan areas, the entire county was included if any part of it was assigned by the OMB.

hard-copy volumes of the Census of Population and Housing. Both sources are based on 100 percent population counts. All dollar values are converted into constant 2000 dollars.[4]

In each data set, we divide the distribution of real family incomes into five categories that are consistent over time. The income categories in the original census data change in each decade. We set the category boundaries equal to 25, 50, 75, and 100 percent of the 1980 family income topcode and populate the resulting five bins using a weighted average of the actual categories in 2000 dollars, assuming a uniform distribution of families within the bins. Since 1980 had among the lowest topcode in real terms, using it as an upper bound reduces miscategorization of families into income bins. We call a family poor if its income is less than $39,179 in 2000 dollars. Middle poor are those families with incomes between $39,179 and $78,358; middle-income families have incomes between $78,359 and $117,537; and middle-rich families lie between $117,538 and $156,716. Finally, rich families have incomes in excess of the 1980 real topcode of $156,716.

Using these data, we begin by detailing the remarkable dispersion—and even skewness—across MSAs in house price growth over the 1950 to 2000 period. Figure 2.1 plots the kernel density of average annual real house price growth between 1950 and 2000 for our sample of 280 metropolitan areas. The tail of growth rates above 2.6 percent is especially thick, and the distribution is right skewed. Table 2.1, which lists the average real annual house price growth rate between 1950 and 2000 for the ten fastest and ten slowest appreciating metropolitan areas out of the fifty MSAs with populations of at least 500,000 in 1950, documents that the dispersion seen in this figure is not an artifact of a few areas that were small initially and then experienced abnormally rapid price growth.[5]

These annual differences in house price growth rates compound to very large price gaps over time, even within the top few markets. For example, San Francisco's 3.5 percent annual house price appreciation implies a 458 percent increase in real house prices between 1950 and 2000, more than twice as large as seventh-ranked Boston at 212 percent, which itself still grew 50 percent more than the sample average of 132 percent for the fifty most populous metropolitan areas.[6] Figure 2.2, which plots a kernel density estimate of the 280 metropolitan areas average house values in 1950 and 2000, shows

4. We also use some data for 1940. Population and housing unit data for that year are based on 100 percent counts, but housing values are averages from the 1940 sample provided by the Integrated Public Use Microdata Series (IPUMS) housed at the University of Minnesota. We do not yet use any family income data for 1940.

5. A complete list of house price appreciation rates by metropolitan area, along with 1950 and 2000 mean housing prices, is reported in the appendix table 2A.1.

6. It is worth emphasizing that the extremely high appreciation seen in the Bay Area, southern California, and Seattle markets is not restricted to the past couple of decades. The top five markets in terms of annual real appreciation rates between 1950 and 1980 are as follows: (a) San Francisco, 3.65 percent; (b) San Diego, 3.49 percent; (c) Los Angeles, 3.20 percent; (d) Oakland, 2.99 percent; and (e) Seattle, 2.88 percent.

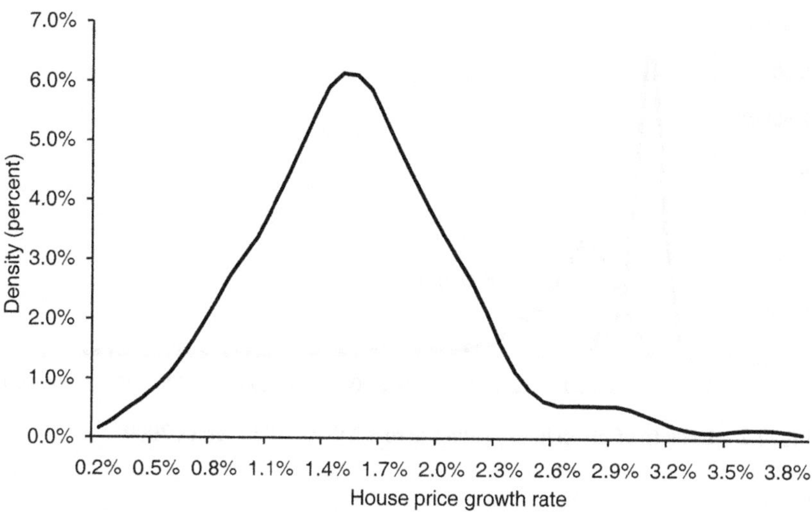

Fig. 2.1 Density of 1950–2000 annualized real house price growth rates across MSAs with 1950 population > 50,000

Table 2.1 **Real annualized house price growth, 1950 to 2000, top and bottom ten MSAs with 1950 population > 500,000**

Top 10 MSAs by price growth Annualized growth rate, 1950–2000		Bottom 10 MSAs by price growth Annualized growth rate, 1950–2000	
San Francisco	3.53	San Antonio	1.13
Oakland	2.82	Milwaukee	1.06
Seattle	2.74	Pittsburgh	1.02
San Diego	2.61	Dayton	0.99
Los Angeles	2.46	Albany (NY)	0.97
Portland (OR)	2.36	Cleveland	0.91
Boston	2.30	Rochester (NY)	0.89
Bergen-Passaic (NJ)	2.19	Youngstown-Warren	0.81
Charlotte	2.18	Syracuse	0.67
New Haven	2.12	Buffalo	0.54

Note: Population-weighted average of the fifty MSAs in this sample: 1.70.

that skewness has increased over the last fifty years, with a relative handful of markets ending up commanding enormous price premiums. Figure 2.3 normalizes the means and standard deviations of the 1950 and 2000 house value distributions so that they are equal and then plots them against each other. In 2000, the right tail of the MSA house value distribution extends to four times the mean, more than twice the highest MSA from the right tail of the 1950 Census. The left tail ends at about half the mean in both years, although it is slightly more skewed in the 2000 Census.

There also is long-run persistence in the markets that exhibit above-average price growth. Across the two thirty year periods from 1940 to 1970

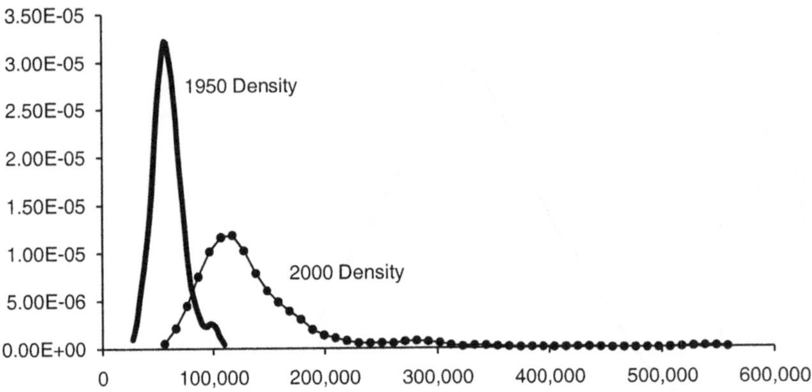

Fig. 2.2 Density of mean house values across MSAs, 1950 versus 2000

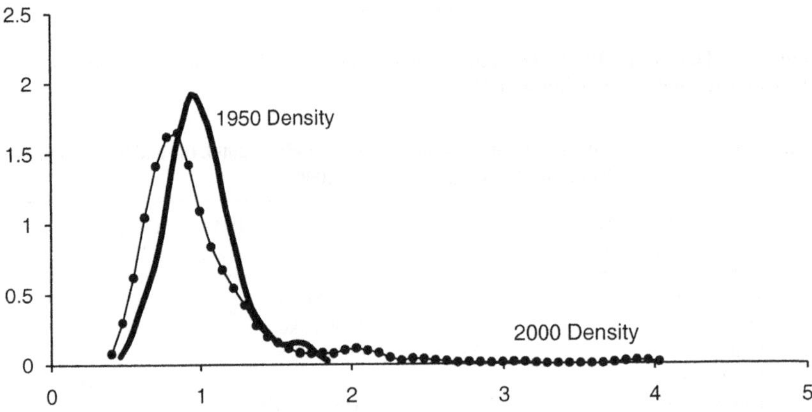

Fig. 2.3 Skewness in mean house values across MSAs, 1950 versus 2000

and 1970 to 2000, average annual percentage house price growth has a positive correlation of about 0.3. The root of this latter result can be seen in table 2.2, which reports the transition matrix for MSAs ranked by their average real house price growth rates computed over the two thirty year periods of 1940 to 1970 and 1970 to 2000. Most high-appreciation areas do not move very far in their relative price growth ranking. For example, of the thirty-two MSAs in the top quartile of annual house price growth between 1940 and 1970, half were still in the top quartile, and nearly two-thirds remained ranked in the top half between 1970 and 2000. Outside of the top growth rate areas, there is more movement across the distribution.[7]

7. Over shorter horizons such as a decade, MSAs can experience large price swings. In fact, the correlation in house price appreciation rates across decades is often negative.

Table 2.2 **Thirty-year house price appreciation rate transition matrix**

	1970 to 2000			
1940 to 1970	Top quartile	Second	Third	Fourth
Top quartile	16	6	6	4
Second	8	8	7	9
Third	4	7	7	14
Fourth	4	11	12	6

Note: The underlying sample for this table includes only 129 metropolitan areas due to limitations on data available back to 1940.

2.2.2 House Price and Housing Unit Growth

Typically, the markets with high long-run house price growth have not experienced much growth in the number of housing units, although that relationship has evolved over time, as housing supply has presumably become more inelastic in some cities. In table 2.3, we document the relationship between housing price and housing unit growth over time for the high price appreciation markets. To estimate this relationship, we regress the decadal growth in the number of housing units at the MSA level on the long-run growth in house price, allowing a different intercept and slope for those areas in the top quartile of the price appreciation distribution. Specifically, we estimate:

$$(1) \qquad \%\Delta H_{i,t} = \alpha + \beta^{*}\%\Delta P_{i} + \gamma^{*}(\text{TopQuartile}_{i}) + \delta^{*}(\%\Delta P_{i}{}^{*}\ \text{TopQuartile}) + \varepsilon_{i,t},$$

where $\%\Delta H_{i,t}$ is the percentage change in housing units in metropolitan area i during decade t, $\%\Delta P_i$ is the percentage house price growth in metropolitan area i between 1960 and 2000, and TopQuartile is a dummy indicator for whether the metropolitan area is among the top quartile of areas in terms of house price appreciation over the 1960 to 2000 period.

These results show that the price growth/unit growth relationship for the top quartile of the price appreciation distribution has essentially disappeared between the 1960s and the 1990s. For the bottom 75 percent of the price growth distribution, the relationship between average price growth and unit growth is positive, and with the exception of the 1980s, it is flat over the decades. The MSAs in the top quartile in terms of price appreciation start out in 1970 with a slightly less positive correlation than for the lower 75 percent (11.12 – 3.12 = 8.0 correlation). By the 1970s, however, the highest price growth markets are already in negative territory (17.18 – 18.14 = –0.96), while there still is a large positive relationship between long-run price growth and housing unit production for the other metropolitan areas. The negative correlation for the top quartile increases over time, to –3.62 in the 1980s and –3.89 in the 1990s.

Table 2.3 **The relationship between high long-run price growth MSAs and the change in the number of housing units, by decade**

	1960s	1970s	1980s	1990s
Average house price growth, 1960–2000	11.12	17.18	11.73	9.37
	(4.76)	(3.77)	(2.19)	(1.51)
In top quartile of average price growth	6.10	35.23	31.99	24.99
	(16.02)	(12.68)	(7.38)	(5.08)
Average price growth × in top quartile	–3.12	–18.14	–15.35	–13.26
	(7.91)	(6.26)	(3.64)	(2.51)
Adjusted R^2	0.04	0.10	0.16	0.15

Notes: The left-hand-side variable is the decadal percent change in the number of housing units. Standard errors in parentheses. To be in the top quartile, average real house price growth must have exceeded 1.75 percent over the 1960 to 2000 period.

2.2.3 Classifying "Superstar Cities"

We now turn to other work we have done (Gyourko, Mayer, and Sinai 2006) to identify those markets with high house price growth and low housing unit growth. Such markets are termed "superstar" markets in that research, and they are markets that are in high demand and those in which something prevents the development of many new homes.[8] Thus, house price growth is very high, but housing unit growth is not.

Because we do not observe the true state of demand and the literature does not provide high quality estimates of the elasticity of supply, the following two measures are combined to determine whether a market is a superstar. First, a market is classified as in high demand if the sum of its housing unit and housing price growth is above the sample median for the relevant period of analysis. Second, a metropolitan area is defined to have a low elasticity of supply if its ratio of housing price growth to housing unit growth is at or above the ninetieth percentile of the distribution for all metropolitan areas over the relevant period of analysis.

Each of these measures is constructed using data from the two decades prior to the year for which a superstar designation is made. Thus, the status of each metropolitan area is classified from 1970 to 2000, with 1970 being the first year, because the underlying data begin in 1950.[9] Figure 2.4 documents the outcome of this methodology for the most recent period—using 1980 to 2000 data to determine superstar status in 2000. Average real annual

8. That something could be a natural constraint such as an ocean or a man-made constraint in the form of binding growth controls on housing development.

9. Because the empirical task here is to document whether equilibrium relationships implied by our model exist in the data rather than to identify causal mechanisms for why a place becomes a superstar, the use of lagged data is not driven by endogeneity concerns (which these lags would not deal with effectively in any event). Rather, we wish to be able to classify superstar status in the most recent census data from the year 2000, and we suspect that any relationship between income segregation and house price effects occur after the superstar market has filled up.

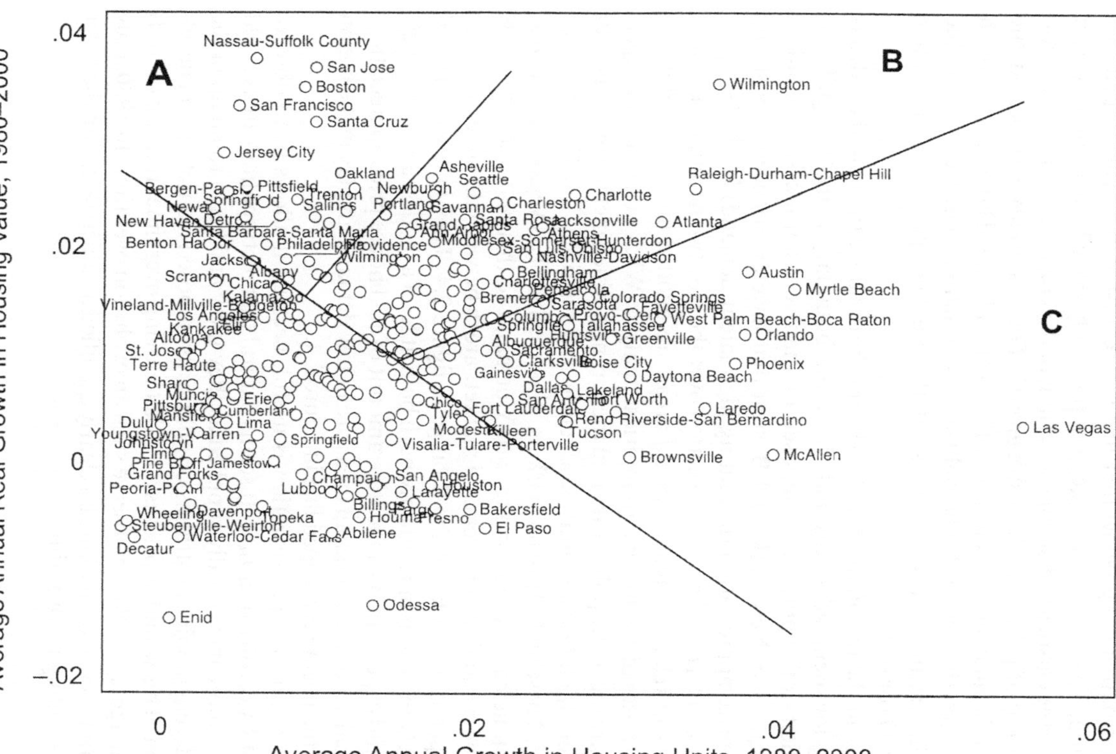

Fig. 2.4 Real annual house price growth versus unit growth, 1980 to 2000

house price growth between 1980 and 2000 is on the y-axis, with housing unit growth over the same two decades on the x-axis. The single downward-sloping line reflects the boundary between markets with a sum of price and unit growth above the sample median across all our MSAs for 1980 to 2000. Any metro area lying below that line is a relatively low-demand place by definition. The left-most and steepest positively sloped line from the origin captures the elasticity of supply at the ninetieth percentile of the distribution of the ratio of price growth to unit growth. For this twenty-year period, the MSA at the ninetieth percentile has a ratio of real annual house price growth to unit growth above 1.7. The right-most and flattest positively sloped line from the origin reflects the inverse of the ninetieth percentile ratio value (i.e., 1/1.7, or 0.59).

Cities in the region marked A, which is both above the boundary determining low-demand status and above the boundary marking significant inelasticity of supply, are composed of many coastal markets including San Francisco, New York, and Boston that have experienced very strong house price appreciation (indicating high latent demand) but little supply response in terms of new construction over the past two decades. The other markets in relatively high-demand areas are divided into two groups for the purposes of the following empirical analysis. What we term "nonsuperstars" are the metropolitan areas in the C range, which include markets with relatively high housing unit production and relatively low housing price growth. These high-demand markets, which include Las Vegas and Phoenix, build sufficient new housing to satisfy demand so that real price growth is low. The remaining high-demand markets are in between the superstars and nonsuperstars and lay in the B range in figure 2.4. They have experienced relatively high demand and have both built at least a modest amount of new units and experienced a moderate amount of real house price appreciation. The final set of metropolitan areas are in low demand and lay in the region below the negatively sloped line in figure 2.4.

This nonlinear categorization is useful, because it allows us to observe how MSAs evolve over time. It seems natural that metropolitan areas could become more inelastically supplied as they grow and begin to fill up in the face of geographic constraints or politically imposed restrictions on development. This would appear as a market moving over time from area C to B to A in figure 2.4. We do observe such an evolution over time. In 1980, only San Francisco and Los Angeles clearly qualified as superstars, with the other markets filling up over time.

2.3 Characteristics of Superstar Market Growth: Decomposing the Roles of Productivity, Amenities, and Housing Supply

As a first pass in understanding what determines the unique price growth of superstar markets, we apply a strategy developed by Glaeser and Tobio

(2008). Their approach uses structure imposed by a Rosen/Roback-style theory to transform MSA differences in house price growth, population growth, and income growth into implied differences in the growth of MSA-specific amenities, productivity, and housing supply. We use this decomposition to see how superstars vary from other cities on these dimensions.

Following Glaeser and Tobio (2008), every market in the United States is characterized by a location-specific productivity level of A and firm output of $AN^{\beta}K^{\gamma}Z^{1-\beta-\gamma}$, where N represents the number of workers, K is traded capital, and Z is nontraded capital. Traded capital always can be purchased for a price of 1. The location has a fixed supply of nontraded capital equal to $\overline{Z}$.

Three equilibrium conditions can be derived involving households, firms, and the housing market. One involves consumers who are presumed to have Cobb-Douglas utility defined over tradable goods and housing, the nontraded good. The next equations assume the following utility function defined over traded goods (C), housing (H), and city amenities (θ): $\theta C^{1-\alpha}H^{\alpha}$. Standard optimizing behavior assumptions yield indirect utility of $\alpha^{\alpha}(1-\alpha)^{1-\alpha}\theta W p_H^{-\alpha}$. Spatial equilibrium requires household utility to be the same everywhere, with the level determined by the utility available (denoted $\underline{U}$) in the reservation market, which always is open to any household or firm.

The second equilibrium condition involves firms, which are presumed to behave competitively, so they cannot earn excess profits in any one market in equilibrium. Hence, their labor demand function is derived from the firm's first-order conditions, as usual.[10]

An important innovation of Glaeser and Tobio (2008) that is quite relevant for this chapter is its introduction of housing supply heterogeneity into the classic urban spatial equilibrium framework. Specifically, housing is produced competitively with height (h) and land (L) so that the total quantity of housing supplied equals hL. There is a fixed quantity of land in the market area, denoted $\overline{L}$, which will determine an endogenous price for land (p_L) and housing (p_H). The cost of producing hL units of structure on L units of land is presumed to be $c_0h^{\delta}L$. Given these assumptions, the developer's profit for producing these hL units of housing is $p_HhL - c_0h^{\delta}L - p_LL$, where $\delta > 1$. Of course, this must equal zero, given that we have presumed free entry of developers. The first-order condition for height then implies the area's housing supply.

The firm's labor demand equation, the equality between indirect util-

10. As in Rosen (1979) and Roback (1982), the spatial equilibrium assumption does not mean that wages corrected for local price (real wages) are equal across space but that higher real wages in some places are offsetting lower amenity levels. However, spatial equilibrium is presumed to hold at every point in time, which does imply that housing prices are sufficiently flexible to offset differences in wages and amenities, not that labor or capital has perfectly adjusted at all times and places.

ity in the town and reservation utility, and the housing price equation are three equations with the three unknowns of population, income, and housing prices. Solving these equations for the unknowns yields equations (2) through (4) from Glaeser and Tobio (2008):

$$(2)\quad \text{Log}(N) = K_N + \frac{(\delta + \alpha - \alpha\delta)\text{Log}(A) + (1-\gamma)[\delta\text{Log}(\theta) + \alpha(\delta-1)\text{Log}(\overline{L})]}{\delta(1-\beta-\gamma) + \alpha\beta(\delta-1)},$$

$$(3)\quad \text{Log}(W) = K_W + \frac{(\delta - 1)\alpha\text{Log}(A) - (1-\beta-\gamma)[\delta\text{Log}(\theta) + \alpha(\delta-1)\text{Log}(\overline{L})]}{\delta(1-\beta-\gamma) + \alpha\beta(\delta-1)},$$

and

$$(4)\quad \text{Log}(p_H) = K_p + \frac{(\delta - 1)[\text{Log}(A) + \beta\text{Log}(\theta) - (1-\beta-\gamma)\text{Log}(\overline{L})]}{\delta(1-\beta-\gamma) + \alpha\beta(\delta-1)},$$

where K_N, K_W, and K_p are constant terms that differ across cities but not over time within a city, and all other terms are as defined previously.

These static relations are transformed into dynamic ones by presuming that changes to productivity, amenities, and housing supply are characterized by the following growth equations:

$$(5)\quad \text{Log}\left(\frac{A_{t+1}}{A_t}\right) = K_A + \lambda_A S + \mu_A,$$

$$(6)\quad \text{Log}\left(\frac{\theta_{t+1}}{\theta_t}\right) = K_\theta + \lambda_\theta S + \mu_\theta,$$

and

$$(7)\quad \text{Log}\left(\frac{\overline{L}_{t+1}}{\overline{L}_t}\right) = K_L + \lambda_L S + \mu_L,$$

where S is a dummy variable reflecting superstar market status as defined previously, the terms K_A, K_θ, and K_L are constants, the terms λ_A, λ_θ, and λ_L are the expected difference in growth rates for superstar markets, and μ_A, μ_θ, and μ_L are standard error terms. Given this, equations (2) through (4) imply the following:

$$(8)\quad \text{Log}\left(\frac{N_{t+1}}{N_t}\right) = K_{\Delta N} + \chi^{-1}\{(\delta + \alpha - \alpha\delta)\lambda_A + (1-\gamma)[\delta\lambda_\theta + \alpha(\delta-1)\lambda_L]\}S + \mu_N,$$

$$(9)\quad \text{Log}\left(\frac{W_{t+1}}{W_t}\right) = K_{\Delta W} + \chi^{-1}\{(\delta - 1)\alpha\lambda_A - (1-\beta-\gamma)[\delta\lambda_\theta + \alpha(\delta-1)\lambda_L]\}S + \mu_W,$$

and

$$(10)\quad \text{Log}\left(\frac{P_{t+1}}{P_t}\right) = K_{\Delta P} + \chi^{-1}(\delta - 1)[\lambda_A + \beta\lambda_\theta - (1 - \beta - \gamma)\lambda_L]S + \mu_P,$$

where $\chi = [\delta(1 - \beta - \gamma) + \alpha\beta(\delta - 1)]$.[11]

Equations (8) through (10) enable us to transform differential changes in population, incomes, and house prices across superstar and other cities into differences in innovations in productivity, amenities, and housing supply over time. Each of the equations can be estimated using ordinary least squares (OLS) by regressing each of log population, income, or house price growth on a constant and a superstar indicator variable, recovering the estimated coefficients on the superstar dummy, which are B_{pop}, B_{inc}, and B_{val}, respectively. Then, some algebra yields that the connection between superstar status and productivity growth (λ_A) equals $(1 - \beta - \gamma)B_{\text{pop}} + (1 - \gamma)B_{\text{inc}}$, where B_{pop} and B_{inc} are the estimated coefficients on a superstar market dummy variable from the population and wage change regressions, respectively. The weight on the population regression coefficient is the share of production associated with immobile capital. The weight on the income regression coefficient is the share of production associated with labor plus immobile inputs.[12]

The connection between superstar status and changing amenities is given by λ_θ, which equals $\alpha B_{\text{val}} - B_{\text{inc}}$, where α is the share of expenditure going toward housing, and B_{val} is the coefficient from the house price change regression. Given that traded goods always cost 1 and that housing is the only nontraded good, this difference reflects the change in real wages. If real wages are decreasing, then amenities are rising, so the basic insight of the static Rosen/Roback compensating differential model also holds in this more dynamic context.[13]

The connection between housing supply growth and superstar status, λ_L, equals $B_{\text{pop}} + B_{\text{inc}} - [\delta/(1 - \delta)]B_{\text{val}}$, where δ reflects the elasticity of housing supply. In this equation, population directly affects housing supply one for one, as everyone in the market has to live in a housing unit. Hence, if superstar markets have relatively low population growth, the B_{pop} term will be negative. The population/housing supply relationship is then adjusted for income and price effects. Higher relative income growth in superstars will raise the estimate of λ_L. However, house price growth that is substantially higher in superstar markets will lower the value of λ_L, with the weight determined by the elasticity of supply.[14]

11. The interested reader should see Glaeser and Tobio (2008) for more detail on the derivation of these equations.

12. In the results reported next, we follow Glaeser and Tobio (2008) in presuming that labor's share of input costs (β) equals 0.6, with that for mobile capital (γ) being 0.3.

13. In the results reported next, we presume that $\alpha = 0.3$, which Glaeser and Tobio (2008) also used, based on their examination of Consumer Expenditure Survey data over time.

14. We presume that $\delta = 3$ in the following analysis. Supply would be perfectly elastic if $\delta = 1$, which clearly is not the case in at least some markets or for the nation on average. Glaeser

To estimate B_{pop}, B_{inc}, and B_{val}, for each decade, we regress the decadal log change in population, mean income, or mean house price on a dichotomous dummy for whether the market *ever* was a superstar during our sample period. Thus, the superstar indicator is constant within each MSA. We also allow for a number of controls, including the beginning of period mean population, mean income, mean house price, and the share of the adult population with a college degree. Those regression coefficients are reported in table 2.4. The results typically were not economically or even statistically different if we omitted the controls.

It is worth noting that our definition of a superstar market as described in the preceding section is a function of the prior two decades' house price and housing unit growth. Since our data starts in 1950, our first decade where superstar status is fully predetermined is 1970. However, since we are using an indicator for whether an MSA *ever* was defined as a superstar, we feel comfortable backcasting the superstar identification to 1960. When we use a time-varying definition of superstar status in the next section, we will restrict our attention to 1970 and later.

In the 1960s, population growth in markets that ultimately became superstars was not materially different from those that did not. However, it has been appreciably lower in every subsequent decade, with the gap widening over time. These estimated coefficients are reported in the first four columns of the top panel of table 2.4. Superstar MSAs had almost 4 percentage points lower population growth (relative to other MSAs) in the 1970s, almost 5 percentage points lower in the 1980s, and almost 8 percentage points lower in the 1990s. To smooth out some decade-to-decade fluctuations, the last two columns of table 2.4 pool the 1960s and 1970s decades and the 1980s and 1990s decades. Over the 1960 to 1980 period, superstars had statistically insignificantly lower population growth. But during 1980 to 2000, superstars' population growth averaged almost 5.5 percentage points lower than other MSAs.

Superstar markets also experienced higher income and house price growth, as can be seen in the middle and bottom panels of table 2.4, respectively. However, all of the higher growth came in the 1960s and 1980s. Indeed, during the 1970s and 1990s, superstar markets had income and price growth below that of other cities (with the exception of house price growth in the 1970s). However, the more rapid growth for superstars in the 1960s exceeded the decline in the 1970s, and the growth in the 1980s exceeded the decline in the 1990s. Thus, in the last two columns of table 2.4, which average across decade pairs, superstars had income and house price growth that typically exceeded that of other MSAs. Over the 1960 to 1980 period, superstars had

and Tobio (2008) also worked with $\delta = 3$. The value of δ does affect the magnitude of the housing supply innovations, although no reasonable value changes the relative magnitudes of the contributions of productivity, amenities, or housing supply.

Table 2.4 **Decadal population, income, and house price growth regressions**

	1960s	1970s	1980s	1990s	1960–1980	1980–2000
		Population growth on superstar market dummy				
B_{pop}	0.0046	–0.0394**	–0.0483**	–0.0771**	–0.0096	–0.0542**
	(0.0159)	(0.0167)	(0.0125)	(0.0146)	(0.0143)	(0.0110)
		Income growth on superstar market dummy				
B_{inc}	0.0205**	–0.0127	0.1085**	–0.0110	0.0016	0.0384**
	(0.0090)	(0.0091)	(0.0125)	(0.0082)	(0.0051)	(0.0063)
		House price growth on superstar market dummy				
B_{val}	0.0773**	0.0284	0.3510**	–0.0777**	0.0492**	0.0794**
	(0.0129)	(0.0247)	(0.0289)	(0.0262)	(0.0132)	(0.0117)

**Significant at the 5 percent level.

almost no excess income growth but had almost 5 percentage points higher house price growth. Over the 1980 to 2000 period, superstars experienced almost 4 percentage points higher income growth and almost 8 percentage points higher house price growth.

The decade-to-decade volatility in the estimated superstar coefficients is not so surprising, given the well-known mean reversion in house prices. If superstars have higher trend income and house price growth but also greater volatility around that trend, then excess growth in one decade should be followed by less growth the next. This effect is compounded by our observing house prices and incomes only once per decade. Instead, what table 2.4 shows is that the *long-run* trends for superstars in income and house price growth are above those of other MSAs, while their long-run population growth is below that of other markets on average.

Next, we apply equations (8) through (10) to convert the estimated coefficients in table 2.4 into innovations in productivity, amenities, and housing supply in table 2.5.[15] At the decadal frequency, superstar markets do not exhibit consistently higher productivity or amenity growth (the first two panels). The estimates are positive in some decades and negative in others. For productivity, only in the 1980s did superstar MSAs seem to experience sizeable excess productivity growth. The decadal amenity results are small in general, indicating that superstar markets are not very different from the average along this dimension.

When we look at the twenty-year periods, in the last two columns of table 2.5, the pattern becomes clearer. Superstars effectively had no excess productivity growth during the 1960 to 1980 period, but they did have 2.2 percentage points higher productivity growth during the 1980 to 2000 period.

15. All regression coefficients and assumptions regarding consumption and sector shares are taken at face value in these calculations, which is why no standard errors are reported for these figures. They should be interpreted as stylized facts, not as precise estimates.

Table 2.5 Growth decomposition: Productivity, amenities, and housing supply

	1960s	1970s	1980s	1990s	1960–1980	1980–2000
Innovations to productivity						
Superstar, with controls	0.019	–0.013	0.071	–0.015	0.0002	0.022
Innovations to amenities						
Superstar, with controls	0.003	0.021	–0.003	–0.012	0.013	–0.015
Innovations to housing supply						
Superstar, with controls	–0.091	–0.095	–0.466	0.029	–0.082	–0.135

By contrast, superstars' amenity growth is not much different from that of other cities and over the 1980 to 2000 period was actually below that of nonsuperstar markets.

Superstar markets are most consistently different from other areas in terms of their housing supply growth, as can be seen in the bottom panel of table 2.5. It was much less (9 percentage points) even in the 1960s, before these places filled up, according to our measure of "superstarness." Relative housing supply was similarly low in the 1970s, with these markets building dramatically less in the 1980s. The results for the 1990s indicate a marked change in this pattern, although the estimate is only slightly positive at 2.9 percentage points. This discrepancy is swamped by the overall trend, as can be seen in the last two columns. Over 1960 to 1980, superstars' supply growth was 8.2 percentage points lower than for other cities. That difference rose to 13.5 percentage points during 1980 to 2000.

In sum, the only clear pattern is that Superstars have long had much less housing production than other markets. There is some evidence that productivity growth was higher for superstars in the last two decades, but as noted before, the productivity growth results are sometimes positive and sometimes negative, with only the 1980s generating the bulk of the higher measured productivity growth. Thus, not only are the magnitudes of the productivity differences smaller than the housing supply effects, but there is less of a clear pattern indicating that superstar markets are more (or less) productive than other markets.

2.4 The Distribution of Income within Metropolitan Areas: Superstars versus Nonsuperstars

What enabled us to distinguish productivity and amenity growth in section 2.3 was the relationship between the growth of average income and average house prices. If house price growth were large relative to income growth in a given MSA, one could conclude that amenities were improving since the after-housing income would have declined. If income or population growth were high, that indicates greater local productivity leading to greater demand for living in the city. In large part, what tables 2.4 and 2.5

tell us is that house price growth and income growth must have been highly correlated within MSA. Indeed, the distribution of income growth rates across MSAs looks very much like that of house price growth, with wide dispersion and some right skew. This partly can be seen in figure 2.5, which plots the kernel density of average annual real income growth over the 1950 to 2000 period by MSA. It shows that growth rates range from 0.8 percent per year to 3.1 percent.

However, another important stylized fact is that the entire distribution of income, not just the average, has been changing differentially for superstar MSAs, even relative to the nation as a whole. Over the last fifty years, the United States has experienced growth in the absolute number, population share, and income share of high-income households (Autor, Katz, and Kearney 2006; Piketty and Saez 2003; Saez 2004). The left panel of figure 2.6 shows that the aggregate distribution of family income across all MSAs in the United States has been shifting to the right in real dollars, as the right tail of the income distribution has grown much faster than the mean. The right panel of figure 2.6 then displays the evolution of the number of families in each of the income bins. Most of the growth in the number of families was among those earning more than the $78,358 median value for our sample.

These changes in the national high-income share were accompanied by very disparate patterns at the metropolitan-area level. Two canonical MSAs—San Francisco and Las Vegas—provide a vivid contrast. San Francisco experienced low levels of new construction and high house price growth (figure 2.7). Between 1950 and 1960, the San Francisco PMSA expanded its population by about 48,000 families. Over the subsequent *four* decades, San Francisco grew by only 44,000 families, with two-thirds of that growth taking place between 1960 and 1970. Real house prices spiked in San

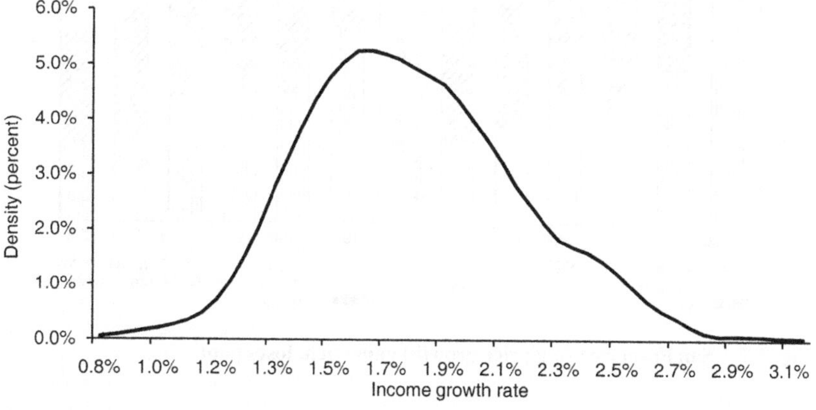

Fig. 2.5 Density of 1950 to 2000 annualized real income growth rates across MSAs with 1950 population > 50,000

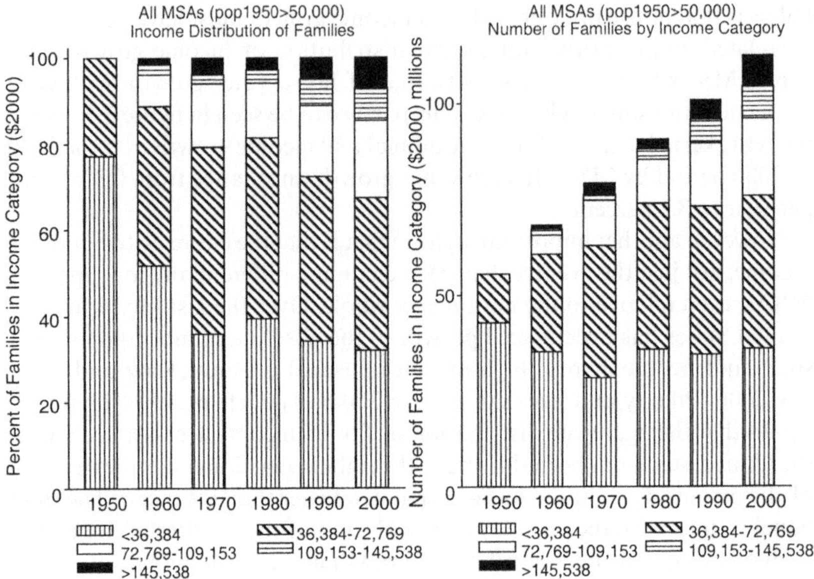

Fig. 2.6 The evolution of the national income distribution

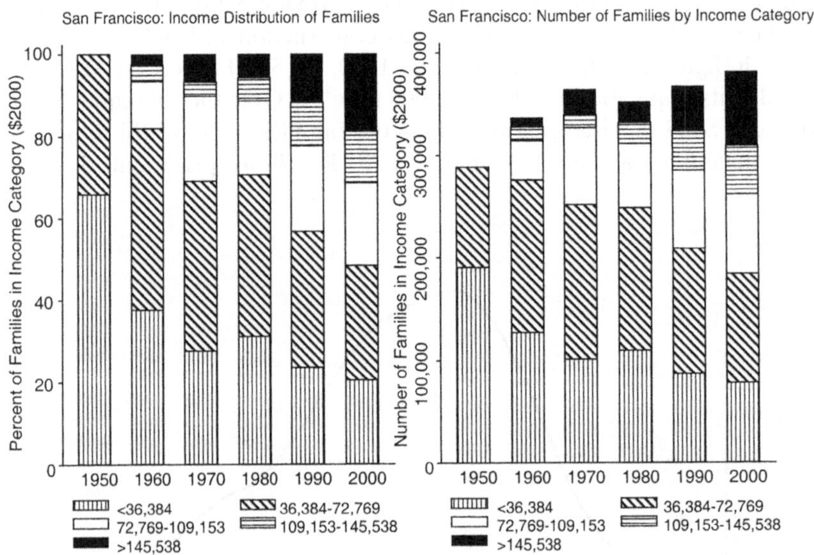

Fig. 2.7 San Francisco (big price growth) gains rich, loses poor

Francisco after 1970, growing between 3 and 4 percent per year between 1970 and 1990—about 1.5 percentage points above the average across all MSAs—and 1.4 percent per year between 1990 and 2000—almost 1 percentage point above the all-MSA average. By contrast, over the same time period, Las Vegas saw explosive population growth, expanding from fewer than 50,000 families in 1960 to the size of the San Francisco PMSA by 2000 (figure 2.8). Yet, it experienced modest real house price growth that was well below the national average.

Note that San Francisco's high-income share grew disproportionately. San Francisco, which always had relatively more rich families and fewer poor families than Las Vegas, became even more skewed toward high-income families between 1960 and 2000. Since the number of families in the San Francisco MSA did not grow by much, the MSA actually experienced an increase in the number of rich families and a reduction in the number of lower-income ones. In fact, only the richest groups with incomes of $78,358 and above increased their share of the number of families in the San Francisco MSA.

In stark contrast, the overall income distribution in Las Vegas did not keep up with the nation (left panel of figure 2.8), leaving that metropolitan area progressively more poor relative to both San Francisco and the U.S. metropolitan-area aggregate. The large numbers of new families in Las Vegas were both rich and poor, leading to substantial growth in the number of families across the income distribution of Las Vegas. Relative

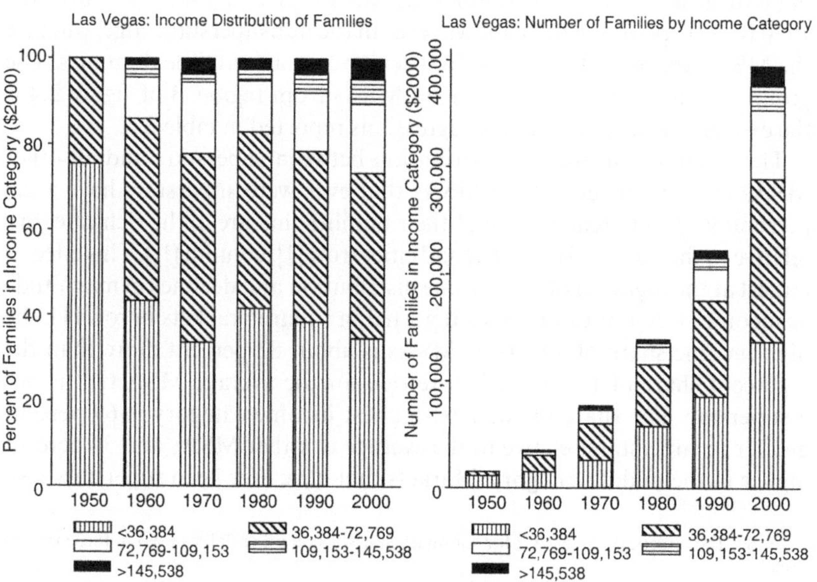

Fig. 2.8 Las Vegas (big unit growth) gains rich and poor, shares stay constant

to the national income distribution, however, the growth in Las Vegas was skewed toward poorer families.

We can generalize this pattern beyond San Francisco and Las Vegas by comparing the evolution of the income distribution in our superstar MSAs to other MSAs. Table 2.6 reports regression results on the link between income distributions and house prices using our earlier categorization of cities into superstar versus nonsuperstar status. We start with the cross-sectional relationship and then examine the data over time. The specification in equation (11) investigates whether a typical superstar market's household income is skewed to the right of the U.S. income distribution, as we saw was the case for San Francisco. Specifically, we estimate the following regression for MSA i in year t:

$$(11)\quad \frac{\#\text{ in Income Bin}_{yit}}{\#\text{ of Households}_{yit}} = \beta_1(\text{Superstar}_i) + \beta_2(\text{Nonsuperstar}_i) + \beta_3(\text{Superstar}_{it}) + \beta_4(\text{Nonsuperstar}_{it}) + \gamma_1(\text{Low Demand}_i) + \gamma_2(\text{Low Demand}_{it}) + \delta_t + \varepsilon_{ir}$$

Essentially, this regression relates the share of an MSA's families that are in each income bin to its superstar status and controls for total demand.[16]

The first column of the top panel of table 2.6 is based on a pooled cross-section of 1,116 MSA × year observations.[17] As in table 2.4, this regression treats superstar status as a (nonexclusive) fixed MSA characteristic, including indicator variables for whether the MSA ever was a superstar over the 1970 to 2000 period, whether it was ever in the nonsuperstar range, whether the MSA ever moved inside the low-demand area, and time dummies. The group of intermediate, high-demand MSAs from region B of figure 2.4 is the excluded category in all the regressions reported in table 2.6.

The difference in income distribution between superstars and all other MSAs is pronounced. Those MSAs that ever were superstars have a 2.5 percentage point greater share of their families that are in the rich category relative to the excluded high-demand cities (row [1], column [1]). This effect is largest at the high end of the income distribution and declines in magnitude as incomes fall. For example, as reported in square brackets in row (1), the high-income share of superstar MSAs is about 83 percent more than the 3 percent share of families who are rich for the average MSA that is not a superstar. The share of the next-highest income category is 69 percent greater in superstars relative to the average of other MSAs and 34 percent higher in the middle category. Markets that have ever been superstars also

16. See the appendix table 2A.2 for summary statistics on all variables used in these regressions.

17. This represents 279 MSAs in each census year from 1970 on.

Table 2.6 **The income distribution in superstar MSAs**

	Left-hand-side variable: Share of MSA families in income bin				
	Rich	Middle rich	Middle	Middle poor	Poor
		Cross-section:			
Superstar_i	0.025	0.022	0.042	–0.004	–0.086
[relative to mean share]	(0.001)	(0.001)	(0.003)	(0.004)	(0.007)
	[0.833]	[0.688]	[0.339]	[–0.010]	[–0.208]
Nonsuperstar_i	0.005	0.003	0.002	–0.023	0.013
	(0.001)	(0.001)	(0.002)	(0.003)	(0.006)
Low demand_i	–0.008	–0.007	–0.010	0.007	0.017
	(0.001)	(0.001)	(0.003)	(0.004)	(0.007)
Adjusted R^2	0.442	0.621	0.377	0.178	0.214
		Time-varying superstar/nonsuperstar status			
Superstar_i	0.013	0.011	0.035	0.013	–0.071
[relative to mean share]	(0.002)	(0.002)	(0.004)	(0.005)	(0.009)
	[0.433]	[0.344]	[0.282]	[0.0325]	[–0.171]
Nonsuperstar_i	0.005	0.005	0.002	–0.022	0.010
	(0.001)	(0.001)	(0.003)	(0.004)	(0.007)
Low demand_i	–0.006	–0.006	–0.009	0.000	0.021
	(0.001)	(0.001)	(0.003)	(0.004)	(0.007)
Superstar_{it}	0.028	0.027	0.017	–0.030	–0.041
[relative to mean share]	(0.003)	(0.002)	(0.006)	(0.008)	(0.015)
	[0.903]	[0.818]	[0.135]	[–0.075]	[–0.100]
Nonsuperstar_{it}	–0.003	–0.006	–0.004	0.010	0.003
	(0.002)	(0.001)	(0.004)	(0.005)	(0.009)
Low demand_{it}	–0.003	–0.003	–0.003	0.015	–0.006
	(0.001)	(0.001)	(0.003)	(0.004)	(0.007)
Adjusted R^2	0.504	0.669	0.383	0.207	0.219
Mean of LHS					
$\text{Superstar}_i = 0$	0.030	0.032	0.124	0.400	0.414
[$\text{superstar}_{it} = 0$]	[0.031]	[0.033]	[0.126]	[0.402]	[0.409]

Notes: Number of observations is 1,116, for four decades (1970 to 2000) and 279 MSAs. Standard errors are in parentheses. All specifications include year dummies. Superstar_{it} is equal to 1 when an MSA's ratio of real annual price growth over the previous two decades to its annual housing unit growth over the same period exceeds 1.7 (the ninetieth percentile) and the sum of price and unit growth over that period exceeds the median. Superstar_i is equal to 1 for an MSA if superstar_{it} is ever equal to 1. Nonsuperstar_{it} is equal to 1 when the price growth/unit growth ratio is below 1/1.7, and nonsuperstar_i is an indicator of whether nonsuperstar_{it} is ever 1. To control for MSA demand, the top panel includes an indicator variable for whether the MSA's sum of annual price growth and unit growth over any twenty year period fell below the median in that period. The bottom panel includes that variable plus a time-varying variable for whether the sum of the growth rates over the preceding twenty years was below the median; LHS = left-hand side.

have a nearly 9 percentage point lower share of families who are poor (row [1], column [5]), almost 21 percent less than the other MSAs.

Nonsuperstar cities appear similar to the in-between group (row [2]). Those coefficients are relatively small and do not exhibit a clear pattern. Low-demand MSAs are less high income and poorer relative to all of the high demand categories of MSAs, although the magnitudes are modest (row [3]).

The second panel of table 2.6 adds time-varying superstar, nonsuperstar, and low-demand indicator variables to the previous specifications. Prior to becoming superstars, MSAs that eventually will become superstars are richer on average, with a 1.3 percentage point greater share of families who are rich and a 7.1 percentage point lower share of families who are poor (row [1] of panel 2). When these areas are actually in the superstar region, the share of families who are rich goes up by an additional 2.8 percentage points, and the share of families who are poor declines further by 4.1 percentage points (row [4] of panel 2). As a baseline, superstar cities have a 43 percent higher share of families who are rich, declining monotonically to a 17 percent lower share of families who are poor, than other MSAs. After their transition to superstar status, these MSAs have an additional 80 to 90 percent greater share of the top two income groups and an 8 to 10 percent lower share of the bottom two income categories. As before, this pattern of results is robust to adding a host of controls for potential unobservables, such as MSA fixed effects, differential time trends for superstars versus not, or separate year dummies for superstars/nonsuperstars/low-demand MSAs.

2.5 Urban Productivity Differences and the Skewing of House Prices and Incomes

We now turn to a discussion of existing theories of urban growth and how consistent they are with the set of stylized facts that we have established. We first consider growth in amenities as an explanation and then turn to differences in productivity across MSAs. Finally, we consider dynamic agglomeration economies. In the next section, we will discuss a less traditional story that links national growth in the high-income population to the presence of housing supply constraints in some labor market areas to induce income-based sorting.

The standard spatial equilibrium model in urban economics developed by Rosen (1979) and Roback (1982) suggests that house price differences across markets are a function of amenity and wage (productivity) differentials. Glaeser and Saiz (2003) and Shapiro (2006) investigate the effect of amenities on the growth of population and employment. Both conclude that the link between education and metro-area population/employment growth largely is due to productivity, with amenities playing a smaller role. Going beyond the reduced-form OLS estimation standard in the literature, Shapiro (2006) calibrates a neoclassical urban growth model and estimates that about 60 percent of the impact of a higher local population share of college graduates on metropolitan-area employment growth is due to productivity, as reflected in wage growth. This does leave room for improvements in the quality of life to play a role, too, and they appear related to "consumer city"-type attributes, as reflected in various local cultural traits (Glaeser, Kolko, and Saiz 2001).

In our context, growth in amenities conceivably could cause the excess growth in house prices in superstar markets. However, this seems unlikely, since the results of the decomposition in section 2.3 indicate that amenities play little—if any—role. This makes intuitive sense: the growth in amenities in some MSAs would have to be substantial in order to match the patterns of long-run house price growth we observe. In addition, the amenities would have to be favored by high-income households in order to generate the cross-MSA changes in income distributions.

An alternative explanation for our stylized facts is that urban productivity differentials are growing sufficiently to account for the increases in house price and income dispersion that we observe in the data. Van Nieuwerburgh and Weill (2006) investigate the role of productivity by developing a dynamic, general equilibrium version of the Rosen-Roback model in which they then run calibration exercises to see whether there has been enough growth in wage dispersion across labor markets to account for the growth in house price dispersion.[18] Essentially, they assume homogeneous physical markets receive unobservable exogenous productivity shocks, and they investigate whether their model can then match the increase in the coefficient of variation in house prices across markets between two steady states. This exercise yields a very good match of the mean annual increase in house prices between 1975 and 2004, as well as a tight fit of the increase in the coefficient of variation in house prices across markets. This simulation also results in a good match of the growth of population in the productive places with higher wages. Although the framework is dynamic, the essential insight of Rosen and Roback still holds—housing costs are the price one has to pay to access the productivity of a given labor market area.[19]

Although the results in Van Nieuwerburgh and Weill (2006) are consistent with growing urban productivity differentials being the cause of the growing house price dispersion across labor market areas, they are not conclusive in proving causality. In particular, their results are not consistent with the empirical fact in our table 2.3 and figure 2.4 that the MSAs that experience

18. Van Nieuwerburgh and Weill (2006) provide one of the first truly dynamic frameworks to analyze spatial equilibria. Glaeser and Gyourko (2006) also have produced a dynamic model, but it is designed to investigate higher frequency movements in house prices.

19. There are a host of other results, ranging from the role of supply-side constraints to the change in the ratio of house prices to construction costs. We do not review those findings here so as to stay focused on the relationship between the skewing of incomes and house prices across markets.

long-run house price growth often have little population growth and vice versa. A careful review of Van Nieuwerburgh and Weill's (2006) data indicates that the productive/high-wage markets to which the model predicts people should move include both high price growth/low population growth cities in the A section of our figure 2.4, as well as high population growth/low price growth cities in the C section. More generally, there is a mixture of both types of markets in Van Nieuwerburgh and Weill's (2006) predicted top-wage quintile. Thus, it appears that their model's ability to match the data is at least partially the result of it picking up much of the growing price dispersion from very high-price (and price appreciation) coastal markets that have very little homebuilding and population growth; analogously, it looks to be picking up much of the housing unit/population growth from large Sunbelt markets that have relatively low house price levels and that have experienced relatively little price appreciation. This suggests that it remains an open question whether the growing dispersion in house prices and matching dispersion in income growth are being driven exclusively by random productivity shocks.

Much has been written in urban economics and in the broader growth literature about agglomeration effects and the potential for increasing returns in some markets that conceivably could causally link the endogenous relationship between house price and income growth previously documented. Indeed, Lucas (1988) explicitly notes that cities are a natural laboratory in which to test growth models involving some type of productivity spillover. Glaeser et al. (1992), Glaeser, Scheinkman, and Shleifer (1995), and Henderson, Kuncoro, and Turner (1995) soon followed with analyses of dynamic agglomeration economies that extend across time. While there is much debate about the precise nature of the spillovers involved, there is widespread agreement that there are long-run effects from urban agglomerations.[20]

Much of the more recent agglomeration research starts with the basic fact that skilled cities grow more quickly, where growth is measured in terms of quantities such as population or employment. For example, Glaeser and Saiz (2003) document that at the metropolitan-area level, a 1 percentage point higher population share for college graduates is associated with about a 0.5 percentage point higher decadal population growth rate. Similarly, Shapiro (2006) shows that from 1940 through 1990, a 10 percent higher concentration of college graduates is associated with a 0.8 increase in future employment growth (also at the metropolitan-area level).

Since Rauch (1993), we have known wages in a market rise with the skill level of that market, holding constant individual worker skills. Moretti (2004) recently confirmed Rauch's basic correlation, identifying human

20. See Rosenthal and Strange (2003) for an extensive review of the urban agglomeration literature.

capital externalities via an instrumental variables estimation that uses the presence of land grant universities as an instrument that proxies for human capital in the area but is plausibly exogenous to wages.[21]

Urban wage premia do appear to be relatively large. Glaeser and Mare (2001) estimate them to be on the order of 20 to 35 percent for workers in larger cities. Those authors also find that long-term residents in bigger cities earn a premium over new arrivals and that when long-term workers leave their city for another, the larger the size of their previous market, the higher their wages are in the new location.[22]

While there is much evidence consistent with the presence of dynamic spillovers, the agglomeration literature has not focused on the relationship between house price and income dispersion. However, it is not hard to see a natural link. If productivity differences across markets are growing, then the higher wages that result in the most productive agglomerations should be capitalized into land values (and thus house price) in markets where the supply of housing is constrained.

This story requires a very high rate of value growth, consistency in the location of agglomeration benefits in areas with inelastic supply sides to their housing markets, and firms that will not move to cheaper places. It certainly is not hard to understand how difficult it would be to recreate somewhere else the production or consumption externalities that lead to increasing returns. In the short run, this probably is impossible, although it seems more open to debate whether we should expect mobility of people and firms to be high over half-century-long periods. In addition, it is not immediately clear why such productivity would tend to occur in supply-constrained markets.

2.6 Household Sorting and Supply Constraints as Explanations for the Spatial Skewing of House Prices and Incomes

While a positive relationship between house prices and incomes across MSAs suggests that there might be innate differences in productivity across locations, it may be that productive people agglomerate rather than agglomerations make people more productive (Glaeser and Mare 2001). In addition, people may value grouping together for various reasons that do not have anything to do with production (Waldfogel 2003).

Given that, an alternative explanation for the stylized facts described earlier can be found in Gyourko, Mayer, and Sinai (2006). In that paper, the

21. That said, there is some debate about the strength of such externalities, with Acemoglu and Angrist (2000) finding small effects but at the state level. See Moretti (2003) for a recent review of the literature on human capital externalities in cities.

22. There is research on the firm side, too. For example, Henderson (1997) shows that concentrations of own-industry employment have measureable impacts on growth many years into the future.

growth in incomes and house prices across MSAs is due to inelastic supply in certain MSAs, heterogeneity in preferences for living in various MSAs across households, and a growing absolute number of high-income households at the national level. Importantly, neither the elasticity of supply nor the distribution of tastes for MSAs need vary over time for the Gyourko, Mayer, and Sinai (2006) hypothesis. Instead, changes in the income distribution at the national level percolate down to differences in the composition of families at the MSA level.

In addition, the comparative statics do not depend on the reasons for location preferences or the inelasticity of supply in the one market. All that is required is that some households prefer one city over the others and that there be some binding limit (natural or regulatory) on the supply of new housing units in some MSAs. Ultimately, the relatively rich with a preference for the market with an inelastic housing supply outbid the poor for the scarce slots. Gyourko, Mayer, and Sinai (2006) conclude that it is increases in the number of rich people nationally that should be correlated with the spatial skewing of prices and incomes. The intuition is that skewing can continue and increase as long as the growth in the number of rich people, at least some of whom have a preference for the supply-constrained market, exceeds the growth in supply in that market. The urban productivity model does not predict any such relationship with national aggregates.

That the right tail of the national income distribution has indeed been getting thicker over time is confirmed in figure 2.9, which reports data from Saez (2004) on the share of U.S. income by population percentile over time. The tax-return data Saez (2004) uses provides a very clear picture of changes

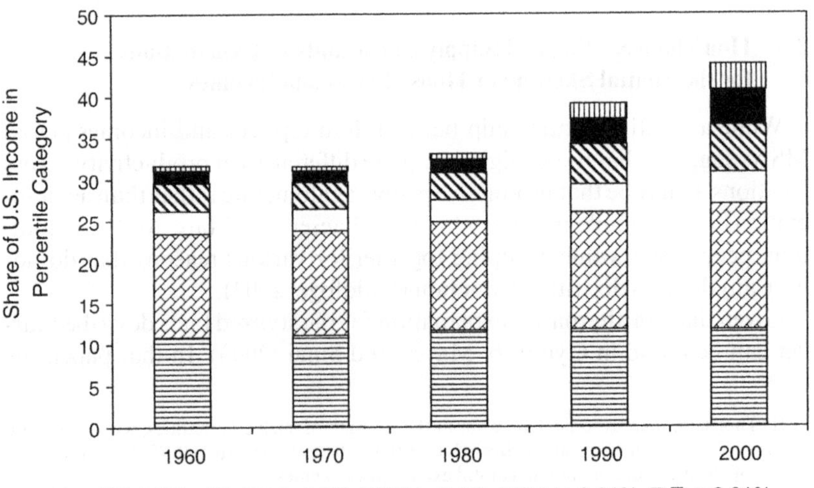

Fig. 2.9 Change in U.S. income distribution, 1960 to 2000 (from Saez [2004])

at the high end of the income distribution. The share of income held by the very top percentiles of the U.S. population—the top one-hundredth or 0.01 percentile, the 0.1 to 0.01 percentile, and the 0.5 to 0.1 percentile—all increased dramatically over the last forty years. The income share of the top 1 percent grew from under 10 percent in 1960 to almost 17 percent in 2000. Even the share of income held by the first to tenth percentiles of the population went up, from about 23 percent in 1960 to about 27 percent in 2000. While the income data reported in the decennial censuses in figure 2.6 are not nearly as fine or detailed as that available to Saez (2004), this source also shows skewing over time similar to that observed in the Internal Revenue Service data.

Gyourko, Mayer and Sinai (2006) show that changes in the national income distribution are correlated with more rapid house price growth in superstar markets. They regress a proxy for the entry price of a home (they use the tenth percentile house value in each metropolitan area) on a set of indicators for superstar/nonsuperstar/low growth status that are also interacted with the national number of rich families. Their findings imply that when the national number of rich families is 10 percent higher, the gap in the tenth percentile house value between MSAs that are ever superstars and those in-between markets is 1.1 percent greater.[23]

2.7 Conclusion

The growing dispersion in house price and income growth rates across MSAs is one of the most important stylized facts about metropolitan areas in America. The spatial sorting by income that it necessarily involves goes to the heart of how we live and organize ourselves socially. Whether these phenomena are due primarily to increasing value from amenities and productivity benefits or are the result of a growing number of high-income families willing to pay increasingly large amounts to live in a few supply-constrained markets is likely to have much to say about how many of us view this ongoing development.

This chapter has documented the basic facts about the spatial distribution of house prices and incomes and has outlined several possible explanations for the patterns we see in the data. Our review concludes that it is unlikely that growth in urban amenities, urban productivity, or agglomeration benefits are the sole causal forces involved. Rather, the skewing of the income distribution nationally is interacting with binding supply-side constraints in certain (primarily coastal) markets to help generate the variation

23. Gyourko, Mayer, and Sinai (2006) report results from several other empirical tests that are designed to distinguish between growth in the value of a location (such as from productivity growth) and growth and willingness to pay for the same utility (such as a greater number of high-income households that must choose between MSAs). We refer the interested reader to that paper for details.

observed. However, the empirical importance of the different explanations remains unresolved. Parsing this out is an essential task for future research that will not be easy but that is important for our understanding of urban markets.[24]

More generally, these changes in the nature of metropolitan America have profound implications for the evolution of urban areas. If the skewing and dispersion continues to grow, even large metropolitan areas could evolve into markets that are affordable only to the rich. In effect, an entire labor market area could have the income distribution of an exclusive resort. We do not know whether such an MSA is sustainable. Moreover, should public policy ensure that living in a particular city is available to all, or, because superstar cities are like luxury goods, should we not care whether lower-income households can buy into those markets any more than we care whether they can buy a Mercedes? The answer also has important implications for views on policy issues such as tax-based subsidies to homeownership. While economists can justify subsidies based on positive externalities involving better citizenship or improved outcomes for children (DiPasquale and Glaeser 1999; Green and White 1997), the case becomes harder if one believes that the high prices in America's coastal markets are due more to preference-based sorting combined with binding local regulation on homebuilding than to productivity. These and other questions will provide fertile ground for thought and research by economists interested in urban agglomerations.

24. Even if preference-based sorting explains the moves of the rich into markets like San Francisco, it is possible that once the rich agglomerate in that market, productivity then increases. Hence, the two forces may interact in various ways.

Appendix

Table 2A.1 **House prices and appreciation**

MSA	% House price appreciation 1950–2000	1950 Mean value (2000 dollars)	2000 Mean value (2000 dollars)
Abilene, TX	34.6	54,917	73,918
Akron, OH	93.9	69,720	135,174
Albany, GA	61.7	60,388	97,630
Albany, NY	62.3	75,522	122,604
Albuquerque, NM	132.6	64,411	149,835
Alexandria, LA	98.9	46,114	91,722
Allentown, PA	110.3	61,811	129,981
Altoona, PA	99.2	43,163	85,966
Amarillo, TX	54.4	61,713	95,299
Ann Arbor, MI	177.2	70,125	194,421
Anniston, AL	132.5	37,222	86,527
Appleton, WI	93.3	63,152	122,098
Asheville, NC	192.3	50,005	146,159
Athens, GA	191.4	49,138	143,184
Atlanta, GA	178.8	61,933	172,667
Atlantic City, NC	128.3	68,581	156,590
Auburn-Opelika, AL	151.5	50,779	127,708
Augusta, GA	138.9	45,543	108,814
Austin, TX	193.8	55,895	164,223
Bakersfield, CA	94.7	57,461	111,850
Baltimore, MD	148.6	65,817	163,594
Bangor, ME	113.3	43,328	92,403
Barnstable, MA	205.5	76,239	232,912
Baton Rouge, LA	115.3	56,276	121,178
Beaumont, TX	47.6	51,200	75,580
Bellingham, WA	276.4	49,780	187,380
Benton Harbor, MI	103.9	59,222	120,727
Bergen-Passic, NJ	196.0	98,065	290,265
Billings, MT	48.4	79,117	117,401
Biloxi, MS	170.4	39,205	106,029
Binghamton, NY	24.4	70,626	87,873
Birmingham, AL	178.1	47,949	133,362
Bismarck, ND	72.0	61,250	105,354
Bloomington, IN	112.1	61,691	130,870
Bloomington, IL	176.3	47,973	132,556
Boise City, ID	142.6	58,231	141,275
Boston, MA	212.4	76,168	237,974
Boulder, CO	377.2	61,206	292,063
Brazoria, TX	123.5	46,086	103,025
Bremerton, WA	280.4	51,233	194,886
Brownsville, TX	73.8	39,569	68,775
Bryan, TX	137.9	48,788	116,046
Buffalo, NY	31.1	79,254	103,880
Burlington, VT	131.9	65,502	151,915

(continued)

Table 2A.1 (continued)

MSA	% House price appreciation 1950–2000	1950 Mean value (2000 dollars)	2000 Mean value (2000 dollars)
Canton, OH	78.4	65,215	116,324
Casper, WY	37.8	72,285	99,579
Cedar Rapids, IA	76.4	69,121	121,942
Champaign, IL	49.6	75,056	112,277
Charleston, SC	236.8	47,790	160,960
Charleston, WV	56.0	67,951	105,994
Charlotte, NC	194.1	53,454	157,233
Charlottesville, VA	158.7	66,377	171,734
Chattanooga, TN	154.3	45,327	115,264
Cheyenne, WY	75.5	68,901	120,934
Chicago, IL	113.7	97,920	209,302
Chico, CA	173.8	53,621	146,827
Cincinnati, OH	76.2	82,734	145,774
Clarksville, TN	146.1	39,349	96,846
Cleveland, OH	57.0	91,687	143,988
Colorado Springs, CO	162.7	67,264	176,709
Columbia, MO	106.2	64,039	132,067
Columbia, SC	109.0	62,560	130,741
Columbus, GA	97.8	52,647	104,113
Columbus, GA	112.5	68,152	144,797
Corpus Christi, TX	60.8	52,261	84,055
Corvallis, OR	190.3	65,383	189,834
Cumberland, MD	78.8	45,269	80,950
Dallas, TX	138.4	60,875	145,125
Danville, VA	79.1	49,789	89,160
Davenport, IA	46.4	69,396	101,616
Dayton, OH	63.9	72,429	118,740
Daytona Beach, FL	100.2	56,285	112,670
Decatur, AL	39.7	59,324	82,878
Decatur, IL	162.9	39,426	103,651
Denver, CO	184.3	75,357	214,261
Des Moines, IA	104.8	59,610	122,069
Detroit, MI	123.8	72,666	162,595
Dothan, AL	132.9	41,834	97,447
Dover, DE	142.0	52,372	126,746
Dubuque, IA	55.7	71,399	111,178
Duluth, MN	77.0	50,214	88,899
Dutchess County, NY	103.9	84,876	173,021
Eau Claire, WI	106.0	53,068	109,346
El Paso, TX	21.9	68,651	83,652
Elkhart, IN	124.8	51,894	116,662
Elmira, NY	19.8	65,681	78,693
Enid, OK	35.4	52,425	70,985
Erie, PA	60.8	63,623	102,287
Eugene, OR	169.8	60,521	163,308
Evansville, IN	104.6	51,168	104,673
Fargo, SD	65.2	64,995	107,401

Table 2A.1 (continued)

MSA	% House price appreciation 1950–2000	1950 Mean value (2000 dollars)	2000 Mean value (2000 dollars)
Fayetteville, NC	163.0	44,821	117,882
Fayetteville, AR	131.1	46,057	106,439
Flagstaff, AZ	226.7	50,500	164,989
Flint, MI	108.4	52,717	109,844
Florence, AL	105.7	53,411	109,874
Florence, SC	143.6	41,008	99,881
Fort Collins, CO	246.9	58,103	201,557
Fort Lauderdale, FL	112.5	76,577	162,733
Fort Myers, FL	224.3	47,951	155,498
Fort Pierce, FL	164.5	55,601	147,065
Fort Smith, AR	123.3	38,849	86,732
Fort Walton Beach, FL	310.2	32,220	132,178
Fort Wayne, IN	81.9	58,417	106,245
Fort Worth, TX	125.2	51,794	116,627
Fresno, CA	110.9	61,792	130,339
Gadsden, AL	95.6	43,564	85,218
Gainesville, FL	131.6	52,261	121,013
Galveston, TX	73.9	62,502	108,689
Gary, IN	79.6	68,478	123,004
Glens Falls, NY	111.5	52,596	111,252
Goldsboro, NC	117.0	48,770	105,809
Grand Forks, ND	84.0	52,702	96,954
Grand Junction, CO	182.4	50,121	141,565
Grand Rapids, MI	122.4	61,120	135,937
Great Falls, MT	60.5	66,267	106,331
Greeley, CO	240.5	47,601	162,079
Green Bay, WI	92.0	69,589	133,603
Greensboro-Winston-Salem, NC	160.4	51,382	133,785
Greenville, NC	126.8	53,496	121,353
Greenville, SC	136.4	51,358	121,431
Hagerstown, MD	128.9	56,392	129,058
Hamilton, OH	101.9	67,859	136,985
Harrisburg, PA	104.5	60,176	123,036
Hartford, CT	85.9	94,780	176,237
Hattiesburg, MS	157.9	37,870	97,658
Hickory, NC	169.4	43,043	115,939
Houma, LA	161.1	36,392	95,011
Houston, TX	100.2	63,203	126,516
Huntington, WV	60.5	52,196	83,751
Huntsville, AL	204.2	41,005	124,754
Indianapolis, IN	123.2	60,474	134,977
Iowa City, IA	101.6	77,367	155,995
Jackson, MI	112.1	47,567	100,887
Jackson, MS	123.8	51,349	114,931
Jackson, TN	77.8	61,374	109,126
Jacksonville, FL	134.7	56,494	132,578

(continued)

Table 2A.1 (continued)

MSA	% House price appreciation 1950–2000	1950 Mean value (2000 dollars)	2000 Mean value (2000 dollars)
Jacksonville, NC	226.7	31,850	104,044
Jamestown, NY	31.3	58,609	76,940
Janesville, WI	76.8	62,627	110,704
Jersey City, NJ	136.8	72,622	171,946
Johnson City, TN	121.3	46,771	103,517
Johnstown, PA	65.9	45,873	76,127
Jonesboro, AR	128.9	43,218	98,938
Joplin, MO	143.5	34,162	83,176
Kalamazoo, MI	97.9	58,856	116,504
Kankakee, IL	70.3	68,181	116,145
Kansas City, MO	118.4	58,259	127,225
Kenosha, WI	93.3	71,148	137,515
Killeen, TX	100.3	44,527	89,207
Knoxville, TN	179.7	44,710	125,053
Kokomo, IN	129.7	45,759	105,114
La Crosse, WI	99.0	56,323	112,078
Lafayette, LA	155.4	39,681	101,363
Lafayette, IN	108.3	59,286	123,521
Lake Charles, LA	95.2	50,583	98,730
Lakeland, FL	101.7	49,523	99,883
Lancaster, PA	100.4	67,637	135,567
Lansing, MI	118.0	56,559	123,283
Laredo, TX	181.2	30,869	86,801
Las Cruces, NM	157.1	43,025	110,607
Las Vegas, NV	147.5	65,114	161,166
Lawrence, KS	187.3	49,050	140,902
Lawton, OK	72.7	48,036	82,946
Lewiston, ME	92.2	52,248	100,434
Lexington-Fayette, KY	113.7	60,367	129,025
Lima, OH	72.7	56,382	97,381
Lincoln, NE	105.5	61,336	126,018
Little Rock, AR	117.1	50,879	110,443
Longview, TX	123.2	37,678	84,102
Los Angeles, CA	236.6	85,150	286,633
Louisville, KY	113.4	60,413	128,893
Lubbock, TX	36.1	62,442	84,999
Lynchburg, VA	124.4	52,348	117,452
Macon, GA	133.0	44,416	103,502
Madison, WI	99.0	86,136	171,383
Mansfield, OH	49.3	64,370	96,099
McAllen, TX	99.9	33,393	66,759
Medford, OR	199.0	56,647	169,383
Melbourne, FL	114.9	55,488	119,262
Memphis, TN	100.7	61,886	124,183
Merced, CA	121.8	58,295	129,318
Miami, FL	95.2	83,286	162,594
Middlesex-Somerset-Hunterdon, NJ	185.6	80,437	229,739

Table 2A.1 (continued)

MSA	% House price appreciation 1950–2000	1950 Mean value (2000 dollars)	2000 Mean value (2000 dollars)
Milwaukee, WI	69.3	92,698	156,918
Minneapolis-St. Paul, MN	117.6	77,421	168,496
Missoula, MT	162.5	59,653	156,573
Mobile, AL	184.0	41,465	117,766
Modesto, CA	162.2	55,669	145,969
Monmouth-Ocean, NJ	160.2	77,938	202,758
Monroe, LA	101.7	49,470	99,781
Montgomery, AL	107.2	55,648	115,307
Muncie, IN	66.8	51,851	86,505
Myrtle Beach, SC	176.3	52,277	144,456
Naples, FL	406.7	51,144	259,155
Nashville-Davidson, TN	178.8	56,363	157,166
Nassau-Suffolk County, NY	167.6	99,692	266,806
New Haven, CT	185.4	103,118	294,297
New London, CT	132.5	74,479	173,185
New Orleans, LA	81.2	71,836	130,140
New York, NY	181.4	103,209	290,412
Newark, NJ	155.2	101,549	259,115
Newburgh, NY	125.2	70,748	159,289
Norfolk, VA	150.2	54,670	136,783
Oakland, CA	300.8	86,596	347,050
Ocala, FL	146.8	40,186	99,169
Odessa, TX	27.4	59,116	75,294
Oklahoma City, OK	65.8	58,078	96,278
Olympia, WA	194.8	57,586	169,788
Omaha, NE	104.3	59,470	121,483
Orange County, CA	356.1	72,185	329,206
Orlando, FL	122.8	61,908	137,919
Owensboro, KY	72.7	55,968	96,648
Panama City, FL	238.7	34,908	118,233
Parkersburg, WV	64.7	56,158	92,516
Pensacola, FL	185.6	40,422	115,431
Peoria-Pekin, IL	59.8	66,167	105,723
Philadelphia, PA	121.6	66,426	147,186
Phoenix, AZ	209.2	53,106	164,191
Pine Bluff, AR	113.6	33,106	70,724
Pittsburgh, PA	66.1	64,015	106,345
Pittsfield, MA	96.9	73,066	143,854
Pocatello, ID	71.7	60,819	104,417
Portland, OR	221.4	63,337	203,578
Portland, ME	169.3	60,377	162,576
Providence, RI	94.1	81,189	157,574
Provo-Orem, UT	207.3	61,174	187,982
Pueblo, CO	120.8	50,635	111,798
Punta Gorda, FL	215.2	39,342	124,010
Racine, WI	72.1	74,706	128,537

(*continued*)

Table 2A.1 (continued)

MSA	% House price appreciation 1950–2000	1950 Mean value (2000 dollars)	2000 Mean value (2000 dollars)
Raleigh-Durham-Chapel Hill, NC	205.7	58,153	177,794
Rapid City, SD	89.5	59,458	112,668
Reading, PA	96.3	59,750	117,313
Redding, CA	168.0	52,416	140,465
Reno, NV	115.4	96,874	208,650
Richland, WA	117.2	60,700	131,811
Richmond-Petersburgh, VA	116.5	64,964	140,677
Riverside-San Bernardino, CA	173.7	59,725	163,483
Roanoke, VA	103.8	60,679	123,680
Rochester, MN	68.1	81,995	137,822
Rochester, NY	56.1	72,348	112,926
Rockford, IL	51.2	73,216	110,727
Rocky Mount, NC	109.4	50,538	105,837
Sacramento, CA	167.9	71,504	191,567
Saginaw, MI	90.4	54,865	104,471
Salem, OR	159.8	59,484	154,551
Salinas, CA	316.6	83,456	347,705
Salt Lake City, UT	157.1	70,810	182,029
San Angelo, TX	52.8	50,539	77,215
San Antonio, TX	75.2	56,397	98,829
San Diego, CA	262.4	78,640	284,952
San Francisco, CA	465.9	96,703	547,206
San Jose, CA	513.3	86,667	531,562
San Luis Obispo, CA	346.0	59,995	267,605
Santa Barbara-Santa Maria, CA	328.4	89,559	383,707
Santa Cruz, CA	522.0	68,494	426,041
Santa Fe, NM	284.9	66,127	254,503
Santa Rosa, CA	362.5	69,007	319,124
Sarasota, FL	166.7	62,131	165,729
Savannah, GA	153.5	53,867	136,552
Scranton, PA	111.5	49,142	103,948
Seattle, WA	285.7	70,684	272,603
Sharon, PA	58.4	56,123	88,901
Sheboygan, WI	84.6	67,042	123,742
Shermon-Denison, TX	119.4	38,321	84,065
Shreveport-Bossier, LA	61.6	57,812	93,411
Sioux City, IA	55.1	57,815	89,660
Sioux Falls, SD	87.5	64,197	120,400
South Bend, IN	66.4	62,322	103,678
Spokane, WA	119.0	60,147	131,739
Springfield, IL	83.1	60,736	111,198
Springfield, MA	93.7	72,294	140,063
Springfield, MO	128.5	47,932	109,543
St. Cloud, MN	135.0	48,134	113,132
St. Joseph, MO	126.5	39,063	88,484
St. Louis, MO	78.6	72,973	130,348

Table 2A.1 (continued)

MSA	% House price appreciation 1950–2000	1950 Mean value (2000 dollars)	2000 Mean value (2000 dollars)
State College, PA	145.6	54,367	133,541
Steubenville-Weirton, OH	34.4	57,706	77,550
Stockton, CA	171.8	60,531	164,517
Sumter, SC	93.4	47,929	92,696
Syracuse, NY	39.8	69,624	97,341
Tacoma, WA	201.6	58,269	175,746
Tallahassee, FL	137.0	53,971	127,889
Tampa-St. Petersburgh, FL	109.4	58,714	122,967
Terre Haute, IN	134.0	36,094	84,467
Texarkana, TX	123.4	35,200	78,620
Toledo, OH	80.4	65,783	118,705
Topeka, KS	72.1	54,593	93,969
Trenton, NJ	189.2	67,916	196,431
Tucson, AZ	130.5	63,094	145,417
Tulsa, OK	99.0	53,533	106,510
Tuscaloosa, AL	178.6	46,197	128,691
Tyler, TX	97.4	52,262	103,168
Utica-Rome, NY	30.6	64,791	84,587
Vallejo, CA	233.4	69,620	232,145
Ventura, CA	319.6	70,971	297,826
Victoria, TX	57.2	55,147	86,680
Vineland-Millville-Bridgeton, NJ	91.2	53,459	102,201
Visalia-Tulare-Porterville, CA	159.7	46,174	119,908
Waco, TX	70.1	48,552	82,577
Washington, DC	112.7	106,235	225,914
Waterloo-Cedar Falls, IA	40.2	64,682	90,685
Wausau, WI	114.3	51,753	110,908
West Palm Beach-Boca Raton, FL	159.7	73,275	190,261
Wheeling, WV	46.3	53,928	78,871
Wichita, KS	62.9	60,499	98,554
Wichita Falls, TX	57.4	47,826	75,266
Williamsport, PA	82.3	53,625	97,759
Wilmington, DE	90.8	82,087	156,661
Wilmington, NC	310.6	42,865	176,011
Yakima, WA	140.7	54,809	131,944
Yolo, CA	205.7	65,842	201,293
York, PA	104.8	60,915	124,730
Youngstown-Warren, OH	49.8	63,044	94,470
Yuba, CA	146.4	51,463	126,793
Yuma, AZ	156.6	44,473	114,101

Note: Decadal Census; all values in 2000 dollars.

Table 2A.2 MSA summary statistics

Variable	Mean	Standard deviation
MSA time-invariant characteristics:		
Average annual real house price growth, 1950–2000 ($N = 279$)	1.57	0.56
Average annual housing unit growth, 1950–2000 ($N = 279$)	2.10	0.98
Average annual real income growth, 1950–2000 ($N = 279$)	1.82	0.35
Ever a superstar	0.165 [46]	0.372
Ever a nonsuperstar	0.337 [94]	0.474
Ever low demand	0.821 [229]	0.384
MSA time-varying characteristics:		
Average 20-year real house price growth	1.50	1.04
Average 20-year housing unit growth	2.10	1.20
Average 20-year house price growth + housing unit growth	3.60	1.86
Average ratio of 20-year price growth to 20-year unit growth	0.936	0.642
Real house value	111,329	54,889
Average price/average annual rent	17.00	3.99
Year	**Number of superstars**	**Number of nonsuperstars**
1970	3	55
1980	3	34
1990	30	43
2000	21	36
Income distribution	**Mean**	**Standard deviation**
Share of an MSA's population that is rich	0.033	0.021
Share middle rich	0.035	0.024
Share middle	0.129	0.043
Share middle poor	0.400	0.050
Share poor	0.402	0.095
National number rich		
1970	1,571,136	
1980	1,312,103	
1990	2,611,178	
2000	4,098,324	

References

Acemoglu, D., and J. Angrist. 2000. How large are human capital externalities? Evidence from compulsory schooling laws. *NBER macroeconomics annual 2000,* ed. B. S. Bernanke and K. Rogoff, 9–59. Cambridge, MA: MIT Press.

Autor, D., L. Katz, and M. Kearney. 2006. The polarization of the U.S. labor market. *American Economic Review* 96 (2): 189–94.

DiPasquale, D., and E. Glaeser. 1999. Incentives and social capital: Are homeowners better citizens? *Journal of Urban Economics* 45 (2): 354–84.

Glaeser, E., and J. Gyourko. 2003. The impact of zoning on housing affordability. *Economic Policy Review* 9 (2): 21–39.

———. 2006. Housing dynamics. NBER Working Paper no. 12787. Cambridge, MA: National Bureau of Economic Research, December.

Glaeser, E., J. Gyourko, and R. Saks. 2005a. Why have house prices gone up? *American Economic Review* 95 (2): 329–33.

———. 2005b. Why is Manhattan so expensive? Regulation and the rise in house prices. *Journal of Law and Economics* 48 (2): 331–70.

Glaeser, E., H. Kallal, J. Scheinkman, and A. Shleifer. 1992. Growth in cities. *Journal of Political Economy* 100 (6): 1126–52.

Glaeser, E., J. Kolko, and A. Saiz. 2001. Consumer cities. *Journal of Economic Geography* 1 (1): 27–50.

Glaeser, E., and D. Mare. 2001. Cities and skills. *Journal of Labor Economics* 19 (2): 316–43.

Glaeser, E., and A. Saiz. 2003. The rise of the skilled city. NBER Working Paper no. 10191. Cambridge, MA: National Bureau of Economic Research, December.

Glaeser, E., J. Scheinkman, and A. Shleifer. 1995. Economic growth in a cross-section of cities. *Journal of Monetary Economics* 36 (1): 117–43.

Glaeser, E., and K. Tobio. 2008. The rise of the Sunbelt. *Southern Economic Journal* 74 (3): 610–43.

Green, R., and M. White. 1997. Measuring the benefits of homeowning: Effects on children. *Journal of Urban Economics* 41 (3): 441–61.

Gyourko, J., C. Mayer, and T. Sinai. 2006. Superstar cities. NBER Working Paper no. 12355. Cambridge, MA: National Bureau of Economic Research, June.

Gyourko, J., A. Saiz, and A. Summers. 2008. A new measure of the local regulatory environment for housing markets. *Urban Studies* 45 (3): 693–721.

Henderson, J. V. 1997. Externalities and industrial development. *Journal of Urban Economics* 42 (3): 449–70.

Henderson, J. V., A. Kuncoro, and M. Turner. 1995. Industrial development in cities. *Journal of Political Economy* 106 (4): 667–705.

Moretti, E. 2003. Human capital externalities in cities. In *Handbook of regional and urban economics,* vol. 4, ed. J. V. Henderson and J.-F. Thisse, 2243–91. Amsterdam: North-Holland.

———. 2004. Estimating the social return to higher education: Evidence from longitudinal and repeated cross-sectional data. *Journal of Econometrics* 121 (1/2): 175–212.

Piketty, T., and E. Saez. 2003. Income inequality in the United States, 1913–1998. *Quarterly Journal of Economics* 118 (1): 1–39.

Rauch, J. 1993. Productivity gains from geographic concentration of human capital: Evidence from the cities. *Journal of Urban Economics* 34 (3): 380–400.

Roback, J. 1982. Wages, rents, and the quality of life. *Journal of Political Economy* 90 (2): 1257–78.

Rosen, S. 1979. Wage-based indexes of urban quality of life. In *Current issues in urban economics,* ed. P. Mieszkowski and M. Straszheim, 74–104. Baltimore, MD: Johns Hopkins University Press.

Rosenthal, S., and W. Strange. 2003. Geography, industrial organization, and agglomeration. *Review of Economics and Statistics* 85 (2): 377–93.

Saez, E. 2004. Reported incomes and marginal tax rates, 1960–2000: Evidence and policy implications. NBER Working Paper no. 10273. Cambridge, MA: National Bureau of Economic Research, February.

Saks, R. 2008. Job creation and housing construction: Constraints on metropolitan area employment growth. *Journal of Urban Economics* 64 (1): 178–95.
Shapiro, J. 2006. Smart cities: Quality of life, productivity, and the growth effects of human capital. *Review of Economics and Statistics* 88 (2): 324–35.
Van Nieuwerburgh, S., and P.-O. Weill. 2006. Why has house price dispersion gone up? NBER Working Paper no. 12538. Cambridge, MA: National Bureau of Economic Research, September.
Waldfogel, J. 2003. Preference externalities: An empirical study of who benefits whom in differentiated-product markets. *RAND Journal of Economics* 34 (3): 557–68.

3

Cities as Six-by-Six-Mile Squares
Zipf's Law?

Thomas J. Holmes and Sanghoon Lee

3.1 Introduction

Economists analyzing urban economics questions commonly use geographic units from the Census Bureau; for example, *metropolitan statistical areas* (MSAs). The Census Bureau, in turn, typically uses arbitrarily defined political boundaries to construct its reporting units. The Census Bureau must satisfy numerous constituents with its reporting. In its determination of reporting unit boundaries, the Census Bureau would not be likely to place a high priority on what would be best for research in urban economics. Put another way, there is a high probability of measurement error between the *economic units* that researchers want and the *reporting units* such as MSAs that the Census Bureau provides.

A question in urban economics that has attracted much attention is the extent to which the size distribution of cities obeys Zipf's law.[1] If Zipf's law holds perfectly, then when we rank cities and plot the log of the rank against the log of the city population, we get a straight line with a slope

Thomas J. Holmes is professor of economics at the University of Minnesota, a visiting scholar at the Federal Reserve Bank of Minneapolis, and a research associate of the National Bureau of Economic Research. Sanghoon Lee is an assistant professor in the Sauder School of Business, University of British Columbia.

We thank NSF Grant 0551062 for research support. We are grateful to conference volume editor Ed Glaeser for his detailed and helpful comments. We thank Joel Waldfogel for his comments as a discussant at the NBER Economics of Agglomeration conference. We received many helpful comments from the conference participants, including, in particular, a comment by Gilles Duranton. We thank Jan Eeckhout, Xavier Gabaix, and Erzo Luttmer for feedback. We thank Julia Thornton and Steve Schmeiser for research assistance. The views expressed herein are solely those of the authors and do not represent the views of the Federal Reserve Bank of Minneapolis or the Federal Reserve System.

1. See Gabaix and Ioannides (2004) for a literature survey.

of 1. Equivalently, the largest city is twice as big as the second largest, three times as big as the third largest, and so on (the *rank-size rule*). Researchers who have used MSAs to define cities, such as Gabaix (1999), have found that Zipf's law holds to a striking degree. But what does it mean to say that Zipf's law holds, when the boundaries are determined by bureaucrats and politicians?

We are concerned about how to interpret Zipf's law results with these data for three reasons. First, MSAs are aggregations of counties, and the county is a crude geographic unit for such a building block. In some parts of the country, counties cover an extremely large land area, and locations get wrapped together as an MSA that clearly does not comprise a coherent metropolitan area.[2] We note that even if measurement error is unsystematic, it causes potential problems for a study of the size distribution, because the distribution *with* measurement error is generally different from the one *without* it. Second, we are particularly concerned about how boundaries are drawn for the largest cities. These cities can often be found in densely populated parts of the country where MSAs form contiguous blocks, such as the Northeast Corridor extending from Washington, DC, to Boston. It is often a tough call determining whether a given area should be classified as one or two MSAs, and if the latter, where to delineate the boundary. If bureaucrats tend to use broad definitions of MSAs that subsume contiguous areas into single large MSAs, this process may itself contribute to the findings of Zipf's law. Third, with MSA data, we leave out approximately 20 percent of the population not living in MSAs. So, we do not see what is going on with small cities, the left tail of the size distribution.[3] Eeckhout (2004) has recently advocated looking at the left tail by using data on census places that include very small towns. But as argued next, census places are heavily dependent on arbitrary political decisions of where to draw boundaries.

Our chapter considers a new approach to looking at population distributions that sweeps out any decisions made by bureaucrats or politicians. When comparing populations of geographic units, we can think of differences as falling along two margins. First, one unit can have a larger population than another because it encompasses more land area, holding population density fixed. Second, a unit can have a larger population on a fixed amount of land; that is, higher population density. In our analysis of the size distribution, we completely eliminate the first margin and allow only the second. We cut the map of the continental United States into a uniform grid of *six-by-six-mile squares* (and some other size grids as well) and examine the distribution of population across the *squares*. We document several regularities that

2. This point about MSAs is well appreciated in the literature. See, for example, Bryan, Minton, and Sarte (2007) for a recent discussion.

3. The Census recently released data on what are called *micropolitan areas,* which are essentially moderate-sized counties that do not qualify as MSAs. So, our concern that the county is a crude geographic unit applies here.

are robust to various ways of cutting the data. We also examine the extent to which Zipf's law holds for squares.

Our first result is that the extreme left tail of the distribution looks approximately lognormal—roughly, a bell curve. With the Zipf distribution, there are always more smaller cities than bigger cities; there is never a bell curve with a modal point below which the density of log population decreases as size decreases. This works well on the right tail of the distribution (e.g., there are more squares with 50,000 people than with 100,000) but does not work well around the left tail. This point can be highlighted by a discussion of the extreme cases of squares with population one and two. There are 713 squares with exactly one person (a bachelor farmer, a forest ranger) living in them. A much larger number of squares (1,285) have exactly two people living in them. (Perhaps a forest ranger couple?) Given priors about scale economies and basic agglomeration benefits, it not surprising that squares with one lonely person in them are rarer than squares with two. The recent literature has not focused on scale economies and agglomeration benefits to try to understand the size distribution; instead, it has focused on the impacts of cumulative random productivity shocks (e.g., Gabaix [1999] and Eeckhout [2004]). We suspect that to understand the shape of the extreme left tail of the distribution of squares, issues of scale economies and agglomeration are of first-order importance.

Our second result throws out the extreme left tail and looks at the distribution of population across squares with population 1,000 or more. Approximately 24,000 squares meet this population threshold, and these squares account for 28 percent of the surface area of the continental United States. We construct a Zipf plot and find a striking pattern. To a remarkable degree, the plot is linear until it hits a kink at square population around 50,000. Below the kink, the slope is approximately 0.75; above the kink, the slope is approximately 2. This piecewise linear function fits the data extremely well. Moreover, when we split the data by region and make a Zipf's plot in each individual region, the same piecewise linear relationship shows up, with the kinks in approximately the same place. Our results are not like the standard Zipf's law findings, and the objects we are looking at—with no variation on the land-area margin—are different from the standard objects people look at. But we find our results intriguing in the same way that the usual Zipf's law findings are intriguing.

The third result concerns the extent that Gibrat's law for growth rates holds with squares. Under a typical statement of Gibrat's law, the mean and variance of growth is independent of initial size. Gibrat's law does not hold for squares. The relationship between growth and size is an inverted U, with the smallest and the largest population squares having the lowest growth rates. It is not surprising that the highest population squares have a low growth rate, since these areas typically are fully developed, and little vacant land is available for further growth.

Our fourth result links our findings to results in the previous literature about Zipf's law for MSAs. As mentioned, the main finding in the literature is that when we look at the upper tail of the MSA's size distribution, the regression coefficient of log rank on log population equals 1. Now, if we were to replace *MSA population* with *MSA average density* in the regression, we do not necessarily expect to get a coefficient of 1, because it depends on the elasticity of MSA surface area to MSA population. If this elasticity equals 0.05 (which is approximately what we find it to be), then the expected slope coefficient on density is actually 2 rather than 1. This is, in fact, our approximate result when we replace MSA population with MSA density. This is also our result when we use the maximum density square rather than the average density in the MSA. We find it interesting that the slope we are getting in the right tail of these *MSA-level* regressions is similar to the slope we get in the right tail of the *square-level* regressions (i.e., the slope to the right of the previously mentioned kink). We interpret this result as evidence of some kind of fractal structure, where the distribution of average density of the right tail of MSAs is similar to the distribution of the right tail of squares *within* MSAs, which in turn is similar to the distribution of the right tail of squares *across* all of the continental United States.

Given our wariness about using the MSA surface-area measure, we are somewhat surprised that when we use it to construct average MSA density, we get numerical results that we can connect to our results with squares. Perhaps the bureaucrats are doing a reasonably good job after all. Even if they are, our analysis of squares rather than MSAs is still interesting, because we are looking at something different from the previous literature with new insights. The fractal pattern of the right tails—across MSAs similar to squares within MSAs similar to squares across the continent—suggests an underlying common explanation. The dominant explanation in the recent literature of the size distribution of MSAs is the random growth explanation of Gabaix (1999),[4] but it certainly cannot explain the size distribution of squares within MSAs and squares across the continent. For one thing, Gibrat's law does not hold for squares, as already noted, and Gibrat's law is needed to get the random growth theory to work. For another, it is clear that the size distribution of squares within MSAs is better understood by economic theories like the Alonzo-Muth-Mills monocentric model of the city than by a random growth theory. We believe that a unified theory of the size distribution of squares within MSAs and across MSAs will have to incorporate economic factors like scale economies and include an explicit spatial structure. See Hsu (2008) for an attempt to do exactly this.

The closely related work of Eeckhout (2004) merits further discussion. He made a compelling case that the use of MSAs truncates out low population areas, and he suggested the use of the *census place* as a way to see what is

4. For related work on firms, see Luttmer (2007).

happening at the bottom tail of the distribution. Interestingly, Eeckhout found that the distribution of places is lognormal rather than Zipf. However, we are even more concerned about the use of census places to define geographic boundaries than we are about the use of MSAs. First, only 74 percent of the 2000 population actually lives in what the Census calls a place; the rest of the population are in unincorporated areas.

Next, consider table 3.1. To construct it, we take a list of all census places from the 2000 Census (Eeckhout's data) and tabulate all those places with population five or less. Two places in the census file have exactly one resident (including Lost Springs, Wyoming), and two places have population equal to two, including Hove Mobile Park City, North Dakota. The arbitrary decision that Lost Springs with its one resident is considered a place, while a farmhouse in an unincorporated area with a family of five living in it is not a place of five people is dependent on legal particulars that are not likely to be of interest in our analysis of city size distributions. These concerns arise at the top of the size distribution as well. Saint Paul and Minneapolis in the Twin Cities are adjacent to each other and are different census places, since they have never merged. Manhattan and Brooklyn are part of the same census place (New York City), because they merged in the nineteenth century. Our six-by-six-square analysis pulls in all of the land in the continental United States and treats it in a uniform way: the one resident of Hove Mobile Park City is on equal footing with a bachelor farmer in an unincorporated area, and New York City is treated the same way as the Twin Cities.

Many others have noted the inadequacies of MSA definitions for vari-

Table 3.1 **Census places with population five or less (2000 Census)**

Place	Population
New Amsterdam town, IN	1
Lost Springs town, WY	1
Hove Mobile Park city, ND	2
Monowi village, NE	2
Hobart Bay CDP, AK	3
East Blythe CDP, CA	3
Hillsview town, SD	3
Point of Rocks CDP, WY	3
Flat CDP, AK	4
Blacksville CDP, GA	4
Prudhoe Bay CDP, AK	5
Storrie CDP, CA	5
Baker village, MO	5
Maza city, ND	5
Gross village, NE	5

Note: CDP = Census designated place.

ous research questions and have used geographical techniques to improve on these boundaries. For example, Duranton and Turner (2008) use buffers around 1976 settlements within MSA boundaries to obtain more meaningful MSA definitions for their analysis of urban growth and transportation. Others have used rich geographic data to determine the location of employment subcenters. (See Anas, Arnott, and Small [1998] and McMillen and McDonald [1998].) In principle, rather than fix squares like we do, it might be possible to draw some kind of optimal city boundaries to let the land margin back in. We view this approach as fruitful and complementary. But once the economists take the job of drawing the metropolitan boundaries away from the bureaucrats, we need to worry about the mistakes the economists might make. For this reason, we think it is useful to nail down what happens when we completely eliminate the land margin across locations, as we do here.

While the focus of our work is the size distribution and Zipf's law, our work also makes a broader point that research in urban economics should not be constrained by standard geographic units handed to us by statistical agencies. The Census releases population data at an extremely high level of geographic precision—the *block level* (which in urban areas is a city block or an apartment building)—so there is great flexibility in choosing boundaries. Moreover, such analysis is facilitated by advances in geographic information system software. We therefore have great flexibility in defining the boundaries to be whatever we want them to be. In many applications in urban economics, researchers might be well served by defining their own boundaries rather than using the off-the-shelf boundaries. The construction of segregation indices is one example. Other papers highlighting the flexibility of continuous geographic data include Duranton and Overman (2005) and Burchfield et al. (2006). Another related work is the G-Econ database, which contains the worldwide geographic distribution of economic activity (gross domestic product; GDP) on a 1-degree-latitude-by-1-degree-longitude grid (Nordhaus et al. 2006).

3.2 Data

We draw a grid of six-by-six-mile squares across the map of the continental United States. A map is a two-dimensional projection of the three-dimensional globe, and the square grid may look different on maps using different projection methods. We use the USA Contiguous Albers Equal Area Conic projection method, which preserves area size: the size of an area on a map is equal to the real size of the area on the globe.[5]

5. This may not be true in maps using other projections. For example, maps using Mercator projections present Greenland as being roughly as large as Africa, but Africa is about fourteen times as big as Greenland.

We use six miles for our baseline, because in the first version of this chapter, we used the original township grid of six-by-six-mile squares. This grid was laid down in the early 1800s by the Public Land Survey System (PLSS) for the purpose of selling federal lands. (See Linklater [2003] and Holmes and Lee [2008].) That was a good place to start, but we eventually realized that drawing our own grid would be much cleaner. That way, we could cover states that were otherwise left out (e.g., the original thirteen states were not surveyed, because there were no federal lands to sell). Moreover, the original survey done with chains and landmarks was sloppy compared to what we can do now on a computer. We have to anchor the grid at some place, but as we show later, shifting the grid up or down or left or right is irrelevant. As discussed in section 3.7, a large enough change in the grid size can make a difference but not a small change.

The grid has 85,527 squares, each exactly thirty-six square miles, summing up to 3.1 million square miles of the continental United States. Figure 3.1 illustrates the grid in the vicinity of New York City. Note the six-by-six squares along the coast project into the water. We treat these areas as full six-by-six-mile squares and do not distinguish between dry land and water when delineating the surface area within the square. We make no distinc-

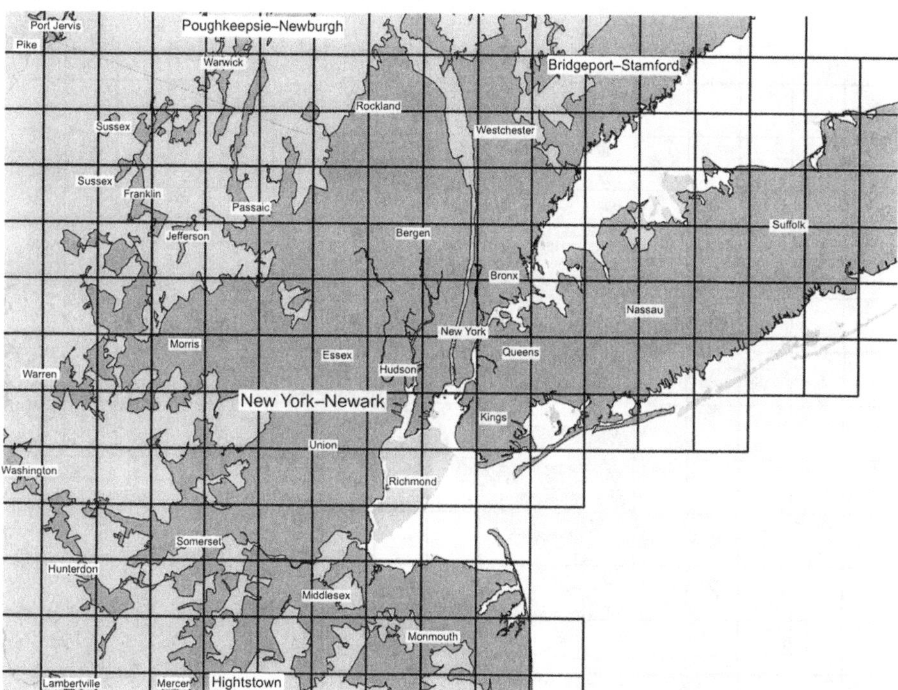

Fig. 3.1 Map of grid lines for six-by-six squares in the vicinity of New York City

tion, because people can live on the water (e.g., on houseboats) in some cases more easily than they can live on dry land, particularly in remote desert areas. We return to the water issue in section 3.7.

We use the population data from the 2000 and 1990 decennial Census reported at the level of the census block. In urban areas, a census block is a city block or an apartment building. For 2000, there are 7 million census blocks in the continental United States. Of those reporting any population, the area of the median census block for 2000 equaled 0.014 square miles, a tiny unit of land compared to a six-by-six square. The ninety-fifth percentile of block area equals 1.43 miles, still a small amount. The Census Bureau reports the longitude and latitude of a point within the boundaries of each census block, and we use this point to map each block into a six-by-six square. Figure 3.2 illustrates the location of census blocks in the vicinity of New York City. In this area, a thousand or more blocks can be assigned to a particular square.

We need to address the possibility of measurement error in the allocation of population to squares. A block boundary might cross the boundaries of a six-by-six square, and when this happens, someone living in the block on one side of the boundary can be mistakenly allocated to the six-by-six square on the other side. Because blocks are typically very small, this issue is negligible,

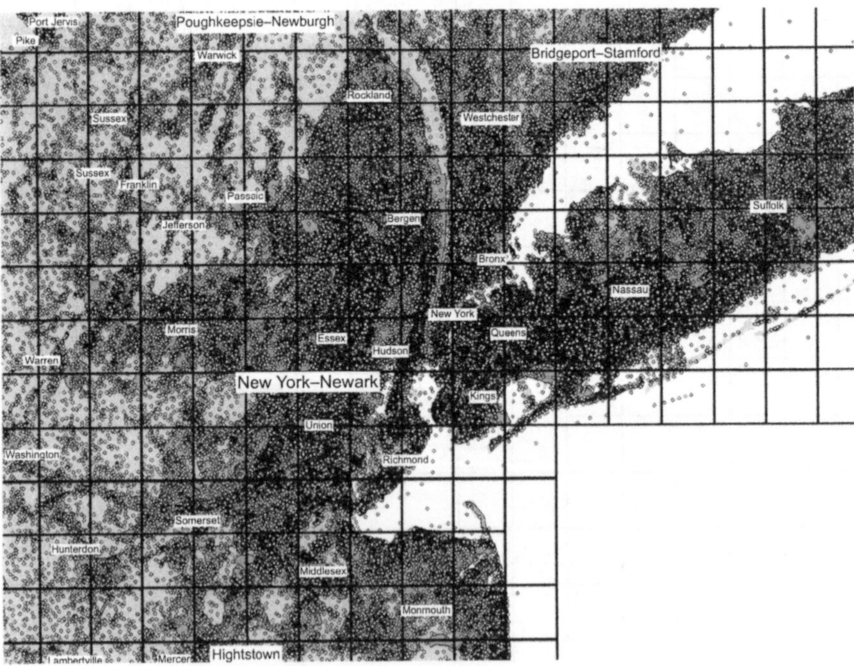

Fig. 3.2 Location of census blocks (2000 Census) in the vicinity of New York City

except in a few extreme cases. To get some sense of this issue, we determine for each of the 280 million people in the population what six-by-six square they are assigned to and the number of block groups assigned to the same six-by-six square. The first percentile of this statistic is thirty-five blocks. This means that all but 1 percent of the population live in six-by-six squares with at least thirty-five blocks assigned to them. Now, thirty-five blocks will trace out a fairly clean square. The fifth percentile is 74 blocks, the fiftieth is 719, and the seventy-fifth is 1609. We are confident that for 99 percent of the population, our assignment is very good. We note that even in remote rural areas, the Census typically defines blocks at a fine level of granularity.[6]

To compare our results with what comes out of the traditional approach with MSA-level data, it is useful to aggregate our squares to MSAs. We allocate squares to the MSAs as defined for the 2000 Census. In certain metropolitan areas, the Census offers a choice of consolidated areas (e.g., the New York CMSA) versus a breakdown into component areas. We use the consolidated definitions. There are 274 different such MSAs in the continental United States. We allocate squares to MSAs according to the following rule. A square gets assigned to an MSA if any block in the square is part of the MSA. In the event a square is at a boundary where MSAs overlap in the square, we assign the square to the MSA with the largest surface area based on blocks.

Table 3.2 presents summary statistics of how population from the 2000 Census varies across squares. Mean population across the 85,527 squares is 3,269. Population is highly skewed, with two squares in the New York MSA having 1.3 million in population. The area unit used in the analysis to calculate density is the six-by-six-mile square. So, each square has one unit of area, and the population density equals the population.

Table 3.2 also presents summary statistics for the 274 MSAs. Mean density is 7,881 per square, which is twice the density of squares overall. The mean number of squares across MSAs is 87, with the minimum being 14 and the maximum being 981 squares. So clearly, the square is a much smaller geographic unit than the MSA. The maximum land area is attained by the Las Vegas MSA, which is a good example of the limitations of Census MSA definitions. The surface areas of counties in Nevada are huge. Since the Census uses the county as a building block unit for MSAs, much of the surrounding area that is not actually part of the Las Vegas metropolitan area is folded into the MSA bearing its name.[7]

6. In a relatively small number of cases, a square has only one block group assigned to it. There are 592 such blocks, accounting for 20,000 people (out of 280 million). These look like unusual and exceptional cases rather than just simply rural cases. Of these 20,000 people, 5,677 are in the 29 Palms military base in California. The base is in a census block covering 272 square miles. Another block is in the Mohave Desert. Others are in national parks and national forests.

7. Another example of this problem with huge counties is the case of the Flagstaff MSA in Arizona. The city of Flagstaff is located in the geographically huge Coconino county (over

Table 3.2 **Summary statistics: Squares and MSAs (population from 2000 Census)**

Unit	Variable	Number	Mean	Standard deviation	Minimum	Maximum	Sum across units
Square	Population	85,527	3,269	18,181	0	1,317,207	279,583,434
	Log(population)	70,590	5.69	2.48	0	14.09	—
	Area (6 × 6 square)	85,527	1	0	1	1	85,527
MSA	Population	274	843,209	1,986,836	60,744	21,343,534	231,039,389
	Population density	274	7,881	7,073	215	55,151	—
	Log(population density)	274	8.67	.80	5.37	10.92	—
	Area (6 × 6 square)	274	87	103	14	981	23,798

3.3 Background Equations

Discussing some background equations on the size distribution is useful. Following the notation of Gabaix and Ioannides (2004), let S_i denote the population size of city i, and suppose the distribution of populations across cities is Pareto:

$$\text{Rank}_i = P(\text{Size}>S_i) = \frac{\alpha}{S_i^{\zeta}}. \tag{1}$$

Taking logs, we get

$$\ln \text{Rank}_i = \ln \alpha - \zeta \ln S_i. \tag{2}$$

The slope ζ is called the *tail coefficient.* Zipf's law is said to hold if $\zeta = 1$.

Let L_i be the land area of city i and the population density D_i be

$$D_i = \frac{S_i}{L_i}.$$

The analysis remains in a log-linear form if there is a constant elasticity η relationship between land and population,

$$L_i = \gamma S_i^{\eta}.$$

Taking logs yields

$$\ln L_i = \ln \gamma + \eta \ln S_i. \tag{3}$$

18,000 square miles). The Census classifies the whole county as the Flagstaff MSA. Flagstaff is the third largest MSA by land area. Cities quite distant from Flagstaff, including Tuba City (78 miles) and Page (119 miles), are folded into the Flagstaff MSA because they happen to be in this county. A large percentage of the Flagstaff MSA population reported by the Census comes from distant places like these that clearly are not part of the economic unit of Flagstaff city. Researchers might be tempted to use the city boundaries of Flagstaff rather than the MSA boundaries. But this raises the issue of the often arbitrary political decisions that determine municipal boundaries.

Solving the preceding for $\ln S_i$ and substituting into equation (2) yields

$$\text{(4)} \qquad \ln \text{Rank}_i = \left[\ln \alpha + \frac{\zeta}{\eta} \ln \gamma\right] - \frac{\zeta}{\eta} \ln L_i.$$

This is a Zipf's relationship using land instead of population. Note the slope is ζ/η, not ζ. In the special case where population density is constant across cities (e.g., each individual inelastically demands one unit of land), then $\eta = 1$, and the slope coefficient for the land regression in equation (4) is identical to the slope coefficient for the population regression in equation (2). But otherwise, in the empirically relevant case where $\eta < 1$, the slope is higher for the land regression than the population regression.

Analogously, using $\ln D_i = \ln S_i - \ln L_i$ and equation (3), we can solve for $\ln S_i$ in equation (2) in terms of $\ln D_i$ to get

$$\text{(5)} \qquad \ln \text{Rank}_i = \left[\ln \alpha - \frac{\zeta \ln \gamma}{(1-\eta)}\right] - \frac{\zeta}{1-\eta} \ln D_i.$$

This is a Zipf's plot for population density. The tail coefficient is $\zeta / (1 - \eta)$. If Zipf's law holds so that $\zeta = 1$, and if $\eta < 1$, then this slope will be greater than 1.

Next, consider squares. Let the squares be indexed by j, and let s_j be the population of square j. Let A_i be the set of squares that are in city i. Then, city population, land area, and density equal

$$S_i = \sum_{j \in A_i} s_j.$$

$$L_i = \text{Number of squares in } A_i,$$

$$D_i = \frac{S_i}{L_i} = \text{mean } s_j, j \in A_i.$$

In general, the relationship between the size distribution of the squares s_j and of the cities S_i is quite complicated, except for the special case where each square is a city. We leave to future research a theoretical analysis of this relationship and focus instead on a descriptive analysis of the distribution of the squares s_j and how it compares to the distribution of MSA-defined cities.

We are able to make one immediate observation. Let $s_i^{\max}$ be the highest population square in city i,

$$s_i^{\max} = \max_{j \in A_i} s_j.$$

If the maximum density square is proportionate to the overall city population density,

$$\text{(6)} \qquad s_i^{\max} = \lambda D_i,$$

and if we replace D_i in equation (5) with $s_i^{\max}$, then we obtain the same slope coefficient. This is interesting, because the maximum population square is more reliably measured than the average population density of an MSA. The latter heavily depends on where the boundaries are drawn. Typically, there is rural land at the boundary of an MSA, so the wider the boundaries are drawn, the lower the overall MSA population density. The s_i^{max} variable is determined in the interior of the MSA, the "central business district," far from the boundaries of the MSA. So, it will not be affected if the MSA boundary is arbitrarily increased twenty miles out or twenty miles in.[8] (The MSA boundaries still impact the s_i^{max} measure if the Census merges two MSAs into one.)

3.4 The Size Distribution of MSAs

As a benchmark, this section examines the size distribution of MSAs. Following Gabaix (1999), we focus on the 135 largest MSAs, treating this area as the upper tail of the distribution.

Figure 3.3 presents three Zipf plots. Panel A is the standard plot where we use population. Panel B replaces population with land area as in equation (4); panel C replaces population with density as in equation (5).[9] Table 3.3 reports estimated slope coefficients. As is common in the literature, we estimate the tail index two ways: standard ordinary least squares (OLS) and the Hill method (the maximum likelihood procedure under the null hypothesis that the distribution is Pareto). See Gabaix and Ioannides (2004) for a discussion of econometric practice in this literature. As recommended in this work, we use simulation methods to estimate the OLS standard errors, because the usual method yields biased estimates. Zipf's law for the population holds in a striking fashion. The OLS estimate of the slope coefficient for the population regression is 1.01. The fit is excellent, as can be seen by the straight line in figure 3.3 and by the R^2 of 0.988 in table 3.3.

The Hill estimate of the population coefficient is 0.94—a little less than 1. But the estimated standard error is 0.07, so we cannot reject that the slope equals one with a standard statistical test. Here and elsewhere in the chapter, the Hill estimates are a little smaller than the OLS estimates and have a higher estimated standard error but are otherwise similar. Since the OLS and Hill estimates are basically telling the same story, for the rest of the chapter, we will discuss just the OLS estimates in the text but report both in the tables.

The OLS slope coefficients on land and density are 1.70 and 1.90, respectively. Straight lines fit reasonably well. To relate this result to the equations in the previous section, we look at the relationship between land area and

8. One issue with s_i^{max} one could raise is that it might depend on where the grid is positioned. We show in the following text that we can shift around the grid and our results with s_i^{max} do not change.

9. Analogous to what we do for population, for land, we take the top 135 MSAs ranked by land, and for density, we take the top 135 MSAs ranked by density.

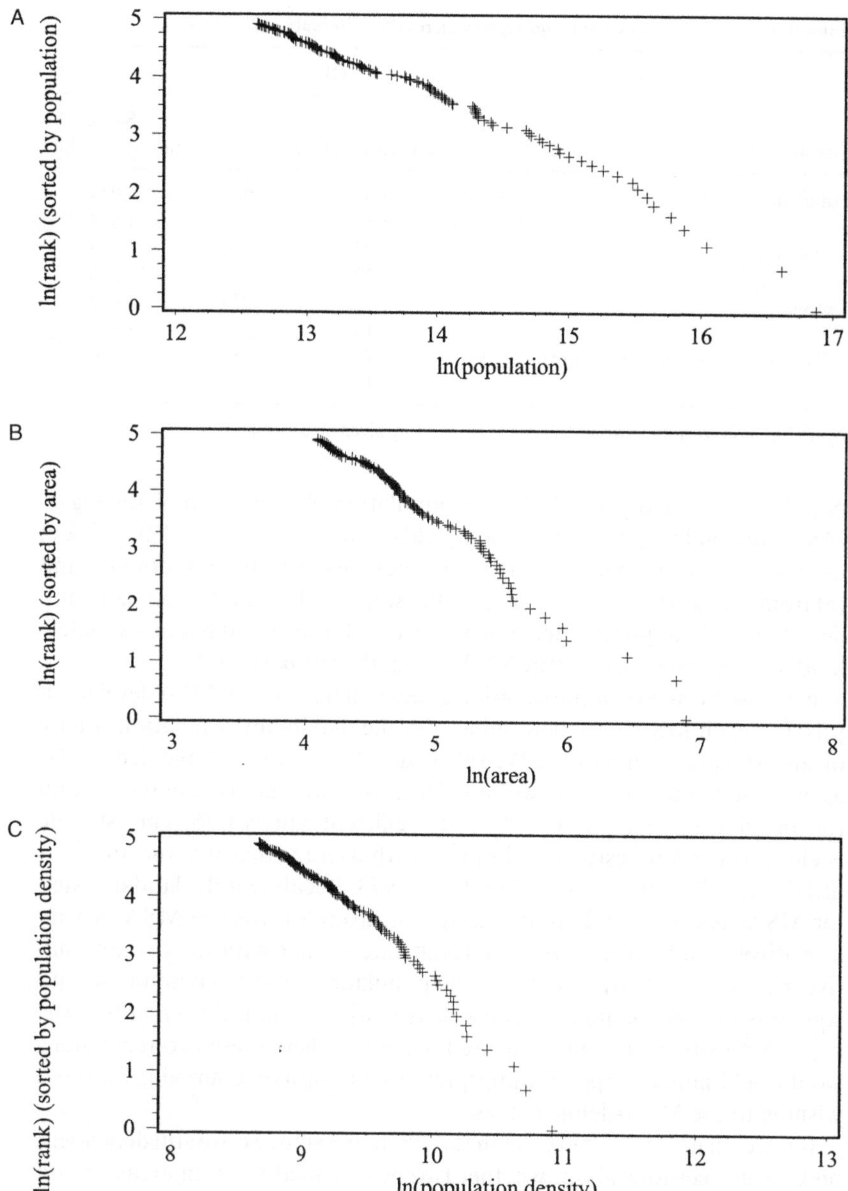

Fig. 3.3 MSA-level Zipf plots: *A*, top 135 MSAs by population; *B*, top 135 MSAs by area; *C*, top 135 MSAs by population density

Table 3.3 MSA-level Zipf regression results: Alternative size measures

	OLS		Hill method
Size measure	Slope (absolute value)	R^2	Slope (absolute value)
Population	1.013 (.12)	.985	.944 (.078)
Land area	1.70 (.12)	.984	1.569 (.176)
Density	1.896 (.12)	.973	1.616 (.120)
s_i^{max} (maximum population square in MSA)	1.761 (.12)	.988	1.546 (.125)

Note: Each regression uses top 135 MSAs ranked by given size measure.

population in the top 135 MSAs by population. A regression of the log of MSA area on log MSA population yields a slope coefficient of 0.52.[10] Let us take this as an estimate of η from the previous section. Equations (4) and (5) from the previous section suggest the slope coefficient on both land and density should approximately equal 2 if $\zeta = 1$ and $\eta = 0.5$ approximately hold. Our estimates of 1.70 and 1.90 are in the ballpark of 2.

Next, we bring in our information about squares into an MSA-level analysis. For each MSA i, we determine s_i^{max}, the maximum population square of all the squares in MSA i. We substitute s_i^{max} for the average density D_i, as discussed in the previous section. The results are reported in the bottom row of table 3.3. The estimated slope coefficient equals 1.76. The estimate is close to the 1.90 estimate obtained with average density, and the fit is little better: $R^2 = 0.988$ instead of $R^2 = 0.973$. Recall that the land measure for MSAs is crude, making the derived measure of average MSA density a relatively crude object. Yet, the results are similar with the two alternative measures of density. Suppose the population of the maximum density square is proportionate to average density as in equation (6) *and* that the average density measure is measured precisely. Then, these two regressions would yield similar slopes. We interpret this finding as encouraging for those wishing to use MSA-defined cities.

It is worth noting that even with the s_i^{max} regression, we are still dependent on Census decisions about whether two nearby metropolitan areas should be grouped into one or two MSAs. The Census groups San Francisco and Oakland into one MSA, so the observation of s_i^{max} is downtown San Francisco. If Oakland were separated into a distinct MSA, we would get another observation of s_i^{max} for downtown Oakland. In our exercise in the next section with squares, we do not depend on such Census classifications.

10. The standard error is 0.04, and the $R^2 = 0.52$.

So far, our focus has been on the upper tail of the MSA distribution. Next, we look at the entire distribution of MSAs. It is known in the literature that Zipf plots of MSAs tend to exhibit a concave shape when the lower tail of the distribution is included. (See, for example, Rossi-Hansberg and Wright [2007].) When a Zipf's plot is not a straight line, a standard density plot of the distribution can be more revealing than a Zipf's plot. As a segue into looking at the whole distribution, we first illustrate in panel A of figure 3.4 a density plot (histogram) of log population for just the upper tail, the 135 highest population MSAs. Also illustrated in the plot is the best-fitting

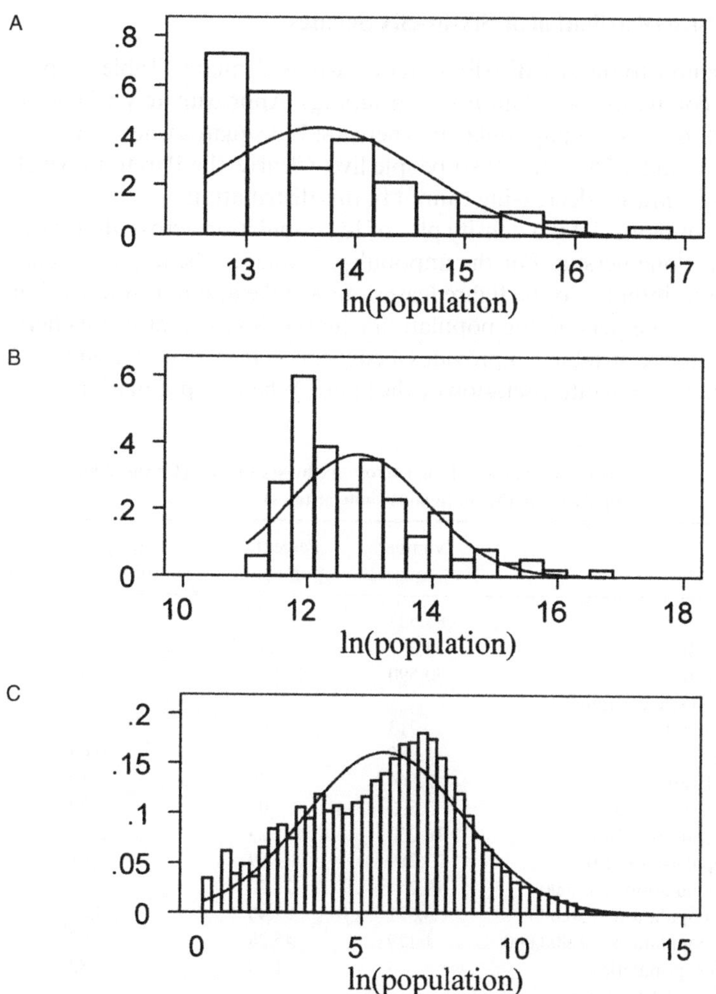

Fig. 3.4 Density plots: *A*, 135 largest MSAs; *B*, all 274 MSAs; *C*, populated squares

normal curve. Clearly, the bell-curved shape of the normal does not fit the distribution within the top 135 MSAs very well. Rather, a Pareto distribution is a good fit here. With the Pareto, the density is a straight line that is strictly decreasing; the smaller the units, the more units there are.

Panel B in figure 3.4 illustrates the distribution of log population for all 274 MSAs. Now, the tendency for monotone decline of the density is not as pronounced as it is with just the top 135, but this is still the clear pattern. Certainly, the bell curve of the normal does not fit the distribution of MSAs very well.

3.5 The Size Distribution of Six-by-Six Squares

We turn now to the size distribution of six-by-six squares. Table 3.4 provides cell counts for population size groupings. Approximately 15,000 of the 86,000 squares are unpopulated. There are 713 squares where only one person lives and 1,285 where two people live. Clearly, the Pareto in which the density is always decreasing cannot fit this distribution.

Panel C of figure 3.4 is a density plot of log population across all squares with at least one person. For the unpopulated squares, the log of population is minus infinity, so the figure leaves out a spike at minus infinity. For squares with one person, log population equals 0, so the plot begins here. The last column of table 3.4 provides a conversion from population to log population to aid in interpretation of the figure. When log population is less

Table 3.4 **Distribution of population across six-by-six squares (Census 2000 population in the contiguous United States)**

	Number of squares	Percent of population	Log(population) at bottom of grouping
All squares	85,527		
Population = 0	14,937	0.00	$-\infty$
Population > 0	70,590	100.00	0.00
By population size grouping			
Population = 1	713	.00	0.00
Population = 2	1,285	.00	0.69
3 ≤ population ≤ 5	2,564	.00	1.10
6 ≤ population < 10	2,532	.01	1.79
10 ≤ population < 100	16,233	.23	2.30
100 ≤ population < 1,000	23,289	3.59	4.61
1,000 ≤ population < 10,000	19,271	21.20	6.91
10,000 ≤ population < 50,000	3,521	27.40	9.21
50,000 ≤ population < 1,000,000	1,179	46.28	10.82
1,000,000 ≤ population	3	1.29	13.82
Size groupings of later interest			
1,000 ≤ population	23,974	96.17	6.91
50,000 ≤ population	1,182	47.57	10.82

than 4 (when population is less than about fifty), the best fit normal curve fits reasonably well, though the fit is choppy. Certainly, the lognormal fits the distribution better than the Pareto on the right tail.

Our finding that the lognormal is a rough approximation to the right tail of the distribution of squares is like Eeckhout's (2004) finding that the lognormal fits the right tail of the distribution of census places. But as argued in the introduction, the census place is a problematic geographic unit to use in examining the size distribution. Eeckhout presents a random growth model with shocks to location productivities that generates a lognormal distribution. We do not attempt any formal analysis in this chapter to try to explain why the size distribution has the shape that it has. But a look at the raw data makes us skeptical that random location-specific productivity shocks are the main driving factor, at least at the extreme left tail. That there are more squares with two people than with one person (1,285 instead of 713) seems to us more likely due to basic agglomeration benefits in the human condition rather than the variance of location-specific productivity shocks. It seems likely that as we move beyond the one- and two-person size classes, related agglomeration forces are also at work.

We now turn our attention away from the extreme left tail and consider what the distribution looks like with the extreme left tail truncated. If any part of the distribution is to look anything like Zipf, it has to be on the downward-sloping portion of the density. Inspection of figure 3.4 (panel C) reveals that the mode of the distribution is approximately at a log population of 7, which corresponds to approximately a population of 1,000. Henceforth, we truncate all squares with population less than 1,000. From table 3.4, we see that there are 23,974 squares with 1,000 people or more and that these account for about 28 percent of the U.S. land mass and 96 percent of the population. The coverage of the population is very significant here. Even with the truncation, we are including areas that are quite remote.

Figure 3.5 is a Zipf's plot of the population distribution of squares with 1,000 or more people. It exhibits a clear pattern. The relationship looks piecewise linear, with a kink around log population of 11 (which corresponds to a population of approximately 50,000). Above the kink, the relationship steepens. We use nonlinear least squares to fit a piecewise linear function to the plot in figure 3.5. The estimates are reported in table 3.5. Because of the large number of observations, the estimated standard errors are quite small, so they are not reported. The estimated kink is at a log population of 10.89. Below the kink, the (absolute value of) the slope is 0.75; above the kink, it is 1.94. The $R^2 = 0.998$ is extremely high, so the piecewise linear function fits very well. For comparison purposes, we also fit a linear function. The slope in the linear case is between the estimates for the piecewise linear case, and the fit is noticeably worse.

The Census groups states into nine different census divisions. Our next exercise is to examine the distribution of population across squares within

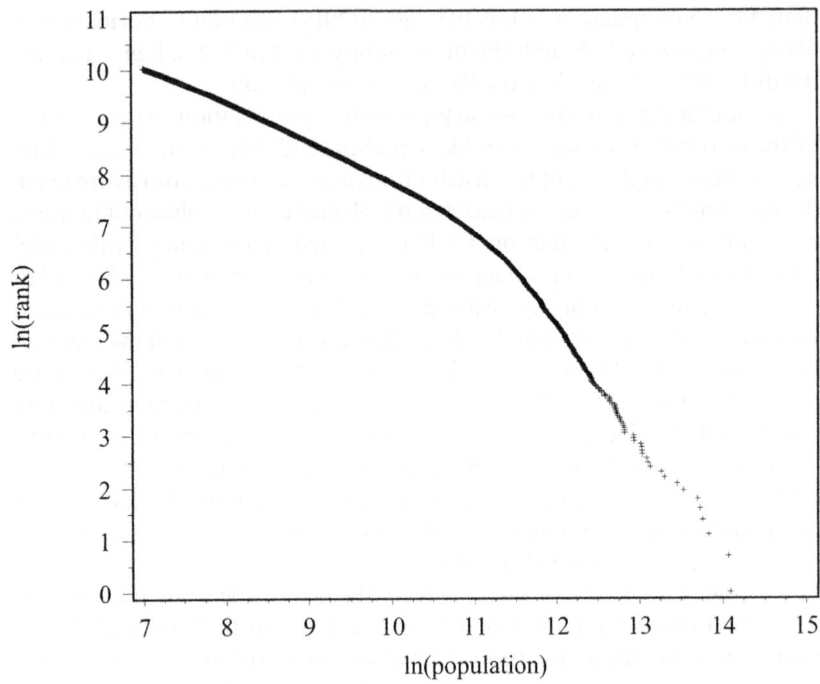

Fig. 3.5 Square-level Zipf plot for continental United States (all 23,974 squares with population at least 1,000)

Table 3.5 Six-by-six-square-level Zipf regression results (squares with population 1,000 and above)

		Piecewise linear				Linear	
Sample of squares	*N*	Kink	Slope1	Slope2	R^2	Slope	R^2
All squares with population ≥ 1,000	23,974	10.89	.747	1.937	.998	.833	.969
By Census division							
New England	1,027	9.96	.569	1.521	.996	.763	.930
Middle Atlantic	2,184	10.28	.669	1.249	.997	.759	.965
East North Central	4,313	10.92	.784	1.982	.999	.861	.975
West North Central	2,337	11.04	.886	2.607	.999	.941	.984
South Atlantic	4,977	10.72	.756	2.175	.995	.857	.959
East South Central	2,898	10.48	1.010	2.357	.997	1.072	.983
West South Central	3,078	11.17	.786	2.834	.997	.857	.969
Mountain	1,383	11.55	.723	3.662	.997	.791	.964
Pacific	1,777	11.21	.521	1.872	.992	.646	.922

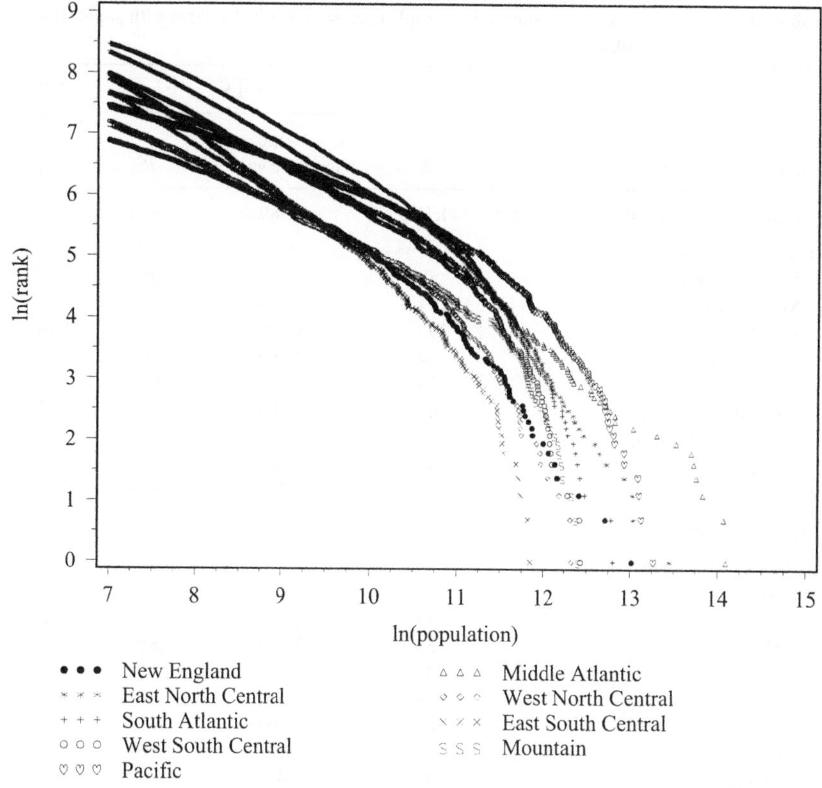

Fig. 3.6 Square-level Zipf plots for census divisions (square population at least 1,000)

each census division. Figure 3.6 contains Zipf plots for all nine divisions, and table 3.5 lists the estimates. To a remarkable degree, the pattern we have established for the country as a whole occurs in each division individually. Table 3.5 shows that the estimated location of the kink varies little across the divisions, roughly eleven for each. In figure 3.6, we see that the slope on the left side of the kink is approximately the same for each division. The plots look something like vertical shifts across the divisions. In all cases, the slope to the right of the kink is strictly greater than 1, and to left of the kink, the slope is less than 1 (with the exception that for the East South Central, the slope actually equals 1 to the left of the kink).

The kink at log population of 10.9 suggests we should explore this upper tail. This corresponds approximately to a population of 50,000. Now, truncate all squares with population less than 50,000. We are left with 1,182 squares, accounting for 48 percent of the population. Table 3.6 reports the

Table 3.6 **Six-by-six-square-level Zipf regression results (squares with population 50,000 and above)**

		OLS		Hill method
Sample of squares	N	Slope (absolute value)	R^2	Slope
All squares with population ≥ 50,000	1,182	1.889	.983	1.569
By Census division				
New England	58	1.865	.989	1.892
Middle Atlantic	154	1.318	.989	1.302
East North Central	193	1.929	.987	1.641
West North Central	74	2.389	.969	2.108
South Atlantic	218	2.271	.972	1.847
East South Central	44	2.763	.923	2.575
West South Central	138	2.286	.918	1.778
Mountain	85	1.951	.853	1.487
Pacific	218	1.597	.931	1.236
Mean across divisions	131.3	2.041	.948	1.763
By MSA (10 largest)				
Boston	26	1.462	.987	1.491
Chicago	54	1.412	.974	1.246
Dallas	35	2.208	.869	1.401
Detroit	35	1.718	.938	1.603
Houston	29	1.751	.894	1.469
Los Angeles	82	1.265	.870	0.986
New York	95	1.139	.981	1.173
Philadelphia	32	1.425	.982	1.612
San Francisco	43	1.451	.935	1.373
Washington	43	1.639	.955	1.336
Mean across top ten MSAs	47.4	1.547	.939	1.369
Mean across top twenty-five MSAs	29.2	1.776	.915	1.556

results of a linear Zipf's regression on this tail of the distribution. Taking the country as a whole, the slope is 1.889. Looking at each census division individually, the variation in the slope is relatively small, and the mean is 2.

We conclude this section by connecting our results from the square-level analysis to the previous section's results for the MSA-level analysis. The bottom of table 3.6 reports the results of Zipf regressions across squares *within* MSAs. For example, there are twenty-six squares with 50,000 people or more in the Boston MSA, and when we estimate the Zipf's regression on this sample, we get a slope of 1.46. The table reports the results of individual regressions for the top ten MSAs (by population), as well as the mean coefficients across these regressions for the top ten and top twenty-five MSAs. (We only do this for large MSAs, since small MSAs have few 50,000+ squares with which to run the regression.)

Recall from table 3.3 that in an *MSA-level* regression with the 135 top MSAs, when we use the maximum population square s_i^{max} as the size measure, we get a slope of 1.761. It is notable that when we take the MSA that is ranked 135 according to this measure, its value of s_i^{max} is 65,000, which approximately equals the 50,000 cutoff we are using here. The 1.761 slope approximately equals the slope of the *within-MSA, square-level* regressions we are doing here. The average slope across the top twenty-five MSAs is in fact 1.776.

The results here are interesting in two ways. First, there is an interesting fractal-like pattern among squares with 50,000 or more in population. Looking *within* a given MSA, the Zipf coefficient across squares is on the order of 1.7. This is approximately what we get when we take the maximum population square in each MSA and look *across* MSAs. It is also approximately what we get when we take all such squares across the whole country and look at them together (the 1.9 estimate in table 3.6), as well as when we look at squares in individual regions.

Second, this coefficient is also approximately the result we get when we do not use the squares and just use average MSA density (the 1.896 coefficient on density in table 3.3). We have raised concerns about the arbitrary way MSAs are defined, and there is certainly measurement error. Yet, our analysis in which MSA definitions play no role whatsoever (1.889 Zipf coefficient in table 3.6) is very close to our results in the MSA density analysis of table 3.3 (again, the 1.896 coefficient in table 3.3). Now, these are different objects that need not be the same, even if with perfect measurement. Yet, the suggestive fractal pattern here hints that they might very well be the same or very close if we did have perfect measurement. And even with the imperfect measurement of MSAs we have to work with, our analysis may not be very far off.

3.6 Growth Rates

The theoretical literature has emphasized the link between the size distribution of cities and their growth rates. In particular, Gabaix has shown a connection between Gibrat's law and Zipf's law. One version of Gibrat's law is that the mean and variance of the growth rate of a city are independent of the initial size of a city. Authors such as Ioannides and Overman (2003) have noted that Gibrat's law is a reasonable first-order approximation to the data. (See also Black and Henderson [2003] for an analysis.)

Table 3.7 shows that Gibrat's law is a reasonable first-order approximation for MSA growth in our data. The measure of growth rate used here is the difference in log population between 2000 and 1990. Mean growth over all MSAs during the period is 0.124. The mean growth varies relatively little over the four different MSA groupings in the table. It takes a low of 0.114 for cities with less than 250,000 people and has a peak of 0.141 for cities in

Table 3.7 **Growth rates (change in log population), 1990 to 2000, by size (MSAs and squares)**

	Number with positive population in 1990 and 2000	Change in log population	
		Mean	Standard deviation
MSAs	274	.124	.100
MSAs by 1990 population			
Population < 250,000	135	.114	.098
250,000 ≤ population < 500,000	66	.127	.093
500,000 ≤ population < 1,000,000	32	.141	.129
1,000,000 ≤ population	41	.139	.094
Squares	65,975	.081	.6186
Squares by 1990 population			
Population < 1,000	43,723	.054	.741
1,000 ≤ population < 2,000	8,057	.129	.228
2,000 ≤ population < 5,000	7,117	.139	.242
5,000 ≤ population < 10,000	2,953	.144	.223
10,000 ≤ population < 50,000	3,118	.149	.204
50,000 ≤ population < 100,000	616	.093	.128
100,000 ≤ population < 250,000	341	.056	.095
250,000 ≤ population < 500,000	39	.046	.071
500,000 ≤ population	11	.060	.061

the 0.5 to 1 million range. Moreover, the standard deviation does not vary much across the different groups.

Table 3.7 shows that Gibrat's law is not a good approximation for the growth of squares. The mean and variance of growth depend on size in a clear pattern. Mean growth in the smallest size category is 0.054—the lowest over all categories. Growth increases with size until it attains a maximum value of 0.149 for squares in the 10,000 to 50,000 range. Beyond this, mean growth decreases, falling to 0.093 in the 50,000 to 100,000 range and to around 0.05 beyond that. The standard deviation is not flat but decreases sharply with population.

These results for the growth rates of squares are not surprising, given what we know about the patterns of urban and rural growth. As is well known, remote rural areas have been declining in their share of population, so not surprisingly, mean growth is lowest in the smallest size category, under 1,000 people in the square. Also well understood is that in large urban areas, population expansions take place at the edges where new housing is constructed. For this reason, the most dense squares (those with more than 100,000 in 1990 population) have the lowest growth rate besides the under-1,000 category. These dense areas are already built up, and additional housing units are hard to squeeze in. Those squares that tend to be on the edge of metropolitan areas (in the range of 10,000 to 50,000 people) have the highest growth rate of 0.149.

It is also easy to see why the highest population squares have the lowest variance of growth. The absence of a large stock of vacant buildable land eliminates the possibility of upside growth, and the existence of a housing stock decreases the downside of population outflow (see Glaeser and Gyourko [2005]). It is easy to see why the smallest locations have the highest variance of growth. If the forest ranger living by himself or herself in a six-by-six square gets married, population in the square doubles.

3.7 Robustness

In setting our grid of squares, we had to determine: (a) what grid size to use (we picked six miles), and (b) where to start the grid. Let us begin by exploring this second decision, which is analogous to the decision of where to put the prime meridian for longitude, an arbitrary placement that by international convention passes through Greenwich. With the way we have placed the grid in figure 3.1, we can see that downtown Manhattan is in the same six-by-six square with Jersey City and other places across the river in New Jersey. If we had shifted the grid two miles to the east, downtown Manhattan would have been in a square with Queens.

One may wonder whether this arbitrary decision on our part impacts our results. Fortunately, the answer is no: where to start the grid has virtually no impact on our results. Table 3.8 shows what happens when we shift the grid two miles and four miles to the north. (Note that if we shift it north six miles, the grid remains the same.) Analogously, it shows what happens when we shift the grid two and four miles to the east. The top row contains the original baseline results. The rows below are the results with the shift and show that they are the same up to two-digit accuracy, and for some columns, up to three digits.

Next, we consider changing the size of the grid. Significant changes in the grid will impact the results. If we make the grid size 1,000 miles, there will be only three squares. If we make the grid one meter by one meter, then our first problem is the Census data are not fine enough for this size. Our second problem is that populations would typically be one if a person happened to be standing in the one-by-one-meter square at the time of the census and zero otherwise, so the size distribution would not be interesting.

Next, we focus on the robustness of our results to relatively small changes in the grid size. We consider two smaller grid sizes (two and four miles) and four larger ones (eight, ten, fifteen, and twenty miles). To a remarkable degree, our results are robust to these changes in grid size. Recall that in the original six-by-six analysis, we used a 1,000 population cutoff for the piecewise linear regression and a 50,000 cutoff in the linear regression. When we change the grid size, we also change the population cutoffs to keep population density at the cutoff the same. For example, the area of a two-by-two square is 1/9 times the area of a six-by-six square. So, for the two-by-two

Table 3.8 **Robustness of results to alternative grids**

	MSA-level regression on s_i^{max}		Square-level piecewise linear regression, population ≥ 1,000 per 6 × 6 square[a]				Square-level linear regression, population ≥ 50,000 per 6 × 6 square[a]	
	OLS slope	R^2	Kink	Slope1	Slope2	R^2	OLS slope	R^2
Baseline 6 × 6 grid	1.761	.988	10.89	.747	1.937	.998	1.889	.983
Shift of baseline grid								
2 miles north	1.790	.986	10.95	.751	1.984	.998	1.892	.980
4 miles north	1.838	.986	10.90	.750	1.923	.998	1.879	.981
2 miles east	1.715	.988	10.90	.745	1.957	.998	1.919	.987
4 miles east	1.774	.989	10.92	.747	1.979	.998	1.924	.983
Alternative grid size								
2 miles	1.981	.977	9.072	.680	2.097	.999	1.800	.968
4 miles	1.873	.992	10.262	.719	2.037	.999	1.886	.979
6 miles	1.761	.988	10.899	.747	1.937	.998	1.889	.983
8 miles	1.595	.981	11.433	.773	1.976	.998	1.959	.986
10 miles	1.483	.978	11.655	.786	1.819	.998	1.914	.987
15 miles	1.325	.979	12.328	.816	1.850	.998	1.959	.994
20 miles	1.246	.969	12.482	.822	1.630	.997	1.994	.983

[a]We adjust the population cutoffs for the squares to keep the population density the same across cutoffs for the different grid sizes. For example, in the two-by-two-square linear regression, we use all the squares with population sizes greater than or equal to 5,556 (= 50,000/9). The 50,000 comes from the base case of the six-by-six-mile square. The nine takes account of the fact that the area of a six-by-six square is nine times as large as a two-by-two square.

case, the linear regression cutoff is 5,556 = 50,000/9. The piecewise linear function fits extremely well throughout all the grid sizes (R^2 = 0.997 and above). The coefficient estimates do not vary much: 0.7 to 0.8 below the kink, and 1.8 to 2.0 above the kink. Moreover, the locations of the kink increase by the expected magnitude. For example, going from a two-by-two grid to a four-by-four grid increases the area by a factor of 4 (ln [4] = 1.39). If density at the kink stayed the same, then the kink should increase by 1.39 when moving from a two-by-two grid to a four-by-four grid. The actual increase of 1.19 = 10.26 – 9.07 is fairly close. We see an analogous pattern for the other grid sizes. We conclude that our results are not an artifact of an arbitrary choice of a six-mile grid length.

One notable pattern in table 3.8 is the decline of the MSA-level regression coefficient on s_i^{max} as the grid size is increased. As grid sizes increase, the squares begin to incorporate the entirety of the MSA. So, the population of the biggest square s_i^{max} begins to approximate the population of the MSA as a whole, and the coefficient gets close to 1 (Zipf's law), as it is in table 3.3.

One last issue concerns what is happening on the coasts with the squares. As can be seen in figure 3.1, some of the squares in the New York metro area are partly in the very dense island of Manhattan and partly in the water. Since the highest population density locations (New York, Chicago, etc.) tend to border bodies of water, one might wonder whether some systematic biases might be present. We think this is an interesting point but not one of much quantitative significance, because we are working with logs rather than levels. We make two distinct arguments. First, in these dense cities, the log population of the squares changes relatively slowly as we move away from the coasts (at least at a six-by-six grid size). The possibility of systematic biases at the coasts is not quantitatively a big problem, because many other squares nearby that are approximately equal in log population will average things out. Second, even at the coast, variations in density are not quantitatively significant. Suppose, for example, that a square at the coast is half in the water (ln [1/2] = –0.3). At the dense squares near or in Manhattan, log population is around 14. If we shifted such a square and put it half in the water, log population would fall to 13.7 = 14 – 0.3. This is a small difference compared to the vast differences in log population between squares close to Manhattan (regardless of whether in the water) and squares in less-dense places, such as upstate New York. Even if the square were 99 percent in the water, this would not matter either, because such a square at a six-by-six resolution would represent a negligible portion of the downtown area.

3.8 Conclusion

Our chapter studies the distribution of population across six-by-six-mile squares, examining the extent to which Zipf's law and Gibrat's law hold. The main results are as follows:

1. At the bottom tail of the distribution, the distribution is roughly lognormal, certainly not Zipf.
2. For squares above 1,000 in population, a Zipf's plot has a piecewise linear shape, with a kink at around a population of 50,000. Below the kink, the slope is 0.75; above the kink, it is around 2. The finding is robust across different regions in the country.
3. Gibrat's law does not hold with squares. Mean growth has an inverted U-shaped relationship with population size. The variance of growth declines with size.
4. The slope of 2 in the upper tail matches what we get with MSA-level data if we substitute population density for population in a Zipf's plot. This is consistent with the usual Zipf coefficient of 1 for the population regression if the land elasticity of population is 0.5. The slope of 2 also matches what we get if we use the maximum population square in the MSA instead of average density, as well as what we get in the upper tail when we look at squares *within* MSAs. All of this suggests some kind of fractal pattern in

the left tail in which the distribution of squares within MSAs looks like the distribution of MSAs across the country, which in turn looks like the distribution of squares across the country and within individual regions.

In our title, we put a question mark after "Zipf's Law." It is clear that the standard Zipf's law does not apply for squares in the upper tail, because the slope is around 2, not 1. Nevertheless, if we take the land elasticity of population to be 0.5 (which roughly fits the data for large MSAs), then a slope coefficient of 2 for squares (where the land margin is fixed) is consistent with a slope coefficient of 1 for regularly defined MSAs (where the land margin varies). In this sense, Zipf's law holds for squares in the right tail. But what about below the kink of a square population of 50,000? For relatively less-populated squares like these, an expansion of the population might not put much pressure on the land margin, as vacant rural land in the square can be converted to housing sites. If the land elasticity were zero, the coefficient on density in equation (5) would be the same as the coefficient on population in equation (2). In this extreme case, the relevant comparison is between the 0.75 slope for squares and the standard slope of 1, and Zipf's law does not hold. If the land elasticity is a little higher than zero, Zipf's law works better. Regardless of this matter, the fact that the Zipf's plot is straight as an arrow for population in the range between 1,000 and 50,000 is very intriguing. The presence of the kink is intriguing, as well.

We believe a joint analysis of the distribution of population of squares within and across metropolitan areas is a fruitful area for further research. We see opportunities for progress in theories that emphasize economic considerations and spatial factors, such as the work of Hsu (2008). In terms of directions for future empirical work, we believe it would be promising to examine the size distribution of squares in an international context.

References

Anas, A., R. Arnott, and K. A. Small. 1998. Urban spatial structure. *Journal of Economic Literature* 36 (3): 1426–64.

Black, D., and V. Henderson. 2003. Urban evolution in the USA. *Journal of Economic Geography* 3 (4): 343–72.

Bryan, K. A., B. D. Minton, and P.-D. G. Sarte. 2007. The evolution of city population density in the United States. *Economic Quarterly* 93 (4): 341–60.

Burchfield, M., H. G. Overman, D. Puga, and M. A. Turner. 2006. Causes of sprawl: A portrait from space. *Quarterly Journal of Economics* 121 (2): 587–633.

Duranton, G., and H. Overman. 2005. Testing for localization using micro-geographic data. *Review of Economic Studies* 72 (4): 1077–106.

Duranton, G., and M. A. Turner. 2008. Urban growth and transportation. University of Toronto, Department of Economics. Manuscript, November.

Eeckhout, J. 2004. Gibrat's law for (all) cities. *American Economic Review* 94 (5): 1429–51.

Gabaix, X. 1999. Zipf's law for cities: An explanation. *Quarterly Journal of Economics* 114 (3): 739–67.

Gabaix, X., and Y. M. Ioannides. 2004. Evolution of city size distributions. In *Handbook of regional and urban economics,* vol. 4, ed. J. V. Henderson and J.-F. Thisse, 2341–78. Amsterdam: Elsevier.

Glaeser, E. L., and J. Gyourko. 2005. Urban decline and durable housing. *Journal of Political Economy* 113 (2): 345–75.

Holmes, T. J., and S. Lee. 2008. Economies of density versus natural advantage: Crop choice on the back forty. University of Minnesota, Department of Economics. Manuscript, October.

Hsu, W.-T. 2008. Central place theory and Zipf's law. University of Minnesota, Department of Economics. Manuscript, January.

Ioannides, Y. M., and H. G. Overman. 2003. Zipf's law for cities: An empirical examination. *Regional Science and Urban Economics* 33 (2): 127–37.

Linklater, A. 2003. *Measuring America: How the United States was shaped by the greatest land sale in history.* New York: Plume.

Luttmer, E. G. J. 2007. Selection, growth, and the size distribution of firms. *Quarterly Journal of Economics* 122 (3): 1103–44.

McMillen, D. P., and J. F. McDonald. 1998. Suburban subcenters and employment density in metropolitan Chicago. *Journal of Urban Economics* 43 (2): 157–80.

Nordhaus, W., Q. Azam, D. Corderi, K. Hood, N. M. Victor, M. Mohammed, A. Miltner, and J. Weiss. 2006. The G-Econ Database on Gridded Output: Methods and data. Yale University, Geographically Based Economic Data (G-Econ). Available at: http://gecon.yale.edu.

Rossi-Hansberg, E., and M. L. J. Wright. 2007. Urban structure and growth. *Review of Economic Studies* 74 (2): 597–624.

4

Labor Pooling as a Source of Agglomeration
An Empirical Investigation

Henry G. Overman and Diego Puga

4.1 Introduction

Spatial concentrations of establishments and workers offer great productivity advantages. Many modern econometric studies have confirmed and quantified this important stylized fact. Estimates of the productivity increase from a doubling in the size of an agglomeration range between 2 and 8 percent, depending on the sector and details of the estimation procedure (see Rosenthal and Strange [2004] and Combes et al. [chapter 1 in this volume]).

Unfortunately, the literature has been far less successful at distinguishing between the different sources of urban increasing returns than at quantifying their overall magnitude. Specifically, while we have sound theoretical models providing microeconomic foundations for the economies of agglomeration, the different mechanisms are hard to distinguish empirically. The main difficulty arises from the "Marshallian equivalence" of these theories (see Duranton and Puga [2004]): they all predict an increase in productivity with spatial concentration but work through mechanisms that are hard to trace.

Henry G. Overman is professor of economic geography at the London School of Economics. Diego Puga is a research professor at the Madrid Institute for Advanced Studies (IMDEA) Social Sciences.

Thanks to Edward Glaeser and seminar participants at the NBER Urban Economics meeting in March 2007 for comments. We are grateful to Roberto Picchizzolu for his help in providing us with data on energy use and research and development expenditures. Funding from the Comunidad de Madrid through the grant PROCIUDAD-CM is gratefully acknowledged. This work contains statistical data from ONS, which is Crown copyright and reproduced with the permission of the controller of HMSO and Queen's Printer for Scotland. The use of the ONS statistical data in this work does not imply the endorsement of the ONS in relation to the interpretation or analysis of the statistical data. This work uses research data sets that may not exactly reproduce National Statistics aggregates.

This chapter focuses on a potential source of agglomeration economies to which Alfred Marshall (1890) devoted particular attention: labor market pooling. While there are various interpretations of labor market pooling as a source of agglomeration economies, Marshall emphasized that "a localized industry gains a great advantage from the fact that it offers a constant market for skill" (Marshall 1890, 271). In section 4.2, we use a simple model to clarify the microeconomic foundations of labor pooling as a source of agglomeration economies and to motivate our empirical analysis. The model is a version of the labor pooling model of Krugman (1991). We consider a series of sectors where establishments experience idiosyncratic shocks. Individual profits are convex in the establishment-specific shock, since each establishment responds to the shock by adjusting its levels of both production and employment. However, changes in the establishment's employment affect local wages, and the more isolated the establishment is from other establishments in the same sector or using similar workers, the greater the effect. If wages are higher when the establishment wants to expand production in response to a positive shock and lower when it wants to contract production in response to a negative shock, this limits the establishment's ability to adapt its employment level to good and bad times. Consequently, establishments that tend to experience substantial changes in their employment relative to other establishments using workers with similar skills will find it advantageous to locate in places where there is a large number of workers with such skills. As a result, the model predicts that sectors whose establishments experience more idiosyncratic volatility will be more spatially concentrated.[1]

To assess the importance of labor market pooling as a source of agglomeration economies empirically, we use establishment-level data from the United Kingdom's Annual Respondents Database (ARD), which underlies the Annual Census of Production. The data is described in section 4.3. We begin by constructing an establishment-level measure of idiosyncratic employment shocks by calculating the difference between the percentage change in the establishment's employment and the percentage change in the sector's employment. We then average this (in absolute value) across time and across establishments in the sector to obtain a sector-level measure of how much idiosyncratic volatility individual establishments in each sector face. We then check whether, consistent with the theory, sectors whose

1. Labor market pooling is not the only theoretical agglomeration mechanism operating through local labor markets. Larger markets also improve the chances of matching between firms and workers, as well as the average quality of matches (see Helsley and Strange [1990]). In addition, larger markets also encourage workers to focus on a narrower set of tasks and to acquire more specialized skills (see Baumgardner [1988], Becker and Murphy [1992], and Duranton [1998]). We focus just on labor pooling, whereby concentrations of employers using similar workers allow labor to move more easily from less-productive to more-productive firms. We maintain this specific focus because only by concentrating on the unique implications of a given agglomeration mechanism can we hope to identify it empirically.

establishments experience more idiosyncratic volatility are more spatially concentrated. We find that this is indeed the case, even after controlling for a range of other industry characteristics that include a novel measure of the importance of localized intermediate suppliers.

4.2 The Theoretical Advantages of Labor Pooling

In this section, we present a simple model of labor pooling. This helps clarify the microeconomic foundations of labor pooling as a source of agglomeration economies. It also allows us to derive an empirically testable prediction about how the importance of labor pooling will vary across sectors. The model is a multisector and multilocation version of the labor pooling model of Krugman (1991).

4.2.1 Setup

Consider a series of sectors indexed by $s = 1, \ldots, S$. Each sector has a discrete number of production establishments distinguished by subindex $i = 1, \ldots, N$ and a continuum of workers with skills specific to that sector. Establishments and workers are risk neutral. After choosing its location, each establishment receives a productivity shock ε_i. The shocks are uncorrelated across establishments and identically distributed over $[-\varepsilon, \varepsilon]$ with mean zero and variance σ_s. Establishments observe these shocks and decide how much labor to hire from the local labor pool in the sector. If establishment i chooses an employment level l_i, it has operating profits given by:

$$\pi_i = [\beta + \varepsilon_i]l_i - \frac{1}{2}\gamma[l_i]^2 - wl_i. \tag{1}$$

4.2.2 Wages

Following Krugman (1991), assume that each establishment takes the local wage as given. Thus, after shocks are realized, each establishment hires labor until its marginal value product equals the wage. This yields establishment i's labor demand:

$$l_i = \frac{\beta - w + \varepsilon_i}{\gamma}. \tag{2}$$

Denote by L the hours of labor effectively supplied in a given city and sector. Labor market clearing, together with equation (2), implies

$$L = \sum_{i=1}^{N} l_i = \frac{\beta - w + \sum_{i=1}^{N}\varepsilon_i}{\gamma}. \tag{3}$$

We can then solve for the market-clearing wage from equation (3):

$$w = \beta - \gamma\frac{L}{N} + \frac{1}{N}\sum_{i=1}^{N}\varepsilon_i. \tag{4}$$

Taking expectations yields the expected wage.[2]

$$E(w) = \beta - \gamma\frac{L}{N}. \tag{5}$$

4.2.3 Profits

Substituting equation (2) into equation (1), this simplifies to:

$$\pi_i = \frac{[\beta - w + \varepsilon_i]^2}{2\gamma}. \tag{6}$$

Note that establishment profits are a convex function of the idiosyncratic productivity shock, since the establishment adjusts its production level in response to the shock. Similarly, profits are convex in the wage.

Taking expectations of the profits in equation (6) yields:

$$E(\pi_i) = \frac{[\beta - E(w)]^2 + \mathrm{var}[\varepsilon_i - w]}{2\gamma}. \tag{7}$$

Substituting equation (5) and $\mathrm{var}[\varepsilon_i - w] = \mathrm{var}[\varepsilon_i] + \mathrm{var}(w) - 2\mathrm{cov}[\varepsilon_i, w]$ into equation (7), this simplifies to:

$$E(\pi_i) = \frac{\gamma}{2}\left(\frac{L}{N}\right)^2 + \frac{\mathrm{var}[\varepsilon_i] + \mathrm{var}(w) - 2\mathrm{cov}[\varepsilon_i, w]}{2\gamma}. \tag{8}$$

The first term of the right-hand side is what establishment profits would be in the absence of shocks. It increases as the ratio of workers to establishments L/N increases, because this lowers the expected wage. The second term captures the labor pooling effect. This shows that expected profits increase with the variance of the establishment-specific productivity shock, $\mathrm{var}[\varepsilon_i]$, and with the variance of the local wage, $\mathrm{var}(w)$, because of the convexity of profits previously discussed. However, they decrease with the covariance of the establishment-specific productivity shock and the local wage, $\mathrm{cov}[\varepsilon_i, w]$. The reason is that if the local wage is higher when an establishment wishes to expand production in response to a positive shock and lower when the establishment wishes to contract production in response to a negative shock, profits become less convex in the shock and fall in expectation. This is the key intuition of the model, which highlights the microeconomic foundations of labor pooling as a source of agglomeration: *establishments prefer locations where their productivity shocks get ironed out rather than heavily reflected in local wages.*

To simplify equation (8) further, we can use equations (4) and (5) to calculate $\mathrm{var}(w) = \sigma_s/N$ and $\mathrm{cov}[\varepsilon_i, w] = \sigma_s/N$. Substituting these and $\mathrm{var}[\varepsilon_i] = \sigma_s$ into equation (8) yields:

2. We assume that the support of the distribution of productivity shocks is not so large that the nonnegative employment constraint for some establishment might be binding under some realization of shocks. In particular, we assume that the restriction $\gamma/\varepsilon \geq [2(N-1)]/L$ holds. This follows from $l_i > 0$ and equations (2) and (4) for a case where $\varepsilon_i = -\varepsilon$ and $\varepsilon_j = \varepsilon\ \forall j \neq i$.

$$(9) \qquad E(\pi) = \frac{\gamma}{2}\left(\frac{L}{N}\right)^2 + \left(1 - \frac{1}{N}\right)\frac{\sigma_s}{2\gamma},$$

where we have dropped subindex i, since expected profits are equal for all establishments in the same location and sector. The labor market pooling effect, as captured by the term $(1 - [1/N])(\sigma_s/2\gamma)$, is stronger when the σ_s in the sector is higher. Thus, *the benefits of labor pooling will be greater when the heterogeneity of establishment-specific shocks in the sector is larger.* This suggests that sectors with more heterogeneous shocks are more likely to be agglomerated. To show this more formally, we now explore two alternative definitions of an urban equilibrium in this model, both of which yield the same key testable prediction.

4.2.4 Equilibrium with Simultaneous Relocation by Firms and Workers

Following Ellison and Fudenberg (2003), let us first treat location and production in this model as a two-stage game. In the first stage, all establishments and workers (whose total number is exogenously given) simultaneously choose their location. In the second stage, each establishment receives its productivity shock ε_i. Since there is a continuum of workers, a relocation by an individual worker has no effect on wages or profits. Provided wages are equalized across locations, no worker has an incentive to relocate. From equation (5), this implies that the equilibrium ratio of workers to establishments L/N must be the same in all locations.

Establishments, unlike workers, are discrete, and this assumption is essential for there to be advantages from labor pooling. Thus, a relocation by an individual establishment alters wages and profits at both the origin and destination of the relocation. In equilibrium, it must be the case that an individual establishment cannot increase the expected profits of equation (9) by deviating and locating elsewhere. An establishment must consider two aspects in deciding whether such a deviation is profitable. First, starting from a situation where wages are equalized across locations, the establishment's relocation would decrease the ratio of workers to establishments in the destination location, making the labor market tighter in expectation and increasing the expected wage, which would reduce the establishment's expected profits. This labor market tightness effect operates through the first term on the right-hand side of equation (9). Second, if after the deviation, the destination has a larger number of establishments, the establishment's productivity shocks (that get translated into employment shocks) will not affect the local wage as much, allowing the establishment to adapt better to circumstances and obtain higher expected profits. This is the labor pooling effect previously discussed, summarized now by the second term on the right-hand side of equation (9).

Suppose that the S sectors differ only in terms of the variance of productivity shocks, σ_s. Then, the labor market tightness effect favoring establishment dispersion is equally strong across all sectors, but the labor market pooling effect is stronger when σ_s in the sector is higher. Thus, the balance of agglomeration and dispersion forces tips more easily in favor of agglomeration when σ_s is higher. In particular, if a location has fewer than $\sigma_s/[2(\gamma^2 R^2 + \sigma_s)]$ times as many establishments as the largest agglomeration in the sector, all remaining establishments find it individually profitable to relocate to the largest agglomeration.[3] Thus, *sectors with more heterogeneous shocks are more likely to be agglomerated.* We will test this prediction empirically in section 4.4.

4.2.5 Equilibrium with Free Entry and an Agglomeration Wage Premium

The urban equilibrium we have just derived already captures the key prediction used next to check the empirical relevance of labor pooling as a source of agglomeration. However, while theoretically elegant, it also has some counterfactual predictions for cities. In particular, in equilibrium, workers capture none of the benefits of agglomeration, whereas in practice, larger cities and denser agglomerations are associated with a significant wage premium (see Glaeser and Maré [2001]; Wheaton and Lewis [2002]; and Combes, Duranton, and Gobillon [2008]).

To capture this wage premium, following Glaeser (2008), we now redefine an equilibrium of the model so that the number of establishments in each city is endogenously determined by free entry and exit, taking the size of local labor markets as given. We let the size of the labor pool differ across cities but keep it fixed for simplicity (although this can be justified through a heterogenous fixed housing stock). The equilibrium number of establishments in each city is then determined by free entry up to the point where a further increase in N would leave each establishment unable to cover the fixed cost of entry, denoted ϕ.[4] Substituting equation (9) into $E(\pi) = \phi$ and solving for N yields the equilibrium number of establishments in each city (ignoring integer constraints):

$$N = \frac{\sqrt{\sigma_s^2 + 4(2\gamma\phi - \sigma_s)\gamma^2 L^2} - \sigma_s}{2(2\gamma\phi - \sigma_s)}. \tag{10}$$

It follows from this expression that a city with a larger local labor market not only has more establishments but also a higher ratio of establishments to workers (or equivalently, a lower ratio of workers to establishments):

3. Stated differently, an equilibrium in this model is an allocation of workers and establishments across locations such that each location is either empty or has at least $\sigma_s/2(\gamma^2 R^2 + \sigma_s)$ as many establishments as the location with most establishments, and the ratio R of workers to establishments is the same in all nonempty locations as in the aggregate economy. See Ellison and Fudenberg (2003) for details.

4. Note that by equation (9), we must have $\phi > \sigma_s/2\gamma$. Otherwise, entry would continue indefinitely without exhausting profits net of ϕ.

$$(11)\quad \frac{\partial(L/N)}{\partial L} = \frac{-2\sigma_s(2\gamma\phi-\sigma_s)}{\sqrt{\sigma_s^2+4(2\gamma\phi-\sigma_s)\gamma^2L^2}\,[\sqrt{\sigma_s^2+4(2\gamma\phi-\sigma_s)\gamma^2L^2}-\sigma_s]}$$
$$= \frac{-\sigma_s}{N\sqrt{\sigma_s^2+4(2\gamma\phi-\sigma_s)\gamma^2L^2}} < 0.$$

By equation (5), this creates a wage premium that offsets the advantages of greater labor pooling in larger markets and ensures that profits are exhausted everywhere:

$$(12)\quad \frac{\partial E(w)}{\partial L} = -\gamma\frac{\partial(L/N)}{\partial L} > 0.$$

The equilibrium with free entry, with its agglomeration wage premium, is quite different from the equilibrium with simultaneous relocation of a fixed number of establishments and workers. Still, the key prediction we wish to take to the data also holds. To see this, differentiate equation (10) with respect to σ_s to obtain:

$$(13)\quad \frac{\partial^2(L/N)}{\partial L\partial\sigma_s} = -\frac{1}{2\gamma^2L^2}\left\{1+\frac{\sigma_s[\sigma_s^2+2\gamma^2L^2(8\gamma\phi-3\sigma_s)]}{[\sigma_s^2+4(2\gamma\phi-\sigma_s)\gamma^2L^2]^{3/2}}\right\} < 0.$$

(The inequality $\phi > \sigma_s/2\gamma$ has been used to sign this derivative; see note 4.) This implies that cities with a larger local labor market attract a disproportionate number of establishments and that the effect is stronger when σ_s in the sector is higher. Thus, once again, *sectors with more heterogeneous shocks tend to be more agglomerated.*

4.3 Data

To examine the role of labor pooling, we will regress a measure of spatial concentration for each sector on a measure of the potential for labor pooling in the sector and a number of sectoral characteristics that are also likely to affect geographic concentration. The measure of geographic concentration and the pooling variable described next are calculated using exhaustive establishment-level data from the Annual Respondents Database (ARD), which underlies the Annual Census of Production in the United Kingdom. We use data from 1994 to 2003. The data set is collected by the Office for National Statistics (ONS) and covers all UK establishments (see Griffith [1999] and Duranton and Overman [2005] for a detailed description of this data).[5] For every establishment, we know its postcode, four-digit industrial classification, and employment. We restrict our attention to production

5. We use the terms establishment and plant interchangeably. Our description of the data is based closely on Duranton and Overman (2005).

establishments in manufacturing industries using the Standard Industrial Classification 92 (SIC 15000 to 36639) for the whole country except Northern Ireland. For the purposes of this exercise, we have plant data from the ARD for 1994 to 2003. We observe 557,595 plants at least once. On average, we observe each plant 4.16 times.

Since the labor pooling mechanism depends on establishments' ability to take more or less workers from the local labor pool without difficulty, we must work with geographical units that correspond as closely as possible to local labor markets. Thus, our geographical units of analysis are the UK travel to work areas (TTWA), 1998 classification. Similar to the labor market areas that the Bureau of Labor Statistics defines for the United States, these TTWA are defined on the basis of commuting patterns to capture local labor markets. Specifically, the boundaries are drawn such that of the resident economically active population, at least 75 percent work in the area, and of everyone working in the area, at least 75 percent live in the area. The classification is exhaustive, with 308 TTWA covering the whole of Great Britain. United Kingdom postcodes can be uniquely mapped to TTWA, so we are able to locate establishments in the ARD according to the TTWA classification. The number of plants per TTWA is rather skewed. There are 15,154 on average, while the median number is 4,545. There are fourteen TTWA with less than one hundred plants, although inclusion of the very large or the very small areas does not affect our results, so we include the whole sample in what follows. One slight complication involves the treatment of plants that move across TTWA or change sector. We treat these as a separate observation.[6]

Our controls for other industry characteristics come mainly from the ONS input-output (IO) tables, available annually from 1994 to 2003.[7] We complement these where necessary with Eurostat's detailed enterprise statistics for the United Kingdom and the ARD itself. We provide more details as we introduce these controls.

4.4 The Importance of Labor Pooling for Industry Concentration

The theoretical model of section 4.2 suggests that sectors whose establishments experience more heterogeneous employment shocks have greater potential to benefit from labor pooling and, to exploit this, will be more

6. Moves across TTWA should not actually happen, as plant identifiers are supposed to designate a unique physical entity. In reality, firms sometimes report under the same plant identifier when they have actually moved plants. This justifies our decision to treat these observations separately. The issue of changing SIC is more problematic, as these classifications are based on the most significant activity undertaken at a given plant and may change over time.

7. The UK input-output tables use a 77-industry classification. This is compatible with NACE (Nomenclature générale des Activités économiques dans les Communautés Européennes) Rev. 1 and corresponds roughly to NACE three digit. We map this to the 237 industries in the UK SIC 92 by assigning the same value to all four-digit industries under any given IO heading.

spatially concentrated. In this section, we consider this prediction empirically by regressing a measure of spatial concentration for each sector on a measure of the potential for labor pooling in the sector. Of course, other characteristics of industries may also affect the extent of concentration, and we will need to control for these. That is, we estimate:

$$C_s = \alpha + \rho P_s + \phi \mathbf{X}_s + \epsilon_s, \tag{14}$$

where C_s is a measure of spatial concentration for sector s, P_s is a measure of the potential for labor pooling in the sector, $\mathbf{X}_i$ is a vector of sector characteristics, α, ρ, and ϕ are parameters to be estimated, and ϵ_i is an identically and independently distributed error term.

This approach to investigating the significance of different motives for spatial concentration has been used before. (See Audretsch and Feldman [1996] and in particular Rosenthal and Strange [2001] to which our regressions are most directly related.) The main novelty of our analysis is that by measuring the heterogeneity of individual establishments' employment shocks in each sector, we are able to look explicitly at the potential for labor pooling of different sectors. In contrast, as discussed next, the existing literature has had to rely on fairly indirect proxies to capture any possible effect. We also offer an important refinement for measuring the importance of the sharing of intermediate input suppliers.

4.4.1 Measuring Each Sector's Potential for Labor Pooling

The argument that labor pooling, by allowing establishments to better adapt to idiosyncratic shocks, can be an important determinant of agglomeration is well known. However, data restrictions mean that previous studies have had to get at this effect indirectly by focusing, for example, on the extent to which workers in an industry are likely to have industry-specific skills. Rosenthal and Strange (2001), for example, use three measures of labor pooling: net labor productivity (the value of shipments less the value of purchased inputs, all divided by the number of workers in the industry), the ratio of management workers to production workers, and the percentage of an industry's workers with doctorates, master's degrees, and bachelor's degrees. These indirect measures are not ideal, because while sectors with a larger share of managers or high-skilled workers may agglomerate partly because of labor pooling, there are many other reasons why they may concentrate geographically. For instance, agglomerations of high-skilled workers may facilitate better matching between jobs and workers (see Helsley and Strange [1990]). Alternatively, large markets may also allow high-skilled workers to specialize in a narrower set of tasks and become more productive (see Baumgardner [1988], Becker and Murphy [1992], and Duranton [1998]), or they may help solve dual-career problems for high-skilled couples (see Costa and Kahn [2000]).

We wish to be able to isolate the role of labor pooling, as motivated by the theoretical argument of section 4.2, from other labor market considerations. The crucial point, as previously discussed, is that a labor pooling advantage only arises if whenever a plant expands employment, many other plants using similar workers are contracting and vice versa. That is, what matters is the plants' idiosyncratic need to alter employment. To capture this effect, we exploit the fact that we have a panel of plants over a long time period to construct a direct measure of the idiosyncratic nature of any given plant's employment adjustments. To measure the idiosyncratic shock to a plant in any given year, we calculate the difference between the percentage change in the plant's employment and the percentage change in the industry's employment (in absolute value). This will take a high value for plants that either expand employment when the rest of the industry is contracting or vice versa. Taking the difference between the plant's change and the industry's change is important, because there is no labor pooling advantage if whenever the plant expands employment, many other plants using similar workers also expand.[8] We then take the average of this variable across all years and across all plants in each sector. The resulting "pooling" measure captures how much idiosyncratic volatility is faced by individual establishments in each sector.

4.4.2 Measuring Each Sector's Spatial Concentration

There are a variety of statistics that can be used to measure the extent of spatial concentration. We adopt the widely used index proposed by Ellison and Glaeser (1997). This measures the amount of clustering in a sector over and beyond that which we would expect to find based on randomness alone. It has the advantage of being comparable across sectors and controlling for both the overall geographic concentration of employment and for the "lumpiness" of employment. This lumpiness arises because industrial concentration means plants are of different sizes. This is a problem when trying to measure spatial concentration, because even random distributions of plants across spatial units can give rise to some places having more employment than others (if they happen, by chance, to get a particularly large plant). Because the Ellison-Glaeser index controls for industrial concentration of the industry, it corrects for this problem. Let s_a be the share of sector's employment that is in area a and x_a be the share of total manufacturing employment that is in area a. Then, the Ellison-Glaeser index of geographical concentration is defined as:

$$C_s \equiv \frac{G_s - (1 - \sum_a x_a^2)H_s}{(1 - \sum_a x_a^2)(1 - H_s)}, \tag{15}$$

8. We are assuming that plants in the same industry use similar workers so that the plant's industry is the appropriate reference group. When we turn to our results, we will also consider the opposite extreme, where the appropriate reference group is manufacturing as a whole.

where G_s is a raw localization index equal to

$$G_s \equiv \sum_a (s_a - x_a)^2, \tag{16}$$

and

$$H_s \equiv \sum_i z_i^2 \tag{17}$$

is the Herfindahl index of the sector's plant size distribution, with z_i denoting plant i's share of sector s's employment. Ellison and Glaeser (1997) show that if plants are randomly distributed across locations with probabilities given by x_a, then the expected value of this measure is zero. A positive value of the index indicates a level of spatial concentration over and above what one would expect by chance.

4.4.3 Results

Although we have panel data for the Ellison-Glaeser index and some of the explanatory variables, preliminary regressions exploiting the panel dimension of the data did not perform well. Perhaps this is unsurprising, as location patterns change only slowly, while some of the industry characteristics (e.g., research and development [R&D] expenditure per worker) can show a considerable amount of year-on-year variation. Furthermore, for the labor pooling measure, it is necessary to take into account plant-level employment shocks relative to the sector for a number of years. Given both these considerations, we choose to average variables over time. Specifically, we split the time period in half and regress the average Ellison-Glaeser index for the six years from 1998 to 2003 on the average of the industry characteristics from 1992 to 1997. This specification has a rather nice economic interpretation whereby plants are able to observe industry characteristics before making their location decisions, so we would actually expect some lag from characteristics to outcomes. It also helps to partially address concerns about the endogeneity of some of the industry characteristics.

Figure 4.1 shows what happens when we plot (time-averaged) values of the Ellison and Glaeser index against our (lagged time-averaged) measure of the importance of labor market pooling.[9] A regression of the Ellison and Glaeser index on a constant and our measure of labor market pooling gives a coefficient on labor pooling of 0.1, significant at the 4 percent level. The upward-sloping line in figure 4.1 plots the predicted values from this regression. Overall, the figure provides preliminary evidence in favor of the importance of labor market pooling in explaining geographic concentration. Of course, many other industry characteristics may be correlated with both

9. The plot and our econometric results drop one four-digit sector—1725: other textile weaving—which is a large outlier in terms of our measure of labor market pooling (it takes a value over three times the next highest value and over 12 standard deviations away from the mean). Dropping this outlier does not affect our regression results but does affect the significance of the univariate correlation coefficient we report in the text.

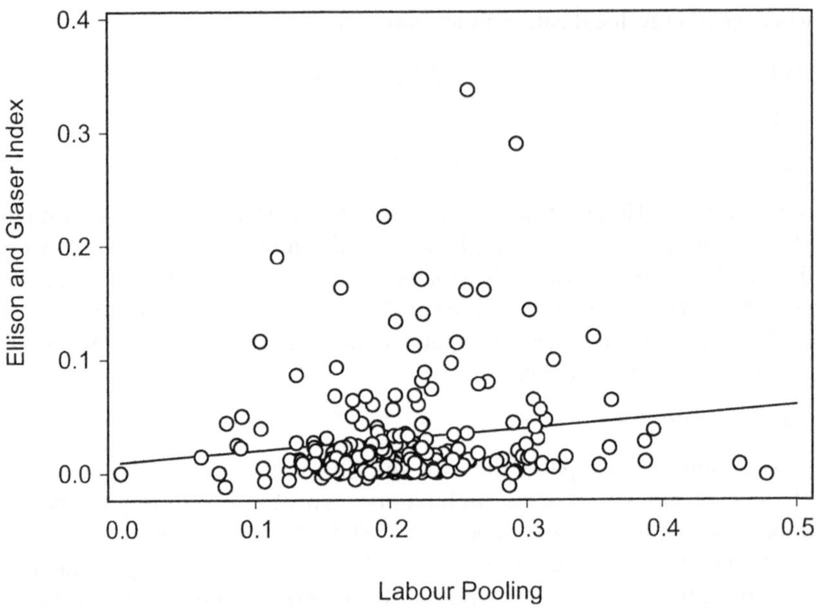

Fig. 4.1 Ellison and Glaeser geographic concentration index against potential for labor pooling

geographic concentration and our measure of labor market pooling, and we will need to control for these to reach a more robust conclusion on the role of labor market pooling.

Before turning to our results, we now briefly consider each of the industry characteristics for which we are able to control. The control variables for our first specification broadly follow Rosenthal and Strange (2001). We briefly motivate all of them but refer the reader to Rosenthal and Strange (2001) for a more detailed discussion.

The availability of natural resources may differ across regions. If natural resources are very spatially concentrated, then we would expect industries that use them intensively to be very spatially concentrated. Of course, if natural resources are very dispersed, then the opposite effect could hold, and industries that use these resources intensively may be dispersed. As we do not have independent information on the distribution of resources, we capture the effect of natural resources on geographic concentration by looking at each industry's primary inputs (from agriculture, forestry, fishing, mining, and quarrying) as a share of total inputs. As the preceding discussion makes clear, we do not have a strong prior on whether the impact will be positive or negative. Industries also differ in the intensity with which they use water and energy. As the price of water and energy may differ across regions, the intensity with which industries use these two inputs may affect their spatial distribution.[10] We capture reliance on water using "collection, purification and distribution of water" (IO 87) as a share of total inputs from the ONS input-output tables. Eurostat's detailed enterprise statistics provide data on the value of energy products purchased at the SIC four-digit level, which we normalize by total inputs to provide a proxy for reliance on energy. We expect the coefficients on these two variables to be positive and significant if price variations across regions are large enough to affect plant location and insignificant otherwise.

Turning to agglomeration forces, we start by following Rosenthal and Strange (2001) and using the purchase of goods and services as a share of inputs to capture the importance of vertical linkages. These are calculated using the input coefficients on manufacturing (IO 8–84) and nonmanufacturing industries (IO 107–115, 118–123), respectively, from the ONS input-output tables. The basic idea is that industries that buy or sell a lot from other plants may have an incentive to cluster near those plants. If the degree to which an industry buys goods and services as inputs captures this effect, then we should expect the coefficient on these two variables to be positive. As emphasized in models of new economic geography, the level of transport costs for an industry will be crucial in determining whether agglomeration forces outweigh dispersion forces leading to the spatial clustering of the industry. We use transport services (IO 93–97) as a share of inputs to capture the impact of transport costs on industry spatial concentration, again using data from the ONS input-output tables. As Rosenthal and Strange (2001) argue, this measure is not ideal, as it is most likely endogenous. Unfortunately, for the United Kingdom, alternative data are not available in the time period that we consider. Finally, we use the share of R&D expenditure in value added to capture the possible role of technological externalities and knowledge spillovers in driving the spatial concentration of high-tech industries. These are calculated on the basis of Eurostat's detailed enterprise statistics for the United Kingdom.[11]

Results from a regression of the Ellison-Glaeser index (averaged over the years 1998 to 2003) on these industry characteristics (averaged over the years 1992 to 1997) are given in column (1) of table 4.1. The main result of interest is the relationship between each sector's potential for labor pooling and the spatial concentration in the sector. As predicted, the role of the labor pooling variable is positive and significant. Thus, industries where, on

10. The UK water industry is comprised of a number of privatized regional monopolies that have different pricing structures. Thus, we allow for the possibility that water usage may play a role in industrial concentration, although the existence of a national regulator is likely to restrict the importance of water in practice.

11. Preliminary data for all these variables were kindly provided by Roberto Picchizzolu, a PhD student in the department of geography and environment at the London School of Economics. The final version of our data continues to use the energy and R&D variables provided by Picchizzolu, but the remaining variables are based on the authors own calculations from the ONS input-output tables from 1992 to 2003.

Table 4.1 Regression of localization and urbanization on industry characteristics

	Ellison-Glaeser localization index				Urbanization
Dependent variable:	(1)	(2)	(3)	(4)	(5)
Pooling (plant to sector)	0.1167 (0.0535)**	0.1261 (0.0521)**		0.1261 (0.0523)**	0.0169 (0.0685)
Pooling (plant to United Kingdom)			0.0196 (0.0113)*		
Pooling (sector to United Kingdom)				0.0002 (0.0106)	0.0026 (0.0068)
Natural resources as share of inputs	–0.1656 (0.0493)***	–0.1782 (0.0571)***	–0.1689 (0.0566)***	–0.1782 (0.0572)***	–0.1496 (0.0708)**
Water as share of inputs	1.7106 (3.0794)	0.7851 (2.7732)	1.8663 (2.7124)	0.7898 (2.7105)	–1.1054 (3.1246)
Energy as share of inputs	–0.0748 (0.3603)	–0.3268 (0.3533)	–0.3615 (0.3472)	–0.3274 (0.346)	–0.7768 (0.3550)**
Goods as share of inputs	–0.1866 (0.0758)**	–0.2453 (0.0847)***	–0.2512 (0.0863)***	–0.2453 (0.0851)***	–0.1621 (0.0707)**
Services as share of inputs	–0.5701 (0.1628)***	–0.4079 (0.1580)**	–0.3803 (0.1546)**	–0.408 (0.1576)**	–0.1773 (0.1966)
Share of R&D expenditure in value added	–1.8371 (1.2614)	–2.0807 (1.2106)*	–2.2511 (1.2184)*	–2.0771 (1.2141)*	–3.3887 (1.1219)***
Transport costs as share of inputs	–0.4248 (0.1403)***	–0.4265 (0.1356)***	–0.4604 (0.1376)***	–0.4261 (0.1387)***	–0.2855 (0.1123)**
Own industry as share of inputs		0.095 (0.0285)***	0.0937 (0.0287)***	0.0949 (0.0285)***	0.0928 (0.0337)***
IO weighted EG index		0.5767 (0.2512)**	0.5422 (0.2541)**	0.5756 (0.2502)**	–0.155 (0.2172)
Constant	0.1501 (0.0459)***	0.1426 (0.0485)***	0.1666 (0.0501)***	0.1425 (0.0490)***	0.1438 (0.0454)***
R^2	0.09	0.14	0.13	0.14	0.13
Observations	235	235	235	235	235

Notes: Errors are robust to heteroscedasticity. The dependent variable for columns (1) through (4) is the Ellison and Glaeser (EG) index of localization or spatial concentration; for column (5), it is the percentage of industry in the three largest UK TTWA in terms of manufacturing employment (London, Manchester, and Birmingham).

***Significant at the 1 percent level.

**Significant at the 5 percent level.

*Significant at the 10 percent level.

average, plants face more idiosyncratic shocks relative to their industry are more spatially concentrated.

Turning to other determinants of spatial clustering, a high natural resource requirement actually causes industries to be less spatially concentrated than they otherwise would be. This may well reflect the fact that agricultural inputs tend to dominate for most industries where natural resource inputs are important, and at least in the United Kingdom, agricultural activity is reasonably dispersed across the country. Water and energy use have no significant effect on spatial concentration. As suggested previously, this is probably because price variations are not that large across UK regions. Ignoring for one moment the role of purchases of goods and services, we see that the share of R&D expenditure in value added does not have a significant effect. The final variable, transport costs, has a negative and significant effect on spatial concentration. As expected, industries with high transport costs are more dispersed.

Perhaps the biggest surprise are the negative and significant coefficients on the purchase of goods and services as a share of inputs. As we already discussed, if these variables are actually capturing vertical linkages, then we would expect them to have a positive significant effect on spatial concentration.[12] How then do we explain the negative coefficients? It may be that sharing intermediate suppliers is not an important motive for agglomeration, but other evidence suggests it is.[13] The answer, it turns out, is similar to that which explains the negative coefficient on natural resources. When an industry buys a lot from other industries, the effect on its concentration in turn will depend on whether those industries are spatially concentrated or dispersed. For instance, the meat processing industry is a large buyer of inputs from farms and from the plastic film industry. However, farms are very dispersed across the country, and so is the plastic film industry, since it supplies many other sectors located in different places, in addition to processing meat. Hence, the meat processing industry has no reason to concentrate spatially, even if it makes large intermediate purchases: it can easily find its inputs everywhere. For a sector to cluster to share intermediate suppliers, it must be the case that the sector not only makes large purchases of intermediates but also that those intermediates are supplied by industries that are themselves very spatially concentrated. Following this line of reasoning, to better capture the importance of vertical linkages for a particular industry, *s*, we calculate the input share weighted sum of the Ellison-Glaeser index across all industries from which industry *s* purchases intermediates. That is, we calculate:

$$V_s = \sum_{j \neq s} I_{sj} C_j, \tag{18}$$

where V_s is our new measure of vertical linkages, I_{sj} is the share of sector *j* in sector *s*'s intermediate inputs from other sectors, and C_s is the Ellison-Glaeser index of spatial concentration for sector *j*. Notice that for obvious reasons, we exclude industry *s*'s own Ellison-Glaeser index from this calculation. However, we would expect ceteris paribus industries that buy a large share of intermediate inputs from their own industry to be more spatially

12. Rosenthal and Strange (2001) find no significant effect for these variables.

13. Holmes (1999) looks at variations in intermediate input purchases within sectors across locations and finds a strong connection between spatial concentration and intermediate purchases.

concentrated. To capture this, we can include I_{ss}, the share of intermediates purchased from own industry, in the regression, in addition to the vertical linkages variable.

Column (2) in table 4.1 shows what happens when we include these two new variables. We see that both the own-industry inputs as a share of inputs and the input-output weighted Ellison-Glaeser index have a positive and significant impact on spatial concentration. Industries that buy a lot of intermediates from other plants in the same industry or that buy a lot of intermediates from other industries that are spatially concentrated are in turn more spatially concentrated. We see that the coefficients on goods purchased and services purchased remain negative and significant. That is, purchasing large amounts of inputs per se has a negative impact on spatial concentration. Finally, note that the coefficient on our main variable of interest, labor market pooling, remains positive and significant.

So far, we have assumed that the appropriate reference group for calculating our measure of labor pooling is the industry. An alternative would be to consider idiosyncratic shocks relative to manufacturing as a whole; that is, to use a measure of labor market pooling that is calculated as before, but this time using the sectoral average of the difference between the percentage change in the plant's employment and the percentage change in UK manufacturing employment (in absolute value). Column (3) of table 4.1 reports results when we use this alternative measure of labor market pooling. As can be seen, the coefficient on this alternative measure is positive and significant. Conceptually, we can think of this alternative measure (plants relative to UK manufacturing as a whole) as being disaggregated into two orthogonal components: plants relative to their industry ("plant to sector") and industries relative to the whole of UK manufacturing ("sector to United Kingdom").[14] From column (4) of table 4.1, we see that the finding of a significant coefficient on the pooling measure calculated using plants relative to UK manufacturing as a whole is purely driven by plants experiencing idiosyncratic shocks relative to their industry ("plant to sector"). Industries that tend to experience idiosyncratic results relative to manufacturing as a whole ("sector to United Kingdom") do not tend to be more geographically concentrated.

This raises the interesting question, however, of whether these industries are more likely to go to larger locations where they can benefit from labor market pooling *across* sectors rather than within their own sector. To consider this possibility, we can undertake a similar exercise, but this time using as our dependent variable a measure of the extent to which the industry is

14. Formally, this decomposition is not exact, but in practice, it holds to a close approximation. As a result, including all three measures does not make any sense, given that they are essentially colinear.

urbanized rather than geographically concentrated. To measure urbanization, we take the share of each industry in the three largest manufacturing cities in the United Kingdom (London, Manchester, and Birmingham).[15] The final column of table 4.1 shows the results when we regress this measure of urbanization on the two components of labor pooling (plant to sector and sector to United Kingdom) and other industry characteristics. We find no significant effect on urbanization of either measure. In results not reported here, we also find no effect if we simply use the combined measure based on plants relative to the whole of UK manufacturing.

Do our findings suggest that labor market pooling plays no role in explaining urbanization? We would argue not. The central problem, of course, is whether our measure is capturing the correct reference group when calculating the importance of idiosyncratic shocks. For localization, our measure is appropriate if workers move easily within four-digit sectors. This seems a reasonable assumption, and so we are able to identify an effect from our labor pooling measure on localization. However, for urbanization, our measure is only appropriate if workers move easily *across* sectors. This is unlikely to be the case, suggesting that our results could easily be explained by the use of an inappropriate reference group when considering urbanization rather than by there being no effect of labor market pooling. Unfortunately, making any progress on defining the appropriate reference group would require data on worker moves between industries. This data is not available from the Annual Respondents Database that we use in this chapter. Finally, we also note that we are only considering manufacturing sectors, and it is often argued that urbanization is more important for services than for manufacturing.

4.5 Conclusions

Since Alfred Marshall talked about labor pooling as a source of agglomeration, it has been the focus of much interest in the urban economics literature. Existing empirical studies tend to find that labor market issues play a key role in leading industries to cluster, but despite the interest in labor pooling, we have so far not had a direct test of whether ironing out plant-level shocks by drawing workers from a large local pool is at least in part an explanation of these labor market effects. In this chapter, we have developed a novel measure that captures precisely this aspect: we calculate the fluctuations in employment of individual establishments relative to their sector and average these across the sector and over time. Our results show

15. Our decision to rank cities in terms of manufacturing employment reflects the fact that the pooling mechanism relies on movements between plants, and such movements are less likely between services and manufacturing than within manufacturing.

that sectors whose establishments experience more idiosyncratic volatility are more spatially concentrated, even after controlling for a range of other industry characteristics.

References

Audretsch, D. B., and M. P. Feldman. 1996. R&D spillovers and the geography of innovation and production. *American Economic Review* 86 (3): 630–40.

Baumgardner, J. R. 1988. The division of labor, local markets, and worker organization. *Journal of Political Economy* 96 (3): 509–27.

Becker, G. S., and K. M. Murphy. 1992. The division of labor, coordination costs, and knowledge. *Quarterly Journal of Economics* 107 (4): 1137–60.

Combes, P.-P., G. Duranton, and L. Gobillon. 2008. Spatial wage disparities: Sorting matters! *Journal of Urban Economics* 63 (2): 723–42.

Costa, D. L., and M. E. Kahn. 2000. Power couples: Changes in the locational choice of the college educated, 1940–1990. *Quarterly Journal of Economics* 115 (4): 1287–315.

Duranton, G. 1998. Labor specialization, transport costs, and city size. *Journal of Regional Science* 38 (4): 553–73.

Duranton, G., and H. G. Overman. 2005. Testing for localization using micro-geographic data. *Review of Economic Studies* 72 (4): 1077–106.

Duranton, G., and D. Puga. 2004. Micro-foundations of urban agglomeration economies. In *Handbook of regional and urban economics,* vol. 4, ed. V. Henderson and J.-F. Thisse, 2063–117. Amsterdam: North-Holland.

Ellison, G., and D. Fudenberg. 2003. Knife-edge or plateau: When do market models tip? *Quarterly Journal of Economics* 118 (4): 1249–78.

Ellison, G., and E. L. Glaeser. 1997. Geographic concentration in US manufacturing industries: A dartboard approach. *Journal of Political Economy* 105 (5): 889–927.

Glaeser, E. L. 2008. *Cities, agglomeration and spatial equilibrium.* Oxford: Oxford University Press.

Glaeser, E. L., and D.C. Maré. 2001. Cities and skills. *Journal of Labor Economics* 19 (2): 316–42.

Griffith, R. 1999. Using the ARD establishment level data: An application to estimating production functions. *Economic Journal* 109 (456): F416–F442.

Helsley, R. W., and W. C. Strange. 1990. Matching and agglomeration economies in a system of cities. *Regional Science and Urban Economics* 20 (2): 189–212.

Holmes, T. J. 1999. Localization of industry and vertical disintegration. *Review of Economics and Statistics* 81 (2): 314–25.

Krugman, P. R. 1991. *Geography and trade.* Cambridge, MA: MIT Press.

Marshall, A. 1890. *Principles of economics.* London: Macmillan.

Rosenthal, S. S., and W. Strange. 2004. Evidence on the nature and sources of agglomeration economies. In *Handbook of regional and urban economics,* vol. 4, ed. V. Henderson and J.-F. Thisse, 2119–71. Amsterdam: North-Holland.

———. 2001. The determinants of agglomeration. *Journal of Urban Economics* 50 (2): 191–229.

Wheaton, W. C., and M. J. Lewis. 2002. Urban wages and labor market agglomeration. *Journal of Urban Economics* 51 (3): 542–62.

5

Urbanization, Agglomeration, and Coagglomeration of Service Industries

Jed Kolko

Services now dominate the United States and other advanced economies, most of all in large cities. Employment in most services industries is strikingly urbanized, while manufacturing is the least urbanized sector of the economy, aside from natural resource-dependent sectors of agricultural support and mining. The economic future of cities depends on services, and understanding why services are in cities is essential to understanding the function of cities in modern economies.

Although services are highly urbanized, they are less concentrated than manufacturing industries are. While there are examples of highly agglomerated services industries—such as investment banking and motion picture production—services are, on average, less agglomerated than manufacturing at the county level and much less so at the state level. Furthermore, nearly all agglomerated services industries are highly urbanized, whereas many manufacturing industries agglomerate in smaller cities or rural areas. The traditional study of agglomeration, which focused on manufacturing, could safely divorce the question of urbanization from agglomeration. To analyze why some services industries are agglomerated, it is important to ask at the same time why services are urbanized.

To assess why services are less agglomerated, yet highly urbanized, this chapter looks at coagglomeration between pairs of industries, which helps reveal the microfoundations for the observed location patterns in services

Jed Kolko is associate director and research fellow of the Public Policy Institute of California.

Thanks to Davin Reed for excellent research help. Thanks for useful comments to Ed Glaeser, Mark Partridge, and to participants at PPIC seminars, the April 2007 Kiel Institute workshop on Agglomeration and Growth in Knowledge-Based Societies, the November 2007 Regional Science meetings, and the December 2007 NBER workshop on Economics of Agglomeration.

and manufacturing and the differences between them. Services differ from manufacturing in that services rely much less on physical inputs, freeing services from having to locate near natural resources, and service transactions often happen in person, making it important for some services industries to be near their customers. Both of these characteristics of services contribute to their tendency to be in larger cities and to be less agglomerated than manufacturing industries.

The main empirical finding is that services industries that trade with each other are more likely to colocate in the same zip code, though not in the same county or the same state; in contrast, manufacturing industries that trade with each other are more likely to colocate in the same county or state but not at the zip code level. This finding is consistent with the in-person delivery of many services, including consumer services like haircuts and professional services like management consulting. Furthermore, services industries that rely more on information technology are even less likely to colocate at the state level, which suggests that the Internet substitutes for phone, mail, and travel in services industries, though not for in-person interactions. The importance of proximity to trading partners underscores the advantages of an urban location for services industries, especially for services whose customers are other businesses.

5.1 Urbanization and Agglomeration Patterns

Services are strikingly urbanized (see table 5.1).[1] Ranking sectors by the average metropolitan population where jobs in that sector are located, the most urbanized sectors are all services, including professional, scientific, and technical services; information; and management of companies and enterprises (see table 5.2). Services that serve households rather than primarily other businesses—such as health care and accommodation and food services—are less urbanized but still more so than the manufacturing sector is. Aggregating all services sectors, 55 percent of services jobs are in metro areas with at least 2 million population, compared with 42 percent of manufacturing jobs. The urbanization of services is even more apparent when considering the county density of the average job, because services are disproportionately clustered in downtowns of metropolitan areas. The county

1. In this chapter, "services" refers to industries involved in the production and distribution of intangible goods. These include the information sector; finance, insurance, and real estate; professional services; education, health care, leisure, and hospitality; and other personal and business services. Together, these are covered by the North American Industry Classification System (NAICS codes 51–81) and accounted for 59 percent of private, nonfarm employment in 2004. Manufacturing, covered by NAICS codes 31–33, accounted for 12 percent. The remainder of private, nonfarm employment is in the natural resources industries, mining, utilities, construction, wholesale and retail trade, and transportation.

Table 5.1 **Share of U.S. private, nonfarm employment by sector, 2004**

Sector	Share (%)	NAICS
Forestry, fishing, hunting, mining, utilities, and construction	7	11, 21–23
Manufacturing	12	31–33
Trade and transportation	22	42–49
Information, finance, insurance, and real estate	10	51–53
Business and personal services	49	54–81

Source: U.S. Census Bureau County Business Patterns.

Table 5.2 **Urbanization, all sectors (NAICS two-digit)**

Sector	Mean metro size
Professional, scientific, and technical services	6,674,642
Information	6,445,303
Management of companies and enterprises	6,212,818
Educational services	6,195,770
Wholesale trade	6,038,354
Real estate and rental and leasing	6,005,790
Finance and insurance	5,955,742
Administrative and support and waste management and remediation services	5,700,440
Arts, entertainment, and recreation	5,456,450
Transportation and warehousing	5,176,784
Other services (except public administration)	5,019,998
Health care and social assistance	4,889,552
Construction	4,704,008
Retail trade	4,572,272
Accommodation and food services	4,359,364
Utilities	4,278,660
Manufacturing	4,049,816
Forestry, fishing, hunting, and agriculture support	1,697,923
Mining	1,591,765

Note: Average metro size refers to the mean population of the Combined Statistical Area (CSA), Core Based Statistical Area (CBSA; if not in a CSA), or county (if not in a CBSA), averaged over all jobs in the sector.

population density of the average services job is 3,583; for manufacturing jobs, the average county density is only 1,400 (see table 5.3).[2]

While services are more urbanized than manufacturing and other sectors on average, the most urbanized industries are spread across multiple sec-

2. Employment data are from the U.S. Census Bureau County Business Patterns (CBP) and the National Establishment Time Series (NETS) database. The NETS was available for California only and is used for calculating zip code-level agglomeration and coagglomeration; CBP is available nationally and is used for all other analyses in the chapter. Details on the data sets are given in the appendix.

Table 5.3 Urbanization and agglomeration (NAICS six-digit industries)

	All	Manufacturing	Services
Average metro size	5,113,050	4,046,245	5,450,653
% in metros over 2 million	.52	.42	.55
Average county population density	2,902	1,400	3,583
County-level agglomeration	.0066	.0132	.0068
State-level agglomeration	.0154	.0406	.0135
Correlation between average metro size and county-level agglomeration	.3487	.2581	.4830
Correlation between average metro size and state-level agglomeration	.0776	–.0773	.2938
N	1,084	471	334

Note: Weighted by six-digit NAICS industry employment.

tors. Among the ten most extremely urbanized industries are four services industries: investment banking, motion picture production, teleproduction and postproduction services, and agents and managers (see table 5.4). The rest of the top ten are apparel manufacturers and wholesalers and related industries. In these most urbanized industries, the metro-area population of the average job is over 12 million, implying that these industries are all highly concentrated in New York and Los Angeles.

Services are less agglomerated than manufacturing at the county level and much less so at the state level.[3] The average Ellison-Glaeser county-level agglomeration index for services industries at the six-digit North American Industry Classification System (NAICS) level, weighted by national employment, is 0.0068, compared with the average for manufacturing of 0.0132. The difference is even larger for state-level agglomeration: the average index for services is 0.0135 and for manufacturing is 0.0406. Services account for most of the nonagglomerated industries: five of the seven industries with agglomeration indices at or below zero are services, including newspaper publishers, monetary authorities, consumer electronics repair and maintenance, blood and organ banks, and sports teams and clubs.[4]

Still, some services industries are highly agglomerated, and services account for five of the ten most agglomerated industries at the county level (see table 5.5). Motion picture and video production, teleproduction and postproduction services, and payroll services are all highly agglomerated and

3. Following earlier work on agglomeration, this chapter uses the Ellison-Glaeser (1997) index of agglomeration, which adjusts for both the distribution of region sizes and the level of establishment-level concentration, allowing comparisons of agglomeration at different levels of geography and of industrial aggregation. The formula is given in the appendix.

4. The Ellison-Glaeser index can be negative if, by design or agreement, establishments are located far from each other to prevent competition (which could explain the negative index for sports teams and clubs) or to provide more uniform geographic coverage than the population (which could explain monetary authorities and blood and organ banks).

Table 5.4 Most urbanized industries (NAICS six-digit)

Sector	Mean metro size
Investment banking and securities dealing	16,545,537
Women's and girls' cut and sew dress manufacturing	15,500,985
Women's, children's, and infants' clothing and accessories merchant wholesalers	14,950,006
Women's and girls' cut and sew blouse and shirt manufacturing	14,907,902
Women's girls', and infants' cut and sew apparel contractors	14,607,557
Motion picture and video production	14,303,119
Teleproduction and other postproduction services	13,652,323
Agents and managers for artists, athletes, entertainers, and other public figures	13,503,575
Jewelry, watch, precious stone, and precious metal merchant wholesalers	12,336,946
Piece goods, notions, and other dry goods merchant wholesalers	12,304,385

Note: Average metro size refers to the mean population of the Combined Statistical Area, Core Based Statistical Area (if not in a CSA), or county (if not in a CBSA), averaged over all jobs in the industry. Only industries with at least 10,000 national employment included.

Table 5.5 Most agglomerated industries: County

Industry	EG Index
Deep sea passenger transportation	.454
Motion picture and video production[a]	.335
Investment banking and securities dealing[a]	.282
Women's cut and sew blouse and shirt manufacturing	.265
Photographic film, paper, plate, and chemical manufacturing	.236
Casino hotels[a]	.205
Teleproduction and other postproduction services[a]	.198
Women's cut and sew apparel contractors	.194
Payroll services[a]	.163
Oil and gas field equipment/machinery manufacturing	.152

Note: Highest Ellison-Glaeser agglomeration values, six-digit NAICS industries, national employment ≥ 10,000.

[a]Denotes services industries (NAICS 51–81).

concentrated in Los Angeles county; investment banking is agglomerated in Manhattan and casino hotels in Clark county, Nevada (Las Vegas). At the state level, services account for only two of the top ten most agglomerated industries (see table 5.6). Motion picture and video production is sufficiently concentrated in Los Angeles that its concentration when averaged with the rest of California still causes it to be agglomerated at the state level. Casino hotels have disproportionately high employment in other parts of Nevada, like Reno, not just in Las Vegas, contributing to its high agglomeration at the state level. Several manufacturing industries, like wineries, carpet and rug mills, and cigarette manufacturing, are much more agglomerated at the state level than at the county level: these industries tend to be agglomerated

Table 5.6 **Most agglomerated industries: State**

Industry	EG Index
Wineries	.448
Deep sea passenger transportation	.437
Oil and gas field equipment/machinery manufacturing	.403
Carpet and rug mills	.381
Other (nonsheer) hosiery and sock mills	.370
Cigarette manufacturing	.333
Motion picture and video production[a]	.327
Casino hotels[a]	.322
Women's cut and sew blouse and shirt manufacturing	.300
Yarn spinning mills	.270

Note: Highest Ellison-Glaeser agglomeration values, six-digit NAICS industries, national employment ≥ 10,000.
[a]Denotes services industries (NAICS 51–81).

over a larger geographic area that covers multiple counties within a state (California, Georgia, and North Carolina, respectively).

A pronounced difference between manufacturing and services is that agglomeration and urbanization are more correlated for services than for manufacturing. The correlation between average metro size and the county-level agglomeration index, weighted by industry employment, is 0.48 for services and 0.26 for manufacturing; using the state-level agglomeration index, the correlations are 0.29 for services and –0.08 for manufacturing (see table 5.3). Nearly all of the agglomerated services industries are highly urbanized, the only exception being casino hotels, where employment is concentrated in Las Vegas rather than in the largest metropolitan areas (see figure 5.1). In contrast, many manufacturing industries are highly agglomerated, even at the county level, without being highly urbanized, such at the photographic equipment manufacturing industry, based in midsized Rochester, New York.

To explain the variation in agglomeration levels across industries, the analysis uses four measures at the industry level: occupational specialization, natural resource inputs, workers with graduate degrees, and share of output going to consumers. This section follows Rosenthal and Strange (2001) and others in using industry-level measures for agglomeration forces as explanations for observed agglomeration.[5] These four measures are also used to explain urbanization. The intuitive meaning of these measures is outlined in

5. Including services industries in the study of agglomeration comes at some cost. Many of the measures used to explain or illustrate agglomeration in manufacturing industries—such as research and development spending, patents, or the importance of natural resource inputs—are harder to interpret in the context of services industries; that is, if they can even be constructed from available data.

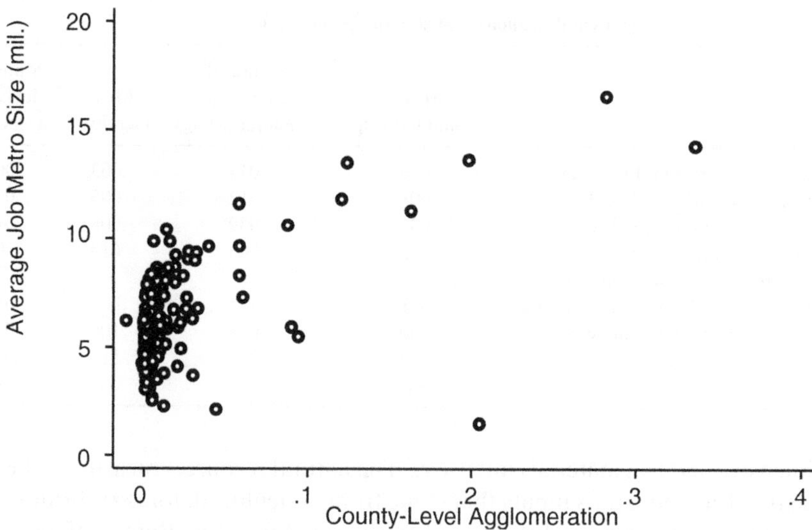

Fig. 5.1 Services six-digit industries

the following paragraphs. The formulas and data sources for these measures are summarized in table 5.7 and detailed in the appendix.

The occupational specialization measure is intended to capture the importance of labor pooling. Intuitively, if an occupation is concentrated in an industry, then the employment opportunities for workers in that occupation are concentrated in that industry, and those workers should be willing to accept a lower wage if that industry is geographically concentrated so that workers could switch employers in the event of a firm-specific shock. In contrast, an industry that hires workers in occupations common to many industries would have less advantage in agglomerating, since workers in that occupation would have opportunities outside that industry. The occupational specialization index captures how much an industry's occupational mix diverges from the national occupational mix and is generated from the Bureau of Labor Statistics (BLS) National Industry-Occupation Employment Matrix (NIOEM).[6]

The second measure, natural resource inputs, is designed to capture whether an industry depends on a location-specific input like coal or lumber and therefore agglomerates to be near that input. The literature on agglomeration, having been developed to explain the geography of manufacturing industries, has focused on these natural resource inputs, even though they are presumably less important for service industries, which are more labor

6. The summary statistics in table 5.7 reveal no difference between services industries and manufacturing industries in their levels of occupational specialization.

Table 5.7 Measures and summary statistics of agglomeration

Measure	Mean (manufacturing)	Standard deviation (manufacturing)	Mean (services)	Standard deviation (services)
Zip code agglomeration (EG index)	.009	.014	.003	.004
County agglomeration (EG index)	.008	.012	.005	.013
State agglomeration (EG index)	.031	.039	.008	.014
Occupational specialization	.625	.045	.619	.103
% natural resource inputs (agriculture, forestry, fishing, logging, and mining)	.088	.175	.005	.018
Share of workers with graduate degrees	.040	.038	.106	.099
Share of output going to consumers	.354	.336	.518	.370
N	64	64	54	54

intensive and less materials intensive.[7] The natural resources measure is the share of an industry's inputs that come from agricultural, forestry, fishing, hunting, and mining industries and is generated from the Bureau of Economic Analysis (BEA) input-output (IO) accounts.

The third measure is the share of workers with graduate degrees, as a proxy for knowledge spillovers; this measure comes from the 2000 Public Use Microdata Sample (PUMS).[8]

The fourth measure is the share of industry output going directly to consumers as opposed to other businesses or government. Although the agglomeration literature has not suggested that the share of output going to consumers should affect industry agglomeration, the finding that business services are generally more urbanized than consumer services raises the possibility that the nature of industry output could affect industry location decisions. This measure comes from the BEA IO accounts.

Because the data sources use different industry classifications, the six-digit NAICS industries were aggregated so that each resulting industry had unique information from each of the data sources. This aggregation process resulted in sixty-four manufacturing industries and fifty-four services industries. Despite the much larger share of employment in services industries, there are more manufacturing industries in the analysis, because the data sources provide information at a finer level of disaggregation for manufacturing than for services industries. In the analysis, manufacturing industries

7. The natural resource inputs that could help explain why—and where—services agglomerate might include location-specific determinants of the supply of specialized labor. These could include natural amenities that raise quality of life, like good weather and proximity to a coast (see Glaeser, Kolko, and Saiz [2001]), as well as institutions, like universities.

8. While these measures are typical proxies for the reasons for agglomeration in the literature, there is no consensus on which theoretical explanations for agglomeration are represented by each measure. Rosenthal and Strange (2001) point out the difficulty of choosing a proxy measure for labor pooling; they use three alternatives, one of which is the percentage of workers with high levels of education, which is arguably as suitable a proxy for knowledge spillovers as it is for labor pooling.

typically correspond to the four-digit NAICS level, whereas services industries usually correspond to the three-digit NAICS level.[9]

The index of agglomeration is regressed on these four measures separately for these manufacturing and services industries by estimating the following:

$$\text{agglom}_{i,k} = \beta X_i + \varepsilon_{i,k},$$

where $\text{agglom}_{i,k}$ is the agglomeration index for industry i at the level of geography k; X_i is the set of industry measures, including occupational specialization, natural resource inputs, workers with graduate degrees, and share of output going to consumers, along with national industry employment as a control; and k refers to zip codes, counties, or states, depending on the specification.[10] Agglomeration is measured at the zip code level in California and at the county and state levels for the United States. The four measures that proxy for agglomeration factors—occupational specialization, natural resource inputs, graduate degrees, and share of output going to consumers—are calculated for each industry at the national level, so their values do not vary with the level of geography at which agglomeration is calculated. The specification is then repeated with urbanization in place of agglomeration, with the average metropolitan population where jobs in that industry are located as the dependent variable.

The purpose of this part of the analysis is twofold: first, to see what, if anything, explains agglomeration and urbanization in services industries; and second, to see if similar forces explain agglomeration in both manufacturing and services. The results for manufacturing and services are in tables 5.8 and 5.9, respectively. For manufacturing, the relationship between occupational specialization and agglomeration is positive and significant at the 5 percent level for both county and state agglomeration. The theory of labor pooling suggests that the workers and therefore firms benefit from agglomerating in the same labor market.[11] Labor markets are larger than either zip codes or counties, so an industry should benefit from labor pooling so long as it is agglomerated within a state, even if spread over multiple counties.[12] That the relationship between occupational specialization and agglomeration is strongest at the state level is consistent with interpreting occupational specialization as a proxy for labor pooling. There is no statistically significant

9. See the appendix for more detail on the industry classification.

10. This setup follows Rosenthal and Strange (2001).

11. Labor pooling mitigates the cost to workers of firm-specific shocks only if other firms in the industry are within the same labor market, so workers can switch firms within the same industry without incurring moving costs to a new labor market.

12. In defining a metropolitan area, the U.S. Office of Management and Budget (OMB) includes territory with a "high degree of social and economic integration with the core as measured by commuting ties," so metropolitan areas are a reasonable approximation for a local labor market. Metropolitan areas consist of one or typically multiple counties, so it is natural to think of labor markets as somewhat larger than a county, though not as large as a state. See the OMB standards for defining metropolitan areas at: http://www.census.gov/population/www/metroareas/metrodef.html.

Table 5.8 Agglomeration and urbanization in manufacturing industries

	Zip code agglomeration	County agglomeration	State agglomeration	Average metro size
Occupational specialization	0.06535	0.07310**	0.41916**	–5.53399
	(0.04265)	(0.03543)	(0.10965)	(4.93500)
Share of natural resource inputs	0.00762	–0.00868	0.00059	–2.97760**
	(0.01009)	(0.00838)	(0.02595)	(1.16769)
Share of workers with grad degrees	0.03481	0.05172	0.13130	15.25900**
	(0.05042)	(0.04189)	(0.12965)	(5.83486)
Fraction of output to consumers	0.00764	0.00450	0.00206	1.31775**
	(0.00520)	(0.00432)	(0.01337)	(0.60169)
R-squared	0.09	0.13	0.24	0.33
N	64	64	64	64

Note: National industry employment included as control but not reported. Standard errors in parentheses.
**Significant at the 5 percent level.

Table 5.9 Agglomeration and urbanization in services industries

	Zip code agglomeration	County agglomeration	State agglomeration	Average metro size
Occupational specialization	0.00039	0.00639	0.00423	1.10561
	(0.00608)	(0.01965)	(0.02179)	(1.81134)
Share of natural resource inputs	0.00538	–0.04528	–0.07347	–4.40207
	(0.03498)	(0.11314)	(0.12548)	(10.42858)
Share of workers with grad degrees	0.01374**	0.00716	0.00718	3.38075*
	(0.00575)	(0.01859)	(0.02061)	(1.71309)
Fraction of output to consumers	0.00129	–0.00298	–0.00348	–1.27118**
	(0.00165)	(0.00532)	(0.00590)	(0.49056)
R-squared	0.15	0.04	0.03	0.24
N	54	54	54	54

Note: National industry employment included as control but not reported. Standard errors in parentheses.
**Significant at the 5 percent level.
*Significant at the 10 percent level.

relationship between either natural resource inputs or knowledge spillovers, as measured by workers' graduate degrees, and agglomeration at any geographic level for manufacturing industries.

For services, the only measure that contributes to agglomeration is the percent of workers with graduate degrees, interpreted as knowledge spillovers, which is positive and statistically significant only at the zip code level. Neither occupational specialization nor natural resource inputs help explain agglomeration at any level of geography. These findings shed little light on why services agglomerate, although they do suggest that services and manufacturing may agglomerate for different reasons, since none of the three factors was significant for both manufacturing and services agglomeration at any level of geography.

Turning to urbanization, for manufacturing industries, the reliance on natural resource inputs is negatively correlated with urbanization. While the coefficient on natural resource inputs is statistically insignificant for urbanization in services industries, this is probably due less to a qualitatively different relationship between natural resources and urbanization in the services sector and due more to the very low mean and variance of natural resource inputs within services (the standard error on the coefficient is quite high). Share of workers with graduate degrees is positively correlated with urbanization for both manufacturing and services, though not quite at the 5 percent level for services. The important difference in explaining urbanization across the sectors, however, is the share of output going to consumers, which is positively correlated with urbanization for manufacturing industries and negatively correlated with urbanization for services industries (and statistically significant for both sectors). This difference between manufacturing and services suggests that the cost of transporting output to customers could affect location decisions differently for manufacturing and for services, which will be explored in greater depth in the coagglomeration analysis.

5.2 Transport Costs in Manufacturing and Services

Comparing the factors affecting location patterns in manufacturing and services, two differences between the sectors stand out: (a) occupational specialization contributes to agglomeration only for manufacturing industries, not services; and (b) the fraction of output going to consumers encourages urbanization for manufacturing industries and discourages urbanization for services industries. This section outlines a theory on why these differences might arise.

First, why does occupational specialization not contribute to agglomeration in services? To the extent that occupational specialization is a proxy for the benefits of labor pooling, industries that are urbanized have less need to agglomerate to take advantage of labor pooling. The theory of labor pooling posits that workers will require higher wages if there are fewer local employment opportunities outside their firm, whereas agglomeration protects workers from firm-specific shocks (though not industry-wide shocks). If being in a large labor market also protects workers from shocks, then the benefits of labor pooling could be weakened for urbanized industries, which tend to be services.

Second, why should the type of customer—consumers or businesses—affect manufacturing and service location decisions differently? This striking difference between the sectors warrants a closer examination of the costs each sector faces in transporting output and of how the nature of output and customers affects location decisions. In fact, the question of transport costs goes to the essence of how manufacturing and services differ, since manufacturing by definition produces tangible output and services produce intangible output. What follows is a simple yet plausible model of transport costs for tangible and intangible goods and—by implication—for manufacturing and services industries.

For tangible goods, transport costs rise linearly with distance and include a fixed cost that reflects the loading and unloading of goods at both ends. Over short distances, the fixed costs are large relative to the portion of costs that vary with distance.[13] Over long distances, the fixed costs diminish relative to the variable cost, so shipping goods coast to coast costs close to twice as much as shipping goods halfway across the country.[14] Firms facing these shipping costs that trade with each other benefit little from being in the same zip code, since the transport cost savings of being in the same zip code is minimal relative to the total transport cost; over longer distances, though, the fixed costs shrink in importance relative to distance costs, and firms that trade manufactured goods can reduce their transport costs by a larger percentage by locating, say, 250 miles apart rather than 500 or 1,000 miles apart. Therefore, we might expect manufacturing firms to be indifferent to the distance from their trading partners within a certain radius and therefore find little advantage in agglomerating at a small geographic level; beyond that radius, firms would be more likely to be sensitive to proximity to trading partners and therefore would exhibit agglomeration at larger geographic levels.[15]

For intangibles, transport costs are quite different. Consider a service that must be consumed in person, like a haircut or a face-to-face legal discussion, where what is transported is a person (the customer to the barber shop or the lawyer to his or her client). Over very short distances, the transport cost equals the opportunity cost of the traveler's time: it costs essentially twice as much to walk four blocks as two blocks or to drive ten miles as five miles.[16] Beyond the distance at which flying becomes the preferred mode, transport cost varies relatively little by distance; for instance,

13. Residential moves, for instance, are priced nearly identically for a one-mile move or a two-mile move: the only difference would be the marginal cost of the time needed to drive the truck the second mile.

14. According to http://www.upsfreight.com, shipping 1,000 pounds by truck from San Francisco (zip = 94111) costs $368 for 15 miles (to Oakland, zip = 94601); $517 for 56 miles (to Santa Rosa, zip = 95401); $627 for 388 miles (to Los Angeles, zip = 90001); $1,167 for 2,132 miles (to Chicago, zip = 60601); and $1,543 for 2,809 miles (to Washington, DC, zip = 20009). This suggests a fixed cost of shipping this weight of over $300 and a per-mile cost of 30 to 40 cents.

15. Here, a firm's trading partners are not necessarily other firms in the same industry. Trading partners could be firms in other industries. The following section on coagglomeration will discuss this in more detail.

16. For some services that must be delivered in person, like management consulting engagements, the value may be sufficiently high to warrant paying the travel and time cost to bring in

for a San Francisco management consultant to attend a client meeting in person, it matters little in cost or time whether that client is in Chicago or New York.[17] If the service output lends itself to being transported by phone or mail—such as a document for signature—over a very short distance, it may still be optimal to deliver it face to face, but beyond that short distance, the cost of the phone call or of using priority mail may be invariant to distance. In these examples, the cost of transporting services rises over short distances when face to face is possible, and beyond the face-to-face distance, transport costs are relatively flat with respect to distance. For services that can be delivered electronically, such as data processing services, the cost of transport is effectively zero, regardless of distance. Generalizing across services industries, the absence of fixed costs over short distances suggests that being in the same building or immediate neighborhood as customers could lower transport costs for services industries considerably relative to being across town from customers, though the advantage of being 500 miles away from a customer over being 2,000 miles away from a customer is relatively small—at least relative to manufacturing.[18] Face-to-face, low-value services, like laundry or haircuts, must be near customers and should exhibit low industry-level agglomeration, but face to face and low value characterize only a subset of the broad category of services. Therefore, we might expect services firms to benefit from proximity to trading partners within a certain radius and therefore find it advantageous to agglomerate at a small geographic level; beyond that radius, firms would be less sensitive to proximity to trading partners and therefore would exhibit less agglomeration at larger geographic levels—the opposite of the logic that applies to manufacturing.

These simple models of transport costs imply that information technology (IT) usage could affect the location decisions of services and manufacturing differently. The direct effect on information technology is to lower the transport cost of intangibles only: a spreadsheet can be e-mailed but a

consultants based in another city; for lower-value in-person services, like haircuts, almost no one travels any significant distance for a haircut, and the cost of transporting the output of haircut services is so high relative to the its value.

17. To attend a 10:00 a.m. meeting in Chicago, the San Franciscan might fly out the day before at 3:00 p.m., arrive in Chicago at 9:00 p.m., and depart Chicago on a 1:00 p.m. flight to arrive at the San Francisco International Airport (SFO) at 3:00 p.m.—a twenty-four hour trip. To attend a 10:00 a.m. meeting in New York, the San Franciscan would leave home at 1:00 p.m. the day before to arrive in New York at 9:00 p.m. and would depart New York at 1:00 p.m. to arrive at the SFO at 4:00 p.m.—a twenty-seven hour trip. Traveling 50 percent farther raises the time cost by three hours—a one-eighth increase. The cost of the ticket, booked in advance, would be in the $300 to $500 range, and even if the New York ticket were 50 percent more expensive, the difference in ticket cost is very small relative to the opportunity cost of the management consultant's time, who might be billed at several hundred dollars per hour.

18. Theoretically, services industries that could rely entirely on phone, mail, or electronic communication with customers would be indifferent to how far away from customers they are, but in practice, it is hard to come up with services industries that never use face-to-face communication.

motor cannot.[19] Advances in IT might be expected to affect services industry location decisions more than manufacturing location decisions. Electronic communication, however, is a closer substitute for mail and telephone communication than it is for face-to-face communication; many interactions, like education or complex negotiations, still are largely face to face, even though the output is intangible.[20] Information technology, therefore, may not reduce the benefits to services industries of very close proximity to customers as much as they reduce the benefits of longer-distance proximity to customers.[21]

5.3 What Coagglomeration Reveals about Transport Costs

To assess how important trading relationships are for industry location decisions, this section analyzes whether industries that trade with each other also agglomerate together and whether trading affects coagglomeration differently for services than for manufacturing. In addition to examining the effect of trading relationships between industries, coagglomeration allows for the possibility that agglomerative forces like labor pooling, knowledge spillovers, or input sharing exist between firms in different industries, as well as between firms in the same industry.[22] One can characterize the degree of similarity of multiple variables between firms in different industries on a continuous scale, so coagglomeration allows for more refined testing of the earlier finding that occupational specialization affects manufacturing location decisions but not those of services.

To measure coagglomeration, this chapter uses the extension of the Ellison-Glaeser (1997) index to coagglomeration.[23] Their coagglomeration

19. Improvements in information technology can lower the transport costs for tangibles indirectly if it is less costly to arrange for shipping on-line than by phone; improvements in information technology can also lower transport costs for the entire distribution system by improving tracking, coordination, and other logistics.

20. The effect of reduced communication costs on location decisions is theoretically ambiguous, and despite predictions in the 1990s to the contrary, the Internet did not cause cities to become obsolete. Gaspar and Glaeser (1998) show that theoretically, electronic and face-to-face communications can instead be complements rather than substitutes. Kolko (2000) and Sinai and Waldfogel (2004) offer empirical evidence that the Internet both substitutes and complements for nonelectronic communications, depending on the nature of the communications.

21. Kolko (2000) finds that the geographic distribution of commercial Internet domains was highest in isolated larger cities, suggesting that the Internet is a complement for face-to-face interactions (that are primarily within-city) and a substitute for longer-distance communication like phone and postal mail.

22. Jacobs (1969) argues that the innovative activity arises in interactions between industries, not within an industry: "When new work is added to older work, the addition often cuts ruthlessly across categories of work, no matter how one may analyze the categories" (62).

23. There has been very little research on industries locating near each other. Three examples are as follows. Ellison and Glaeser (1997) find coagglomeration to be higher between pairs of manufacturing industries where one is a significant input to the other. Also, Duranton and Puga (2005) show that functional specialization is increasingly important rather than industrial specialization, which implies greater linkages between rather than within industries. Most

index measures the extent to which multiple industries are clustered together geographically in excess of the agglomeration of each of the industries. Like the agglomeration index, their coagglomeration index adjusts for both the distribution of region sizes and the level of establishment-level concentration. The formula for the coagglomeration index is provided in the appendix.

As with agglomeration, coagglomeration can be measured at different levels of geography. For example, (a) tobacco manufacturing and (b) fiber, yarn, and thread mills are highly coagglomerated at the state level but not at the county or zip code level; these two industries are both concentrated in North Carolina, but each is concentrated in different counties and zip codes within North Carolina. The same is true for (a) audio and video equipment manufacturing and (b) motion picture, video, and sound recording: both are concentrated in California, but the former is in the Bay Area and the latter is in Los Angeles. At the zip code level, (a) accommodations and (b) museums, historical sites, and similar institutions are highly coagglomerated, though not at either the county or state level; most counties and states have both of these industries, but within a county, the two types of industries tend to concentrate in the same immediate neighborhoods.[24]

The empirical strategy for measuring coagglomeration is:

$$\text{coagglom}_{i,j,k} = \beta X_{i,j} + \Lambda + \varepsilon_{i,j,k}.$$

Whereas the agglomeration analysis uses the industry as the unit of observation, the coagglomeration analysis uses the pair of industries (i,j) as the unit of observation. Coagglomeration is measured at level of geography k, which refers to zip codes, counties, or states, depending on the specification. The vector Λ captures industry fixed effects, and the elements of the vector equal 1 for industries i and j and 0 for all other industries. The vector $X_{i,j}$ is a set of variables capturing the reasons for coagglomeration between industries i and j, which are independent of geography, and these are discussed next.

The main variable of interest is direct trade, measured using the volume of direct trade between industries i and j as a share of overall inputs and outputs of both industries. The expectation is that trading intensity should contribute to services coagglomeration for smaller geographies and to manufacturing coagglomeration only for larger geographies. Because one of the key differences between services and manufacturing is the nature of transport costs, and because information technology is hypothesized to affect

---

recently, Ellison, Glaeser, and Kerr (2007) analyze the reasons for agglomeration, including direct trading relationships, through the lens of coagglomeration by using a framework closely related to the one in this chapter. Their study, however, only includes manufacturing industries and therefore does not address the question of whether the different nature of transport costs in service industries affects services' location patterns.

24. Since zip code data were available only in California, these industries are coagglomerated at the zip code level within California; their county- and state-level coagglomerations were measured using CBP, which is available for the nation.

transport costs, the levels of information technology intensity in industries i and j are interacted with the direct trade measure. It is further hypothesized that information technology affects the location decisions of services more than of manufacturing, because information technology lowers the cost of transporting many intangible outputs. Thus, for services, the relationship of direct trade between two industries on coagglomeration is expected to be weaker for more information technology-intensive industries; for manufacturing, the relationship between direct trade and coagglomeration should not be affected by how information technology-intensive the industries are. The level of information technology intensity is proxied using the share of employees in computing-specialty occupations.[25]

The other variable of interest is the occupational similarity between the industry pair. Industries with similar workers could coagglomerate for labor pooling if they have workers in occupations facing thin labor markets; industries with similar workers could coagglomerate also, because they benefit from knowledge spillovers between similarly skilled workers. To attempt to separate out these factors and to isolate whether labor pooling indeed specifically applies uniquely to manufacturing, occupational similarity enters the model twice: once interacted with the average of the occupational specialization of each industry (to reflect labor pooling) and once interacted with the average of the share of workers with graduate degrees in each industry (to reflect knowledge spillovers).[26]

In addition, three further measures are included as controls. The measure of demographic similarity of workers is designed to capture the possibility that firms follow workers: namely, that industries locate where their workers want to live and that local amenities serve as a compensating differential that enables firms to pay less for labor than they would in lower-amenity locations. Rather than attempt to identify high-amenity places, this chapter assumes that different workers put a different amenity value on different places, and age and education help predict which amenities workers demand. Industries with workers that are demographically similar are hypothesized

25. An alternative measure would be the percentage of workers using a computer, the Internet, or e-mail at work. While the Current Population Survey (CPS) does ask these questions sporadically, the number of responses is very low for many industries, so using CPS data would require aggregating an already-small number of industries further.

26. Although Rosenthal and Strange (2001) use education level as a measure of the potential for labor pooling, it seems more plausible that labor pooling could arise from specialized labor at any skill level, whereas the knowledge spillovers that contribute to innovative activity arise from highly skilled labor, regardless of whether that skilled labor is uniquely employed by a given industry. Ellison, Glaeser, and Kerr (2007) use patent citation data and Scherer technology flows to proxy for knowledge spillovers between pairs of industries rather than use any workforce measures. Both patent data and technology flows are available in greater detail for manufacturing than for services industries; for instance, the U.S. Patent and Trademark Office correspondence between patent codes and industry codes combines all nonmanufacturing Standard Industrial Classifications into a single category. Analyzing both manufacturing and services therefore restricts the set of usable data sources to those that are meaningful and disaggregated for both sectors, such as the industry-occupation matrix.

to coagglomerate, because their workers consider the same locations to be high amenity.[27] The other two controls—the similarity of the industries' inputs and the similarity of the industries' outputs—capture whether the two industries in the pair have similar suppliers and customers. Table 5.10 summarizes all of these measures and their interpretations, and the appendix defines them in detail.

The results of the coagglomeration analysis for manufacturing are presented in table 5.11 and for services in table 5.12. The regressions include all of the measures previously described.[28] With sixty-four manufacturing industries, the number of unique manufacturing pairs is (64*63)/2 = 2,016, and with fifty-four services industries, the number of unique services pairs is 1,431. In each table, columns (1), (2), and (3) show the results for zip code, county, and state coagglomeration with all variables except the interaction between direct trade and information technology intensity, and columns (4), (5), and (6) repeat the analysis with the interaction between direct trade and information technology intensity.

The most notable difference between manufacturing and services is the effect of trading intensity. For manufacturing, the coefficient on the direct trading relationship between the industries is positive and significant at the 5 percent level only for state coagglomeration; for county coagglomeration, it is positive and significant at the 10 percent level, and it is not significant for zip code coagglomeration. For services, however, the direct trading relationship contributes to the coagglomeration of services at the zip code level and is *negatively* and significantly related to coagglomeration at the state level. This difference between services and manufacturing is consistent with the simple models of transport costs sketched previously, which predicted that direct trade would lead services to coagglomerate only at small geographies and manufacturing only over larger geographies.[29]

The interaction between trading intensity and information technology usage is more complicated. For manufacturing, the interaction between

27. Implicit in this interpretation is the assumption that demographics—not occupation—influence tastes for location amenities, and occupation—not demographics—contributes to labor pooling. However, occupational categories do not fully describe how skilled or specialized a worker is, and demographic characteristics are probably correlated with the portion of skills and specialization not fully captured by occupational categories. Nonetheless, the inclusion of this demographic similarity measure is an improvement on past research in the field that did not consider an amenity-driven explanation for firm location decision. Furthermore, omitting the demographic similarity variable has essentially no effect on the coefficient estimates for the labor pooling variable.

28. The industry-level values for occupational specialization, graduate degrees, and information technology intensity are absorbed in the industry fixed effects variables. The uninteracted occupational similarity measure for the pair of industries is included in every specification but is not shown.

29. The model of transport costs in services industries suggests that the effect of the direct trading relationship on coagglomeration for services at the state level would be small or zero. The model did not suggest that it could be negative; the negative sign on this coefficient is surprising and remains unexplained.

Table 5.10 **Forces, measures, and summary statistics of coagglomeration**

Measure	Notation	Mean (manufacturing)	Standard deviation (manufacturing)	Mean (services)	Standard deviation (services)
Zip code coagglomeration (EG index)		.0012	.0026	–.00002	.0007
County coagglomeration (EG index)		.0006	.0018	.0002	.0020
State coagglomeration (EG index)		.0033	.0114	.0004	.0036
Occupational similarity of industry pair, uninteracted	Occsim_{ij}	.522	.144	.263	.131
Occupational similarity of industry pair interacted with occupational specialization of each industry	$\text{Occsim}_{ij} \times (\text{occspec}_i + \text{occspec}_j)/2$	.326	.089	.158	.073
Occupational similarity of industry pair interacted with worker graduate degrees of each industry	$\text{Occsim}_{ij} \times (\text{grad}_i + \text{grad}_j)/2$	.021	.014	.029	.026
Demographic similarity of industry pair	Demosim_{ij}	.805	.100	.673	.127
Direct trade between industry pair	Trade_{ij}	.006	.015	.008	.014
Input similarity of industry pair	Inputsim_{ij}	.455	.122	.535	.101
Output similarity of industry pair	Outputsim_{ij}	.302	.222	.449	.266
Direct trade between industry pair interacted with information technology intensity in each industry	$\text{Trade}_{ij} \times (\text{tech}_i + \text{tech}_j)/2$	.0003	.0011	.0010	.0017
N		2016	2016	1431	1431

Note: See appendix for definitions of notations.

Table 5.11 **Coagglomeration in manufacturing industries**

	Zip code	County	State	Zip code	County	State
Direct trade	0.00831	0.01055*	0.10587**	–0.00000	0.00570	0.10255**
	(0.00571)	(0.00573)	(0.03545)	(0.00473)	(0.00625)	(0.04165)
Occupational similarity × specialization	0.06974**	0.05853**	0.38056**	0.06629**	0.05652**	0.37918**
	(0.01832)	(0.02233)	(0.12590)	(0.01832)	(0.02228)	(0.12812)
Occupational similarity × graduate degrees	0.09157**	0.03214*	0.01191	0.06618**	0.01732	0.00177
	(0.02072)	(0.01759)	(0.08766)	(0.02025)	(0.01800)	(0.09420)
Demographic similarity	0.00507**	0.00299**	0.01431**	0.00496**	0.00292**	0.01426**
	(0.00091)	(0.00076)	(0.00406)	(0.00091)	(0.00076)	(0.00408)
Similarity of outputs	–0.00034	–0.00003	0.00028	–0.00031	–0.00001	0.00030
	(0.00027)	(0.00025)	(0.00152)	(0.00027)	(0.00025)	(0.00152)
Similarity of inputs	0.00228**	0.00253**	0.02809**	0.00244**	0.00262**	0.02815**
	(0.00078)	(0.00073)	(0.00585)	(0.00075)	(0.00074)	(0.00586)
IT × direct trade				0.51463**	0.30023**	0.20550
				(0.12484)	(0.10774)	(0.49637)
Observations	2,016	2,016	2,016	2,016	2,016	2,016
R-squared	0.32	0.21	0.28	0.33	0.21	0.28

Note: See table 5.10 for variable definitions. Robust standard errors in parentheses. Industry fixed effects for industries *i* and *j* included in all specifications. Occupational similarity (uninteracted) also included but not shown in all specifications.

**Significant at the 5 percent level.

*Significant at the 10 percent level.

Table 5.12 Coagglomeration in services industries

	Zip code	County	State	Zip code	County	State
Direct trade	0.00604**	0.00142	–0.02568**	–0.00003	0.00274	–0.01131
	(0.00233)	(0.00558)	(0.00953)	(0.00277)	(0.00668)	(0.01030)
Occupational similarity × specialization	0.00174	–0.00454	–0.00047	0.00154	–0.00450	0.00000
	(0.00239)	(0.00564)	(0.00787)	(0.00240)	(0.00560)	(0.00780)
Occupational similarity × graduate degrees	0.01234**	0.00746	–0.00276	0.01147**	0.00765	–0.00069
	(0.00246)	(0.00471)	(0.00899)	(0.00240)	(0.00477)	(0.00890)
Demographic similarity	0.00018	0.00196**	0.00437**	0.00020	0.00196**	0.00433**
	(0.00019)	(0.00054)	(0.00109)	(0.00019)	(0.00054)	(0.00108)
Similarity of outputs	0.00037**	0.00023	0.00122**	0.00033**	0.00025	0.00133**
	(0.00009)	(0.00018)	(0.00039)	(0.00009)	(0.00018)	(0.00040)
Similarity of inputs	0.00090**	0.00187**	0.00684**	0.00083*	0.00188**	0.00701**
	(0.00043)	(0.00087)	(0.00268)	(0.00043)	(0.00087)	(0.00270)
IT × direct trade				0.15834**	–0.03438	–0.37499**
				(0.06041)	(0.05444)	(0.15011)
Observations	1,431	1,431	1,431	1,431	1,431	1,431
R-squared	0.30	0.18	0.17	0.32	0.18	0.17

Note: See table 5.10 for variable definitions. Robust standard errors in parentheses. Industry fixed effects for industries *i* and *j* included in all specifications. Occupational similarity (uninteracted) also included but not shown in all specifications.

**Significant at the 5 percent level.

*Significant at the 10 percent level.

trade and information technology intensity is positive and significant for both zip code and county coagglomeration. This means that manufacturing industries that trade with each other are more likely to locate in the same zip codes and counties if the industries rely more on information technology. In other words, high-tech manufacturing industries that trade with each other are more likely to be neighbors than low-tech manufacturing industries that trade with each other.

For services, the interaction between direct trade and information technology intensity is also positively related to coagglomeration at the zip code level but negatively at the state level. This means that as in manufacturing, services industries that trade with each other are more likely to locate in the same zip codes and counties if the industries rely more on information technology. However, unlike manufacturing industries, service industries that trade with each other are *less* likely to locate in the same state if the industries rely more on information technology. The fact that the interaction coefficient is smaller for services than manufacturing at the county and state levels is consistent with the hypothesis that information technology should lower the transport cost for services output and not for manufacturing output: it is less important for firms that trade to be near each other if they can trade electronically. The positive coefficient on the interaction term for services at the zip code level suggests that information technology might not be a good substitute for the face-to-face interactions that cause services firms that trade to cluster in the zip code, block, or building.

However, the simple model previously outlined would imply that the coefficient on the interaction term between direct trade and information technology should be zero (not positive) when looking at manufacturing industries; if IT does not affect the cost of face-to-face communication, then the interaction term should be zero (not positive) for services industries at the zip code level, as well. The positive coefficient on the interaction term for manufacturing at the zip code and county levels and for services at the zip code level is unexplained by the simple model of transport costs. This suggests that information technology intensity could affect location decisions for reasons other than its effect on transport costs. Trade between information technology-intensive industries may require more coordination between the supplier and the customer if the output is more abstract or complex than in noninformation technology-intensive industries.[30] Furthermore, the information technology itself could add complexity if the supplier and customer need to agree on electronic formats or application standards.

30. This appears to be the effect of information technology per se and not complexity or technical detail in a general sense. When an interaction term between the direct trading relationship and the percent of workers in the industries with graduate degrees is included, the signs and significance on the interaction between direct trade and IT intensity do not change for services; for manufacturing, the coefficient in the county-level coagglomeration regression (table 5.11, column [5]) remains positive but is no longer statistically significant.

If some of this coordination happens face to face, this could explain why coefficient on the interaction between information technology intensity and direct trade could be positive and larger in magnitude for coagglomeration at smaller levels of geography.[31]

Turning to the other variable of interest: occupational similarity interacted with specialization contributes to manufacturing coagglomeration at all levels of geography (table 5.11) and to services coagglomeration at none (table 5.12). There is, however, little difference between manufacturing and services in the effect on coagglomeration of occupational similarity interacted with worker graduate degrees. For both sectors, this interaction term is positive and statistically significant at the 5 percent level only for zip code coagglomeration, and the standardized betas are similar for the two sectors (tables 5.13 and 5.14). These findings reinforce the initial finding that the labor pooling explanation applies specifically to manufacturing, though there are reasons other than labor pooling that encourage industries with similar occupational mixes to coagglomerate (table 5.15).

5.4 Conclusions

These findings on urbanization, agglomeration, and coagglomeration reveal why services are more urbanized yet less agglomerated than manufacturing. First, transport costs for services output encourage services to locate near their customers. This acts as a force against industry-level agglomeration. Further, because services industries often have business customers across diverse industries, it is optimal for many services to locate within a dense, diverse set of businesses, which explains not only the tendency for services to urbanize but also for services to be in the denser portions of urban areas. Second, services industries rely less on natural resources than manufacturing industries do, which allows services to urbanize to a greater extent than manufacturing. Third, although the level of occupational specialization is as high in the average services industry as in the average manufacturing industry, occupational specialization does not lead to agglomeration for services as it does for manufacturing, suggesting that labor pooling does not affect services industries' location decisions as it does manufacturing. In fact, the tendency for services to urbanize due to transport costs and nonreliance

31. These conclusions about services industries are based on regressions that include all services industries. It is possible that many consumer-facing services simply locate where consumers are, without regard to agglomerative forces; table 5.15 therefore repeats the analysis in table 5.12, excluding industries in which 95 percent or more of output goes to consumers. The results in table 5.15 are nearly identical to those in table 5.12, with the exception that similarity of inputs and similarity of outputs are no longer significant for any level of geography in table 5.15 (columns [1] to [3]), knowledge spillovers become statistically significant at the county level, and direct trade becomes statistically insignificant at the state level. Also, the interaction between IT and direct trade becomes statistically significant only at the 10 percent level at the zip code level.

Table 5.13 **Coagglomeration in manufacturing industries: Standardized betas**

	Zip code	County	State	Zip code	County	State
Direct trade	0.05	0.09	0.14	0.00	0.05	0.14
Occupational similarity × specialization	2.43	2.99	3.00	2.31	2.89	2.99
Occupational similarity × graduate degrees	0.52	0.27	0.02	0.37	0.14	0.00
Demographic similarity	0.20	0.17	0.13	0.19	0.17	0.13
Similarity of outputs	–0.03	0.00	0.01	–0.03	0.00	0.01
Similarity of inputs	0.11	0.18	0.30	0.12	0.18	0.30
IT × direct trade				0.11	0.10	0.01

Note: Standardized betas correspond to results from regressions in table 5.11.

Table 5.14 **Coagglomeration in services industries: Standardized betas**

	Zip code	County	State	Zip code	County	State
Direct trade	0.12	0.01	–0.10	0.00	0.02	–0.04
Occupational similarity × specialization	0.18	–0.17	–0.01	0.16	–0.17	0.00
Occupational similarity × graduate degrees	0.44	0.10	–0.02	0.41	0.10	0.00
Demographic similarity	0.03	0.13	0.15	0.04	0.13	0.15
Similarity of outputs	0.14	0.03	0.09	0.12	0.03	0.10
Similarity of inputs	0.13	0.10	0.19	0.12	0.10	0.20
IT × direct trade				0.21	–0.02	–0.10

Note: Standardized betas correspond to results from regressions in table 5.12.

on natural resources may itself make labor pooling less important, since urbanized services industries are already in thick labor markets, even in the absence of industry agglomeration.

These results also suggest that the increasing reliance on information technology could continue to change business location decisions but in a way that could favor cities. Information technology can either encourage or discourage coagglomeration between industries that trade with each other. Information technology encourages coagglomeration for services that trade with each other at the zip code level and discourages it at the state level, while it encourages coagglomeration for manufacturing at both the zip code and county levels, with no effect at the state level. This chapter argues that the differential effect of information technology on manufacturing and services is because electronic communication dramatically lowers the cost of transporting intangibles, especially over longer distances, but not the cost of transporting tangible goods. However, because information technology encourages coagglomeration, information technology appears to have other effects on firms that trade with each other. While information technology lowers transport costs, high-IT industries appear to benefit more from face-to-face coordination than low-IT industries do. As information technology becomes further integrated into business processes, the benefit for

Table 5.15 Coagglomeration in services industries, excluding consumer services

	Zip code	County	State	Zip code	County	State
Direct trade	0.00739**	0.00337	–0.01389	0.00257	0.00514	0.01107
	(0.00266)	(0.00629)	(0.01243)	(0.00345)	(0.00794)	(0.01340)
Occupational similarity × specialization	0.00599*	–0.00653	–0.01918*	0.00566	–0.00641	–0.01747*
	(0.00347)	(0.00850)	(0.01063)	(0.00350)	(0.00844)	(0.01056)
Occupational similarity × graduate degrees	0.01081**	0.01510**	0.01484	0.01064**	0.01517**	0.01573
	(0.00320)	(0.00723)	(0.01212)	(0.00320)	(0.00724)	(0.01202)
Demographic similarity	0.00031	0.00197**	0.00410**	0.00032	0.00197**	0.00407**
	(0.00027)	(0.00092)	(0.00155)	(0.00027)	(0.00092)	(0.00155)
Similarity of outputs	0.00025*	–0.00034	–0.00018	0.00024*	–0.00034	–0.00013
	(0.00014)	(0.00047)	(0.00087)	(0.00014)	(0.00047)	(0.00087)
Similarity of inputs	0.00047	0.00073	0.00392	0.00044	0.00074	0.00407
	(0.00059)	(0.00117)	(0.00340)	(0.00059)	(0.00117)	(0.00340)
IT × direct trade				0.10656*	–0.03919	–0.55236**
				(0.06419)	(0.07443)	(0.18933)
Observations	820	820	820	820	820	820
R^2	0.28	0.23	0.28	0.29	0.23	0.29

Note: See table 5.10 for variable definitions. Robust standard errors in parentheses. Industry fixed effects for industries *i* and *j* included in all specifications. Occupational similarity (uninteracted) also included but not shown in all specifications. Excludes industries in which 95 percent or more of output goes to consumers: elementary and secondary schools, health care, museums and historical sites, personal care services, death care services, and religious organizations.

**Significant at the 5 percent level.

*Significant at the 10 percent level.

services of proximity in dense areas increases, even though IT enables some types of output to be transported more cheaply—good news for the future of cities.

Appendix

Data Sources and Variable Definitions

County Business Patterns

County Business Patterns (CBP) is the source for employment counts at the county and state levels. The CBP is an annual tabulation of the Census Bureau's register of all business establishments, which is generated from the quinquennial Economic Censuses, the annual Company Organization Survey, the Annual Survey of Manufactures, and administrative records. The CBP covers all private-sector nonfarm employment in establishments with at least one paid employee. The total employment covered by CBP was around 115 million employees in 2004.

A record in CBP is a county-industry cell, where industries are reported down to the four-digit SIC level. For each industry-county cell, an employment figure is given, which is either an exact figure or a range (1 to 4, 5 to 9, 10 to 19, etc.). A range rather than an exact figure is given when the number of establishments is sufficiently small that an exact figure would disclose information about a particular establishment. Also reported for each industry-county cell is the total number of establishments and the number of establishments in each of several establishment-size ranges (1 to 4, 5 to 9, etc.). These establishment counts are always exact, never ranges. To impute industry-county employment figures when only a range is given, a second range is constructed using the establishments-by-establishment-size count. Thus, the exact employment count lies with certainty in the intersection of the two ranges. For each industry, a point in the intersection of the ranges was chosen such that the resulting estimates, when added to the exact figures for other cells, added up to the industry's national employment total. That point was a uniform distance between the lower and upper bound of each cell's range (say, 40 percent from the lower bound) for each industry; for each industry, a separate distance was calculated.

The actual (or where necessary, estimated) employment count for industry i in county x is $\text{emp}_{i,x}$ in the following variable definitions. Total employment across industries in county x is emp_x, and total employment across counties in industry i is emp_i. Total national employment in all industries and in all counties is emp.

Documentation for the CBP is available on-line at: http://www.census.gov/econ/cbp/index.html.

The National Establishment Time Series (NETS) Database

The NETS is the source for employment counts at the zip code level. The NETS is a longitudinal file created by Walls and Associates from the register of business establishments tracked by Dun and Bradstreet. For this research only, a subset of California data were available. The NETS provides uncensored employment counts and addresses at the establishment level, so no imputation is necessary in creating employment counts at the zip code-industry level. Detailed information about the NETS and an assessment of its quality is available in Neumark, Zhang, and Wall (2007).

The CBP is the basis for calculating agglomeration and coagglomeration at the county and state levels. The NETS is the basis for calculating agglomeration and coagglomeration at the zip code level. The agglomeration and coagglomeration measures follow Ellison and Glaeser (1997).

Ellison-Glaeser measure of agglomeration (following their notation):

$$\gamma = \frac{G - (1 - \sum_i x_i^2)H}{(1 - \sum_i x_i^2)(1 - H)}$$

$$G = \sum_i (s_i - x_i)^2$$

$$H = \sum_j z_j^2 \text{ (industry Herfindahl index)},$$

where s_i = share of industry employment in geographic area i, x_i = share of national employment in geographic area i, and z_j = share of industry employment in establishment j.

The index is the sum of squared differences between industry and national employment shares across geographic areas, adjusted for (a) the size distribution of geographic areas and (b) the Herfindahl index of the industry establishment size distribution.

Ellison-Glaeser measure of coagglomeration (following their notation) across J industries, $j = 1$ to J, which constitute an industry group:

$$\gamma^c = \frac{[G/(1 - \sum_i x_i^2)] - H - \sum_j \hat{\gamma}_j w_j^2 (1 - H_j)}{1 - \sum_j w_j^2}$$

$$H = \sum_j w_j^2 H_j \text{ (weighted Herfindahls of industry establishment size distributions)},$$

where G is the raw concentration (as defined previously) for industry group employment, H_j is the Herfindahl index of industry j's establishment size distribution, W_j is industry j's share of industry group employment, and γ_j is the agglomeration index for industry j (as defined previously).

Input-Output Accounts

The 2004 input-output (IO) accounts are the source for information on customer-supplier relationships among industries and consumption by final users (consumers and government). The IO accounts estimate the value of commodity flows between pairs of industries. The IO accounts are developed by the Bureau of Economic Analysis based on the quinquennial Economic Censuses conducted by the Census Bureau and numerous other sources. Both physical (i.e., manufacturing) and nonphysical (i.e., services) goods are included. Additional input sources and output destinations are included; namely, labor is included as an input source, and households and government are included as output destinations.

Documentation for the IO accounts is available on-line at: http://www.bea.gov/papers/pdf/IOmanual_092906.pdf.

In the IO accounts, industries can use their own output as an input in the production process. These "circular flows" are excluded. The key variables generated from the IO accounts are the direct trade variable, the similarity of inputs, and the similarity of outputs for the coagglomeration analysis, as well as the natural resource inputs variable for the agglomeration analysis.

Between any pair of industries *i* and *j*, there are four possible measures of the strength of direct trade between them. Let input_k and output_k represent the total inputs from other industries consumed in industry *k*'s production process and the total outputs generated by industry *k*'s production process, excluding output from industry *k* that is also an input for industry *k*. If $b_{i \to j}$ equals the value of industry *i*'s output used as an input by industry *j*, and $b_{j \to i}$ equals the value of industry *j*'s output used as an input by industry *i*, then the four measures of direct trade are:

1. $b_{i \to j}/\text{input}_j$
2. $b_{i \to j}/\text{output}_i$
3. $b_{j \to i}/\text{input}_i$
4. $b_{j \to i}/\text{output}_j$

These four measures reflect the fact that industry *i* and *j* might be of different size, and the amount of trade $b_{j \to i}$, for instance, could reflect a very different share of industry *i*'s overall inputs than it does of industry *j*'s overall outputs.

The *direct trade* (trade_{ij}) variable is calculated as the average of the four underlying measures, and the results of the analysis are not changed when using only the maximum of the four measures.

The *output similarity* variable, outputsim_{ij}, is equal to the sum of absolute differences between the shares of industries *i* and *j*'s outputs going to each customer *k*, where *k* = all other industries, consumers, and government:

$$\text{outputsim}_{ij} = \left(2 - \sum_k \left| \frac{b_{i \to k}}{\text{output}_i} - \frac{b_{j \to k}}{\text{output}_j} \right| \right)/2,$$

which equals 1 if industries *i* and *j* have perfectly overlapping distributions of customers and 0 if they have nonoverlapping distributions of customers.

The *input similarity* variable, inputsim_{ij}, is equal to the sum of absolute differences between the shares of industries i and j's inputs coming from each supplier k, where k = all other industries:

$$\text{inputsim}_{ij} = \left(2 - \sum_k \left| \frac{b_{i \to k}}{\text{input}_i} - \frac{b_{j \to k}}{\text{input}_j} \right| \right) / 2,$$

which equals 1 if industries i and j have perfectly overlapping distributions of suppliers and 0 if they have nonoverlapping distributions of suppliers.

The *natural resource inputs* (nature_i) measure is the share of inputs to industry i that come from crop or animal production, forestry, logging, fishing, or mining (NAICS 11 and 21, with the exception of support activities within those categories).

National Industry-Occupation Employment Matrix

The National Industry-Occupation Employment Matrix 2004 (NIOEM) is the source for occupation data. The Bureau of Labor Statistics produces the NIOEM from Occupational Employment Statistics, Current Employment Statistics, and the Current Population Survey.

The NIOEM presents employment counts in industry-occupation cells for around 300 industries and around 700 occupations. This chapter uses the summary occupation codes, which aggregate the 700 occupations into ninety-three occupational groups.

The *occupational similarity* variable, occsim_{ij}, is equal to the sum of absolute differences between the shares of industries i and j's workforces in occupation k, where occ_{ik} = share of industry i's workforce in occupation k:

$$\text{occsim}_{ij} = \frac{(2 - \sum_k |\text{occ}_{ik} - \text{occ}_{jk}|)}{2},$$

which equals 1 if industries i and j have perfectly overlapping distributions of occupations and 0 if they have nonoverlapping distributions of occupations.

The *occupational specialization* variable, occ_i, is equal to the sum of absolute differences between the share of occupation k in the economy (occ_k) and the share of occupation k of employment in industry i:

$$\text{occspec}_i = \frac{(2 - \sum_k |\text{occ}_{ik} - \text{occ}_k|)}{2},$$

which equals 1 if industry i has a distribution of occupations identical to the economy in aggregate.

The NIOEM also provides the *share of workers within computer specialist occupations* (tech_i) used in the coagglomeration analysis, interacted with the direct trade measure.

Documentation for the NIOEM is available on-line at: http://www.bls.gov/emp/nioem/empioan.htm.

Public Use Microdata Sample

The 2000 Public Use Microdata Sample (PUMS) of the U.S. Census Bureau provides individual-level data on age and education level of workers by industry. Using six age groups and eight education categories, the distribution of workers across forty-eight age-education cells was calculated by industry.

The *demographics similarity* variable, demosim_{ij}, is equal to the sum of absolute differences between the shares of industries *i* and *j*'s workforces in each age-education cell *k*, where demo_{ik} = share of industry *i*'s workforce in age-education cell *k*:

$$\text{demosim}_{ij} = \frac{(2 - \sum_k |\text{demo}_{ik} - \text{demo}_{jk}|)}{2},$$

which equals 1 if industries *i* and *j* have perfectly overlapping distributions of age-education cells and 0 if they have nonoverlapping distributions of age-education cells.

The PUMS also provides the *share of workers with graduate degrees* (grad_i) used in the agglomeration analysis and in the coagglomeration analysis, interacted with the occupational similarity measure.

Industry Definitions

Data on employment in the CBP and the NETS are available at the six-digit NAICS level. The other data sources—the IO accounts, NIOEM, and the PUMS—are available at the four-digit NAICS level, or for many industries, only at the three- or two-digit level. In creating the industry classification used in this chapter, the classifications from all four data sources were aggregated so that each industry has a unique value from each data set.

For instance, one industry used in this chapter is NAICS 722, "Food Services and Drinking Places," rather than using the underlying four-digit industries: NAICS 7221 ("Full Service Restaurants"), 7222 ("Limited Service Restaurants"), 7223 ("Special Food Services," like caterers), and 7224 ("Drinking Places"). The CBP, NETS, and NIOEM provide separate data for NAICS 7221, 7222, 7223, and 7224. However, the Census industry code 868 used in the PUMS combines NAICS 7221, 7222, and 7223, and Census code 869 corresponds to NAICS 7224. The IO accounts use the Bureau of Labor Statistics (BLS) industry code 168, which corresponds to NAICS 722 in aggregate. Thus, in order to avoid measurement error from assigning values from Census code 868 or BLS code 168 to all the component four-digit NAICS codes, the industry classification in this chapter uses NAICS 722 for which data is available for every source. The greater precision in the CBP, NETS, and NIOEM is lost, of course, by not using their data at the finest level of disaggregation available.

Table 5A.1

	Manufacturing	Services
County business patterns and NETS (NAICS based)	86	109
NIOEM (NAICS based)	84	100
IO accounts (BLS sectors)	86	66
PUMS (Census based)	77	83
Classification in this chapter	64	54

Table 5A.1 shows the number of industries that each data source uses within the manufacturing and services sector.

For manufacturing, the Census classification used in the PUMS provides the least detailed breakdown; for services, the BLS sector classification used in the IO accounts is the least detailed. Aggregating across all four sources results in sixty-four manufacturing industries and fifty-four services industries, which is the maximum number of codes such that none is a subset of any industry code in any of the data sources.

References

Duranton, G., and D. Puga. 2005. From sectoral to functional urban specialization. *Journal of Urban Economics* 57 (2): 343–70.

Ellison, G., and E. Glaeser. 1997. Geographic concentration in U.S. manufacturing industries: A dartboard approach. *Journal of Political Economy* 105 (5): 889–927.

Ellison, G., E. Glaeser, and W. Kerr. 2007. What causes industry agglomeration? Evidence from coagglomeration patterns. NBER Working Paper no. 13068. Cambridge, MA: National Bureau of Economic Research, April.

Gaspar, J., and E. Glaeser. 1998. Information technology and the future of cities. *Journal of Urban Economics* 43 (1): 136–56.

Glaeser, E., J. Kolko, and A. Saiz. 2001. Consumer city. *Journal of Economic Geography* 1 (1): 27–50.

Jacobs, J. 1969. *The economy of cities.* New York: Vintage.

Kolko, J. 2000. The death of distance? The death of cities? Evidence from the geography of commercial Internet usage. In *The Internet upheaval,* ed. I. Vogelsang and B. Compaine, 73–99. Cambridge, MA: MIT Press.

Neumark, D., J. Zhang, and B. Wall. 2007. Employment dynamics and business relocation: New evidence from the National Establishment Time Series. In *Research in labor economics* vol. 26, *Aspects of worker well-being,* ed. S. O. Polachek and O. Bargain, 39–83. Amsterdam: Elsevier.

Rosenthal, S., and W. Strange. 2001. The determinants of agglomeration. *Journal of Urban Economics* 50 (2): 191–229.

Sinai, T., and J. Waldfogel. 2004. Geography and the Internet: Is the Internet a substitute or complement for cities? *Journal of Urban Economics* 56 (1): 1–24.

6

Who Benefits Whom in the Neighborhood?
Demographics and Retail Product Geography

Joel Waldfogel

It is well understood that because of fixed costs, retail product provision requires agglomeration of consumers.[1] As a result, places with more people tend to have more retail outlets, while places with insufficient demand have none.[2] In this sense, additional people nearby confer a benefit on each other by helping to make more products available. Yet, because product preferences differ across groups of consumers, it is not simply the *amount* of nearby demand that determines what's available but the *mix* of consumers according to their preferences. If product preferences relate to consumer characteristics such as race, income, age, and ethnicity, then product availability will be stimulated by concentration of like individuals. Additional group members nearby benefit each other, while additional persons preferring other things do not.

The sensitivity of available products to the demographic mix of consumers has been documented for products whose market area is an entire metropolitan area, such as newspapers, radio, and television. The mechanism may also operate at the neighborhood level; Waldfogel (2008) documents that neighborhoods with large populations in particular groups (black, college educated, etc.) are more likely to have chain restaurant outlets appealing specifically to those groups. Based on evidence for the restaurant market, this indicates a product market benefit of agglomeration with persons of

Joel Waldfogel is the Joel S. Ehrenkranz Family Professor of Business and Public Policy at the Wharton School, University of Pennsylvania, and a research associate of the National Bureau of Economic Research.

1. See, for example, Fujita and Thisse (2002) for an extensive discussion on the role of increasing returns in explaining agglomeration, as well as for many references.

2. This is one way to interpret much of the empirical work on firm entry. See Bresnahan and Reiss (1990) and a host of other studies.

like preferences. While it is conventional to think of publicly provided goods as the rationale for neighborhood sorting, privately provided goods may provide an additional benefit to agglomeration with like types. The goal of the present exercise is to revisit this question for a much broader group of local establishments.

The possibility that product markets reward agglomeration of like individuals has possible implications for residential segregation. A large volume of social scientific research documents a long legacy of residential segregation in the United States.[3] Other research shows that residential segregation by race is harmful to blacks.[4] Even as formal barriers to integration have declined, segregation has remained puzzlingly strong.

Notwithstanding the important negative effects of segregation for some groups, agglomeration of like individuals benefits them from helping to make the agglomerating groups' preferred products available nearby. It is a small instrumental leap to suggest that residential segregation persists in part because the agglomeration of like individuals provides them some benefit through product markets. Race is an important motivating example, but the product market motive for local agglomeration is not limited to race. Rather, agglomeration could provide product market benefits to any group with product preferences distinct from the remainder of the population.

The chapter addresses three empirical questions. First, how do "preferences" differ across groups (race, education, income)?[5] For this, we use the 2004 Consumer Expenditure Survey (CEX), which shows how households allocate their expenditures across narrow product categories. Second, using the 2000 Census and the 2000 ZIP Business Patterns, we ask how the availability of outlets in a category varies with the number of persons, by type, in local areas (five-digit zip codes). Finally, we ask whether the mix of products is sensitive to the mix of local preferences or whether people derive benefit through the product market from agglomerating with persons of similar preferences.

Section 6.1 provides a brief theoretical background. Section 6.2 describes the data used in the study, and section 6.3 presents results.

6.1 Theoretical Background

Our underlying question is whether the mix of nearby products affects the mix of available products and consumers' ensuing satisfaction from retail product markets. The following framework in the spirit of Hotelling (1929)

3. See Cutler, Glaeser, and Vigdor (1999) and Massey and Denton (1988) for two prominent examples.

4. See Cutler and Glaeser (1997).

5. "Preferences" is in quotation marks because what matters to products that are brought forth is not what people want absent price and income constraints but rather what they are able and inclined to purchase.

is helpful for fixing ideas. Think of a one-dimensional retail product spectrum, where the dimension represents the relative appeal of the product to one group versus another. For example, if the groups are blacks and non-blacks, the dimension measures the relative appeal of the product to blacks as opposed to non-blacks. There is a large but finite number of possible retail outlets, such as shoe stores, fish markets, and so on. We have in mind the hundreds of different kinds of retail establishments in the North American Industry Classification System (NAICS) coding system. Let's suppose that we have some way of measuring the extent to which a type of outlet is black targeted (I propose an approach to this in the following text). Then, the possible types of outlets can be arrayed in order along the spectrum.

Firms must choose whether to enter at each of the possible establishment types along the spectrum. Because of fixed costs, the number of outlets that can profitably operate is finite. And indeed, because of fixed costs, an outlet requires some density of nearby (in product space) consumers to make it viable. Places—corresponding to market areas—differ in their mix of consumers, who in turn differ by their preferences. Some places are heavily black; others are heavily white.

Consider figure 6.1. The top panel depicts the distribution of the most preferred varieties in a place where the distribution of tastes is skewed toward "black" products; the second panel depicts a place where tastes are skewed "white." Suppose the consumers patronize the nearest outlet to their ideal. The market can support more outlets in regions of product space where demand is denser. As a result, the market in the top panel has more black-targeted products, while the market in the bottom panel supports more white-targeted products.

This setup then yields the nonsurprising implication that places with

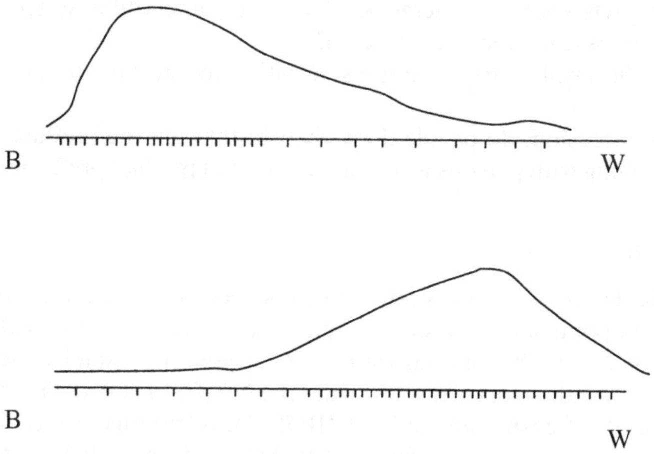

Fig. 6.1 Consumer density and retail outlet availability

more people preferring a particular type of products are more likely to have outlets—or to have more outlets—offering that type of product. As a result, the welfare of consumers—at least from the standpoint of nearby product availability—is higher when they live among others sharing their preferences.

A few important caveats are in order. The forgoing discussion ignores issues of pricing that conventionally assume larger importance in the discussion of entry. As the large literature on entry makes clear, products isolated in product space generally fetch higher prices, allowing them to cover their fixed costs with less nearby consumer density. From the standpoint of product availability, pricing issues attenuate problems of relatively less provision in sparse regions of product space. At the same time, inclusion of prices also suggests notions of welfare reflecting product availability net of prices rather than availability alone. The only prediction we seek to derive from this setup, however, is that regions of product space with denser demand have more outlets; and it is difficult to imagine this not being true (especially in light of the following evidence).

Second, consumers do not literally patronize one sort of outlet. Rather, consumers patronize both clothing and food and auto parts stores. One can think of a spectrum specific to each category of products (e.g., new cars versus used cars).

Third, outlets are not literally mutually exclusive in their product coverage. Grocery stores sell many of the items available at meat markets, fruit and vegetable markets, and fish and seafood stores. Similarly, department stores sell many of the items available at stores specializing in women's apparel.

Notwithstanding these caveats, this framework can fruitfully guide our empirical work, which seeks to answer the following questions:

1. Do preferences for different kinds of retail outlets differ systematically across groups (race, income, age, etc.)?
2. Is the availability of outlets sensitive to the mix of consumers nearby?
3. By extension, do people derive benefit through the product market from dwelling with persons who share their retail product preferences?

6.2 Data

The basic data set for the study is a zip code-level cross-section with information on population and demographic characteristics, along with information on the number of retail outlets, by category. The establishment data exist for 1,082 distinct categories under the NAICS. These data are drawn from the 2000 Census and the 2000 ZIP Business Patterns. We seek to map these categories to groupings for which we have evidence on how preferences differ by groups.

Separately, we have calculations from the Consumer Expenditure Survey showing how expenditure is distributed across groups of people (for example, by race and income) and over categories of goods and services. We examine the following distinctions: race (black/non-black), Asian (Asian/non-Asian), Hispanic (Hispanic/non-Hispanic), income (low income/non-low income)[6], education (college educated/not college educated), and age (over 65/not over 65).

Although the Economic Census and CEX data exist for different purposes, they contain many categories that correspond with one another. That is, many of the expenditure categories in the CEX correspond to categories—or groups of categories—of establishments in the NAICS coding system. For example, the expenditure category "food away from home" maps reasonably to the NAICS categories for full-service restaurants (722110), limited-service restaurants (722211), cafeterias (722212), snack and nonalcoholic bars (722213), mobile food services (722330), and drinking places (alcoholic beverages; 722410). Similarly, the CEX category for footwear maps to the NAICS category for shoe stores (448210). The CEX provides fairly detailed information on the categories of establishments included in each expenditure category at the CEX glossary of terms (available at: http://www.bls.gov/cex/csxgloss.htm). The appendix presents the mapping we create from this information in conjunction with the full NAICS list.

In most cases, CEX expenditure categories include multiple types of NAICS establishments. In two cases, CEX categories are narrower that NAICS categories. For example, the CEX separately reports expenditure on beef, pork, poultry, and other meats. The NAICS includes only meat markets (445210). Our matching procedure yields thirty-six distinct categories.

Table 6.1 describes the entry (supply) data. The first column shows the mean number of category outlets in a zip code. The second column shows the share of zip codes with at least one outlet in the category. These are our two basic measures of product availability. As the table shows, some of the most commonly available categories are food at home, food away from home, gas stations, and health care (chiefly doctors and dentists offices). Less commonly available establishments are bakeries, apparel shops for children underage two, fruit and vegetable stores, fish and seafood markets, and tobacco stores. Of course, table 6.1 indicates the presence of establishments dedicated to the particular category. Many specialized items are available not only at specialized stores (such as bakeries and butcher shops) but also at more general grocery stores (which are included in the "food at home" category).

Table 6.2 shows basic demand characteristics. The mean (median) zip

6. The low-income group in the CEX includes households with income below $20,000, and the most similar low-income household category in the Census includes households with income below $25,000.

Table 6.1 Establishment presence by category

Modified CEX categories	Mean	Presence (%)
Alcoholic beverages	0.97	38.42
Apparel and services	0.70	23.33
Bakery products	0.18	13.05
Cars and trucks, new	0.88	30.84
Cars and trucks, used	0.83	31.94
Children under two (apparel)	0.19	10.09
Drugstores	1.39	46.15
Fees and admissions	2.24	52.98
Fish and seafood	0.06	4.96
Floor coverings	0.54	26.10
Food at home	3.34	71.54
Food away from home	15.52	83.15
Footwear	1.01	24.10
Fruits and vegetables	0.11	8.02
Fuel oil and other fuels	0.18	11.83
Furniture	1.01	32.90
Gasoline and motor oil	4.06	75.75
Health care	14.50	61.67
Household textiles	0.08	6.46
Maintenance and repairs	7.01	69.18
Major appliances	0.33	20.08
Meat and poultry	0.22	15.03
Men and boys (apparel)	0.36	14.55
Miscellaneous household equipment	1.26	42.19
Other apparel products and services	2.32	38.58
Other entertainment supplies, equipment, and services	1.49	40.01
Other household expenses	0.40	22.35
Other vehicles	0.21	14.32
Personal care products and services	3.18	46.28
Personal services	2.24	53.93
Pets, toys, hobbies, and playground equipment	0.88	30.63
Postage and stationery	0.29	16.82
Reading	0.46	21.07
Television, radios, and sound equipment	0.93	29.48
Tobacco products and smoking supplies	0.19	12.81
Women and girls (apparel)	1.21	27.25

code population is 9,697 (3,472). The mean (median) percentage black is 7.8 (0.8), and the mean and median percentages with household income below $25,000 are both 32. The mean (median) percentage Hispanic is 6.5 (1.6), and the mean (median) percent Asian is 1.5 (0.3). The mean (median) percent college educated is 13.3 (9.4), and the mean (median) percent over age sixty-five is 12.4 (11.9). On average, a zip code is eighty-eight (thirty-nine) square miles. The mean (median) radius is 4.1 (3.5) miles if they were circular. In addition, as table 6.2 indicates, there is substantial variation

Table 6.2 **Demand characteristics of five-digit zip codes**

	Mean	Median	75th percentile	90th percentile
Population (000)	9,697	3,472	13,451	28,885
Square miles	88	39	94	193
Radius	4.1	3.5	5.5	7.8
Percent:				
Black	7.7	0.8	5.9	25.9
Hispanic	6.5	1.6	5.1	16.9
Asian	1.5	0.3	1.0	3.4
Low-income household	32.0	31.7	41.0	49.6
College educated	13.3	9.5	15.3	25.8
Over 65	12.4	11.9	14.8	18.1

across zip codes in their composition by age, race, and so forth, suggesting the possibility to separately measure the relationship of establishment availability to different populations.

6.3 Results

6.3.1 Do Preferences Differ across Groups?

It is well known from other contexts that preferences for many products differ sharply by groups. For example, radio station formats attracting two-thirds of black listeners attract 2 to 3 percent of non-black listeners. Likewise, Spanish-language radio attracts half of U.S. Hispanics but less than 1 percent of non-Hispanic listeners.[7] Similarly sharp differences exist for other media products. With the exception of *Monday Night Football,* top-rated shows among whites tend to be bottom rated among blacks and vice versa.[8]

Demographic differences in product preferences are not limited to media products. In the restaurant market, blacks and non-blacks patronize chain restaurants offering systematically different cuisines. Even after accounting for income as well as zip code of residence, blacks patronize restaurants offering Southern cuisine far more heavily than non-blacks. Educated consumers patronize coffee/bagel restaurants, as well as more expensive chain restaurants, at elevated levels relative to their less-educated—and lower-income—counterparts.[9] While many products remain to be studied, it seems

7. See Waldfogel (2003) for evidence on how radio preferences differ by group.

8. Waldfogel (2004) provides data on television viewing by race and Hispanic status.

9. Waldfogel (2008) provides evidence on how chain restaurant patronage varies by race, Hispanic status, and education.

clear that preferences for food and cultural products differ sharply across groups.

The findings that preferences differ sharply across groups are derived from consumption data at the narrow product—brand—level. That is, the data indicate which radio station, television program, or chain restaurant consumers patronize. Our data for this study are at a far higher level of aggregation, and these data may obscure intergroup differences in preferences. To see this, consider a category such as food. Everyone eats food, so virtually everyone allocates a substantial share of expenditure to food. Two persons who share a willingness to eat none of the same particular foods might still allocate similar amounts of money to food. As the product categories grow narrower, their capacity to show differences grows. For example, devout Hindus, Moslems, and Orthodox Jews might spend similar amounts on meat; but their expenditures on beef, lamb, and pork would differ sharply. Here, I trade off precision for reach. I include many categories of expenditure and types of establishments, but my information on spending patterns are at a highly aggregative level.

Beyond this, the question of whether preferences differ across groups is more accurately rephrased as, do expenditure patterns differ across groups? I am not interested in underlying preferences—what people want, absent the constraints imposed by their means. Rather, I am interested in what people find useful and appealing, given both their preferences and their means. Table 6.3 presents data from the 2004 CEX table 2100, "Race of Reference Person: Average Annual Expenditure and Characteristics."[10] As table 6.3 shows, the answer to the preceding question is yes—at least to some extent. The first column shows the ratio of black to non-black household expenditure. This is our measure of *relative preference* by group. The remaining columns show analogous relative preference measures for other groups relative to their complements: Asians (versus non-Asians), over age sixty-five, Hispanics, college educated, and low income (under $20,000).

Some of the differences in expenditure patterns—relative preferences—between groups are striking. For example, blacks spend 32 percent less than non-blacks overall, reflecting their lower average income. We would therefore expect the viability of retail outlets to be less sensitive to the black population than to the white, since black households spend less. Despite black households' lower overall expenditures, blacks actually spend absolutely more on some products, including footwear (167 percent as much) and fish and seafood (134 percent). Blacks also spend more than non-blacks on two subcategories of meat, included separately in the CEX but not listed separately in the table: poultry (124 percent) and pork (118 percent). At the other end of the spectrum, blacks spend substantially less than non-blacks on pets, toys, hobbies, and playground equipment (29 percent); health care

10. Available at: http://www.bls.gov/cex/#tables.

Table 6.3 **Household relative expenditures by group and category**

Modified CEX category	Black[a]	Asian[b]	Age[c]	Hispanic[d]	Education[e]	Income[f]
Alcoholic beverages	0.34	0.71	0.52	0.67	1.98	0.36
Apparel and services	0.97	1.04	0.45	1.00	1.65	0.39
Bakery products	0.74	0.93	0.88	1.03	1.16	0.56
Cars and trucks, new	0.42	1.32	0.57	0.91	1.35	0.18
Cars and trucks, used	0.58	0.86	0.50	1.18	1.09	0.33
Children under two (apparel)	0.61	1.04	0.22	2.03	1.38	0.53
Drugstores	0.48	0.71	2.26	0.54	1.21	0.69
Fees and admissions	0.32	1.16	0.63	0.56	3.18	0.20
Fish and seafood	1.27	2.38	0.77	1.28	1.36	0.50
Floor coverings	0.45	1.23	0.81	0.40	3.42	0.15
Food at home	0.80	1.10	0.78	1.18	1.19	0.56
Food away from home	0.59	1.25	0.56	0.82	1.68	0.33
Footwear	1.67	0.95	0.33	1.34	1.41	0.52
Fruits and vegetables	0.77	1.55	0.89	1.31	1.33	0.58
Fuel oil and other fuels	0.40	0.33	1.48	0.58	1.04	0.64
Furniture	0.76	1.23	0.51	0.83	2.00	0.27
Gasoline and motor oil	0.75	1.02	0.55	1.04	1.21	0.42
Health care	0.50	0.82	1.73	0.59	1.38	0.54
Household textiles	0.65	0.61	0.97	0.67	1.75	0.30
Maintenance and repairs	0.63	1.08	0.71	0.87	1.59	0.41
Major appliances	0.50	0.68	0.83	1.00	1.43	0.31
Meat and poultry	0.98	0.94	0.74	1.39	1.01	0.58
Men and boys (apparel)	0.80	1.35	0.45	1.02	1.70	0.32
Miscellaneous household equipment	0.38	0.81	0.58	0.73	2.14	0.26
Other apparel products and services	0.77	0.85	0.43	0.94	2.28	0.35
Other entertainment supplies, equipment, and services	0.13	0.43	0.55	0.43	1.64	0.17
Other household expenses	0.46	0.96	1.11	0.51	2.64	0.31
Other vehicles	0.18	0.23	0.06	0.11	0.91	0.07
Personal care products and services	0.85	0.87	0.77	0.88	1.55	0.41
Personal services	0.78	1.50	0.62	1.12	1.99	0.32
Pets, toys, hobbies, and playground equipment	0.29	0.41	0.48	0.60	1.55	0.33
Postage and stationery	0.60	0.90	0.95	0.58	1.85	0.44
Reading	0.38	0.86	1.15	0.38	2.49	0.39
Television, radios, and sound equipment	0.82	1.01	0.65	0.82	1.37	0.45
Tobacco products and smoking supplies	0.67	0.36	0.46	0.51	0.43	0.74
Women and girls (apparel)	0.89	0.97	0.53	0.77	1.56	0.39

[a]Black/non-black
[b]Asian/all
[c]Over 65/under 65
[d]Hispanic/non-Hispanic
[e]College educated/non-college educated
[f]Household income < $20,000/household income ≥ $20,000

(50 percent); alcoholic beverages (34 percent); reading materials (38 percent); and new cars (42 percent).[11]

Other columns reveal similar differences in relative preferences between groups and their complements. For example, Asian households outspend non-Asian households on new cars (132 percent), fish and seafood (232 percent), and fruits and vegetables (155 percent). Asians spend about one-third as much as non-Asians on tobacco products.

The old outspend the young by more than double on drugs and medical supplies (at drugstores). Similarly, the old outspend the young by 73 percent on health care. On the other hand, the old spend much less than the young on clothing and footwear.

Hispanic and non-Hispanic households also spend differently. While Hispanic households spend 12 percent less than non-Hispanic households overall, Hispanic households outspend non-Hispanics on clothing for children under age two (203 percent), fish and seafood (128 percent), footwear (134 percent), fruits and vegetables (131 percent), and meat and poultry (139 percent). By contrast, Hispanic households spend much less than others on tobacco (51 percent); pets, toys, hobbies, and playground equipment (60 percent); and reading materials (38 percent).

College-educated households outspend their less-educated counterparts more than three to one on fees and admissions and floor coverings and more than double on furniture, reading materials, and various other household expenditures.

Low-income households (with household income under $20,000) spend about two-thirds less than others overall and outspend higher-income households in no category. Still, the low-income households' expenditures are relatively high on tobacco (74 percent).

Even with these data, it appears that preferences differ across groups. Each of the two-way comparisons leaves open a large possibility that the difference along the dimension of comparison actually reflects other causes. For example, some of the racial differences may reflect income rather than race. Whatever their cause, however, it is clear that persons in different groups by race and income tend to allocate their expenditures across categories differently. As a result, different groups benefit from the availability of establishments offering different products for sale.

We can summarize the differences between groups' preferences systematically. One measure is the Euclidean distance between groups' expendi-

11. Using data on consumption choices as measures of preference runs the risk of confusing supply with demand. That is, different groups' differing consumption patterns may arise, because the different groups have access to (live near stores offering) different products. In unpublished work on restaurant patronage in New York City, the large differences between black and white chain patronage patterns remain, even when controlling for individuals' zip codes of residence. This suggests different consumption choices among people facing the same options.

Table 6.4 **Preferences and segregation**

Group (complement)	Correlation of expenditures	Euclidean distance	Duncan dissimilarity index
Black	0.940	0.070	0.617
Hispanic	0.952	0.065	0.595
College educated	0.971	0.048	0.309
Asian	0.974	0.047	0.535
Over 65	0.834	0.130	0.171
Low income	0.934	0.080	0.256

ture shares. Define p_i^k as the share of group *i*'s expenditure on good *k*. The distance between groups *k* and *j* is then $\sum_{i=1}^{N}(p_i^k - p_i^j)^2$, which is bounded between 0 and 1. Alternatively, we can calculate the correlation between groups' expenditure share vectors. Table 6.4 reports these measures for groups (such as blacks, Asians, etc.) and their complements (non-blacks, non-Asians, etc.)

By both of these measures, the old (over age sixty-five) and the young have the most dissimilar preferences, followed by the low household income (under $25,000) and higher income and then by blacks and Hispanics and their respective complements. Asians and non-Asians—and college-educated and non-college educated persons—have more similar preferences.

Using expenditure data as an indicator of preferences runs the risk of confusing what's available with what people actually want. People can more easily purchase what is available near them. Hence, their expenditure on items available nearby may increase mechanically with supply driving demand rather than the other way around. One response to this concern is independent evidence showing that items with high expenditure shares for a particular group are important to the group. The independent evidence might be of a historical or cultural nature for, say, food preferences by ethnic group. Or, it might relate to other features of group differences. (For example, do older people spend more on health care? If so, it would presumably be driven by heightened medical need rather than, say, proximity to doctors offices.)

Here, we see that older persons outspend younger persons on health care. Lower-income groups also spend relatively more on inferior goods (e.g., used cars as opposed to new), and higher-income college-educated persons outspend others on luxuries, such as fees and admissions. These patterns that are reflective of prior ideas about who wants what lend support to the idea that the direction of causality runs from consumer preferences to patterns of product availability rather than the other way around.

6.3.2 The Size of the Relevant Market

We treat population as a rudimentary measure of demand, and we ask how the number of establishments operating in a category relates to population. The question is, what is the right level of geographic aggregation? Introspection suggests that the overwhelming majority of demand for, say, a typical restaurant in a large area is drawn from persons in that area. Three-digit zip codes contain an average (median) of 323,400 (200,000) persons and average 3,200 square miles. If they were circular, their radii would average twenty-seven miles. To the extent that population measures demand, the demand measure in the three-digit zip code regression is essentially measured without error. Hence, this regression of outlets on population gives an accurate estimate of the number of additional outlets that an additional person (or million persons) attracts. Call the coefficient on population β^3. Now, imagine examining the same relationship—between population and establishments—at finer levels of geographic disaggregation. At some level, the catchment area will be too small to support local supply. At that level, local population will become an erroneous measure of demand. Regressions of establishments on population will therefore yield β coefficients biased toward zero. To determine whether five-digit zip codes are a reasonable measure of the market area, we compare the coefficients from regressions of three-digit and five-digit zip code areas. Table 6.5 reports β^3 and β^5 as well as the ratio β^5/β^3. If the five-digit area is not too small, then the ratio will be close to 1. Inspection of table 6.1 shows that most of these ratios are close to 1. The two categories with the lowest estimates of β^5/β^3 are fruits and vegetables and fish and seafood, which—see table 6.1—are the least prevalent categories included in the study. We retain these as separate categories for two reasons. First, while lower than other categories' β^5/β^3 estimates, at roughly 0.85, they are still both absolutely rather close to 1. Second, these categories have large group differences in apparent preferences.

That the vast majority of the estimates of β^3 are similar to the estimates of β^5 provide some evidence that five-digit zip codes, in addition to being conveniently available, are also a reasonable geographic area for analysis.

6.3.3 Demand and Entry

One feature of table 6.5 that is difficult to miss is the uniformly positive relationship of the number of outlets in the zip code to demand. Similar patterns arise when the presence as opposed to the number of outlets serves as the dependent variable. This is, of course, not surprising, in light of both common sense and the industrial organization literature on entry.[12] Still, its meaning for us is that places with more people are more likely to have outlets nearby—and outlets in more categories—so that in general, additional people provide each other a benefit in helping to bring forth more nearby product outlets. But as the evidence of table 6.3 indicates, different people make use of different products, so people really only benefit from products they value.

12. See Bresnahan and Reiss (1990) or Berry (1992) for early studies. See Seim (2006) for recent work that takes location seriously.

Table 6.5 **Population and entry, five- and three-digit zip codes**

Modified CEX category	Five-digit zip code population	Standard error	Three-digit zip code population	Standard error	β^5/β^3
Alcoholic beverages	93.55	0.63	95.74	2.38	0.98
Apparel and services	68.23	0.83	67.75	1.36	1.01
Bakery products	20.99	0.21	20.66	0.47	1.02
Cars and trucks, new	74.91	0.75	56.12	1.28	1.33
Cars and trucks, used	74.64	0.71	56.84	1.49	1.31
Children under two (apparel)	21.47	0.30	23.44	0.48	0.92
Drugstores	132.76	0.83	130.63	2.13	1.02
Fees and admissions	188.22	1.08	177.55	2.78	1.06
Fish and seafood	7.28	0.13	8.38	0.37	0.87
Floor coverings	51.57	0.45	46.32	0.80	1.11
Food at home	314.96	1.35	347.88	5.10	0.91
Food away from home	1,481.21	7.57	1,540.09	21.37	0.96
Footwear	116.36	1.10	109.14	1.69	1.07
Fruits and vegetables	13.31	0.20	15.87	0.67	0.84
Fuel oil and other fuels	9.55	0.25	8.08	1.05	1.18
Furniture	101.40	0.82	96.97	1.32	1.05
Gasoline and motor oil	307.48	1.61	264.22	5.27	1.16
Health care	1,565.14	10.75	1,606.53	20.79	0.97
Household textiles	8.70	0.13	9.34	0.22	0.93
Maintenance and repairs	676.79	3.36	615.01	6.16	1.10
Major appliances	30.66	0.31	22.18	0.48	1.38
Meat and poultry	24.05	0.27	28.96	0.88	0.83
Men and boys (apparel)	39.50	0.52	44.12	1.06	0.90
Miscellaneous household equipment	111.90	0.74	110.85	1.59	1.01
Other apparel products and services	253.02	2.01	277.08	4.85	0.91
Other entertainment supplies, equipment, and services	130.97	1.11	126.02	2.85	1.04
Other household expenses	40.93	0.36	42.25	0.70	0.97
Other vehicles	17.61	0.24	12.68	0.41	1.39
Personal care products and services	339.92	1.96	347.32	6.06	0.98
Personal services	213.44	0.98	203.51	2.80	1.05
Pets, toys, hobbies, and playground equipment	92.67	0.67	88.06	1.53	1.05
Postage and stationery	30.87	0.30	30.27	0.54	1.02
Reading	47.03	0.49	47.47	1.45	0.99
Television, radios, and sound equipment	104.75	0.74	99.84	1.35	1.05
Tobacco products and smoking supplies	19.17	0.23	18.82	0.53	1.02
Women and girls (apparel)	127.72	1.38	138.27	2.73	0.92

We have two measures of outlet availability, whether the zip code contains an outlet in the category and how many outlets. Both provide a measure of outlet availability; with the number of outlets, larger numbers suggest more outlets nearby.

Table 6.6 revisits the relationship between establishments and demand, dividing population into blacks and others (succinctly but inaccurately labeled "whites"). In each half of the table, each row represents a regression

Table 6.6 **Entry and group population by race**

Modified CEX category	No controls				With controls			
	Black	Standard error	Non-black	Standard error	Black	Standard error	Non-black	Standard error
Alcoholic beverages	132.22	2.11	86.43	0.72	94.65	2.60	68.49	1.14
Apparel and services	21.09	2.81	76.91	0.97	15.37	2.06	53.82	1.49
Bakery products	9.71	0.72	23.07	0.25	4.84	0.49	16.31	0.42
Cars and trucks, new	26.44	2.52	83.84	0.86	20.37	1.94	61.11	1.32
Cars and trucks, used	64.83	2.42	76.45	0.83	27.38	1.73	65.55	2.12
Children under two (apparel)	8.01	1.02	23.95	0.35	13.58	1.73	31.84	0.95
Drugstores	137.27	2.81	131.93	0.96	62.16	1.86	77.89	1.13
Fees and admissions	10.66	3.51	220.92	1.21	53.12	4.28	222.60	2.39
Fish and seafood	17.52	0.45	5.39	0.15	9.89	0.76	9.65	0.55
Floor coverings	12.43	1.5	58.77	0.52	13.99	1.37	47.77	0.90
Food at home	455.5	4.52	289.08	1.55	202.92	3.49	185.97	1.95
Food away from home	633.28	25.17	1,637.35	8.64	450.99	20.08	1,271.08	14.72
Footwear	85.95	3.75	121.96	1.29	66.83	3.79	92.21	2.12
Fruits and vegetables	13.08	0.67	13.35	0.23	29.77	2.11	54.26	2.22
Fuel oil and other fuels	3.17	0.86	10.73	0.29	4.66	1.05	11.40	0.78
Furniture	61.02	2.78	108.83	0.95	43.52	2.34	78.31	1.48
Gasoline and motor oil	256.12	5.47	316.94	1.88	163.51	4.88	243.25	3.99
Health care	464.98	35.87	1,767.71	12.31	549.14	36.37	1,533.58	21.61
Household textiles	–0.56	0.45	10.41	0.16	0.47	0.59	11.51	0.35

Maintenance and repairs	466.26	11.35	715.56	3.89	336.79	11.81	679.53	11.87
Major appliances	4.18	1.04	35.54	0.36	1.73	0.55	21.13	0.47
Meat and poultry	30.22	0.92	22.92	0.31	20.01	1.17	30.87	1.14
Men and boys	35.33	1.75	40.27	0.6	22.87	1.65	32.12	0.99
Miscellaneous household equipment	12.42	2.45	130.21	0.84	24.03	2.46	116.56	1.57
Other apparel products and services	154.09	6.81	271.24	2.34	178.88	8.77	260.17	4.56
Other entertainment supplies, equipment, and services	–9.97	3.67	156.93	1.26	7.01	3.81	144.11	2.40
Other household expenses	23.65	1.22	44.11	0.42	18.18	1.14	35.31	0.75
Other vehicles	3.23	0.81	20.26	0.28	1.40	0.46	12.80	0.39
Personal care products and services	81.03	6.48	387.59	2.22	140.55	7.91	401.70	4.40
Personal services	295.86	3.28	198.26	1.13	376.77	6.66	214.01	2.36
Pets, toys, hobbies, and playground equipment	–7.79	2.18	111.17	0.75	15.24	3.42	135.51	1.89
Postage and stationery	5.59	1	35.53	0.34	8.45	1.06	31.34	0.67
Reading	16.56	1.67	52.64	0.57	12.93	1.38	40.99	0.99
Television, radios, and sound equipment	51.06	2.49	114.64	0.85	40.99	2.32	93.22	1.64
Tobacco products and smoking supplies	1.39	0.76	22.44	0.26	1.65	0.62	17.65	0.49
Women and girls	82.01	4.69	136.14	1.61	68.57	4.65	108.03	2.58

Notes: Regressions without controls are linear regressions of the number of establishments in the zip code on black and non-black population, respectively. Regressions with controls include zip code characteristics (income, age, education, and geographic size) entered multiplicatively.

of zip code entry in a category on population groups. Population is measured in millions, allowing the following interpretation of the no-controls specification in the first row. An additional million non-black persons bring forth 86 additional liquor stores, while an additional million blacks bring forth 132 additional liquor stores. In general, as with this first row, the non-black coefficients exceed the black coefficients. We expect this, given that whites have larger expenditures than blacks.

While the white coefficients are generally larger, the ratio of white to black coefficients is not constant. For example, some of the black coefficients (e.g., fish and seafood) are absolutely larger than white coefficients. Others are substantially lower (e.g., pets, toys, etc).

The regressions in the first half of table 6.6 are very parsimonious. The goal of the regressions is to determine what is experienced in zip codes that differ in their mix of, say, blacks and others. As an alternative strategy, we can add observables to the regression to control for the differences between, say, blacks and whites relevant to entry. Our goal is to determine whether entry patterns are responsive to preferences. If blacks were poor, then the mix of establishments could differ across neighborhoods simply because of differences in income rather than differences in preferences distinct from income. To address this—at least through observables—we repeat the exercises in table 6.6, adding zip code-level controls for education, income, age, and land area of the zip code.

Our basic notion is that entry is responsive to market size, and the basic measure of market size is population. We allow the other variables to enter multiplicatively via the following specification:

$$N_z = (\alpha_0 + \alpha_1 \, \text{bpop}_z + \alpha_2 \, \text{wpop}_z) \times \exp(\beta_1 \, \%\text{lowinc}_z + \beta_2 \%\text{college}_z + \beta_3 \%\text{old}_z + \beta_4 \, \text{sq\_miles}) + \varepsilon_z.$$

The latter half of table 6.6 reports partial results, the coefficients on black and white population. As before, entry depends—possibly—differently on black and non-black population. But here, variables like the share of households in the zip code with low income enter multiplicatively via the exponential function. If the black coefficient in the basic entry equations is lower simply because heavily black zip codes tend to be poor, then controlling for income directly lessens the effect of, say, income that is measure through race.

When we do this, the multiplicative controls are generally significant, often with economic importance. However, the resulting linear coefficients on black and white population are quite similar to the coefficients in the raw equation. If we create vectors of ratios of black/white coefficients across categories, the correlation of these vectors across the raw and with-controls equation is 0.78. Because the demographic controls do not change the results, we proceed with the parsimonious specifications in what follows.

Because blacks, Hispanics, and Asians are concentrated in particular regions, we also estimated these models with Metropolitan Statistical Area (MSA) fixed effects. To avoid the possibility that the coefficients on these groups are picking up features of the areas where they live, we ran regressions including just MSA zip codes in the sample and including MSA fixed effects as regressors, with nearly identical results.

We repeat the exercise of the first half of table 6.6 for five additional breakdowns: Asians versus non-Asians, people under age sixty-five and those over age sixty-five, Hispanic status, college educated by non-college educated, and low versus high income. While these regressions produce too many numbers to easily examine directly, they reveal some interesting patterns. For example, the Asian coefficients on food away from home, fruits and vegetables, and fish and seafood far exceed the non-Asian coefficients. The over age sixty-five coefficients for health care, alcoholic beverages, drugstores, fees and admissions, and food away from home far exceed younger persons' coefficients.

Finally, we also estimated each of the models previously described using the binary dependent variable indicating the presence of a category outlet in the zip code (as opposed to the number of establishments). For economy of exposition, they are not reported, but the results from these regressions will be incorporated next.

6.3.4 Is Entry Sensitive to Preferences?

It is clear from the evidence like that in table 6.6 that entry patterns vary across zip codes with different mixes of population by age, race, and so on. The question of interest to us is whether entry is sensitive to preferences. That is, in places with large agglomerations of blacks, college-educated persons, or so forth, do the agglomerating groups get access to more of the products they prefer? We examine this by comparing our crude measure of relative preferences (relative expenditure) to a simple measure of relative entry sensitivity. To be clear, we measure *relative preference* as the ratio of a group's average household expenditure on this category to the average household category expenditure of the group's complement. We measure *relative entry sensitivity* as the ratio of the group's entry coefficient to the entry coefficient for the group's complement. Here, we have two possible measures of entry sensitivity based on numbers of outlets and on whether an outlet exists. We use the term *relative presence sensitivity* as opposed to *relative entry sensitivity* for the latter.

Figures 6.2 through 6.7 show how relative preferences relate to relative entry sensitivity, and figures 6.8 through 6.13 relate relative preferences to relative presence sensitivity. Many of these figures depict an unmistakably positive relationship. Table 6.7 reports measures of association between relative preferences and relative entry (and presence) sensitivity for each pair of groups. We report both the correlation and the Spearman rank correlation. Ranks are attractive, because the cardinal value of the relative

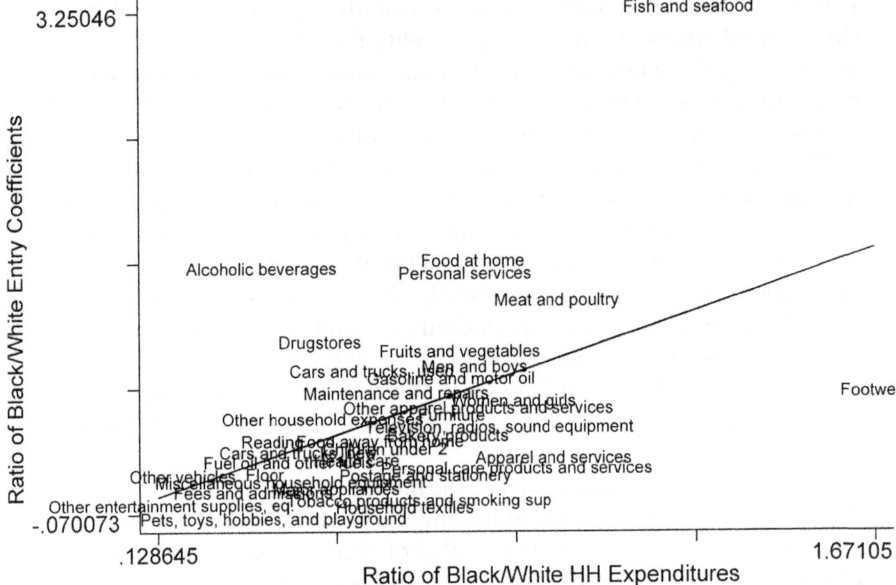

Fig. 6.2 Relative entry versus relative preference

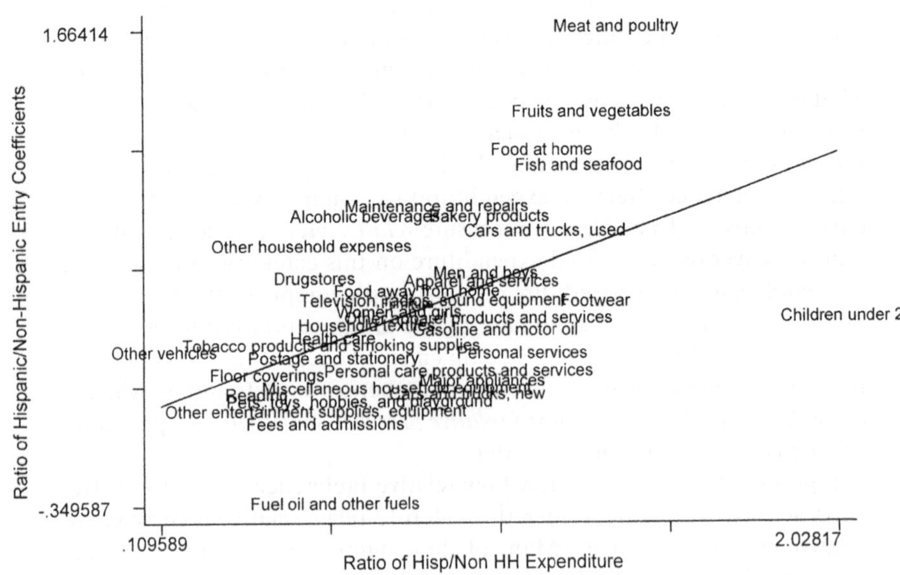

Fig. 6.3 Relative entry versus relative preference

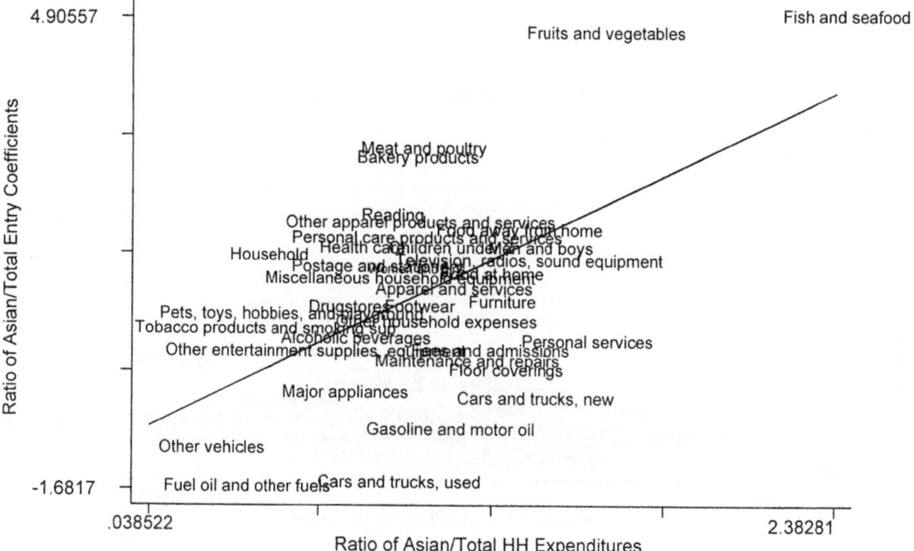

Fig. 6.4 Relative entry versus relative preference

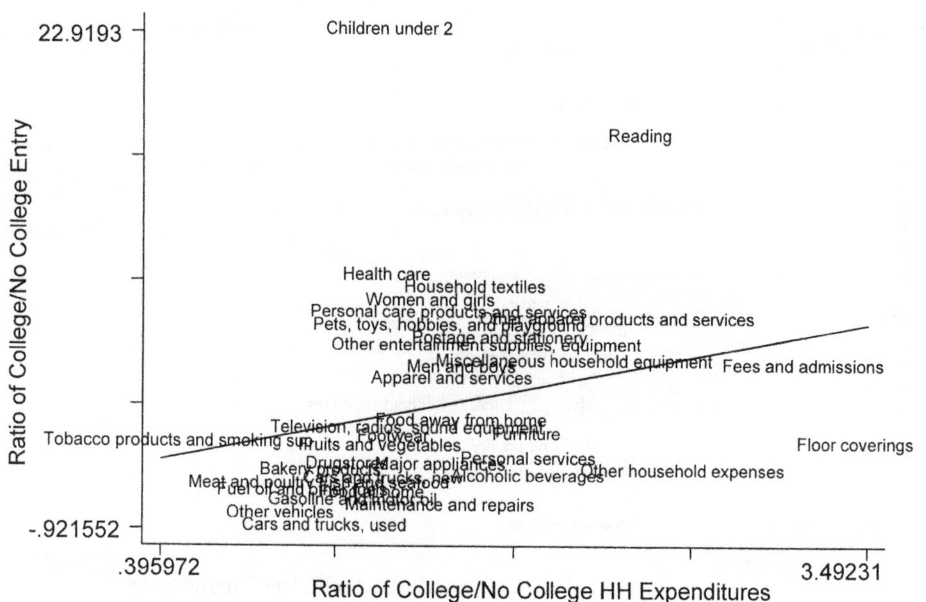

Fig. 6.5 Relative entry versus relative preference

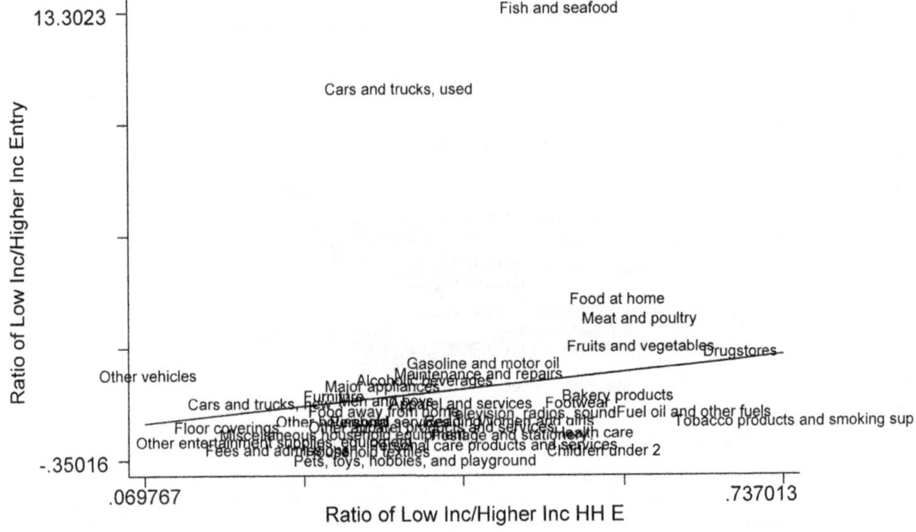

Fig. 6.6 **Relative entry versus relative preference**

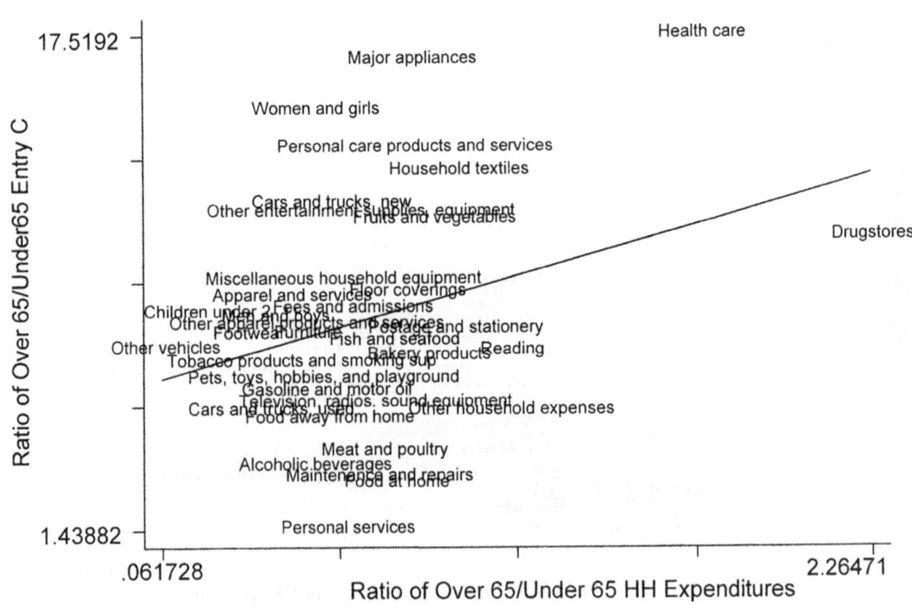

Fig. 6.7 **Relative entry versus relative preference**

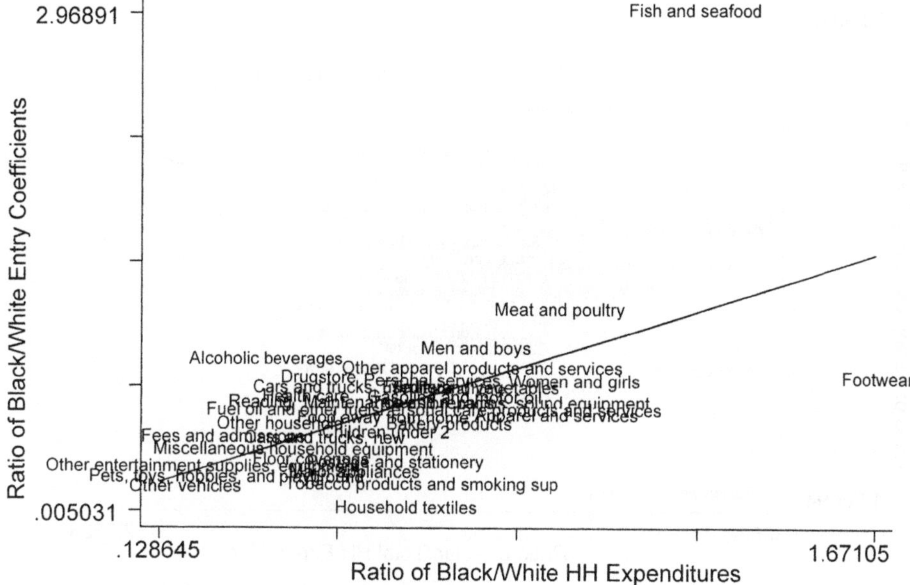

Fig. 6.8 Relative presence versus relative preference

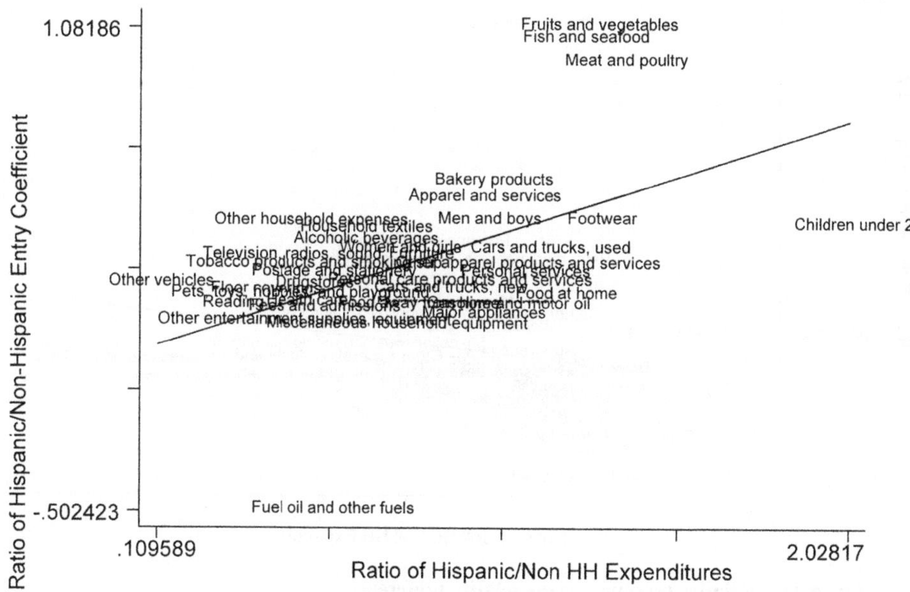

Fig. 6.9 Relative presence versus relative preference

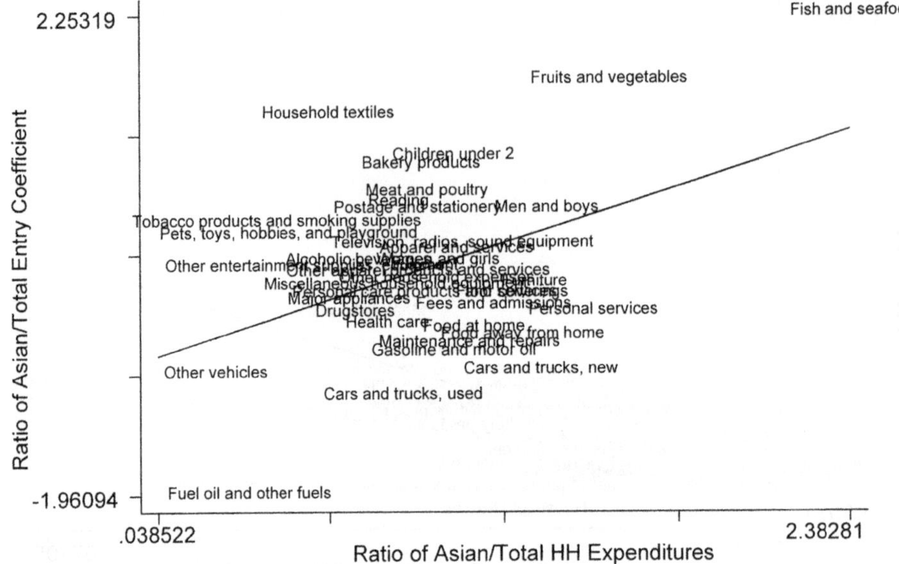

Fig. 6.10 Relative presence versus relative preference

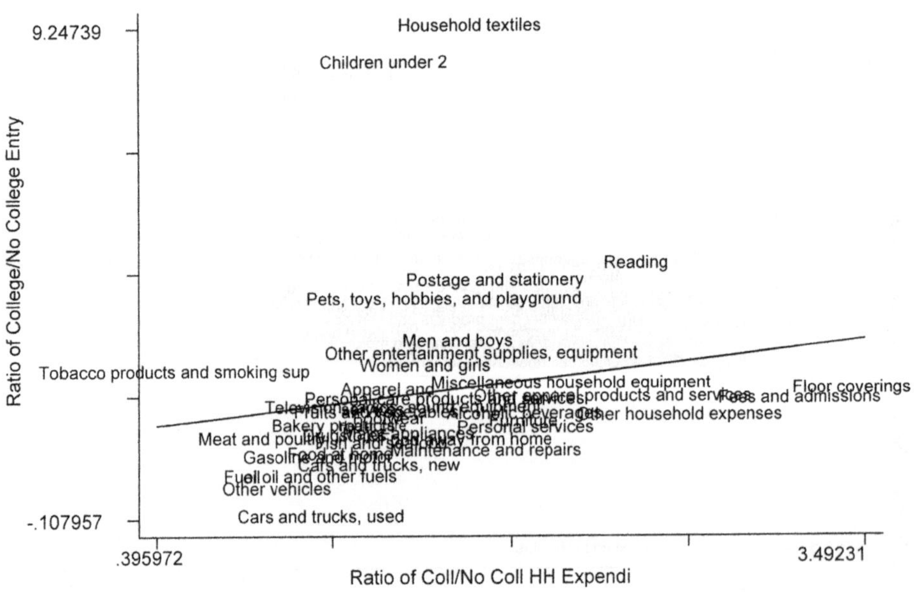

Fig. 6.11 Relative presence versus relative preference

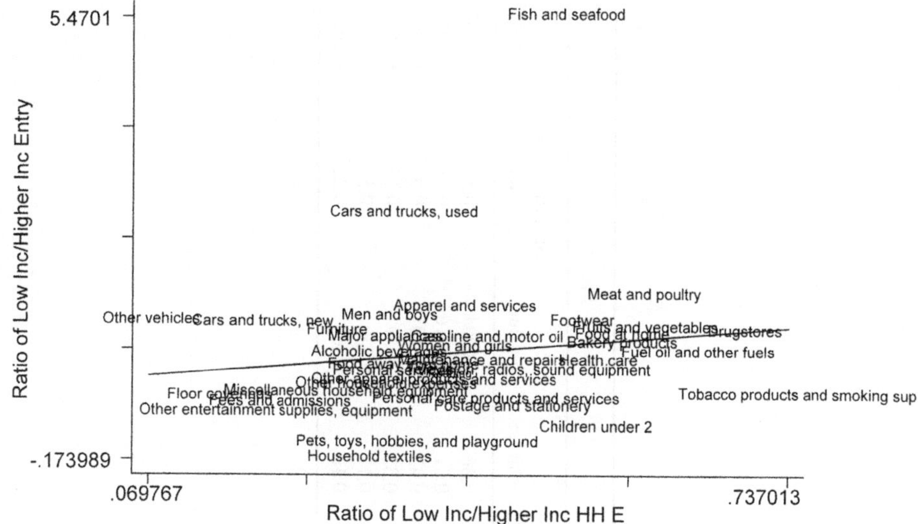

Fig. 6.12 Relative presence versus relative preference

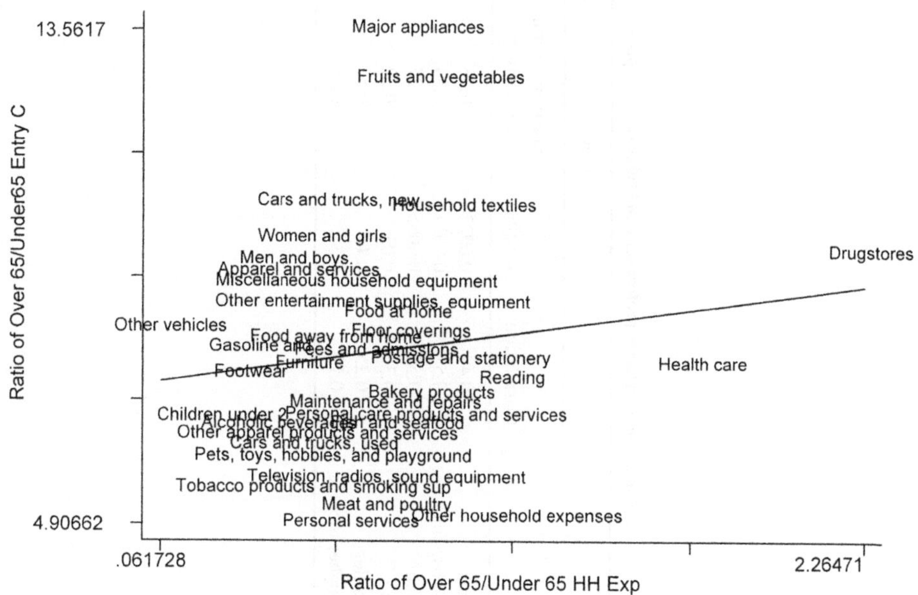

Fig. 6.13 Relative presence versus relative preference

Table 6.7 **Correlation of relative preferences and relative entry/presence sensitivity**

	Entry				Presence			
	Correlation	*p*-value	Spearman rank correlation	*p*-value	Correlation	*p*-value	Spearman rank correlation	*p*-value
Black/non-black	0.49	0.0022	0.53	0.0004	0.56	0.0004	0.59	0.0002
Hispanic/non-Hispanic	0.51	0.0017	0.54	0.0006	0.51	0.0016	0.51	0.001
Asian/non-Asian	0.55	0.0005	0.27	0.114	0.42	0.010	0.08	0.083
Over 65/under 65	0.36	0.03	0.22	0.219	0.32	0.059	0.19	0.269
College/non-college	0.25	0.14	0.51	0.0015	0.17	0.330	0.52	0.001
Low income/higher income	0.17	0.31	0.28	0.101	0.16	0.363	0.22	0.192

entry sensitivity measure (constructed from the ratio of regression coefficients) is somewhat sensitive to small (and sometimes negative) coefficient estimates.

Regardless of the measures used, there are statistically significant relationships between what's available and what's desired for blacks and Hispanics. Across other dimensions, the relationships are less clear. Two of four correlation measures are significant for age and college education. None are significant by income.

6.4 Conclusion

In a context with highly aggregated expenditure patterns—and therefore one biased against revealing effects—we document a sensitivity of the nearby availability of products to preferences, measured along multiple dimensions. This evidence indicates that agglomeration rewards members of agglomerating groups via the availability of products in the local market. This in turn may provide part of the explanation for residential segregation. To be sure, our mechanism of product availability is no more than part of the answer. Schools and other publicly provided amenities certainly loom large. But the evidence in this chapter shows that the economics of retail distribution in the presence of substantial fixed costs too may help explain who lives with whom.

Residential segregation by race rose over time in the United States until the 1960s and today stands nearly at its peak. Using zip codes as the unit of analysis, the Duncan "dissimilarity index" (Duncan and Duncan 1955) of black/non-black dissimilarity for 2000 was 0.62, meaning that 62 percent of blacks would have to move in order for the share of the black population to be equal across zip codes. Interestingly, the index is not only high for blacks compared to non-blacks; it is similarly high for Hispanics versus non-Hispanics (0.60) and for Asians versus non-Asians (0.54). Along other dimensions also explored in this chapter, the index is smaller: college versus non-college educated (0.31), over age sixty-five versus under age sixty-five (0.17), and household income below $25,000 (0.26). While we provide no evidence that product availability causes residential segregation patterns, it is nevertheless interesting that the groups whose sorting seems most demonstrably to produce targeted entry are the most segregated.

Public economists typically think of government-provided goods such as schools and police services as the determinants of residential sorting. Another strand of literature has people choosing neighborhoods on the basis of housing, and some more recent work has individuals choosing neighborhoods based on peers. All of these factors are likely to be important. But goods provided through private markets are important as well.

To the extent that goods and services provided by local governments determine the nature of neighborhoods, individuals can be thought to find communities appropriate to their preferences by finding jurisdictions where the median voter shares their preferences over government-provided goods. The market-provided goods discussed in this chapter suggest that in their quest for satisfaction, consumers need to agglomerate with consumers as well as citizens who share their preferences.

The ideas explored in this chapter have additional implications that would be useful to pursue in subsequent research. First, it is important to note that this chapter provides only a first step toward assessing the impact of private goods and the tendency to agglomerate. That is, we show that persons of similar preferences who agglomerate experience greater availability of goods targeted to their tastes. While we provide evidence that such agglomeration rewards like-minded agglomerators, we provide no direct evidence that this mechanism *causes* the agglomeration. Second, the idea that agglomeration benefits consumers through supply-side nonconvexities suggests a possibility of nonlinear effects of group size on welfare. That is, if an important good or service is produced with fixed costs, then it will be available when a group's local population passes a threshold, suggesting that subsequent work on agglomeration may focus on tipping and discontinuities. Of course, the threshold differs across goods and services due to different minimum scales, so such effects may be difficult to identify.

Appendix

CEX-NAICS Mapping

NAICS	NAICS category name	CEX category
441110	New car dealers	Cars and trucks, new
441120	Used car dealers	Cars and trucks, used
441210	Recreational vehicle dealers	Other entertainment supplies, equipment, and services
441221	Motorcycle dealers	Other vehicles
441222	Boat dealers	Other entertainment supplies, equipment, and services
441229	All other motor vehicle dealers	Other vehicles
441310	Automotive parts, accessories, and tire stores	Maintenance and repairs
441320	Tire dealers	Maintenance and repairs
442110	Furniture stores	Furniture
442210	Floor covering stores	Floor coverings
442291	Window treatment stores	Household textiles
443111	Household appliance stores	Major appliances
443112	Radio, television, and other electronics stores	Television, radios, sound equipment
443120	Computer and software stores	Miscellaneous household equipment

NAICS	NAICS category name	CEX category
443130	Camera and photographic supplies stores	Other entertainment supplies, equipment, and services
445110	Grocery (except convenience) stores	Food at home
445120	Convenience stores	Food at home
445210	Meat markets	Beef
445210	Meat markets	Other meats
445210	Meat markets	Pork
445210	Meat markets	Poultry
445220	Fish and seafood markets	Fish and seafood
445230	Fruit and vegetable markets	Fruits and vegetables
445291	Baked goods stores	Bakery products
445310	Beer, wine, and liquor stores	Alcoholic beverages
446110	Pharmacies and drug stores	Drugs
446110	Pharmacies and drug stores	Medical supplies
446120	Cosmetics, beauty supplies, and perfume stores	Personal care products and services
447110	Gasoline stations with convenience stores	Gasoline and motor oil
447190	Other gasoline stations	Gasoline and motor oil
448110	Men's clothing stores	Men and boys
448120	Women's clothing stores	Women and girls
448130	Children's and infants' clothing stores	Children under two
448140	Family clothing stores	Apparel and services
448190	Other clothing stores	Other apparel products and services
448210	Shoe stores	Footwear
448310	Jewelry stores	Other apparel products and services
451110	Sporting goods stores	Other entertainment supplies, equipment, and services
451120	Hobby, toy, and game stores	Pets, toys, hobbies, and playground equipment
451211	Book stores	Reading
451212	News dealers and newsstands	Reading
451220	Prerecorded tape, CD, and record stores	Television, radios, sound equipment
453110	Florists	Miscellaneous household equipment
453210	Office supplies and stationery stores	Postage and stationery
453910	Pet and pet supplies stores	Pets, toys, hobbies, and playground equipment
453991	Tobacco stores	Tobacco products and smoking supplies
454311	Heating oil dealers	Fuel oil and other fuels
512131	Motion picture theaters (except drive-ins)	Fees and admissions
512132	Drive-in motion picture theaters	Fees and admissions
532230	Video tape and disc rental	Fees and admissions
621111	Offices of physicians (except mental health)	Health care
621112	Offices of physicians, mental health	Health care
621210	Offices of dentists	Health care

(*continued*)

NAICS	NAICS category name	CEX category
621310	Offices of chiropractors	Health care
621320	Offices of optometrists	Health care
621330	Offices of other mental health practitioners	Health care
621340	Offices of PT, OT, speech therapy, and audiology	Health care
621391	Offices of podiatrists	Health care
621399	Offices of all other miscellaneous health practitioners	Health care
621410	Family planning centers	Health care
621420	Outpatient mental health, substance abuse centers	Health care
621491	HMO medical centers	Health care
621492	Kidney dialysis centers	Health care
621493	Freestanding ambulatory surgery, emergency centers	Health care
621498	All other outpatient care centers	Health care
624410	Child day care services	Personal services
713110	Amusement and theme parks	Fees and admissions
713910	Golf courses and country clubs	Fees and admissions
713920	Skiing facilities	Fees and admissions
713930	Marinas	Other entertainment supplies, equipment, and services
713940	Fitness and recreational sports centers	Fees and admissions
713950	Bowling centers	Fees and admissions
722110	Full-service restaurants	Food away from home
722211	Limited-service restaurants	Food away from home
722212	Cafeterias	Food away from home
722213	Snack and nonalcoholic beverage bars	Food away from home
722330	Mobile food services	Food away from home
722410	Drinking places (alcoholic beverages)	Food away from home
811111	General automotive repair	Maintenance and repairs
811112	Automotive exhaust system repair	Maintenance and repairs
811113	Automotive transmission repair	Maintenance and repairs
811118	Other automotive mechanical and electrical R&M	Maintenance and repairs
811121	Automotive body, paint, and interior R&M	Maintenance and repairs
811122	Automotive glass replacement shops	Maintenance and repairs
811191	Automotive oil change and lubrication shops	Maintenance and repairs
811412	Appliance repair and maintenance	Other household expenses
811420	Reupholstery and furniture repair	Other household expenses
812111	Barber shops	Personal care products and services
812112	Beauty salons	Personal care products and services
812113	Nail salons	Personal care products and services
812320	Drycleaning and laundry services (except coin-operated)	Other apparel products and services
812910	Pet care (except veterinary) services	Pets, toys, hobbies, and playground equipment

NAICS	NAICS category name	CEX category
812921	Photofinishing laboratories (except one-hour)	Other entertainment supplies, equipment, and services
812922	One-hour photofinishing	Other entertainment supplies, equipment, and services

References

Berry, S. T. 1992. Estimation of a model of entry in the airline industry. *Econometrica* 60 (4): 889–917.

Bresnahan, T. F., and P. C. Reiss. 1990. Entry in monopoly markets. *Review of Economic Studies* 57 (4): 531–53.

———. 1991. Entry and competition in concentrated markets. *Journal of Political Economy* 99 (5): 977–1009.

Cutler, D., and E. Glaeser. 1997. Are ghettos good or bad? *Quarterly Journal of Economics* 112 (3): 827–72.

Cutler, D., E. Glaeser, and J. Vigdor. 1999. The rise and decline of the American ghetto. *Journal of Political Economy* 107 (3): 455–506.

Duncan, O., and B. Duncan. 1955. A methodological analysis of segregation indices. *American Sociological Review* 20 (2): 210–17.

Fujita, M., and J.-F. Thisse. 2002. *Economics of agglomeration.* Cambridge: Cambridge University Press.

Hotelling, H. 1929. Stability in competition. *Economic Journal* 39 (153): 41–57.

Massey, D., and N. Denton. 1988. The dimensions of residential segregation. *Social Forces* 67 (2): 281–315.

Seim, K. 2006. An empirical model of firm entry with endogenous product-type choices. *RAND Journal of Economics* 37 (3): 619–40.

Waldfogel, J. 2003. Preference externalities: An empirical study of who benefits whom in differentiated-product markets. *RAND Journal of Economics* 34 (3): 557–68.

———. 2004. Who benefits whom in local television markets? In *Brookings-Wharton papers on urban affairs: 2004,* ed. J. R. Pack and W. G. Gale. Washington, DC: Brookings Institution Press.

———. 2008. The median voter and the median consumer: Local *private* goods and population composition. *Journal of Urban Economics* 63 (2): 567–82.

7

Understanding Agglomerations in Health Care

Katherine Baicker and Amitabh Chandra

7.1 Introduction

Understanding the drivers of productivity differences across areas is crucial to designing effective public policies to promote growth and efficient use of resources. Knowledge spillovers and economies of scale may be key causes of differences in productivity across space. The agglomeration economies literature explores the positive link between productivity and city size or density: cities, by virtue of their density, may facilitate the generation, transmission, and acquisition of new ideas. This is the Marshallian notion of "knowledge spillovers," where one's neighbors influence one's adoption of new technologies so that cities should be more productive places. Most of this research, however, focuses on aggregate productivity measures, such as average income. These measures can be both crude and affected by common local factors, such as price levels, which makes it difficult to discern from them the mechanisms that drive productivity differences.

In this chapter, we explore the drivers of differences in medical sector productivity to understand agglomeration economies better—particularly, the role that information spillovers play in making some places more productive. The medical sector is one of the largest in the U.S. economy (comprising 17 percent of gross domestic product in 2008) and exhibits dramatic differences in productivity across space. The enormous variation in the quantity and

Katherine Baicker is professor of health economics at the Harvard School of Public Health and a research associate of the National Bureau of Economic Research. Amitabh Chandra is professor of public policy at the John F. Kennedy School of Government, Harvard University, and a faculty research fellow of the National Bureau of Economic Research.

Paper prepared for the NBER conference on Cities in February 2008. We have benefited from conversations with Ed Glaeser, Ashish Jha, and Jonathan Skinner and acknowledge research support from the Taubman Center at the Harvard Kennedy School.

quality of care received by patients in different geographic areas is not just due to different health insurance coverage or patient characteristics. Even within Medicare, the public insurance program for the elderly that provides relatively uniform incentives to providers and patients, there is enormous geographic variation in the use of productive and unproductive health care (Dartmouth Atlas Project). Some of this variation occurs at the level of hospital referral regions (HRRs), which are empirically defined markets for health care, but a large portion may occur within these regions. In Baicker and Chandra (2004a), we demonstrate that areas with the highest quality care are often not the areas that spend the most intensively on health care: in states where Medicare spends more on beneficiaries, they are less likely to receive high-quality care. Furthermore, it is not the case that areas that "do more" do more of everything. Rather, U.S. health care is characterized by variation in both the *overuse* of intensive, costly care that is often of dubious clinical benefit (Fisher et al. 2003a, 2003b) and the *underuse* of effective, high-quality care, such as the administration of beta-blockers after heart attacks, mammograms for older women, influenza vaccines, and eye exams for diabetics. These underused procedures are relatively inexpensive, are known to have significant medical benefits, and are rarely contraindicated. Whether cities are better are avoiding the problems of underuse and overuse in health care is not known. The combined evidence on the overuse of dubious care and the underuse of effective care strongly suggests the opportunity for productivity improvements in health care.

While ideally, all patients would receive the highest possible quality of care, in the presence of variation in care, there may be spillover benefits to any particular hospital providing higher-quality care: one hospital's investment in quality might drive learning across organizations, improving the quality of care provided in neighboring hospitals. By the same token, the use of financially lucrative interventions of dubious therapeutic value may diffuse through a similar process. Prior work in other industries suggests that organizations often learn from each other and that innovations at one company can drive similar innovations in its neighbors. While this potential learning mechanism has been found in many settings, however, it remains largely unexplored in understanding changes in health care quality. Whether that occurs in clinical care and whether high-performing hospitals drive improvements in care among neighbors is largely unknown.

Understanding the primary sources of variation in quality and the role that learning might play in driving improvements is critically important in developing effective public policies: policymakers will be best able to craft interventions that enhance the productivity of American health care spending if they understand the factors that cause some hospitals to lag behind and the channels through which they might catch up. For example, if the variation in care occurs primarily at the hospital level, understanding the degree to which hospital characteristics (such as teaching or profit status) affect the quality of care can help target interventions toward those organizations where improvements are most needed. If the variation is primarily regional, other approaches will be needed. Finally, understanding the role that learning plays can provide insight into policies that might optimize the quality of care delivered across an entire community: if quality enhancements at one hospital are adopted by others, then this positive externality might suggest that it would be optimal to subsidize the investment in quality. On the other hand, if utilization of more expensive but lower-value care also diffuses though a similar learning process, then policies might aim to discourage hospital investments in technologically intensive care of dubious value. In order to better understand the roles of variation and learning in the hospital setting, we seek to answer three questions. First, how much variation in hospital care (measured by both quality and the use of low-value care) is due to differences across regions versus differences within regions? Second, how much of the variation within and across regions can be explained by readily identifiable factors? And finally, what is the role of agglomeration in generating quality? Is there evidence that the quality of care in an institution is influenced by the care at neighboring institutions?

7.2 Background

There is a vast economic literature on diffusion of innovation (e.g., Jovanovic and Nyarko 1995, 1996); see Hall (2004) for a recent survey and synthesis. Nearly all of these economic models posit that diffusion evolves as a profit-maximizing strategy, such as because some producers are waiting for the price of the innovation to drop, or because they had invested in the previous technology, or because of capital-labor complementarity. For example, Zucker, Darby, and Brewer (1998) link the timing of entry and location of biotechnology firms to the presence of academics that publish in basic science journals, while Jaffe, Trajtenberg, and Henderson (1993) document that inventors tend to cite patents that were developed in the same geographic region. In medical care, there is a large literature on knowledge spillovers, beginning with Coleman, Katz, and Menzel (1957), who found that doctors who were more integrated with colleagues were the first to adopt a new drug.

In a world where the barriers to adoption are financial, individual health providers each make decisions about whether to adopt the new innovation. Their incentives to adopt the innovation depend critically on the nature of their own perceived production function—which in turn reflects how rapidly they themselves absorb new clinical evidence on treatments—and the financial structure and rewards of the innovation. When the innovation is both financially remunerative and perceived to be highly effective, the speed of adoption will be rapid; as, for example, the rapid diffusion of tetracycline in the 1950s, documented in the classic Coleman, Katz, and Mendel study (1957). If there are few economic incentives to adopt, as in the case of beta-blockers for the treatment of heart attacks, then diffusion will depend almost entirely on the extent to which individual perceptions of physicians change over time (Skinner and Staiger 2006). In other words, one needs to consider the convergence of physician-specific production functions $f_j(t)$, where t is time, toward the "true" production function f^*. This is similar to how diffusion is modeled in the sociological literature (Rogers 1995), where the emphasis is not on economic factors or profit maximizing but instead on a cultural or intrinsic inability to perceive the benefits of new technologies, despite evidence of their effectiveness. Parente and Prescott (1994) have focused on the importance of relatively minor differences in barriers to technology adoption in explaining differences in income growth across countries. This view emphasizes the view that cross-country differences in productivity arise from variation in technology adoption (Comin and Hobijn 2004).

There is certainly historical precedent for the inexplicably slow adoption of new medical innovations, and Donald Berwick (2003) has written a remarkable account of why this may be the case. In 1601, Captain James Lancaster administered lemon juice to the crew of just one of his fleet of four ships. Halfway through the trip, 40 percent of the sailors in the "control" ships had died of scurvy compared to no deaths in the "treatment" ship. Despite the strength of the evidence and affordability of the intervention, citrus fruits became required for British Navy sailors only in 1795, a mere 194 years after Lancaster's trial. Perhaps even more striking is Joseph Lister's recommendation that surgeons wash their hands, use gloves, and swab wounds with carbonic acid (Lister 1867). Lister acknowledged that his research was influenced by the Austrian physician Ignaz Semmelweis. Semmelweis demonstrated that maternal mortality from puerperal fever (an infection of the genital tract after giving birth) could be reduced from 12.2 percent to 2.4 percent by making physicians wash their hands with chlorinated lime between autopsy and obstetrical rotations. That Semmelweis did not "have a model" (which in medical parlance would correspond to a germ theory of disease to explain his results) is thought to have contributed to the medical establishment's reluctance to embrace his findings.

It is even more difficult to explain in standard economic models the lethargy with which some pernicious treatments are dropped: Heidenrich and McClellan (2001) found that a substantial fraction of the improvement in survival for heart attacks could be explained by the gradual decline in the use of lidocaine, a treatment that actually tended to increase mortality. More recently, a randomized control trial found that providing information to "opinion leaders" in a hospital resulted in large increases in the use of appropriate medications following heart attacks and decreases in the use of outdated therapies (Soumerai et al. 1998). There may also be heterogeneity in diffusion because of intrinsic differences in abilities of physicians (as in Jovanovich and Nyarko [1995, 1996]).

In summary, the adoption and use of health care innovations will be influenced by financial rewards, the perceived benefit from the innovation, and organizational structure. Low-value care of dubious clinical benefit may be adopted quickly if economic incentives encourage adoption. High-value treatment may not be adopted without financial incentives or if the efficacy of the treatment is difficult to observe. The sociological factors that moderate these channels may vary based on physician or hospital characteristics.

The degree to which different factors affect the level and diffusion of best and worst practices is an inherently empirical question. We turn next to the data that we will bring to bear in exploring the nature of variation in the utilization of high-quality and low-value care.

7.3 Data

Our analysis requires hospital-level measures of both high-quality and low-value care. Because we will be performing analysis at the hospital rather than patient level, it is important that we construct measures of each that are not contaminated by unobserved patient characteristics such as severity of illness—especially if those patient characteristics are likely to be correlated across hospitals within a geographic area.

To measure high-value health care, we use hospital compliance with a number of technical "process of care" measures. These measures use samples of patient discharge records for the treatment and capture interventions "for which there is strong scientific evidence and professional consensus that the process of care either directly improves outcomes or is a necessary step in a chain of care that does so," such as the prescription of warfarin for atrial fibrillation or biennial eye examination for diabetics (U.S. Department of Health and Human Services, Centers for Medicare and Medicaid Services; Jha et al. 2005). The advantage of these measures is that detailed risk adjustment (based on how sick a hospital's patient pool is) is not critical, as few patients are contraindicated for these procedures. The inability to perform high-quality risk adjustment at the hospital level is the principal reason that many other direct measures of quality, such as survival or the use of intensive interventions such as rescue angioplasty after a heart attack, are not utilized in this literature.

To construct a measure of the utilization of low-value care, we follow previous work that suggests that hospital expenditures on Medicare beneficiaries at the end of life can proxy for this high-intensity, low-benefit spending. These measures abstract from confounders such as unobserved illness by focusing on the set of patients who are terminally ill. Fisher et al. (2003a, 2003b) established that this end-of-life (EOL) spending is pervasive in areas that have a lot of beds, specialists, and health care facilities. They have also demonstrated that higher EOL spending does not improve patient outcomes or satisfaction. Finally, this work has shown a correlation between a hospital's EOL spending and its treatment of acute conditions such as hip fracture and acute myocardial infarction (AMI), suggesting that hospitals treat many different patients with similar intensity. We next describe both measures in greater detail.

7.3.1 Measuring High-Value Care

The Hospital Quality Alliance, a public-private collaboration between the Centers for Medicare and Medicaid Services (CMS) and several hospital organizations, began reporting individual hospitals' performance on select process-of-care measures through an on-line Web site, "*Hospital Compare,*" on April 1, 2005; See U.S. Department of Health and Human Services, CMS, and Jha et al. (2005) for details. These measures focus on three major conditions for which evidence-based treatments are supported by a solid body of evidence: acute myocardial infarction, pneumonia, and congestive heart failure (CHF). We analyzed data from 2004 to 2006, as 2004 is the first full year of reported data on these measures. We chose to retain only those measures for which a majority of hospitals reported at least twenty-five observations, a cutoff used in previous work to ensure sufficient statistical precision. Eleven process measures yielded at least twenty-five observations for a majority of hospitals: Aspirin at arrival and at discharge and beta-blocker prescription at arrival and at discharge (for AMI patients); assessment of left ventricular function, the provision of discharge instructions, and angiotensin-converting enzyme (ACE) inhibitor or angiotensin receptor blocker (ARB) prescription for patients with left ventricular systolic dysfunction (LVSD; for CHF patients); blood culture performed before receiving the first antibiotic in the hospital, first dose of antibiotics within four hours of admission, initial antibiotic selected appropriately, and assessment of arterial oxygenation within twenty-four hours of arrival (for pneumonia patients). We computed quality scores for 6,917 hospital-year observations.

To create condition-specific quality scores for AMI, pneumonia, and CHF, we used a common methodology prescribed by the Joint Commission, which suggests a summary score calculated as the sum of the number of times a hospital performed the appropriate action across all measures for that condition (numerator), divided by the number of "opportunities" the hospital had to provide appropriate care (denominator). Composite scores were only calculated if a hospital had at least twenty-five patients for at least one measure in that condition. We also calculated an overall quality measure that used information for all three clinical conditions by taking the mean of summary scores across conditions for each hospital. (As a specification test, we also used factor analysis to combine the three composite measures for each hospital, but the correlation between the factor index and the simple average was 0.98, so we used the average.) We thus have four measures of the quality of care: the condition-specific scores for AMI, pneumonia, and CHF patients, and the composite score that aggregates these three. The correlations between the condition-specific scores and the composite-quality score were 0.62 for heart attacks (AMI), 0.82 for congestive heart failure (CHF), and 0.77 for pneumonia. We focus primarily on the composite measure in our analysis, but results using the component measure are similar and are summarized next.

7.3.2 Measuring Low-Value Spending

Our measure of the use of high-intensity but low-value care is based on the intensity of inpatient care for Medicare beneficiaries in the six months preceding death (EOL). By focusing on variation in the treatment of patients with identical life expectancies, the EOL spending measure better reflects the portion of spending that is attributable to differences in practice patterns as opposed to differences in severity of illnesses. End-of-life expenditures have been shown to be highly correlated with both total Medicare spending and spending for specific disease cohorts. Another advantage of focusing on EOL spending is that the sample size is large enough to calculate measures at the hospital level.

To construct our measure of EOL spending, we used Medicare part A (hospital) and part B (outpatient) spending and utilization data for hospital and physician services for chronically ill Medicare beneficiaries who died during the years 1999 to 2003. At death, each of these patients was assigned to the hospital in which he or she had received the majority of care in the previous six months. All of the expenditure and utilization data from that patient's claims were then assigned to that hospital. The vast majority of patients' care occurred at the assigned hospital; the average percent of inpatient days spent at the assigned hospital was 89.6 percent. Spending data were adjusted for differences in age, sex, race, and the relative frequency of chronic illness among the beneficiaries studied.

7.3.3 Hospital and Area Characteristics

We linked the hospital-level quality and EOL data to the American Hospital Association Annual Survey Database that has information on each hospital's nurse-to-patient (Census) ratio, profit status (public, not for profit, for profit), membership in the Council of Teaching Hospitals, bed size, location (region, county, health referral region [described next], and urban versus rural), percentage of Medicare and Medicaid patients, and presence of a medical intensive care unit. Nurse/Census ratios were calculated by dividing the number of full-time equivalent nurses on staff by 1,000 patient days.

We used each hospital's county to link these data to area-level population characteristics from the U.S. Department of Health and Human Services, Health Resources and Services Administration Area Resource File. This data set contains information on residents' characteristics, such as education, race, income, and age. It also contains information on county-level health care providers, such as the number of physicians broken down by specialty practicing in the county.

7.3.4 Defining Geographic Areas

To construct local markets for health care, we adopt the methodology of the "Dartmouth Atlas of Health Care," which divides the United States into 306 hospital referral regions (HRRs) based on attributing zip codes to HRRs by the use of an algorithm reflecting commuting patterns and the location of major referral hospitals. The HRRs may cross state and county borders, because they are determined solely by migration patterns of patients. For example, the Evansville, Indiana HRR encompasses parts of three states, because it draws patients so heavily from Illinois and Kentucky. The HRRs are best viewed as the level at which tertiary services such as cardiac surgeries are received (although they are not necessarily the appropriate geographical level for primary care services).

Analysis at the HRR level is preferable to analysis at the city or state level, since it uses the empirical pattern of patient commuting to determine the geographic boundaries of each referral region rather than assuming that the arbitrary political boundaries of states and cities also define the level at which the health care is delivered. Furthermore, for the purpose of studying geographic productivity spillovers, an analysis at the HRR level is superior to one at the level of the individual hospital for two reasons. First, patients can be assigned to an HRR based on their residence rather than on the hospital at which they received treatment (which may be endogenous). In addition, productivity spillovers are likely to operate at a broader level than that of a given hospital; for example, these spillovers are expected to reach beyond the boundary of the firm to affect productivity at all firms in a region. Physicians often have operating privileges in multiple hospitals and interact (socially and professionally) with other doctors who may or may not practice in their hospital, and patients are commonly referred to other hospitals within the HRR for treatment. The HRR encompasses a physician's likely peers and a hospital's natural competitors.

7.4 Agglomerations in High-Value and Low-Value Care

In the two panels of figure 7.1, we illustrate the degree of variation at the hospital level in high-value, high-quality care (panel A) and in the intensity of end-of-life, low-value spending (panel B). In panel A, the quality measure used is the composite measure that puts equal weight on treatments for heart attacks, pneumonia, and congestive heart failure. In principal, this rate should ideally be close to 1 (100 percent) for all hospitals, as very few patients are contraindicated for the measures that comprise the quality index. Panel

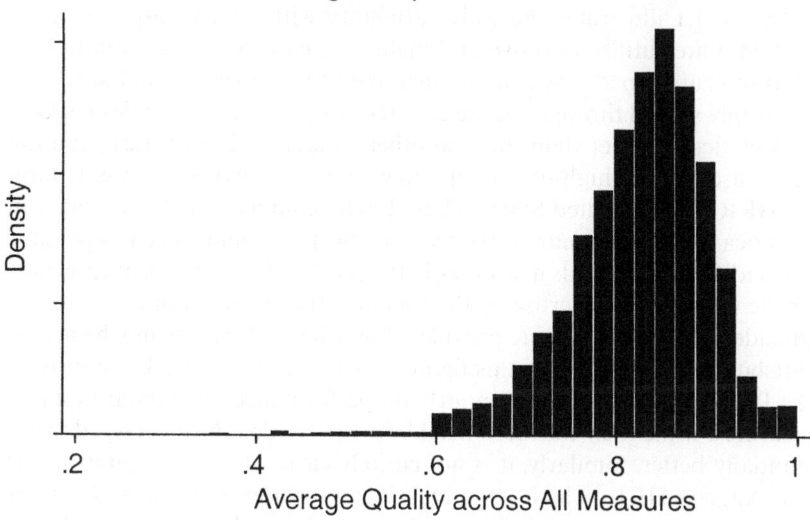

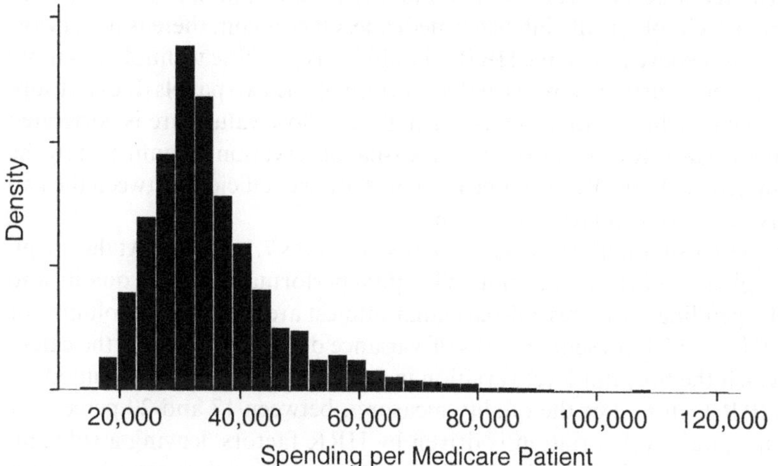

Fig. 7.1 Distribution of quality (panel A) and end-of-life spending (panel B) for Medicare patients in U.S. hospitals

Note: Quality measures refer to a composite measure of quality that puts equal weight on treatments for heart attacks, pneumonia, and congestive heart failure. Spending data is deflated to 2006 dollars.

B shows the roughly log-normal distribution of the use of technologically intensive, low-value EOL care across hospitals.

Figure 7.1 illustrates the wide variability with which hospitals in the United States utilize effective and ineffective care. This variation in hospital utilization patterns is not constrained to particular small areas nor uniformly spread throughout the country: hospitals in some cities perform systematically better than those in others. Figure 7.2 illustrates variation in the use of both high-quality and low-value care across the twenty largest HRRs in the United States. These HRRs comprise the largest cities in America—each has a number of teaching hospitals, and while it is possible that individual hospitals may differ in the severity of their patient caseloads or the managerial expertise of their administrators, it is not obvious why Philadelphia should ex ante provide a lower level of care than Chicago or Pittsburgh. As panel A of this figure illustrates, the hospitals comprising the Philadelphia HRR score poorly on performance on standard quality measures, while their northern neighbors in Camden, New Jersey, do substantially better. Similarly, it is not entirely clear why the hospitals in the Los Angeles HRR, which serve high-income patients and include places such as the University of California, Los Angeles, and Cedars Sinai, should perform so poorly relative to those next door in the Orange county HRR. In panel B of figure 7.2, we graph the analogous use of EOL spending across the twenty largest HRRs. There is similarly wide variation in the use of this form of technologically intensive medicine. Once again, there is no a priori reason to believe that some HRRs should be using these technologies more than others. Furthermore, casual inspection of the two panels does not support the conclusion that the use of high- and low-value care is correlated (either negatively or positively). This casual observation is confirmed by the estimated (statistically insignificant) correlation coefficient between the two measures across all HRRs of –0.06.

Table 7.1 summarizes the key insights of figures 7.1 and 7.2. At the hospital level, we report the variation in hospital performance on the quality and EOL spending measures. Of particular interest are the last two columns of this table, which present analysis of variance decompositions of the extent to which the hospital-level variation in figures 7.1 and 7.2 is accounted for by HRR factors. For the quality measures, between 17 and 20 percent of the hospital-level variation is driven by HRR factors, leaving a substantial amount of within variation. With EOL spending, the opposite is true: here, there is substantial between HRR variation in use, with HRR effects accounting for over 70 percent of the hospital variation. This is another way of saying that when it comes to EOL spending, hospitals in the same HRR practice a similar type of medicine, resulting in agglomerations of regions where intensive medicine is practiced. But when it comes to quality, there is much more disagreement between providers, even those who are within the same HRR. In the following analysis, we will estimate regression models to

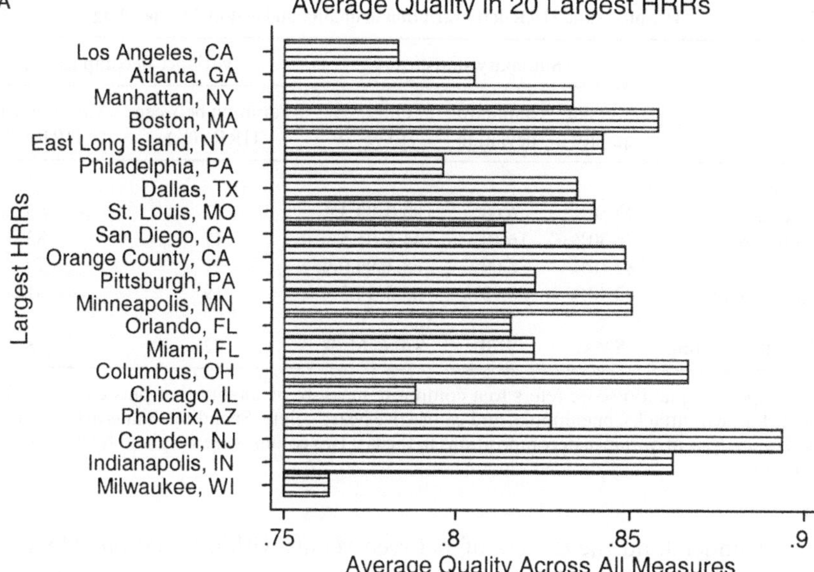

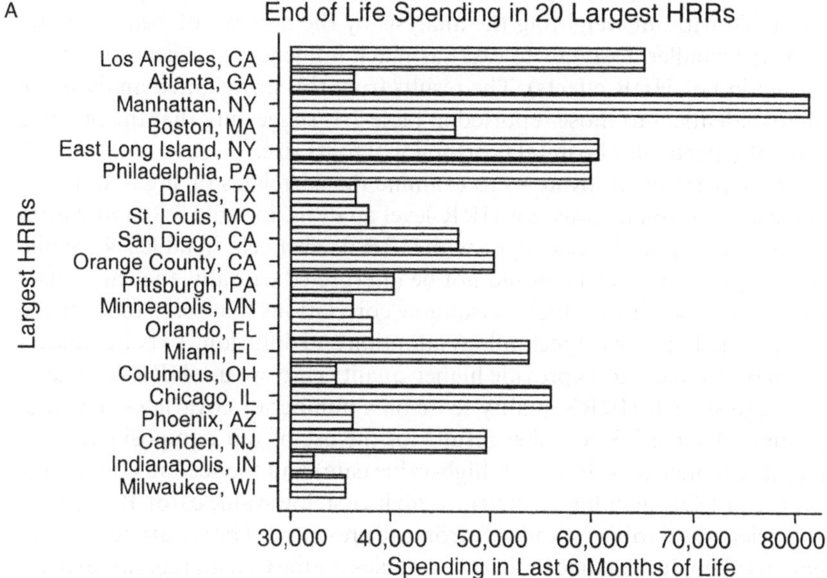

Fig. 7.2 Distribution of quality (panel A) and end-of-life spending (panel B) for Medicare patients in the largest twenty HRRs

Note: Quality measures refer to a composite measure of quality that puts equal weight on treatments for heart attacks, pneumonia, and congestive heart failure. Spending data is deflated to 2006 dollars.

Table 7.1 **Hospital- and HRR-level variation in quality and end-of-life spending**

	Summary statistics			Variance decomposition	
	Average quality	Standard deviation	Range (5% to 95%)	Variation between HRRs (%)	Variation within HRRs (%)
High-value care					
Heart attack	92.50%	6.60%	80.0–99.3%	17	83
Heart failure	75.30%	16.10%	44.4–95.5%	17	83
Pneumonia	82.10%	8.00%	68.3–94.0%	21	79
Composite score	82.40%	8.90%	66.5–94.3%	19	81
Low-value care					
End-of-life spending	$36k	$13k	$20.6–61.0k	72	28

Notes: Composite (quality) score refers to a composite measure of quality that puts equal weight on treatments for heart attacks, pneumonia, and congestive heart failure. Spending data is deflated to 2006 dollars. The analysis of variance decompositions in the last two columns are weighted by the number of hospital beds.

better understand the drivers of between versus within variation. Means and standard deviations for the variables that we use as regressors are shown in table 7.2. While not reported, we also performed the decompositions in this table without weighting the analysis by the number of beds (thereby allowing smaller hospitals to exert as much influence as larger ones in the estimation of HRR effects). The results from this unweighted analysis are almost identical to those reported in table 7.1, suggesting that the practice style of a particular hospital is orthogonal to its size.

These patterns motivate us to examine the correlates of high- and low-value care across regions (an HRR-level analysis, in table 7.3) and within regions (a hospital-level analysis with HRR fixed effects, in table 7.4). While these regression models should not be interpreted causally, they are a useful framework within which to examine correlations that serve to motivate more formal theories of technology adoption and diffusion. To better understand why some HRRs provide higher-quality care, we use HRR-level data and regress each HRR's quality score on a number of covariates. The first column of table 7.3 describes results for the use of our composite quality measure (a metric of low-cost, high-value care) and the second column for the use of EOL spending (a metric of high-cost, low-value care). Regression coefficients and robust standard errors are presented. The covariates that we have used (including nine indicator variables for the Census regions) explain only 30 percent of the between-HRR variation in quality but over 70 percent of the between-HRR variation in EOL spending. Because we have included Census region fixed effects, our results are not driven by explanations that are unique to states in New England or the South, for example. Holding the composition of the physician workforce (the mix of specialists and generalists) constant, adding one more physician to an HRR raises quality but also

Table 7.2 **Summary statistics**

	HRR-level data		Hospital-level data	
	Mean	Standard deviation	Mean	Standard deviation
Percent age > 65	0.13	0.03	0.15	0.06
Percent < high school	0.19	0.06	0.21	0.11
In largest 100 cities	0.16	0.27	0.18	0.38
Publicly owned	0.16	0.19	0.17	0.38
Teaching hospital	0.14	0.19	0.09	0.28
Log(beds)	7.48	0.84	5.02	0.92
RNs per capita	1.25	0.27	1.21	0.66
Percent black	0.09	0.10	0.10	0.15
Percent Medicaid	0.20	0.07	0.18	0.14
Per capita MDs	0.00	0.00	0.00	0.00
Percent specialists	0.57	0.14	0.58	0.14
Overall quality	0.84	0.04	0.82	0.09
EOL spending	36.19	9.02	36.10	12.93

Notes: HRR refers to hospital referral regions as defined by the "Dartmouth Atlas of Health Care." Covariates are from the American Hospital Association and the Area Resource File. Quality of care is from the Hospital Quality Association. End-of-life spending is from Medicare claims data. Data sources are described in more detail in the text.

EOL spending. Interestingly, if we were to hold the size of the workforce constant and simply replace a generalist with a specialist, there would be no change in quality but a substantial increase in the use of EOL spending (consistent with some of our previous research). Also noteworthy is the fact that HRRs with a greater share of teaching hospitals perform substantially better on quality and are no more profligate in their use of EOL care. Large cities are not more likely to offer one type of care vis-à-vis smaller cities. But HRRs with larger shares of minority patients, less-educated patients, and low-income patients (as measured by the percent receiving Medicaid) are all less likely to offer high-quality care and slightly more likely to spend on EOL care. These findings caution against the explanation that richer places spend more on EOL care simply because the marginal utility of health care in the end of life, however small, exceeds the marginal utility of other consumption (as in Hall and Jones [2007]).

In addition to the variation between HRRs in quality and the use of low-value care, the variance decompositions in table 7.1 also hinted at substantial variation within areas, especially in the use of high-quality care. To examine the correlates of this variation, in table 7.4, we estimate models with data at the hospital level that include HRR fixed effects, isolating within-HRR variation in quality and spending. Regression coefficients and standard errors clustered at the HRR level are presented. In these regressions, it is not possible to control for the specialist composition of a hospital's

Table 7.3 **Association between composite quality, EOL spending, and HRR characteristics**

	HRR-level regressions	
	Overall quality	Low-value EOL spending
Per capita total active nonfederal MDs	5.96	4,779.78
	(2.90)	(862.85)
Share of MDs who are specialists	–0.04	12.05
	(0.03)	(4.61)
HRR in one of 100 largest cities	–0.01	1.67
	(0.01)	(1.63)
Share of hospitals that are public (nonfederal)	–0.01	–0.38
	(0.01)	(1.65)
Share of hospitals that are teaching hospitals	0.03	3.85
	(0.01)	(2.69)
Total beds of hospitals in HRR (log)	–0.01	1.40
	(0.00)	(0.55)
Full-time employed RNs per patient Census day	0.00	2.78
	(0.01)	(1.34)
Percent of patients who are black	–0.04	18.36
	(0.03)	(4.80)
Share of inpatient days by Medicaid patients	–0.01	–5.59
	(0.05)	(5.25)
Percent of population over age 65	0.00	–2.84
	(0.06)	(9.81)
Percent of population with less than high school	–0.13	30.19
	(0.05)	(11.25)
Region dummies	Yes	Yes
R^2	0.29	0.72
Observations	262	262

Notes: Regression coefficients from between-HRR regressions are shown, along with robust standard errors; HRR refers to hospital referral regions as defined by the "Dartmouth Atlas of Health Care." Covariates are from the American Hospital Association and the Area Resource File. Quality of care is from the Hospital Quality Association. Composite quality is based on treatment for heart attack, heart failure, and pneumonia patients. End-of-life spending is from Medicare claims data. Data sources are described in more detail in the text.

area, since that is a characteristic of the area that is absorbed by the HRR fixed effect. Table 7.4 shows that hospitals with a larger share of minority, poor, and less-educated patients offer lower-quality care. Once again, it is important to note that our measures of quality do not require the presence of costly investments in new technology: these are primarily low-cost, high-value interventions. On the other hand, EOL spending, which is expensive and technologically intensive, is more likely to be offered at hospitals that serve minority and less-educated populations. It is surprising that teaching hospitals do not offer higher-quality care—some of this effect is simply a consequence of their urban location, a large component of which we have

Table 7.4 Association between composite quality, EOL spending, and hospital characteristics

	Within-HRR regressions	
	Overall quality	Low-value EOL spending
In one of 100 largest cities	0.01	3.63
	(0.00)	(0.69)
Public nonfederal hospital dummy	–0.01	–1.17
	(0.01)	(0.42)
Teaching hospital dummy	0.00	2.99
	(0.00)	(0.76)
Log(hospital beds)	0.02	3.61
	(0.00)	(0.20)
Full-time employed RNs per patient Census day	0.01	0.77
	(0.00)	(0.43)
Percent of patients who are black	–0.09	8.96
	(0.02)	(2.12)
Share of inpatient days by Medicaid patients	–0.02	–4.68
	(0.01)	(1.29)
Percent of zip over age 65	0.00	–4.57
	(0.03)	(3.74)
Percent of zip with less than high school	–0.05	4.68
	(0.02)	(1.98)
Region dummies	Yes	Yes
R^2	0.247	0.759
Observations	6,917	9,751

Notes: Regression coefficients from within-HRR regressions are shown, along with standard errors clustered at the HRR level; HRR refers to hospital referral regions as defined by the "Dartmouth Atlas of Health Care." Covariates are from the American Hospital Association and the Area Resource File. Quality of care is from the Hospital Quality Association. Composite quality is based on treatment for heart attack, heart failure, and pneumonia patients. End-of-life spending is from Medicare claims data. Data sources are described in more detail in the text.

adjusted for by controlling with an indicator variable for hospitals located in one of the largest one-hundred cities. This fact is consistent with the work of Fisher et al. (2004), who note substantial variations in the efficiency of academic medical centers. And contrary to many assertions in the literature, a greater presence of nurses does not seem to result in higher-quality care being provided.

At the bottom of table 7.4, we note that these covariates explain only 25 percent of the within-HRR variation in quality but over 75 percent of the within-HRR variation in EOL spending. So, while the provision of quality, even of the low-cost, high-value kind, may be a function of physician beliefs or idiosyncratic factors at the hospital level, the same explanation does not apply to the phenomena of using low-value, high-cost care. Here, a basic set of hospital and HRR characteristics accounts for a large share of the variation.

7.5 The Role of Learning

These facts point to a world where the use of high-quality care is idiosyncratically dispersed through the health care sector in ways that are uncorrelated with geographic region. Yet, geography at the level of the hospital market is a powerful descriptor of the use of low-value care. But this (within-region) variation in the use of high-quality care also suggests an interesting hypothesis: if high-quality hospitals are located right next to low-quality hospitals, do they learn from their high-quality neighbors? This question is extremely difficult to resolve empirically, as demonstrated in the substantial "peer-effects" literature (Sacerdote 2001). Our goal is less ambitious—we simply ask if the evidence is consistent with learning, and we rely on the use of simple ordinary least squares (OLS) regressions to explore the case for learning. We exploit the panel structure of our data to ask if investments in quality made by a hospital's neighbors last year predict that hospital's performance this year. The obvious concern with this approach is that investments in quality made by neighboring hospitals are correlated but do not causally affect each other's performance. To address this concern, we condition on a hospital's own performance last year. In other words, we compare two hospitals with similar quality in a given year and ask if the one with higher-quality neighbors improves by more than the one with lower-quality neighbors. We perform the parallel analysis for the use of EOL spending. The fact that quality and EOL spending are measured on separate scales makes it difficult to compare the regression coefficients on neighbors' performance across these two different outcomes. We address this concern by standardizing both variables (that is, we take each variable, subtract its mean, and divide by its standard deviation). These standardized variables are both mean 0 and variance 1 (z-scores).

We construct each hospital's neighbors based on a composite of all other hospitals in the HRR. That is, neighbor quality for each hospital is just the average value of that variable for all of the other hospitals in the same HRR. Results using alternate specifications (such as choosing only the largest nearby hospital as the neighbor or focusing on the best performing hospital as the critical neighbor) produce very similar results.

Our exploration of the possibility of learning from neighbors is shown in table 7.5 (high-quality care) and table 7.6 (low-value end-of-life spending). We present regression coefficients and standard errors clustered at the HRR level. In both tables, the first four columns use the dependent variable Y_{it} (composite quality or EOL spending) directly, while the last four columns substitute the standardized (z-score) version of the dependent variable (to present results that are more easily compared across variables). The first

Table 7.5 Hospital-level association between quality and neighbors' quality

	Overall quality				Overall quality: Standardized			
	Base (1)	Add neighbors (2)	Add lagged dependent variable (3)	Instrumental variable for neighbors (4)	Base (5)	Add neighbors (6)	Add lagged dependent variable (7)	Instrumental variable for neighbors (8)
In one of 100 largest cities	0.001	0.003	–0.001	–0.002	0.012	0.025	–0.002	–0.001
	(0.005)	(0.004)	(0.002)	(0.002)	(0.040)	(0.036)	(0.023)	(0.023)
Public nonfederal hospital dummy	–0.006	–0.011	–0.008	–0.008	–0.079	–0.084	–0.033	–0.033
	(0.005)	(0.005)	(0.003)	(0.003)	(0.046)	(0.047)	(0.024)	(0.024)
Teaching hospital dummy	0.005	0.000	–0.004	–0.004	0.041	0.013	–0.010	–0.010
	(0.005)	(0.005)	(0.003)	(0.003)	(0.040)	(0.039)	(0.021)	(0.021)
Ln(total hospital beds)	0.019	0.022	0.009	0.009	0.144	0.158	0.074	0.074
	(0.002)	(0.002)	(0.001)	(0.001)	(0.020)	(0.021)	(0.011)	(0.011)
Full-time employed RNs per patient Census day	0.013	0.012	0.004	0.004	0.119	0.106	0.031	0.031
	(0.004)	(0.004)	(0.002)	(0.002)	(0.032)	(0.034)	(0.018)	(0.018)
Percent black patients	–0.094	–0.075	–0.026	–0.029	–0.527	–0.429	–0.191	–0.190
	(0.016)	(0.016)	(0.009)	(0.010)	(0.131)	(0.129)	(0.076)	(0.076)
Percent of inpatient days by Medicaid patients	–0.018	–0.022	–0.003	–0.003	–0.215	–0.273	–0.116	–0.116
	(0.013)	(0.012)	(0.007)	(0.007)	(0.118)	(0.121)	(0.064)	(0.064)
Per capita total active nonfederal MDs	6.679	2.978	0.933	1.766	58.159	33.566	17.732	17.464
	(2.940)	(1.592)	(0.999)	(1.172)	(24.430)	(16.149)	(9.404)	(10.485)
Percent of MDs who are specialists	–0.086	–0.065	–0.021	–0.028	–0.707	–0.717	–0.386	–0.385
	(0.028)	(0.015)	(0.011)	(0.011)	(0.233)	(0.159)	(0.101)	(0.101)

(continued)

Table 7.5 (continued)

	Overall quality				Overall quality: Standardized			
	Base (1)	Add neighbors (2)	Add lagged dependent variable (3)	Instrumental variable for neighbors (4)	Base (5)	Add neighbors (6)	Add lagged dependent variable (7)	Instrumental variable for neighbors (8)
Percent of zip over age 65	–0.030	–0.018	0.002	0.001	–0.465	–0.401	–0.112	–0.112
	(0.025)	(0.026)	(0.017)	(0.018)	(0.220)	(0.235)	(0.154)	(0.153)
Percent of zip with less than high school	–0.075	–0.058	–0.017	–0.020	–0.764	–0.632	–0.198	–0.197
	(0.017)	(0.016)	(0.009)	(0.009)	(0.141)	(0.142)	(0.082)	(0.082)
Quality in neighboring hospitals		0.556	0.213	0.071		0.462	0.162	0.167
		(0.045)	(0.031)	(0.063)		(0.060)	(0.032)	(0.071)
Lagged dependent variable			0.680	0.696			0.659	0.659
			(0.019)	(0.020)			(0.033)	(0.033)
R^2	0.140	0.227	0.597	0.594	0.148	0.194	0.548	0.547
N	6,917	4,353	4,353	4,353	6,917	4,353	4,353	4,353

Notes: Regression coefficients and standard errors clustered at the HRR level are shown; HRR refers to hospital referral region as defined by the "Dartmouth Atlas of Health Care." Covariates are from the American Hospital Association and the Area Resource File. Quality of care is from the Hospital Quality Association. Composite quality is based on treatment for heart attack, heart failure, and pneumonia patients. Standardized quality is expressed as z-scores. Data sources are described in more detail in the text.

Table 7.6 Hospital-level association between EOL spending and neighbors EOL spending

	End-of-life low-value care				End-of-life low-value care: Standardized			
	Base (1)	Add neighbors (2)	Add lagged dependent variable (3)	Instrumental variable for neighbors (4)	Base (5)	Add neighbors (6)	Add lagged dependent variable (7)	Instrumental variable for neighbors (8)
In one of 100 largest cities	4.009	2.970	0.721	0.722	0.303	0.220	0.051	0.051
	(0.868)	(0.601)	(0.199)	(0.199)	(0.066)	(0.044)	(0.014)	(0.014)
Public nonfederal hospital dummy	–1.119	–1.320	–0.475	–0.465	–0.084	–0.099	–0.035	–0.034
	(0.415)	(0.391)	(0.134)	(0.133)	(0.031)	(0.029)	(0.010)	(0.010)
Teaching hospital dummy	3.272	2.656	–0.027	–0.047	0.249	0.198	–0.005	–0.007
	(0.869)	(0.784)	(0.273)	(0.267)	(0.066)	(0.058)	(0.021)	(0.020)
Ln(total hospital beds)	4.242	3.968	1.057	1.035	0.321	0.295	0.076	0.074
	(0.270)	(0.196)	(0.091)	(0.090)	(0.020)	(0.015)	(0.007)	(0.007)
Full-time employed RNs per patient Census day	0.895	1.132	0.304	0.292	0.068	0.085	0.023	0.021
	(0.550)	(0.445)	(0.141)	(0.140)	(0.042)	(0.033)	(0.011)	(0.010)
Percent black patients	10.602	6.663	1.744	1.781	0.803	0.494	0.123	0.127
	(2.581)	(1.886)	(0.622)	(0.623)	(0.195)	(0.140)	(0.046)	(0.046)
Percent of inpatient days by Medicaid patients	–7.454	–5.110	–1.244	–1.256	–0.563	–0.379	–0.087	–0.089
	(1.477)	(1.265)	(0.462)	(0.458)	(0.112)	(0.094)	(0.035)	(0.034)
Per capita total active nonfederal MDs	4,900.000	787.954	288.773	370.209	369.956	57.030	17.144	26.385
	(879.786)	(272.110)	(119.069)	(141.113)	(66.490)	(20.382)	(9.014)	(10.614)
Percent of MDs who are specialists	19.641	0.869	0.828	1.226	1.483	0.056	0.043	0.088
	(5.470)	(1.865)	(0.872)	(0.962)	(0.414)	(0.138)	(0.063)	(0.072)

(continued)

Table 7.6 (continued)

	End-of-life low-value care				End-of-life low-value care: Standardized			
	Base (1)	Add neighbors (2)	Add lagged dependent variable (3)	Instrumental variable for neighbors (4)	Base (5)	Add neighbors (6)	Add lagged dependent variable (7)	Instrumental variable for neighbors (8)
Percent of zip over age 65	–6.829	–4.690	–1.906	–1.928	–0.517	–0.348	–0.138	–0.141
	(3.684)	(3.123)	(0.922)	(0.906)	(0.278)	(0.232)	(0.068)	(0.066)
Percent of zip with less than high school	11.872	7.882	3.009	3.061	0.895	0.586	0.219	0.225
	(3.259)	(2.014)	(0.750)	(0.743)	(0.247)	(0.149)	(0.054)	(0.054)
EOL spending in neighboring hospitals		0.711	0.170	0.151		0.700	0.172	0.142
		(0.026)	(0.014)	(0.020)		(0.026)	(0.014)	(0.019)
Lagged dependent variable			0.762	0.770			0.753	0.764
			(0.017)	(0.017)			(0.017)	(0.017)
R^2	0.624	0.718	0.875	0.875	0.628	0.719	0.877	0.877
N	9,751	7,312	7,312	7,312	9,751	7,312	7,312	7,312

Notes: Regression coefficients from within-HRR regressions are shown, along with standard errors clustered at the HRR level; HRR refers to hospital referral regions as defined by the "Dartmouth Atlas of Health Care." Covariates are from the American Hospital Association and the Area Resource File. End-of-life spending is from Medicare claims data. Standardized spending is expressed as z-scores. Data sources are described in more detail in the text.

column does not include neighbors' performance, constraining the effect to be zero. The second column adds in the performance of neighbors, and the third column adds the lagged dependent variable for a hospital's own performance in the previous year. With X_i denoting the characteristics of hospital i, N_{-it} the performance of hospital i's neighbors in year t, and $Y_{i(t-1)}$ the lagged performance of hospital i, this last specification is formally expressed as:

$$(1) \qquad Y_{it} = \alpha + X_i\beta + \delta N_{-it} + \lambda Y_{i(t-1)} + e_{it}.$$

This specification may understate the effect of neighbors on performance, for it effectively rules out any lagged neighbor effect on current outcomes. Such an effect is absorbed by the coefficient λ, which through back substitution can be shown to capture the role of lagged neighbor performance on contemporaneous outcomes. The identifying assumption here is that $E(e_{it} \mid X_i, N_{-it}, Y_{i(t-1)}) = 0$ or that unobserved shocks to hospital performance aren't predictable in controlling for hospital characteristics and lagged performance (which includes lagged neighbors' performance). In other words, we are assuming that there is not a common process that contemporaneously improves a hospital's performance and that of its neighbors. This would be violated if, for example, a local quality improvement effort was implemented and affected a hospital and its neighbors or if hospitals and their neighbors were learning about a new technology from a common source. To begin to explore this possibility, in the fourth column, we instrument for neighbors' performance using the characteristics of the neighbors that are described in table 7.3 (such as location in one of the largest one-hundred cities, number of beds, specialist composition in the area, and patient characteristics). In this specification, we are identifying the effect of neighbors' performance on a hospital's performance by only utilizing variation in neighbors' performance that can be attributed to those neighbors' attributes. This source of identification is valid only insofar as those attributes are not correlated with unobserved characteristics that affect both neighbors' performance and the changes in a hospital's own performance. In other words, we need the fact that a greater share of a hospital's neighbors are teaching hospitals (for example) to be uncorrelated with the *unobservable* determinants of that hospital's quality—having controlled for that hospital's own teaching status and its quality performance last year. This assumption is untestable, but it becomes more difficult to tell a story about the relationship being driven by unobservable common factors. Unfortunately, it is difficult to isolate a source of variation that is not subject to similar concerns.

We present results both for the simple composite quality measure and for the standardized measures. It is easiest to compare coefficient estimates across these specifications in the panels on the right, since the variables of interest are measured in similar units. Examining column (6) of table 7.5, we see that a 1 standard deviation increase in neighbors' quality raises a given hospital's quality score by 0.46 standard deviations. As noted earlier, this effect probably overstates the effect of neighbors on learning. In column (7), where we control for own performance last year, the effect of a hospital's neighbors having quality that is 1 standard deviation higher quality than average (a z-score of 1, with mean equal to 0 by construction) is an increase in quality of 0.16 standard deviations (our preferred specification). The instrumental variable (IV) results in column (8) cannot reject the OLS estimates. This is not the consequence of weak instruments: the first stage of our two-stage least squares regression has an F-statistic of 45.

The analogous results for EOL spending are reported in table 7.6. Here, having neighbors whose EOL spending is 1 standard deviation higher raises a hospital's EOL spending by 0.70 (column [6]) standard deviations when we do not include a lagged dependent variable and 0.17 standard deviations (column [7]—our preferred specification) when we do. These are large spillover effects. In this case, the IV results are virtually identical to our preferred OLS specification—column (8) suggests that having neighbors whose EOL spending is 1 standard deviation higher raises a hospital's own EOL spending by 0.14 standard deviations.

The magnitude of learning is thus quite similar across the two outcomes. This might seem at odds with the fact that there is much more variation within HRRs in quality than in EOL care—a phenomenon that may cause one to think that there is greater within-earning with EOL spending. But it is possible for learning to occur for quality and EOL spending at similar rates even while there is less within-area variation in EOL spending if there is faster innovation in low-value EOL care. This seems consistent with highly intensive care being based on adoption of the latest rapidly developing technology, while most of the quality measures used here have been in existence for much longer.

We performed a number of specification tests to rule out alternative explanations. First, we also estimated models that included the lead (instead of or in addition to lag) of neighbors' performance. Our concern was that if quality is noisily measured from year to year, it may be possible to see a correlation between neighbors' scores last year and performance today. But a pure measurement error story would also imply a correlation between performance today and neighbors' quality a year from today (a model that by construction cannot be causal). In general, we found that the largest effects of neighbors' performance loaded onto lagged performance (results available on request). This specification check suggests that the associations identified in these tables could be causal. As previously discussed, we also tested several other methods of constructing a hospital's neighbors, which produced quite similar results. We also estimated a number of specifications with interaction effects to explore whether certain hospitals (such as teaching hospitals or publicly owned hospitals) had stronger spillover effects on neighbors, but we were not able to estimate these second-order effects with enough precision. Last, instead of our composite measure of quality, we reestimated the model with the subcomponent measures (such as the treatment of heart attack patients only), again with quite similar results. For example, the increase in standardized quality of treatment for heart attacks (using the IV specification of column [8]) associated with a 1 point increase in neighbors' quality is 0.19 (HRR-clustered standard error 0.09) and for treatment of pneumonia is 0.11 (HRR-clustered standard error 0.07). While it is clearly still possible that our findings are driven by alternative explanations, these results are quite suggestive of agglomeration effects.

7.6 Discussion

The measures that we have used are subject to several limitations. The first is an aspect of the quality measures themselves, since quality measures may in theory penalize hospitals that treat sicker patients. While this concern may be true of quality measures for acute treatments (such as the use of angioplasty after heart attacks), the measures used in this chapter were chosen in part because they are not sensitive to the ability to perform detailed risk adjustment. Moreover, Higashi et al. (2007) have noted that patients with more comorbidities are no less likely to receive higher-quality care of the type used in our quality measures.

Second, we examined process-of-care measures (such as use of beta-blockers) rather than outcome measures (such as mortality). Policymakers have focused on process-of-care measures because they are less sensitive to risk adjustment, but these measures recently have come under fire, with some critics claiming that they do not actually predict health outcomes such as mortality after AMI and CHF (see, for example, the work of Bradley et al. [2006] and Werner and Bradlow [2006]. More recent work by Jha et al. (2007), however, has demonstrated that there is indeed a significant positive relationship between performance on these measures and risk-adjusted survival rates for each of the three conditions measured here and that hospitals with higher performance on these measures achieve better outcomes for their patients.

A third concern is the validity of the end-of-life measure: a very sick patient treated in a high-intensity hospital may have an increased chance of survival and thus not end up in the end-of-life sample. Presumably, this individual experienced above-average expenditures, thus excluding him or her from the sample and thus attenuating the measured differences in spending. Bach, Schrag, and Begg (2004) have also noted that regions with more "low-cost" diseases will appear to experience lower expenditures in the end-of-life cohorts. However, our spending data have already been adjusted for the relative frequency of diseases in each hospital's patient population, mitigating these concerns. Additionally, previous work has shown a correlation between a hospital's EOL spending and its treatment of acute conditions such as hip fracture and AMI, suggesting that these hospitals treat many different patients with similar intensity.

One might interpret these findings in the context of Baicker and Chandra (2004a, 2004b) and Chandra and Staiger (2007). In this work, we argued that there are two types of health care—one technologically intensive and provided by specialists and the other less intensive. Specialization in one type of care crowds out the ability to deliver the other type of care. This tradeoff is best illustrated in the context of competing treatments for the same condition—angioplasty (intensive) versus thrombolytics (less intensive) for heart attacks. It is, however, difficult to view EOL spending as being an alternative therapy for anything; few physicians view it as being productive in almost any setting.

Last, while we have referred to the spillover effects between neighboring hospitals as "learning," we have not demonstrated that this is the best characterization of the spillover. Competition for local patients could spur hospitals to improve their quality more quickly once their neighbors have done so, for example. This shorthand masks a number of different underlying channels for spillovers that will only be distinguishable with further research.

7.7 Conclusion

Analysis of the health care sector provides a valuable window into the causes of variation in productivity across areas and the role of agglomeration in generating innovation and efficiency. This investigation into variation in the use of high-value, low-cost health care and high-cost, low-value health care has yielded a number of surprising facts. First, there is large variation in the use of both innovations but with different patterns across areas. Variation in the use of high-quality care is not restricted to certain markets—there is variation in care within Boston, Massachusetts, as well as within Birmingham, Alabama—but there is much less variation in the use of low-value care within hospital markets. Second, hospitals seem to learn from their neighbors about both forms of care at similar rates.

This local diffusion has important policy implications. If quality improvements at one hospital diffuse to others in the same hospital market, then there is a case for subsidizing investment in high-quality care, as this positive externality suggests that private investment will be too low. On the other hand, if less productive practice patterns also diffuse through a similar process, then that suggests that hospitals should be discouraged from investing in technologically intensive health care of questionable value. These findings thus have implications both for the optimal design of public subsidization of quality-improving investment and for payments for lower-value care through public insurance programs like Medicare. Both promoting the use of underutilized high-quality care and discouraging the use of overused low-value care would improve the productivity of health care spending. Understanding the mechanisms through which these practices diffuse and the role that agglomeration economies play in that diffusion is crucial for designing policies that achieve these aims and should further inform the design of a wide array of reforms.

References

Bach, P. B., D. Schrag, and C. B. Begg. 2004. Resurrecting treatment histories of dead patients: A study design that should be laid to rest. *Journal of the American Medical Association* 292 (22): 2765–70.

Baicker, K., and A. Chandra. 2004a. Medicare spending, the physician workforce, and beneficiaries' quality of care. *Health Affairs,* April 7 (Web Exclusive, W4-184–W4-197).

———. 2004b. The productivity of physician specialization: Evidence from the Medicare program. *American Economic Review* 94 (2): 357–61.

Berwick, D. M. 2003. Disseminating innovations in health care. *Journal of the American Medical Association* 289 (15): 1969–75.

Bradley, E. H., J. Herrin, B. Elbel, R. L. McNamara, D. J. Magid, B. K. Nallamothu, Y. Wang, S.-L. T. Normand, J. A. Spertus, and H. M. Krumholz. 2006. Hospital quality for acute myocardial infarction: Correlation among process measures and relationship with short-term mortality. *Journal of the American Medical Association* 296 (1): 72–78.

Chandra, A., and D. O. Staiger. 2007. Productivity spillovers in health care: Evidence from the treatment of heart attacks. *Journal of Political Economy* 115 (1): 103–41.

Coleman, J. S., E. Katz, and H. Menzel. 1957. The diffusion of an innovation among physicians. *Sociometry* 20 (4): 253–70.

Comin, D., and B. Hobijn. 2004. Cross-country technology adoption: Making the theories face the facts. *Journal of Monetary Economics* 51 (1): 39–83.

Dartmouth Atlas Project. The Dartmouth Atlas of Health Care. Available at: http://www.dartmouthatlas.org.

Fisher, E. S., D. E. Wennberg, T. A. Stukel, and D. J. Gottlieb. 2004. Variations in the longitudinal efficiency of academic medical centers. *Health Affairs,* October 7 (Web Exclusive, VAR-19–VAR-32).

Fisher, E. S., D. E. Wennberg, T. A. Stukel, D. J. Gottlieb, F. L. Lucas, and E. L. Pinder. 2003a. The implications of regional variations in Medicare spending, part 1: The content, quality, and accessibility of care. *Annals of Internal Medicine* 138 (4): 273–87.

———. 2003b. The implications of regional variations in Medicare spending, part 2: Health outcomes and satisfaction with care. *Annals of Internal Medicine* 138 (4): 288–98.

Hall, B. 2004. Innovation and diffusion. In *The Oxford handbook of innovation,* ed. J. Fagerberg, D.C. Mowery, and R. R. Nelson, 459–84. Oxford: Oxford University Press.

Hall, R., and C. I. Jones. 2007. The value of life and the rise in health spending. *Quarterly Journal of Economics* 122 (1): 39–72.

Heidenreich, P. A., and M. McClellan. 2001. Trends in treatment and outcomes for acute myocardial infarction: 1975–1995. *American Journal of Medicine* 110 (3): 165–74.

Higashi, T., N. S. Wenger, J. L. Adams, C. Fung, M. Roland, E. A. McGlynn, D. Reeves, S. M. Asch, E. A. Kerr, and P. G. Shekelle. 2007. Relationship between number of medical conditions and quality of care. *New England Journal of Medicine* 356 (24): 2496–504.

Jaffe, A. B., M. Trajtenberg, and R. Henderson. 1993. Geographic localization of knowledge spillovers as evidenced by patent citations. *Quarterly Journal of Economics* 108 (3): 577–98.

Jha, A. K., Z. Li, E. J. Orav, and A. M. Epstein. 2005. Care in U.S. hospitals: The Hospital Quality Alliance program. *New England Journal of Medicine* 353 (3): 265–74.

Jha, A. K., E. J. Orav, Z. Li, and A. M. Epstein. 2007. The inverse relationship between mortality rates and performance in the Hospital Quality Alliance measures. *Health Affairs* 26 (4): 1104–10.

Jovanovic, B., and Y. Nyarko. 1995. A Bayesian learning model fitted to a variety of empirical learning curves. *Brookings papers on economic activity, microeconomics:* 247–305.

———. 1996. Learning by doing and the choice of technology. *Econometrica* 64 (6): 1299–310.

Lister, J. 1867. On the antiseptic principle in the practice of surgery. *Lancet* 90 (2299): 353–6.

Parente, S. L., and E. C. Prescott. 1994. Barriers to technology adoption and development. *Journal of Political Economy* 102 (2): 298–322.

Rogers, E. M. 1995. *Diffusion of innovations.* 4th ed. New York: Free Press.

Sacerdote, B. I. 2001. Peer effects with random assignment: Results for Darmouth roommates. *Quarterly Journal of Economics* 116 (2): 681–704.

Skinner, J., and D. Staiger. 2006. The diffusion of health care technology. Dartmouth College, Department of Economics. Unpublished Manuscript.

Soumerai, S. B., T. J. McLaughlin, J. H. Gurwitz, E. Guadagnoli, P. J. Hauptman, C. Borbas, N. Morris, et al. 1998. Effect of local medical opinion leaders on quality of care for acute myocardial infarction: A randomized controlled trial. *Journal of the American Medical Association* 279 (17): 1358–63.

U.S. Department of Health and Human Services, Centers for Medicare and Medicaid Services. Hospital compare. Available at: http://www.hospitalcompare.hhs.gov.

Werner, R. M., and E. T. Bradlow. 2006. Relationship between Medicare's Hospital Compare performance measures and mortality rates. *Journal of the American Medical Association* 296 (22): 2694–702.

Zucker, L. G., M. R. Darby, and M. B. Brewer. 1998. Intellectual human capital and the birth of U.S. biotechnology enterprises. *American Economic Review* 88 (1): 290–306.

8 The Agglomeration of U.S. Ethnic Inventors

William R. Kerr

8.1 Introduction

Economists have long been interested in agglomeration and innovation. In his seminal outline of the core rationales for industrial clusters, Marshall (1920, 271) emphasized the theory of intellectual spillovers by arguing that in agglomerations, "the mysteries of the trade become no mystery, but are, as it were, in the air." Workers can learn skills quickly from each other in an industrial cluster, and this proximity can speed the adoption of new technologies or best practices. Glaeser and Kahn (2001) argue that the urbanization of high human capital industries, like finance, is evidence for the role that density plays in the transfer of ideas, and studies of patent citations highlight the importance of local proximity for scientific exchanges (e.g., Jaffe, Trajtenberg, and Henderson 1993; Thompson and Fox-Kean 2006). Moreover, evidence suggests that agglomeration increases the rate of innovation itself. Saxenian (1994) describes how entrepreneurial firms locate near one another in Silicon Valley to foster new technology development. Carlino, Chatterjee, and Hunt (2007) show that higher urban employment density is correlated with greater patenting per capita within cities.

Strong quantitative assessments of the magnitudes and characteristics of intellectual spillovers and agglomeration are essential. Such studies inform

William R. Kerr is assistant professor and MBA Class of 1961 Fellow at Harvard Business School.

Comments are appreciated and can be sent to wkerr@hbs.edu. An earlier version of this chapter was released as HBS Working Paper no. 09-003. I am grateful to William Lincoln and Debbie Strumsky for data assistance. I thank Ed Glaeser, Jeff Furman, and participants in the NBER Economics of Agglomeration conferences for helpful comments and research ideas. This research is supported by Harvard Business School, the National Science Foundation, the Innovation Policy and the Economy Group, and the MIT George Schultz Fund.

business managers of the advantages and costs for locating in areas that are rich in ideas but most likely come with higher rents and wages as well. Moreover, these studies are important for understanding short-run and long-run urban growth and development. They help inform whether industrial specialization or diversity better foster regional development (e.g., Jacobs 1970; Glaeser et al. 1992; Henderson, Kuncoro, and Turner 1995; Duranton and Puga 2001; Duranton 2007) and the role of local knowledge development and externalities in generating sustained growth (e.g., Romer 1986, 1990; Furman, Porter, and Stern 2002). Rosenthal and Strange (2003) note that intellectual spillovers are strongest at the very local levels of proximity.[1]

This study contributes to our empirical understanding of agglomeration and innovation by documenting patterns in the city-level agglomeration of ethnic inventors (e.g., Chinese, Indian) within the United States from 1975 through 2007. The contributions of these immigrant groups to U.S. technology formation are staggering: while foreign-born account for just over 10 percent of the U.S. working population, they represent 25 percent of the U.S. science and engineering (SE) workforce and nearly 50 percent of those with doctorates. Even looking within the PhD level, ethnic researchers make exceptional contributions to science, as measured by Nobel Prizes, elections to the National Academy of Sciences, patent citation counts, and so on.[2] Recent work relates immigration and growth in U.S. invention (e.g., Peri 2007; Hunt and Gauthier-Loiselle 2008; Kerr and Lincoln 2008). Moreover, ethnic entrepreneurs are very active in commercializing new technologies, especially in high-tech sectors (e.g., Saxenian et al. 2002; Wadhwa et al. 2007).

The spatial distribution of ethnic inventors across U.S. cities, however, is not uniform or random. This agglomeration reflects the general tendency of both high-skilled and low-skilled immigrants to concentrate in certain U.S. cities. Larger cities are often favored for their greater opportunities for assimilation. Geographical distances of cities to home countries and past immigration networks are also important for location decisions. Edin, Fredriksson, and Åslund (2003) and Pedace and Rohn (2008) provide recent evidence on the employment effects of enclaves at both the city and subcity levels. A number of studies in labor economics use spatial differences across cities and occupations in immigrant shares to estimate the impact of higher immigration rates on native workers (e.g., Card 1990, 2001).[3]

1. Several studies assess the relative importance of intellectual spillovers versus other rationales for industrial agglomeration (e.g., lower transportation costs, labor market pooling). Representative papers include Audretsch and Feldman (1996), Rosenthal and Strange (2001), Henderson (2003), Ellison, Glaeser, and Kerr (2007), and Glaeser and Kerr (2008). Porter (1990) emphasizes how vertically related industries may colocate for knowledge sharing.

2. For example, Stephan and Levin (2001), Burton and Wang (1999), Johnson (1998, 2001), and Streeter (1997).

3. General surveys of immigration include Borjas (1994), Friedberg and Hunt (1995), Freeman (2006), and Kerr and Kerr (2008).

The study of how U.S. ethnic inventors agglomerate is thus very important, given (a) the disproportionate contributions of immigrant researchers and (b) their nonrandom spatial distribution across the United States. Such a characterization is necessary for understanding the geography of U.S. innovation and economic growth. Moreover, the spatial variation of immigrant researchers across cities allows for stronger quantitative assessments of the role of innovation in city growth. This chapter is a first step in this direction.

Econometric studies quantifying the role of ethnic scientists and engineers for technology formation and diffusion are often hampered, however, by data constraints. It is very difficult to assemble sufficient cross-sectional and longitudinal variation for large-scale panel exercises.[4] This chapter describes a new approach for quantifying the ethnic composition of U.S. inventors with previously unavailable detail. The technique exploits the inventor names contained on the microrecords for all patents granted by the United States Patent and Trademark Office (USPTO) from January 1975 to May 2008.[5] Each patent record lists one or more inventors, with 8 million inventor names associated with the 4.5 million patents. The USPTO grants patents to inventors living within and outside of the United States, with each group accounting for about half of the patents over the 1975 to 2008 period.

This study maps into these inventor names an ethnic-name database typically used for commercial applications. This approach exploits the idea that inventors with the surnames Chang or Wang are likely of Chinese ethnicity, those with surnames Rodriguez or Martinez of Hispanic ethnicity, and so on. The match rates are 92 percent to 98 percent for U.S.-domestic inventor records, depending on the procedure employed, and the process affords the distinction of nine ethnicities: Chinese, English, European, Hispanic/Filipino, Indian/Hindi, Japanese, Korean, Russian, and Vietnamese. Moreover, because the matching is done at the microlevel, greater detail on the ethnic composition of inventors is available annually on multiple dimensions: technologies, cities, companies, and so on. Section 8.2 describes this data development in greater detail.

Section 8.3 then documents the growing contribution of ethnic inven-

4. While the decennial Census provides detailed cross-sectional descriptions, its longitudinal variation is necessarily limited. The annual Current Population Survey, however, provides poor cross-sectional detail and does not ask immigrant status until 1994. The Scientists and Engineers Statistical Data System database offers a better trade-off between the two dimensions but suffers important sampling biases with respect to immigrants (Kannankutty and Wilkinson 1999).

5. The project initially employed the National Bureau of Economic Research Patent Data File, compiled by Hall, Jaffe, and Trajtenberg (2001), that includes patents granted by the USPTO from January 1975 to December 1999. The current version now employs an extended version developed by Harvard Business School research that includes patents granted through May 2008.

tors to U.S. technology formation. The rapid increase during the 1990s in the share of high-tech patents granted to Chinese and Indian inventors is particularly striking. This section also uses the patenting data to calculate concentration indices for U.S. innovation. Ethnic inventors have higher levels of spatial concentration than English inventors throughout the thirty year period studied. Moreover, the spatial concentration of ethnic inventors increases significantly from 1995 to 2004, especially in high-tech sectors like computer-related patenting. The combination of greater ethnic shares and increasing agglomeration of ethnic inventors helps stop and reverse the 1975 to 1994 declines in the overall concentration of U.S. invention. These trends are confined to industrial patents; universities and government bodies—that are constrained from agglomerating—do not show recent increases in spatial clustering.

The final section concludes. The higher agglomeration of immigrants in cities and occupations has long been noted. For example, Mandorff (2007) highlights how immigrant entrepreneurs tend to agglomerate in selected industries, a process that increases their business impact for specific sectors. Examples within the United States are Korean entrepreneurs in dry cleaning, Vietnamese in nail salons, Gujarati Indians in traveler accommodations, Punjabi Indians in gas stations, Greeks in restaurants, and so on. The higher natural social interactions among these ethnic groups aid in the acquisition and transfer of sector-specific skills; scale economies lead to occupational clustering by minority ethnic groups.

To date, there has been very little work, theoretically or empirically, on the agglomeration of U.S. ethnic scientists and engineers, with the notable exception of Agrawal, Kapur, and McHale (2007).[6] This scarcity of research is disappointing, given the scale of these ethnic contributions and the importance of innovation to regional economic growth. Moreover, the large shifts in ethnic inventor populations, often driven in part by U.S. immigration restrictions, may provide empirical footholds for testing agglomeration theories in a natural experiment framework. It is hoped that the empirical platform developed in this study provides a foothold for furthering such analyses.

8.2 Ethnic-Name Matching Technique

This section describes the ethnic-name matching strategy, outlines the strengths and weaknesses of the name database selected, and offers some

6. Agrawal, Kapur, and McHale (2007) jointly examine knowledge diffusion through colocation and coethnicity using domestic patent citations made by Indian inventors living in the United States. While being in the same city or the same ethnicity both encourage knowledge diffusion, their estimations suggest that the marginal benefit of colocation is four times larger for inventors of different ethnicities. This substitutability between social and geographic proximity can create differences between a social planner's optimal distribution of ethnic members and what the inventors themselves would choose.

validation exercises using patent records filed by foreign inventors with the USPTO. Kerr (2007) further describes the name-matching process, the international name distribution technique, and the apportionment of nonunique matches that are highlighted next.

8.2.1 Melissa Ethnic-Name Database and Name-Matching Technique

The ethnic-name database employed in this study was originally developed by the Melissa Data Corporation for use in direct-mail advertisements. Ethnic-name databases suffer from two inherent limitations: not all ethnicities are covered, and included ethnicities usually receive unequal treatment. The strength of the Melissa database is in the identification of Asian ethnicities—especially Chinese, Indian/Hindi, Japanese, Korean, Russian, and Vietnamese names. The database is comparatively weaker for looking within continental Europe. For example, Dutch surnames are collected without first names, while the opposite is true for French names. The Asian comparative advantage and overall cost effectiveness led to the selection of the Melissa database, as well as the European amalgamation employed in the matching technique. In total, nine ethnicities are distinguished: Chinese, English, European, Hispanic/Filipino, Indian/Hindi, Japanese, Korean, Russian, and Vietnamese.[7]

The second limitation is that commercial databases vary in the number of names they contain for each ethnicity. These differences reflect both that coverage is uneven and that some ethnicities are more homogeneous in their naming conventions. For example, the 1975 to 1999 Herfindahl indices of foreign inventor surnames for Korean (0.047) and Vietnamese (0.112) are significantly higher than Japanese (0.013) and English (0.016) due to frequent Korean surnames like Kim (16 percent) and Park (12 percent) and Vietnamese surnames like Nguyen (29 percent) and Tran (12 percent).

Two polar matching strategies are employed to ensure coverage differences do not overly influence ethnicity assignments.

Full matching: This procedure utilizes all of the name assignments in the Melissa database and manually codes any unmatched surname or first name associated with one-hundred or more inventor records. This technique further exploits the international distribution of inventor names within the patent database to provide superior results. The match rate for this restricted procedure is 98 percent (98 percent U.S., 98 percent foreign). This rate should be less than 100 percent with the Melissa database, as not all ethnicities are included.

Restricted matching: A second strategy employs a uniform name database using only the 3,000 and 200 most common surnames and first names, respectively, for each ethnicity. These numerical bars are the lowest common denominators across the major ethnicities studied. The match rate

7. The largest ethnicity in the U.S. SE workforce absent from the ethnic-name database is Iranian, which accounted for 0.7 percent of bachelor-level SEs in the 1990 Census.

for this restricted procedure is 89 percent (92 percent U.S., 86 percent foreign).

For matching, names in both the patent and ethnic-name databases are capitalized and truncated to ten characters. Approximately 88 percent of the patent name records have a unique surname, first-name, or middle-name match in the full matching procedure (77 percent in the restricted matching), affording a single ethnicity determination, with priority given to surname matches. For inventors residing in the United States, representative probabilities are assigned to nonunique matches using the masters-level SE communities in metropolitan statistical areas (MSAs). Ethnic probabilities for the remaining 3 percent of records (mostly foreign) are calculated as equal shares.

8.2.2 Inventors Residing in Foreign Countries and Regions

Visual confirmation of the top 1,000 surnames and first names in the USPTO records confirms the name-matching technique works well. The appendix documents the one-hundred most common surnames of U.S.-based inventors for each ethnicity, along with their relative contributions. These counts sum the ethnic contribution from inventors with each surname. These counts include partial or split assignments. Moreover, they are not necessarily direct or exclusive matches (e.g., the ethnic match may have occurred through the first name). While some inventors are certainly misclassified, the measurement error in aggregate trends building from the microdata is minor. The full matching procedure is the preferred technique and underlies the trends presented in the next section, but most applications find negligible differences when the restricted matching data set is employed instead.

The application of the ethnic-name database to the inventors residing outside of the United States provides a natural quality-assurance exercise for the technique. Inventions originating outside the United States account for just under half of USPTO patents, with applications from Japan comprising about half of this foreign total. The appendix documents the results of applying the ethnic-matching procedures for countries and regions grouped to the ethnicities identifiable with the database. The results are very encouraging. First, the full matching procedure assigns ethnicities to a large percentage of foreign records, with the match rates greater than 93 percent for all countries. In the restricted matching procedure, a matching rate of greater than 74 percent holds for all regions.

Second, the estimated inventor compositions are reasonable. The own-ethnicity shares are summarized in the fourth and fifth columns. The weighted average is 86 percent in the full matching procedure, and own-ethnicity contributions are greater than 80 percent in the United Kingdom, China, India, Japan, Korea, and Russia, regardless of the matching procedure employed. Like the United States, own-ethnicity contributions should be less than 100 percent due to foreign researchers. The high success rate using the restricted matching procedure indicates that the ethnic-name database performs well without exploiting the international distribution of names, although power is lost with Europe. Likewise, uneven coverage in the Melissa database is not driving the ethnic composition trends.

8.2.3 Advantages and Disadvantages of the Name-Matching Technique

The matched records describe the ethnic composition of U.S. scientists and engineers with previously unavailable detail: incorporating the major ethnicities working in the U.S. SE community, separating out detailed technologies and manufacturing industries, providing city-level statistics, and providing annual metrics. Moreover, the assignment of patents to corporations and institutions affords firm-level and university-level characterizations that are not otherwise possible (e.g., the ethnic composition of IBM's inventors filing computer patents from San Francisco in 1985). The next section studies the agglomeration of invention along these various dimensions.[8]

The ethnic-name procedure does, however, have two potential limitations for empirical work on agglomeration that should be highlighted. First, the approach does not distinguish foreign-born ethnic researchers in the United States from later generations working as SEs. The procedure can only estimate total ethnic SE populations, and concentration levels are to some extent measured with time-invariant error due to the name-matching approach. The resulting data are very powerful, however, for panel econometrics that employ changes in these ethnic SE populations for identification. Moreover, Census and the Immigration and Naturalization Service records confirm Asian changes are primarily due to new SE immigration for this period, substantially weakening this concern when examining these groups.

The name-matching technique also does not distinguish finer divisions within the nine major ethnic groupings. For some analyses (e.g., network ties), it would be advantageous to separate Mexican from Chilean scientists within the Hispanic ethnicity, to distinguish Chinese engineers with ethnic ties to Taipei versus Beijing versus Shanghai, and so on. These distinctions are not possible with the Melissa database, and researchers should understand that measurement error from the broader ethnic divisions may bias their estimated coefficients downward, depending on the application. Nevertheless, the upcoming sections demonstrate how the deep variation available with the ethnic patenting data provides a rich description of U.S. ethnic invention.

8. Sample applications are Kerr (2008a, 2008b), Kerr and Lincoln (2008), and Foley and Kerr (2008).

8.3 The Agglomeration of U.S. Ethnic Invention

This section starts by describing the broad trends in ethnic contributions to U.S. technology formation. The spatial concentration of ethnic invention is then closely analyzed, including variations by technology categories and institutions.

8.3.1 Ethnic Composition of U.S. Inventors

Table 8.1 describes the ethnic composition of U.S. inventors for 1975 to 2004, with granted patents grouped by application years. The trends demonstrate a growing ethnic contribution to U.S. technology development, especially among Chinese and Indian scientists. Ethnic inventors are more concentrated in high-tech industries like computers and pharmaceuticals and in gateway cities relatively closer to their home countries (e.g., Chinese in San Francisco, Europeans in New York, and Hispanics in Miami). The final three rows demonstrate a close correspondence of the estimated ethnic composition to the country-of-birth composition of the U.S. SE workforce in the 1990 Census. The estimated European contribution in table 8.1 is naturally higher than the immigrant contribution measured by foreign-born.

Figure 8.1 illustrates the evolving ethnic composition of U.S. inventors from 1975 to 2004. The omitted English share declines from 83 percent to 70 percent during this period. Looking across all technology categories, the European ethnicity is initially the largest foreign contributor to U.S. technology development. Like the English ethnicity, however, the European share of U.S. domestic inventors declines steadily from 8 percent in 1975 to 6 percent in 2004. This declining share is partly due to the exceptional growth over the thirty years of the Chinese and Indian ethnicities, which increases from under 2 percent to 8 percent and 5 percent, respectively. As shown next, this Chinese and Indian growth is concentrated in high-tech sectors, where Chinese inventors supplant European researchers as the largest ethnic contributor to U.S. technology formation. The Indian ethnic contribution declines somewhat after 2000.[9]

Among the other ethnicities, the Hispanic contribution grows from 3 percent to 4 percent from 1975 to 2004. The level of this series is likely mismeasured due to the extensive overlap of Hispanic and European names, but the positive growth is consistent with stronger Latino and Filipino scientific contributions in Florida, Texas, and California. The Korean share increases dramatically from 0.3 percent to 1.1 percent over the thirty years, while the Russian share climbs from 1.2 percent to 2.2 percent. Although difficult to see with the scaling of figure 8.1, much of the Russian increase occurs

9. This decline is mostly due to changes within the computer technology sector, as seen in the following text. Recent applications to the USPTO suggest the Indian trend may not have declined as much as the granted patents through early 2008 portray. Kerr and Lincoln (2008) investigate the role of H-1B visa reforms for explaining these patterns.

Table 8.1 **Descriptive statistics for inventors residing in United States**

	Ethnicity of inventor								
	English	Chinese	European	Hispanic	Indian	Japanese	Korean	Russian	Vietnam.
	A. Ethnic inventor shares estimated from U.S. inventor records, 1975–2004 (%)								
1975–1979	82.5	2.2	8.3	2.9	1.9	0.6	0.3	1.2	0.1
1980–1984	81.1	2.9	7.9	3.0	2.4	0.7	0.5	1.3	0.1
1985–1989	79.8	3.6	7.5	3.2	2.9	0.8	0.6	1.4	0.2
1990–1994	77.6	4.6	7.2	3.5	3.6	0.9	0.7	1.5	0.4
1995–1999	73.9	6.5	6.8	3.9	4.8	0.9	0.8	1.8	0.5
2000–2004	70.4	8.5	6.4	4.2	5.4	1.0	1.1	2.2	0.6
Chemicals	73.4	7.2	7.5	3.6	4.5	1.0	0.8	1.7	0.3
Computers	70.1	8.2	6.3	3.8	6.9	1.1	0.9	2.1	0.7
Pharmaceuticals	72.9	7.1	7.4	4.3	4.2	1.1	0.9	1.8	0.4
Electrical	71.6	8.0	6.8	3.7	4.9	1.1	1.1	2.1	0.7
Mechanical	80.4	3.2	7.1	3.5	2.6	0.7	0.6	1.6	0.2
Miscellaneous	81.3	2.9	7.0	3.8	2.1	0.6	0.6	1.4	0.3
Top MSAs as a percentage of MSA's patents	KC (89)	SF (13)	NOR (12)	MIA (16)	SF (7)	SD (2)	BAL (2)	BOS (3)	AUS (2)
	WS (88)	LA (8)	STL (11)	SA (9)	AUS (7)	SF (2)	LA (2)	NYC (3)	SF (1)
	NAS (88)	AUS (6)	NYC (11)	WPB (7)	PRT (6)	LA (2)	SF (1)	SF (3)	LA (1)
	B. Ethnic scientist and engineer shares estimated from 1990 U.S. Census records (%)								
Bachelor's share	87.6	2.7	2.3	2.4	2.3	0.6	0.5	0.4	1.2
Master's share	78.9	6.7	3.4	2.2	5.4	0.9	0.7	0.8	1.0
Doctorate share	71.2	13.2	4.0	1.7	6.5	0.9	1.5	0.5	0.4

Notes: Panel A presents descriptive statistics for inventors residing in the United States at the time of patent application. Inventor ethnicities are estimated through inventors' names using techniques described in the text. Patents are grouped by application years and major technology fields. Metropolitan statistical areas include AUS (Austin), BAL (Baltimore), BOS (Boston), KC (Kansas City), LA (Los Angeles), MIA (Miami), NAS (Nashville), NOR (New Orleans), NYC (New York City), PRT (Portland), SA (San Antonio), SD (San Diego), SF (San Francisco), STL (St. Louis), WPB (West Palm Beach), and WS (Winston-Salem). The MSAs are identified from inventors' city names using city lists collected from the Office of Social and Economic Data Analysis at the University of Missouri, with a matching rate of 99 percent. Manual recoding further ensures all patents with more than one-hundred citations and all city names with more than one-hundred patents are identified. Panel B presents comparable statistics calculated from the 1990 Census using country of birth for scientists and engineers. Country groupings follow table 8A.3; English provides a residual in the Census statistics.

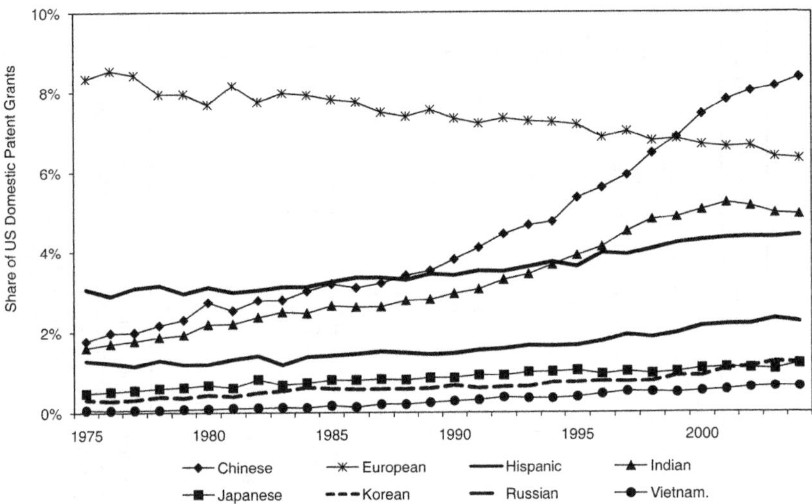

Fig. 8.1 Ethnic share of U.S. domestic patents

in the 1990s following the dissolution of the Soviet Union. The Japanese share steadily increases from 0.6 percent to 1.0 percent. Finally, while the Vietnamese contribution is the lowest throughout the sample, it does exhibit the strongest relative growth from 0.1 percent to 0.6 percent.

The 1975 to 2004 statistics employ patents granted by the USPTO through May 2008. Due to the long and uneven USPTO review process, statistics are grouped by application year to construct the most accurate indicators of when inventive activity occurs. The unfortunate consequence of using application years, however, is substantial attrition in years immediately before 2008. As many patents are in the review process but have yet to be granted, the granted-patent series is truncated at the 2004 application year. The USPTO began publishing patent applications in 2001. These applications data also show comparable ethnic contributions.

8.3.2 Spatial Locations of U.S. Ethnic Inventors

Table 8.2 examines the 1975 to 2004 ethnic inventor contributions by major MSAs. A total of 283 MSAs are identified from inventors' city names, using city lists collected from the Office of Social and Economic Data Analysis at the University of Missouri, with a matching rate of 99 percent. Manual coding further ensures all patents with more than one hundred citations and all city names with more than one hundred patents are identified. The first four columns document each MSA's share of U.S. patenting. Not surprisingly, these shares are highly correlated with MSA size, with the three largest patenting centers for 1995 to 2004 found in San Francisco (12 percent), New York (7 percent), and Los Angeles (6 percent), where the percentages indicate U.S. domestic patent shares.

Table 8.2 **Ethnic inventor contributions by MSA (%)**

	Total patenting share				Non-English ethnic patenting share				Chinese and Indian patenting share			
	1975–1984	1985–1994	1995–2004	2001–2006 (A)	1975–1984	1985–1994	1995–2004	2001–2006 (A)	1975–1984	1985–1994	1995–2004	2001–2006 (A)
Atlanta, GA	0.6	1.0	1.3	1.5	0.3	0.7	1.0	1.1	0.3	0.7	1.0	1.2
Austin, TX	0.4	0.9	1.8	2.0	0.5	1.2	1.9	2.0	0.4	1.6	2.3	2.3
Baltimore, MD	0.8	0.8	0.7	0.7	0.7	0.7	0.6	0.5	0.4	0.5	0.6	0.5
Boston, MA	3.6	3.8	3.9	4.6	3.9	4.2	4.1	4.8	4.0	4.0	3.6	4.3
Buffalo, NY	0.6	0.5	0.4	0.3	0.8	0.6	0.4	0.3	1.1	0.7	0.4	0.3
Charlotte, NC	0.3	0.3	0.3	0.3	0.2	0.2	0.2	0.2	0.1	0.2	0.1	0.2
Chicago, IL	6.0	4.6	3.5	3.2	6.9	5.0	3.5	3.0	5.6	3.9	2.9	2.8
Cincinnati, OH	1.0	1.1	1.0	1.0	0.9	0.9	0.7	0.7	0.7	1.0	0.6	0.6
Cleveland, OH	2.3	1.7	1.3	1.1	2.5	1.5	1.0	0.8	2.5	1.4	0.9	0.6
Columbus, OH	0.7	0.5	0.5	0.4	0.6	0.6	0.4	0.3	0.8	0.7	0.3	0.3
Dallas-Fort Worth, TX	1.6	2.0	2.3	2.1	1.1	1.9	2.3	2.2	1.5	2.4	2.9	2.8
Denver, CO	1.0	1.2	1.3	1.3	0.8	1.0	0.9	0.8	0.8	1.0	0.6	0.5
Detroit, MI	3.1	3.3	2.9	2.8	3.1	3.1	2.6	2.6	3.2	2.8	2.5	2.5
Greensboro-Winston-Salem, NC	0.2	0.3	0.3	0.2	0.1	0.2	0.2	0.1	0.2	0.2	0.1	0.1
Hartford, CT	0.9	0.9	0.6	0.6	1.0	0.8	0.5	0.5	0.8	0.6	0.3	0.4
Houston, TX	2.3	2.5	1.9	2.0	1.8	2.3	1.8	1.9	2.2	2.8	1.8	1.9
Indianapolis, IN	0.8	0.7	0.7	0.5	0.6	0.4	0.4	0.3	0.7	0.5	0.4	0.3
Jacksonville, NC	0.1	0.1	0.1	0.1	0.1	0.1	0.1	0.1	0.1	0.1	0.1	0.1
Kansas City, MO	0.4	0.3	0.4	0.3	0.2	0.2	0.2	0.2	0.2	0.1	0.2	0.2
Las Vegas, NV	0.1	0.1	0.2	0.3	0.1	0.1	0.2	0.2	0.0	0.1	0.1	0.1
Los Angeles, CA	6.6	6.1	6.0	5.7	7.2	7.2	7.9	7.3	6.7	6.9	7.5	7.0
Memphis, TN	0.1	0.2	0.2	0.3	0.1	0.1	0.1	0.2	0.1	0.1	0.1	0.1
Miami, FL	0.8	0.9	0.7	0.7	1.0	1.3	1.0	0.9	0.5	0.6	0.5	0.4
Milwaukee, WI	1.0	0.9	0.8	0.7	0.8	0.8	0.6	0.5	0.5	0.4	0.5	0.4
Minneapolis-St. Paul, MN	1.9	2.4	2.7	2.8	1.6	2.0	2.0	2.0	1.5	1.7	1.7	1.8
Nashville, TN	0.1	0.2	0.2	0.2	0.0	0.1	0.1	0.1	0.1	0.1	0.1	0.1

(continued)

Table 8.2 (continued)

	Total patenting share				Non-English ethnic patenting share				Chinese and Indian patenting share			
	1975–1984	1985–1994	1995–2004	2001–2006 (A)	1975–1984	1985–1994	1995–2004	2001–2006 (A)	1975–1984	1985–1994	1995–2004	2001–2006 (A)
New Orleans, LA	0.3	0.2	0.2	0.1	0.3	0.3	0.1	0.1	0.2	0.2	0.0	0.0
New York, NY	11.5	8.9	7.3	6.9	16.6	13.1	10.1	8.9	16.6	13.3	9.7	9.0
Norfolk-Virginia Beach, VA	0.2	0.2	0.2	0.1	0.1	0.1	0.1	0.1	0.1	0.1	0.1	0.1
Orlando, FL	0.2	0.3	0.3	0.3	0.1	0.2	0.3	0.3	0.1	0.2	0.3	0.3
Philadelphia, PA	4.6	4.0	2.7	2.8	5.6	4.9	2.8	2.9	6.2	5.8	2.8	3.0
Phoenix, AZ	1.0	1.2	1.4	1.3	0.6	1.1	1.3	1.2	0.4	1.0	1.4	1.3
Pittsburgh, PA	2.0	1.3	0.8	0.7	2.2	1.4	0.6	0.5	2.2	1.3	0.5	0.5
Portland, OR	0.5	0.8	1.4	1.6	0.3	0.6	1.4	1.6	0.2	0.6	1.7	2.0
Providence, RI	0.3	0.3	0.3	0.2	0.3	0.4	0.3	0.2	0.2	0.3	0.2	0.2
Raleigh-Durham, NC	0.3	0.6	1.1	1.5	0.3	0.6	1.0	1.3	0.3	0.8	1.0	1.2
Richmond, VA	0.3	0.3	0.2	0.2	0.3	0.3	0.2	0.2	0.3	0.4	0.2	0.2
Sacramento, CA	0.2	0.4	0.5	0.5	0.2	0.4	0.5	0.5	0.2	0.3	0.5	0.5
Salt Lake City, UT	0.4	0.5	0.6	0.6	0.2	0.4	0.3	0.3	0.2	0.3	0.3	0.3
San Antonio, TX	0.1	0.2	0.2	0.2	0.1	0.2	0.2	0.2	0.2	0.1	0.1	0.1
San Diego, CA	1.1	1.6	2.2	2.8	1.1	1.6	2.6	3.6	0.8	1.4	2.4	3.9
San Francisco, CA	4.8	6.6	12.1	13.2	6.2	9.3	19.3	19.9	8.4	13.0	25.4	24.0
Seattle, WA	0.9	1.3	1.9	3.4	0.8	1.1	1.8	3.5	0.6	1.0	1.8	3.7
St. Louis, MO	1.0	0.9	0.8	0.8	0.9	0.8	0.8	0.7	1.0	0.8	0.4	0.4
Tallahassee, FL	0.4	0.5	0.4	0.4	0.3	0.4	0.3	0.3	0.2	0.2	0.2	0.2
Washington, DC	1.5	1.5	1.4	1.6	1.6	1.6	1.5	1.7	1.6	1.7	1.5	1.7
West Palm Beach, FL	0.3	0.5	0.4	0.4	0.3	0.5	0.4	0.4	0.3	0.3	0.2	0.2
Other 234 MSAs	21.8	22.3	20.7	18.4	18.1	18.1	15.6	13.6	19.7	18.2	14.6	12.7
Not in an MSA	9.0	8.2	6.6	6.2	6.3	5.4	3.7	4.1	5.2	3.8	2.5	2.7

Notes: See table 8.1. The first three columns of each grouping are for granted patents. The fourth column, marked with (A), is for published patent applications.

Comparing these total patenting percentages with the ethnic patenting shares—listed in the second set of four columns—reveals the more interesting fact that ethnic patenting is more concentrated than general innovation. The 1995 to 2004 ethnic patent shares of San Francisco, New York, and Los Angeles are 19 percent, 10 percent, and 8 percent, respectively. Similarly, 81 percent of ethnic research occurs in the major MSAs listed in table 8.2, compared to 73 percent of total patenting. The final three columns list the Chinese and Indian patenting share by MSA, highlighting the exceptional growth of San Francisco, from 8 percent of 1975 to 1984 patenting to 25 percent in 1995 to 2004. These concentration levels and trends are further examined next.[10]

Table 8.3 presents simple least squares estimations of ethnic inventor locations and MSA characteristics. The variables of interest are MSA shares of U.S. ethnic inventors during 1985 to 2004, with column headers indicating ethnicities. These shares are calculated over the 244 MSAs for which full covariate information are assembled. The dropped observations are small cities not separately identified in 1990 Census of Population. For ease of interpretation, variables are transformed to have unit standard deviation in these cross-sectional estimations. Estimations are weighted by MSA populations.

To establish a baseline, the first two columns consider MSA inventor shares of the English ethnicity. In column (1), MSA size and urban density strongly predict higher English inventor shares. A 1 standard deviation increase in the population share of the MSA correlates with a 0.57 standard deviation increase in the share of English ethnic invention. Coastal access does not predict greater inventor concentration in multivariate frameworks, although a univariate correlation exists. On the other hand, MSA demographics have a statistically and economically significant relationship with inventor concentrations. The MSA traits are calculated from the 1990 Census of Population. MSAs with more educated workforces are associated with greater inventor concentrations. Higher shares of English invention are also found in MSAs with relatively more people between the ages of thirty and sixty (the omitted group) and more men. All told, this parsimonious set of covariates explains 84 percent of the variation in English invention shares.

Table 8.2 suggests that inventor shares are relatively persistent over time for MSAs. Column (2) of table 8.3 confirms this observation for English inventors. The estimation incorporates the share of English ethnic patenting in the MSA for 1975 to 1984. This ten year period predates the major growth in ethnic inventors highlighted in figure 8.1. The spatial distribution

10. Each of these trends appears to have strengthened in the recent applications data (i.e., the columns marked with A in table 8.2). While suggestive, these statistics should be treated with caution. Some technology fields and firm types are more likely to publish their patent applications than others. Likewise, probabilities of patent grants conditional on application vary by field. Lemley and Sampat (2007) discuss these limitations further.

Table 8.3 **Ethnic inventors and MSA characteristics, weighted estimations**

	English		Chinese		Indian		European		Hispanic	
	(1)	(2)	(3)	(4)	(5)	(6)	(7)	(8)	(9)	(10)
1975–1984 share of ethnic patents in MSA		0.842		0.865		0.796		0.646		0.526
		(0.284)		(0.501)		(0.186)		(0.053)		(0.185)
Log population of MSA	0.573	–0.132	0.475	–0.273	0.457	–0.176	0.650	0.117	0.812	0.268
	(0.076)	(0.260)	(0.099)	(0.495)	(0.199)	(0.186)	(0.191)	(0.066)	(0.071)	(0.200)
Log population density of MSA	0.251	–0.063	–0.140	–0.253	0.143	–0.223	0.329	–0.004	–0.080	–0.100
	(0.105)	(0.134)	(0.129)	(0.166)	(0.238)	(0.146)	(0.211)	(0.084)	(0.106)	(0.078)
Coastal access of MSA	0.029	0.177	0.378	0.294	0.240	0.327	0.063	0.190	0.331	0.269
	(0.137)	(0.161)	(0.266)	(0.160)	(0.237)	(0.221)	(0.146)	(0.132)	(0.135)	(0.106)
Share of population with bachelor's education	0.429	0.268	0.505	0.184	0.602	0.353	0.498	0.301	0.303	0.220
	(0.257)	(0.163)	(0.399)	(0.163)	(0.378)	(0.253)	(0.270)	(0.201)	(0.216)	(0.174)
Share of population under 30 in age	–0.779	–0.711	–1.320	–1.031	–1.291	–1.161	–0.641	–0.667	–0.558	–0.581
	(0.566)	(0.456)	(1.150)	(0.684)	(0.980)	(0.824)	(0.569)	(0.519)	(0.535)	(0.493)
Share of population over 60 in age	–0.452	–0.567	–0.757	–0.804	–0.703	–0.844	–0.175	–0.432	–0.275	–0.400
	(0.347)	(0.325)	(0.704)	(0.535)	(0.598)	(0.549)	(0.362)	(0.326)	(0.334)	(0.327)
Share of population female	–0.313	–0.451	–0.576	–0.968	–0.090	–0.632	0.155	–0.295	–0.128	–0.375
	(0.256)	(0.268)	(0.516)	(0.592)	(0.485)	(0.489)	(0.340)	(0.251)	(0.247)	(0.285)
R^2	0.84	0.88	0.54	0.69	0.61	0.74	0.82	0.91	0.90	0.92

Notes: Estimations provide partial correlations for ethnic patenting undertaken in 244 MSAs over the 1985 to 2004 period. The dependent variable is the MSA's share of indicated ethnic invention relative to the MSA sample. Explanatory regressors are from the 1990 Census of Population, except for coastal access and the lagged ethnic patenting share. The latter is ethnic specific and is calculated for the 1975 to 1984 preperiod from the ethnic patenting database. Estimations are weighted by MSA populations. Variables are transformed to unit standard deviation for interpretation. Robust standard errors are reported in parentheses. Dependent variable is share of 1985–2004 ethnic patenting in the MSA.

of English invention over 1975 to 1984 is a very strong predictor for 1985 to 2004 concentration, with an elasticity of 0.84. The MSA populations and density levels do not exhibit a well-measured relationship with 1985 to 2004 English inventor concentrations after controlling for these past levels. Partial correlations with MSA demographics, however, are more robust. Incorporating the past concentration lag explains 88 percent of the MSA-level variation in inventor shares (83 percent by itself).[11]

The subsequent eight columns of table 8.3 consider major non-English inventor shares. The estimation framework remains the same, except for the 1975 to 1984 MSA inventor shares in the even-numbered columns that are adjusted to match the dependent variable. Most explanatory variables (e.g., MSA demographics) demonstrate similar elasticities across ethnic groups. Coastal access tends to be more important, although it is of borderline statistical significance. This reflects the well-known tendency for immigrants to locate in port cities closer to their home countries.

However, several interesting differences emerge. First, the overall explanatory power of these regressors varies across ethnic groups. The R^2 values for the Chinese and Indian ethnicities are substantially lower than those for the European and Hispanic ethnicities. These Asian ethnicities thus have more idiosyncratic spatial patterns than this limited set of covariates modeled. This is confirmed when the even-numbered columns incorporate the lagged ethnic inventor shares. The gain in the variation explained through past MSA-specific placements is strongest for Chinese and Indian inventors. This strength suggests that lagged spatial patterns for Asian inventors may offer an empirical foothold for predicting future MSA-level innovation, even conditional on other MSA-level traits.

These even-numbered columns also show that lagged ethnic inventor shares tend to have weaker predictive power for subsequent MSA-level concentration compared to the English ethnicity in column (2). The elasticities range from 0.87 for Chinese patents to 0.53 for Hispanic patents (which is lowest among the nine ethnic inventor groups). This lower explanatory power has at least two explanations. First, spatial distributions for ethnic inventors over 1975 to 1984 may have greater measurement error than English inventor distributions due to smaller counts of relevant patents. Such measurement error would downward bias estimated elasticities.

Nonetheless, it is also true that ethnic inventors facilitate shifts in invention locations across U.S. MSAs. For example, immigrant SE students graduating from elite U.S. universities enter a national labor market. Hispanic inventors have supported broader growth in Florida and the southwestern

11. Unreported specifications further incorporate mean wages in manufacturing, mean family income levels, and mean housing prices by MSA. Positive correlations between inventor shares and manufacturing wages are generally found; family income levels and housing prices do not exhibit robust relationships in multivariate settings. The inclusion of these three covariates has very limited influence on the reported outcomes.

states. While past immigration cities are favored, ethnic inventors also have an inherent capacity to facilitate regional adjustments. Unreported estimations further test this conclusion by controlling simultaneously for each MSA's 1975 to 1984 English inventor share and ethnic-specific inventor share. With the exception of the European and Russian ethnicities, lagged ethnic spatial distributions have stronger predictive power for subsequent agglomeration than lagged English spatial distributions.

Table 8.4 repeats the estimations without the MSA population weights. The measured partial correlations decline in magnitude somewhat, reflective of the greater attention paid to smaller MSA shares, but the patterns of coefficients and explanatory power are comparable to the weighted outcomes. Several additional specification checks are also undertaken. Incorporating regional fixed effects finds anticipated spatial patterns—midwestern U.S. MSAs tend to have higher invention rates conditional on the covariates modeled, while southern MSAs have lower rates. The East and West Coasts are often not statistically distinguishable from each other conditionally. Performing the share estimations on an annual basis, which circumvents growth in recent patent application rates, yields similar outcomes to the cross-sectional results. Likewise, log specifications produce outcomes similar to the share specification framework.

Finally, the appendix documents specifications that model lagged ethnic population shares across MSAs as the historical regressor rather than the distribution of lagged ethnic patenting. These shares are calculated over working-age populations for 203 cities through the 1980 Census of Population by country of birth. In general, the spatial distribution of lagged ethnic patenting in tables 8.3 and 8.4 is a stronger predictor than general ethnic population distributions; R^2 values also decline. The one exception is for the Chinese ethnicity, where the general Chinese population distribution is an exceptionally strong predictor of recent patenting. These patterns also hold when jointly modeling the lagged regressors together.

These comparisons are interesting in that they begin to quantify the relative roles of production versus consumption benefits for the agglomeration of ethnic inventors. The productive benefits of being near other inventors of one's ethnicity appear stronger than the general consumption benefits of being in ethnic enclaves, but the latter are surprisingly strong. To properly address this issue, future work hopes to examine the subcity level to the extent possible with the patenting data. The high correlation between lagged Chinese inventor and population distributions depends, for example, on the decision to model the San Francisco Bay Area as a single MSA. Splitting San Jose and Silicon Valley from San Francisco and/or Oakland would reduce the correlation. Undertaking such an analysis would be informative for the specific question of location decisions by ethnic inventors; it would also contribute to recent work on ethnic enclaves at the subcity level (e.g., Pedace and Rohn 2008).

Table 8.4 Ethnic inventors and MSA characteristics, unweighted estimations

	English		Chinese		Indian		European		Hispanic	
	(1)	(2)	(3)	(4)	(5)	(6)	(7)	(8)	(9)	(10)
1975–1984 share of ethnic patents in MSA		0.884		0.968		0.726		0.643		0.655
		(0.255)		(0.586)		(0.262)		(0.107)		(0.271)
Log population of MSA	0.810	–0.029	0.647	–0.230	0.684	0.037	0.845	0.261	0.901	0.250
	(0.106)	(0.171)	(0.145)	(0.431)	(0.185)	(0.134)	(0.166)	(0.102)	(0.075)	(0.189)
Log population density of MSA	0.053	0.026	–0.047	–0.019	–0.002	–0.018	0.020	0.016	–0.043	–0.003
	(0.034)	(0.026)	(0.029)	(0.039)	(0.051)	(0.030)	(0.050)	(0.020)	(0.023)	(0.015)
Coastal access of MSA	–0.027	0.022	0.052	0.067	0.012	0.046	–0.009	0.020	0.054	0.043
	(0.035)	(0.039)	(0.057)	(0.047)	(0.050)	(0.055)	(0.033)	(0.030)	(0.033)	(0.026)
Share of population with bachelor's education	0.123	0.091	0.084	0.041	0.113	0.087	0.094	0.080	0.070	0.067
	(0.034)	(0.023)	(0.050)	(0.025)	(0.048)	(0.035)	(0.034)	(0.026)	(0.029)	(0.025)
Share of population under 30 in age	–0.151	–0.145	–0.115	–0.152	–0.139	–0.150	–0.078	–0.110	–0.045	–0.090
	(0.064)	(0.056)	(0.111)	(0.104)	(0.100)	(0.091)	(0.065)	(0.055)	(0.056)	(0.061)
Share of population over 60 in age	–0.102	–0.135	–0.078	–0.151	–0.086	–0.140	–0.015	–0.081	–0.012	–0.076
	(0.051)	(0.053)	(0.086)	(0.103)	(0.078)	(0.084)	(0.053)	(0.045)	(0.047)	(0.056)
Share of population female	–0.056	–0.050	–0.055	–0.058	–0.055	–0.057	–0.032	–0.039	–0.033	–0.042
	(0.023)	(0.021)	(0.037)	(0.033)	(0.033)	(0.033)	(0.021)	(0.019)	(0.021)	(0.021)
R^2	0.79	0.85	0.45	0.65	0.54	0.64	0.78	0.86	0.83	0.87

Notes: See table 8.3. Estimations are unweighted. Dependent variable is share of 1985–2004 ethnic patenting in the MSA.

Of course, these estimations must be interpreted as partial correlations rather than causal assessments. Clearly, ethnic inventors directly influence many of the determinants modeled (e.g., education shares) and may also have local spillover effects through their work (e.g., local technology gains that generate city population growth). Omitted factors may also be correlated with past immigrant placements. Future work hopes to further refine these determinants in a causal assessment.

Ongoing research is further evaluating how shifts in the geographic concentration of ethnic inventors facilitate changes in the geographic composition of U.S. innovation. Not only are ethnic scientists disproportionately concentrated in major MSAs, but growth in an MSA's share of ethnic patenting is highly correlated with growth in its share of total U.S. patenting. Annual regressions across the full 1975 to 2004 MSA sample find that an increase of 1 percent in an MSA's ethnic patenting share correlates with a 0.6 percent increase in the MSA's total invention share. This coefficient is remarkably high, as the mean ethnic share of total invention during this period is around 20 percent. Of course, additional study is required before causal assessments are possible. The ethnic-name approach will also need to be complemented with external data to distinguish ethnic inventor shifts due to new immigration, domestic migration, or occupational changes.

8.3.3 Spatial Concentration of U.S. Ethnic Inventors

To refine the earlier visual observations made regarding agglomeration levels in table 8.2, table 8.5 presents three concentration indices for U.S. domestic patenting. The first concentration metric studied is the Herfindahl-Hirschman index, defined by $\text{HHI}_t = \sum_{m=1}^{M} \text{Share}_{mt}^2$, where M indexes 283 MSAs, and Share_{mt} is the share of patenting in MSA m in period t. Of course, patenting is undertaken outside of MSAs, too. The share of patenting outside of these 283 MSAs declines from 9 percent in 1975 to 1984 to 7 percent in 1995 to 2004. In 2001 to 2006 applications, this share further declines to 6 percent. This portion of U.S. invention is excluded from the remainder of this chapter, with concentration metrics being calculated over MSA patenting only.

The top panels of table 8.5 and figure 8.2 highlight several important levels differences. First, U.S. invention is more concentrated than the general population across these MSAs.[12] Moreover, ethnic inventors are substantially more agglomerated than English-ethnicity inventors throughout the thirty years considered. The mean population HHI is 0.024 over the period, compared with 0.037 for invention and 0.059 for all non-English inventors. The agglomeration of Chinese inventors further stands out at 0.081. This

12. MSA populations are calculated through county populations collected in 1977, 1982, 1987, 1992, and 1997. These are midpoints of the five-year increments studied. The 2000 to 2004 period uses the 1997 MSA population.

Table 8.5 **Concentration ratios of invention**

	Total population	Total invention	English invention	Non-English invention	Chinese invention	Indian invention
			A. Herfindahl-Hirschman index			
1975–1979	0.025	0.040	0.037	0.061	0.062	0.059
1980–1984	0.024	0.037	0.034	0.055	0.066	0.051
1985–1989	0.024	0.034	0.030	0.051	0.063	0.052
1990–1994	0.024	0.032	0.028	0.048	0.068	0.046
1995–1999	0.023	0.038	0.031	0.065	0.106	0.072
2000–2004	0.023	0.040	0.030	0.075	0.119	0.075
Mean	0.024	0.037	0.032	0.059	0.081	0.059
			B. Share in top 5 MSAs from 1975–1984 (%)			
1975–1979	28.2	37.8	35.9	46.7	48.0	43.4
1980–1984	27.5	35.7	33.8	44.0	49.5	40.1
1985–1989	27.4	33.7	31.4	43.0	49.2	41.2
1990–1994	27.1	32.2	29.6	41.2	48.6	38.5
1995–1999	26.5	33.7	29.8	44.6	53.3	43.3
2000–2004	26.5	33.1	28.0	45.1	53.8	41.6
Mean	27.2	34.4	31.4	44.1	50.4	41.4
			C. Ellison-Glaeser index relative to MSA populations			
1975–1979	n.a.	0.003	0.002	0.011	0.014	0.011
1980–1984	n.a.	0.003	0.002	0.010	0.019	0.011
1985–1989	n.a.	0.003	0.003	0.009	0.018	0.011
1990–1994	n.a.	0.004	0.004	0.010	0.027	0.012
1995–1999	n.a.	0.012	0.009	0.029	0.067	0.038
2000–2004	n.a.	0.016	0.010	0.041	0.082	0.047
Mean		0.007	0.005	0.018	0.038	0.022

Notes: Metrics consider agglomeration of U.S. domestic invention across 283 MSAs, with invention in rural areas excluded. Top five MSAs are kept constant from 1975 to 1984 rankings: New York City, Los Angeles, Chicago, Philadelphia, and San Francisco. Ellison and Glaeser metrics consider agglomeration of invention relative to MSA populations. These latter metrics abstract from plant Herfindahl corrections. General population counts from 1995 to 1999 are used for 2000 to 2004; n.a. = not applicable.

higher ethnic concentration certainly reflects the well-known concentration of immigrant groups but is not simply due to the smaller sizes of some ethnicities. Chinese, Japanese, and Vietnamese are consistently the most agglomerated of ethnic inventor groups. European and Hispanic inventors are the least concentrated, but all ethnic groups are more agglomerated than the English ethnicity.[13]

Moving from the levels to the trends evident in table 8.5 and figure 8.2,

13. Calculations from the 1990 and 2000 Census of Population find that the aggregate concentration of immigrant SEs is slightly less than the agglomeration of all immigrants. Substantial differences in immigrant shares are evident in larger cities. New York City, Los Angeles, and Miami have larger overall immigration pools relative to SE, while San Francisco, Boston, Seattle, and Washington, DC, have greater SE shares.

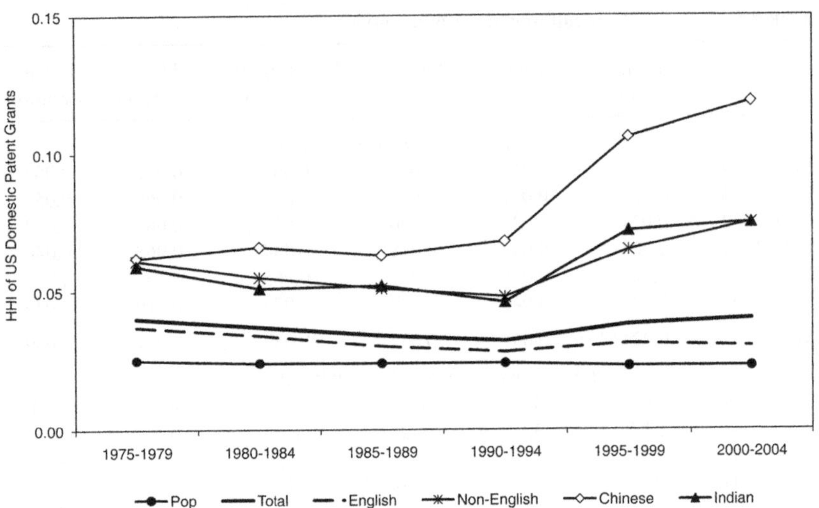

Fig. 8.2 HHI concentration of U.S. patents

the HHI for all U.S. inventors consistently declines from 1975 through 1979 to 1990 through 1994. This trend is reversed, however, with greater levels of invention agglomeration in 1995 to 1999 and 2000 to 2004. This reversal toward greater patenting concentration is not reflected in the overall population shares. Ethnic inventors, however, show a sharp increase in these latter ten years. This upturn is strongest among Asian ethnic groups, with European and Hispanic inventors showing limited change in agglomeration.

A second agglomeration metric is calculated as the share of total U.S. patenting in the top five MSAs for 1975 to 1984: New York City (12 percent), Los Angeles (7 percent), Chicago (6 percent), Philadelphia (5 percent), and San Francisco (5 percent). Boston (4 percent) and Detroit (3 percent) have the next two largest shares in 1975 to 1984. These five MSAs account for about 37 percent of MSA patenting during this initial period and 34 percent of total U.S. patenting that includes rural areas. The share accounted for by these five MSAs behaves similarly to the HHI metric, declining until 1990 to 1994 before growing during 1995 to 2004. While less formal, this second technique highlights how ethnic agglomeration shifts across the major U.S. MSAs. By 1995 to 2004, San Francisco (12 percent) leads New York City (7 percent) and Los Angeles (6 percent). Boston and Chicago would complete a new top-five MSAs list for 1995 to 2004.

Our final agglomeration metric is taken from Ellison and Glaeser (1997),

$$\gamma_e^{\text{Agg}} = \frac{\sum_{m=1}^{M}(s_{m,e} - x_m)^2}{1 - \sum_{m=1}^{M} x_m^2},$$

where M indexes MSAs. The variables $s_{1,e}, s_{2,e}, \ldots, s_{M,e}$ are the shares of ethnicity e's patenting contained in each of these geographic areas. The

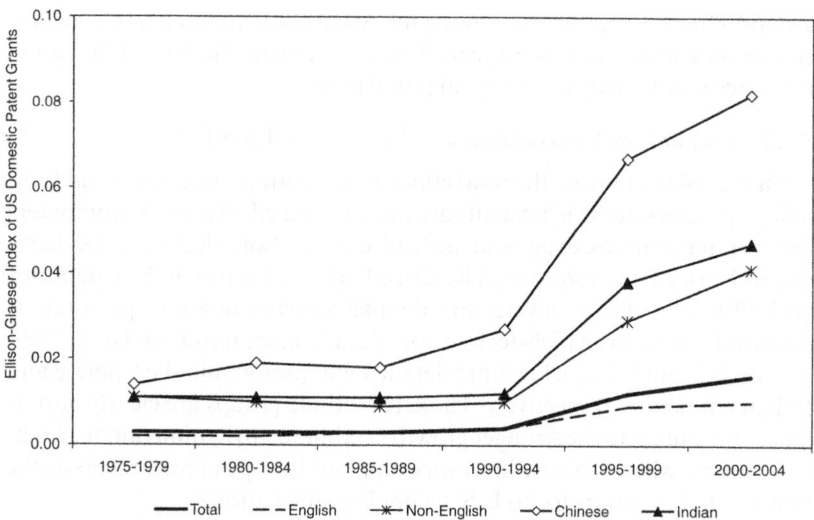

Fig. 8.3 Ellison and Glaeser concentration of U.S. patents

variables $x_1, x_2, \ldots, x_M$ are each area's share of population.[14] This metric estimates the agglomeration of invention relative to the baseline established by the MSA populations. If invention is randomly distributed among the population, the Ellison and Glaeser metric will not show concentration. The bottom panels of table 8.5 and figure 8.3 report these indices. When judged relative to the overall population's distribution, the trends in the agglomeration of invention look a little different. The 1975 to 1994 periods are found to have fairly consistent levels of concentration, with a strong upturn in the 1995 to 2004 years. This pattern is predicted by the growing deviations with time in the HHI trends in panel A.

Following Ellison, Glaeser, and Kerr (2007), the pairwise coagglomeration of invention between ethnicity e_1 and e_2 is analyzed with the simple formula

$$\gamma_{e_1 e_2}^{\text{Coagg}} = \frac{\sum_{m=1}^{M}(s_{m,e_1} - x_m)(s_{m,e_2} - x_m)}{1 - \sum_{m=1}^{M} x_m^2}.$$

This index measures the covariance of ethnic invention across MSAs, with the denominator rescaling the covariance to eliminate a sensitivity to the fineness of the geographic breakdown. The coagglomeration indices are contained in the appendix. Coagglomeration among non-English ethnic inventors is substantially higher than between English inventors and these

14. The full Ellison and Glaeser (1997) formula also controls for the HHI index of plant size. This feature is ignored in this examination of individual inventors. The ethnic patenting data do not easily support continuous estimators like Duranton and Overman (2005), although future research hopes to approximate these metrics, too.

groups. This is especially true among the Asian ethnicities. These coagglomeration measures rise in recent years, behaving similarly to the agglomeration measures when relative to the total population.

8.3.4 Technology Concentration of U.S. Ethnic Inventors

Figure 8.4 documents the total ethnic contribution by the six broad technology groups into which patents are often classified: chemicals, computers and communications, drugs and medical, electrical and electronic, mechanical, and miscellaneous/others. The miscellaneous group includes patents for agriculture, textiles, furniture, and the like. Growth in ethnic patenting is noticeably stronger in high-tech sectors than in more traditional industries. Figures 8.5 and 8.6 provide more detailed glimpses within the Chinese and Indian ethnicities, respectively. These two ethnic groups are clearly important contributors to the stronger growth in ethnic contributions among high-tech sectors, where Chinese inventors supplant European researchers as the largest ethnic contributor to U.S. technology formation.[15]

One possible explanation for the aggregate gains in concentration in table 8.5 is compositional shifts in the volume and nature of granted patents rather than a shift in underlying innovation per se. There has been a substantial increase in the number of patents granted by the USPTO over the last two decades. While this increase is partly due to population growth and higher levels of U.S. innovation, institutional factors also play an important role.[16] The heightened agglomeration may be driven by greater patenting rates by certain technology groups, reflecting either true changes in the underlying innovation rates or simply a greater propensity to seek patent protection. The latter is especially relevant for the recent rise of software patents (e.g., Graham and Mowery 2004). Microsoft, Oracle, and other software companies are among the United States' largest firms today in terms of patent applications, but historically, this industry did not seek patent protection.

Table 8.6 considers the geographic concentration of invention that exists within each of the six broad technology groupings. Panel A presents HHI measures calculated over all patents within each technology. The exceptional rebounds for 1995 to 2004 are strongest within the computers and communications and electrical and electronic groupings. Drugs and medical and mechanical categories also demonstrate weaker gains, while chemicals and miscellaneous show steady trends for less spatial agglomeration throughout the 1975 to 2004 period.

15. The USPTO issues patents by technology categories rather than by industries. Combining the work of Johnson (1999), Silverman (1999), and Kerr (2008a), concordances can be developed to map the USPTO classification scheme to the three-digit industries in which new inventions are manufactured or used. Scherer (1984) and Keller (2002) further discuss the importance of interindustry research and development flows.

16. For example, Griliches (1990), Kortum and Lerner (2000), Kim and Marschke (2004), Hall (2004), and Jaffe and Lerner (2005).

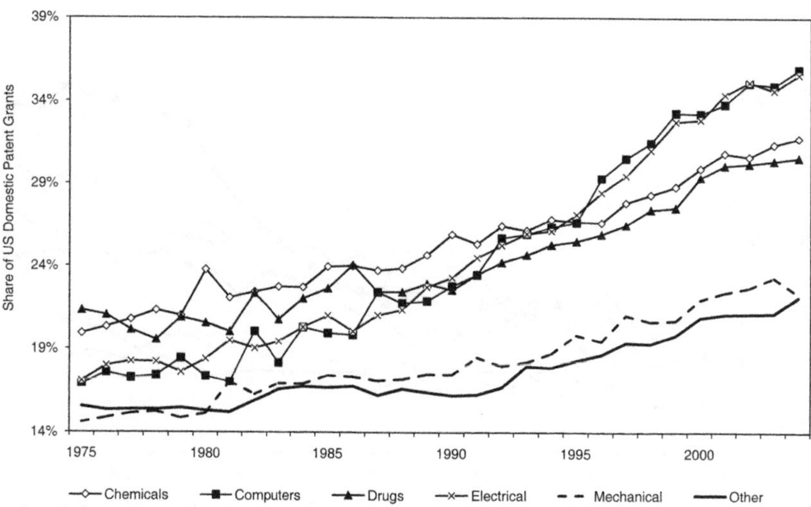

Fig. 8.4 Total U.S. ethnic share by technology

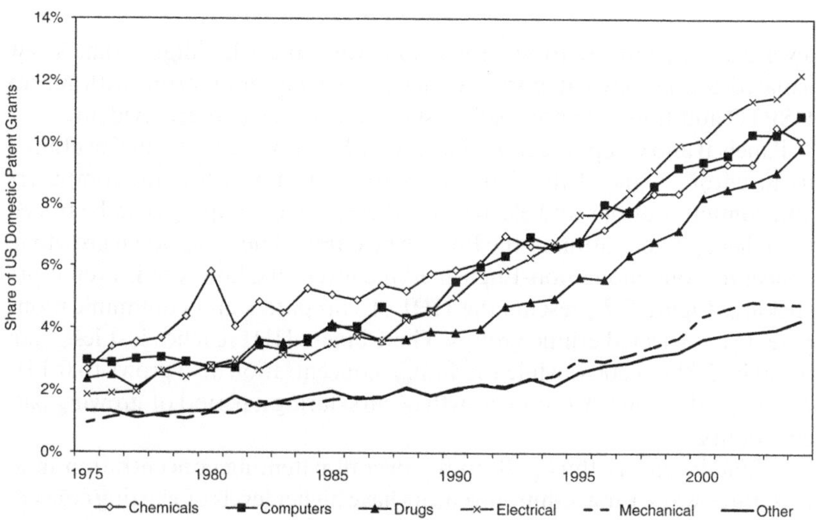

Fig. 8.5 Chinese contribution by technology

The dual responses within the computers and communications and electrical and electronic groupings suggest that the greater agglomeration is more of a high-tech phenomena than software in particular. This conclusion is further confirmed in the appendix. In these estimations, agglomeration is calculated for each subcategory within the six broad technology divisions; there are four to nine subcategories within each division. In both weighted and unweighted estimations, the concentration metrics at the subcategory

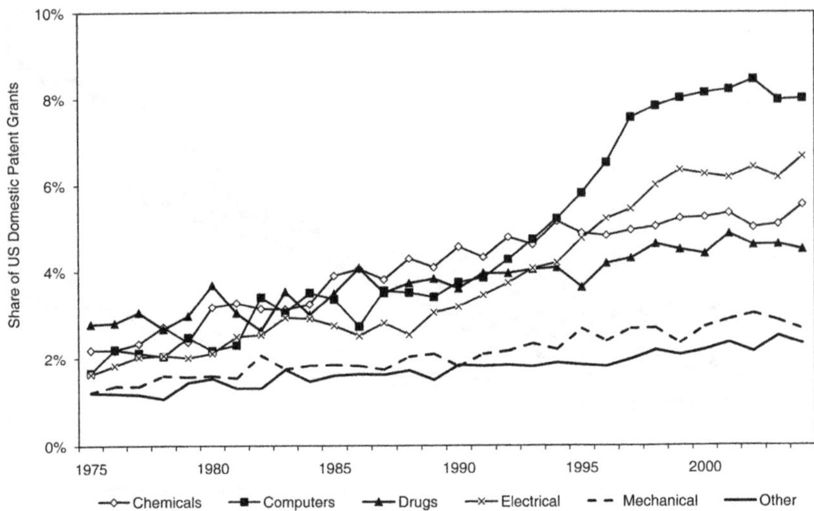

Fig. 8.6 Indian contribution by technology

level behave similarly to table 9.6. This robustness highlights that a few isolated technology categories, either preexisting or entering with recent USPTO additions, are not solely responsible for the patterns evident.

Panels B and C report similar indices for English and non-English ethnicity inventors. Some of the sharp concentration gains within the computers and communications and electrical and electronic groupings can be traced to higher agglomeration of the English inventors. The exceptional growth in concentration among non-English ethnic inventors, however, is even more striking. Figure 8.7 presents the HHI of computers and communications patents for selected ethnic groups. The Chinese HHI reaches just less than 0.200 by 2000 to 2004, while the Indian concentration also grows to 0.141. Note that this concentration growth occurs during a period of growing patent counts.

Ethnic inventors thus pull up the overall patenting concentration in at least three ways. First, ethnic inventors have higher levels of existing concentration and are becoming a larger share of U.S. patenting (figure 8.4). Even if their own concentration holds constant, this should lead to an increase in the agglomeration of U.S. patenting. Second, ethnic inventors are themselves becoming more spatially concentrated in high-tech fields. This force also leads to an increase in overall agglomeration levels. Ethnic inventors are also more concentrated in fields that have experienced greater rates of recent patenting, yielding a mechanical link as well.[17]

17. These effects appear to continue in the 2001 to 2006 applications data cataloged in table 8.2.

Table 8.6 Concentration ratios of invention by technology group

	Chemicals	Computers and communications	Drugs and medical	Electrical and electronic	Mechanical	Miscellaneous
	A. Herfindahl-Hirschman index for all patents within technology group					
1975–1979	0.053	0.055	0.070	0.043	0.032	0.039
1980–1984	0.048	0.050	0.061	0.039	0.030	0.035
1985–1989	0.043	0.048	0.055	0.036	0.029	0.031
1990–1994	0.038	0.054	0.047	0.037	0.028	0.028
1995–1999	0.033	0.075	0.050	0.052	0.029	0.027
2000–2004	0.034	0.078	0.053	0.059	0.032	0.026
Mean	0.041	0.060	0.056	0.044	0.030	0.031
	B. HHI for English patents within technology group					
1975–1979	0.049	0.051	0.063	0.040	0.030	0.036
1980–1984	0.043	0.046	0.056	0.035	0.028	0.032
1985–1989	0.038	0.043	0.050	0.033	0.027	0.028
1990–1994	0.033	0.046	0.044	0.032	0.026	0.025
1995–1999	0.029	0.059	0.046	0.038	0.026	0.023
2000–2004	0.028	0.055	0.048	0.040	0.028	0.022
Mean	0.037	0.050	0.051	0.036	0.028	0.028
	C. HHI for non-English patents within technology group					
1975–1979	0.073	0.079	0.103	0.061	0.048	0.062
1980–1984	0.067	0.069	0.087	0.057	0.041	0.053
1985–1989	0.062	0.074	0.078	0.053	0.042	0.047
1990–1994	0.053	0.084	0.060	0.057	0.039	0.043
1995–1999	0.047	0.126	0.065	0.095	0.042	0.044
2000–2004	0.051	0.141	0.067	0.109	0.050	0.043
Mean	0.059	0.095	0.077	0.072	0.044	0.049

Notes: See table 8.5. Patents are grouped into the major technology categories given in the column headers.

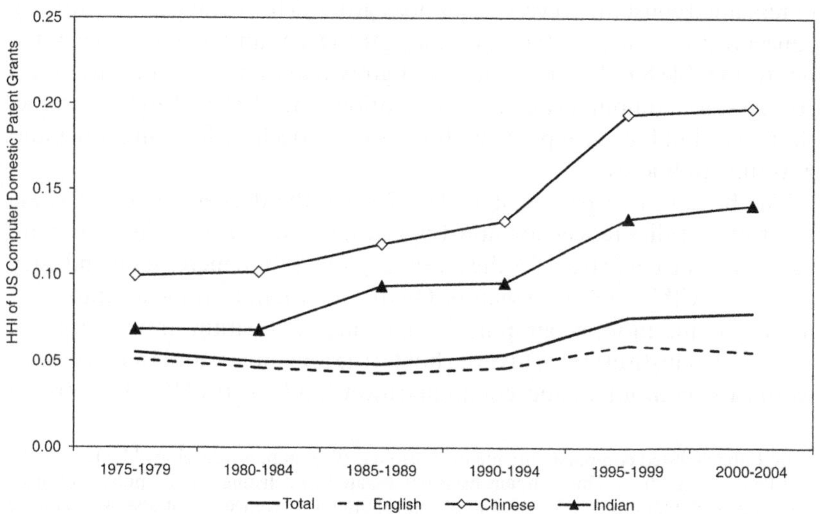

Fig. 8.7 Ethnic concentration in computers

8.3.5 Institutional Concentration of U.S. Ethnic Inventors

Patents are granted to several types of institutions. Industrial firms account for about 70 percent of patents granted from 1980 to 1997, while government and university institutions are assigned about 4 percent of patents. Unassigned patents (e.g., individual inventors) represent about 26 percent of U.S. invention. Public companies account for 59 percent of the industry patents during this period. With the exception of unassigned patents, institutions are primarily identified through assignee names on patents.

Figure 8.8 demonstrates that intriguing differences in ethnic scientific contributions also exist by institution type. Over the 1975 to 2004 period, ethnic inventors are more concentrated in government and university research labs and in publicly listed companies than in private companies or as unaffiliated inventors. Part of this levels difference is certainly due to immigration visa sponsorships by larger institutions. Growth in ethnic shares are initially stronger in the government and university labs, but publicly listed companies appear to close the gap by 2004. The other interesting trend in figure 8.8 is for private companies, where the ethnic contribution sharply increases in the 1990s. This rise coincides with the strong growth in ethnic entrepreneurship in high-tech sectors.[18]

Panels A and B of table 8.7 document the evolution of the HHI concentration for industry and university/government patenting, respectively. The column headers again indicate different technology groups. Despite having fairly similar levels of spatial concentration, the differences between institutions in the agglomeration trends for patenting are striking. The concentration of invention within universities and governments has either weakened or remained constant in every technology group. The recent gains in industry concentration, on the other hand, are stronger than the aggregate statistics from table 8.6. Whereas the recent growth in industry concentration is strongest for computers and communications and electrical and electronic, the two technology groups show above-average declines for universities and government bodies.

The bottom two panels of table 8.7 show the deeper impact of these institutional differences for non-English invention. Ethnic inventors are again very strong drivers for the recent agglomeration increases in industry patenting within high-tech sectors. On the other hand, ethnic inventors are not becoming more geographically agglomerated within universities and government institutions. This even holds true for Chinese and Indian groups within the computers and communications and electrical and electronic

18. Publicly listed companies are identified from a 1989 mapping developed by Hall, Jaffe, and Trajtenberg (2001). This company list is not updated for delistings or new public offerings. This approach maintains a constant public grouping for reference, but it also weakens the representativeness of the public and private company groupings at the sample extremes for current companies.

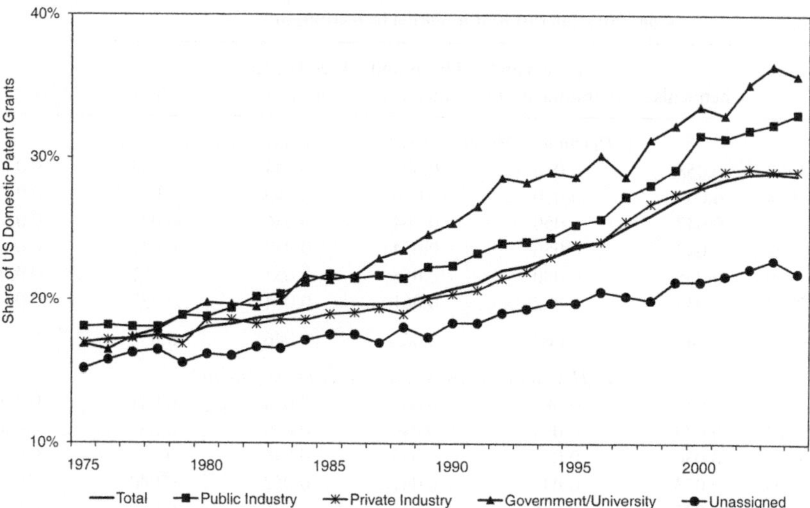

Fig. 8.8 Total U.S. ethnic share by institution

technology sectors. Figures 8.9 and 8.10 summarize these differences. As universities and government bodies are more constrained from agglomerating than industrial firms, these differences provide a nice falsification check on the earlier trends and the role of ethnic inventors.[19]

8.4 Conclusions

Ethnic scientists and engineers are an important and growing contributor to U.S. technology development. The Chinese and Indian ethnicities, in particular, are now an integral part of U.S. invention in high-tech sectors. The magnitude of these ethnic contributions raises many research and policy questions: debates regarding the appropriate quota for H-1B temporary visas, the possible crowding out of native students from SE fields, the brain drain or brain circulation effect on sending countries, and the future prospects for U.S. technology leadership are just four examples.[20] While the answers to these questions must draw from many fields within and outside of economics, valuable insights can be developed through agglomeration theory and empirical studies.

19. Trends in concentration ratios of unassigned inventors fall in between industry and university/government, behaving more closely like the latter. While there is some recent growth in ethnic inventor concentration within this class, the upturn is much weaker than in industrial firms. Figure 8.8 also highlights that ethnic inventors are a smaller fraction of unassigned patents, leading to a smaller impact on aggregate statistics.

20. Representative papers are Lowell (2000), Borjas (2004), Saxenian (2002), and Freeman (2005), respectively.

Table 8.7 **Concentration ratios of invention by institution**

	Chemicals	Computers and communications	Drugs and medical	Electrical and electronic	Mechanical	Miscellaneous
		A. Herfindahl-Hirschman index for all industry patents				
1975–1979	0.058	0.056	0.086	0.044	0.033	0.040
1980–1984	0.053	0.050	0.076	0.040	0.031	0.037
1985–1989	0.047	0.050	0.064	0.036	0.030	0.030
1990–1994	0.042	0.056	0.054	0.038	0.031	0.027
1995–1999	0.035	0.080	0.058	0.055	0.031	0.025
2000–2004	0.037	0.082	0.061	0.064	0.037	0.025
Mean	0.045	0.062	0.066	0.046	0.032	0.031
		B. HHI for all university and government patents				
1975–1979	0.043	0.088	0.043	0.054	0.041	0.040
1980–1984	0.039	0.068	0.046	0.050	0.039	0.040
1985–1989	0.036	0.059	0.044	0.046	0.041	0.029
1990–1994	0.033	0.049	0.047	0.052	0.040	0.031
1995–1999	0.035	0.048	0.041	0.045	0.040	0.027
2000–2004	0.033	0.044	0.038	0.042	0.039	0.029
Mean	0.036	0.059	0.043	0.048	0.040	0.033
		C. HHI for non-English industry patents				
1975–1979	0.078	0.079	0.118	0.061	0.046	0.061
1980–1984	0.072	0.068	0.110	0.057	0.042	0.052
1985–1989	0.067	0.078	0.091	0.053	0.042	0.045
1990–1994	0.058	0.089	0.071	0.060	0.041	0.038
1995–1999	0.050	0.133	0.076	0.103	0.044	0.038
2000–2004	0.056	0.148	0.077	0.118	0.055	0.038
Mean	0.064	0.099	0.091	0.075	0.045	0.045
		D. HHI for non-English university and government patents				
1975–1979	0.052	0.123	0.055	0.075	0.048	0.063
1980–1984	0.046	0.108	0.057	0.067	0.041	0.060
1985–1989	0.047	0.066	0.049	0.060	0.048	0.040
1990–1994	0.039	0.058	0.055	0.059	0.055	0.037
1995–1999	0.039	0.057	0.051	0.048	0.050	0.033
2000–2004	0.031	0.049	0.043	0.049	0.046	0.034
Mean	0.042	0.077	0.052	0.060	0.048	0.044

Notes: See table 8.5. Patents are grouped into the major technology categories given in the column headers.

This chapter builds a new empirical platform for these research questions by assigning probable ethnicities for U.S. inventors through the inventor names available with USPTO patent records. The resulting data document with greater detail than previously available the powerful growth in U.S. Chinese and Indian inventors during the 1990s. At the same time, these ethnic inventors became more spatially concentrated across U.S. cities. The combi-

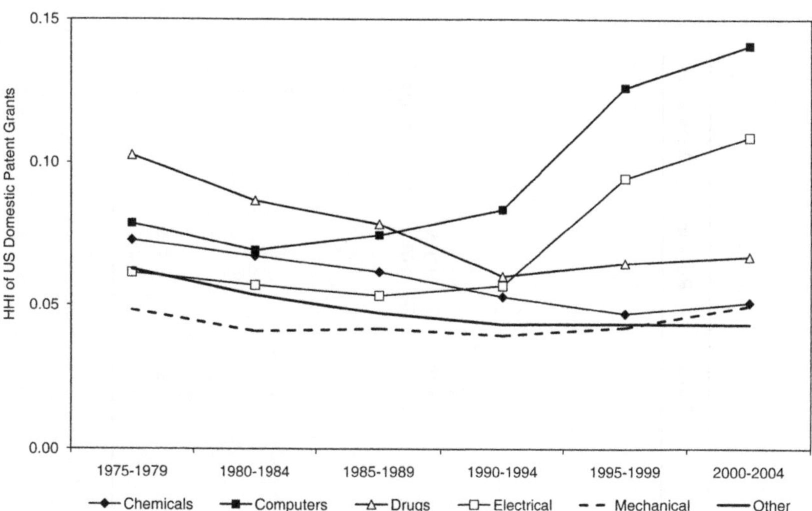

Fig. 8.9 Ethnic HHI, all inventors

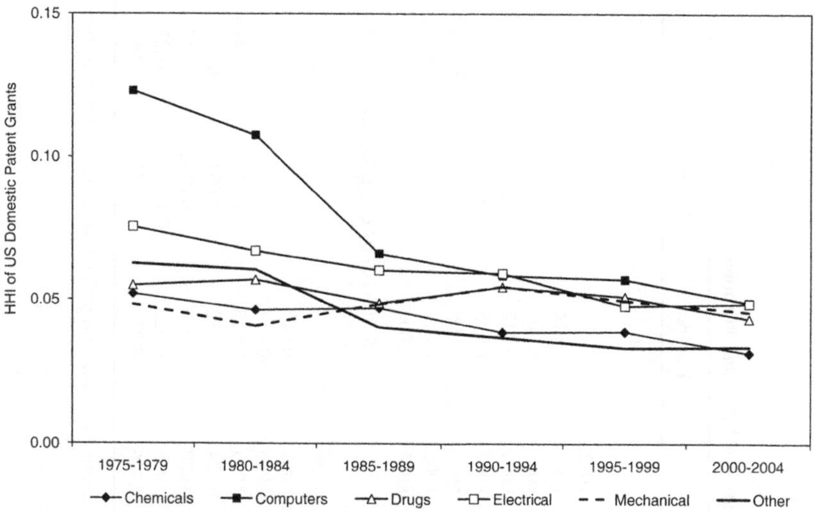

Fig. 8.10 Ethnic HHI, university and government

nation of these two factors helps stop and reverse long-term declines in overall inventor agglomeration evident in the 1970s and 1980s. The heightened ethnic agglomeration is particularly evident in industry patents for high-tech sectors, and similar trends are not found in institutions constrained from agglomerating (e.g., universities, government).

Appendix

Table 8A.1 **Coagglomeration of U.S. ethnic invention**

	Chinese	English	European	Hispanic	Indian	Japanese	Korean	Russian	Vietnamese
				A. 1975–1979 Coagglomeration of ethnic invention					
Chinese	0.014								
English	0.004	0.002							
European	0.011	0.004	0.014						
Hispanic	0.010	0.003	0.009	0.011					
Indian	0.011	0.004	0.012	0.009	0.011				
Japanese	0.010	0.005	0.005	0.011	0.005	0.034			
Korean	0.009	0.004	0.009	0.008	0.008	0.012	0.012		
Russian	0.011	0.005	0.012	0.011	0.011	0.012	0.010	0.015	
Vietnamese	0.011	0.004	0.009	0.012	0.008	0.020	0.010	0.013	0.024
				B. 2000–2004 Coagglomeration of ethnic invention					
Chinese	0.082								
English	0.024	0.010							
European	0.033	0.011	0.016						
Hispanic	0.034	0.010	0.014	0.016					
Indian	0.059	0.019	0.025	0.025	0.047				
Japanese	0.082	0.024	0.032	0.034	0.058	0.084			
Korean	0.075	0.020	0.030	0.031	0.053	0.075	0.071		
Russian	0.051	0.015	0.022	0.022	0.037	0.051	0.048	0.034	
Vietnamese	0.086	0.026	0.033	0.035	0.062	0.087	0.078	0.051	0.097

Notes: Metrics consider coagglomeration of ethnic invention relative to MSA populations.

Table 8A.2 **Concentration ratios at subcategory levels**

	Chemicals	Computers and communications	Drugs and medical	Electrical and electronic	Mechanical	Miscellaneous
	A. Herfindahl-Hirschman index for all patents within technology group					
1975–1979	0.053	0.055	0.070	0.043	0.032	0.039
1980–1984	0.048	0.050	0.061	0.039	0.030	0.035
1985–1989	0.043	0.048	0.055	0.036	0.029	0.031
1990–1994	0.038	0.054	0.047	0.037	0.028	0.028
1995–1999	0.033	0.075	0.050	0.052	0.029	0.027
2000–2004	0.034	0.078	0.053	0.059	0.032	0.026
Mean	0.041	0.060	0.056	0.044	0.030	0.031
	B. Unweighted HHI average across subcategory technology groups					
1975–1979	0.057	0.059	0.072	0.051	0.044	0.052
1980–1984	0.053	0.059	0.069	0.048	0.040	0.050
1985–1989	0.050	0.064	0.063	0.046	0.042	0.042
1990–1994	0.041	0.073	0.054	0.046	0.049	0.040
1995–1999	0.039	0.095	0.057	0.057	0.048	0.041
2000–2004	0.040	0.102	0.062	0.060	0.049	0.051
Mean	0.047	0.075	0.063	0.051	0.045	0.046
	C. Weighted HHI average across subcategory technology groups					
1975–1979	0.060	0.059	0.083	0.047	0.038	0.047
1980–1984	0.053	0.055	0.071	0.044	0.035	0.044
1985–1989	0.047	0.055	0.066	0.043	0.036	0.038
1990–1994	0.041	0.062	0.054	0.045	0.040	0.035
1995–1999	0.037	0.085	0.058	0.064	0.041	0.035
2000–2004	0.038	0.088	0.062	0.072	0.047	0.042
Mean	0.046	0.068	0.066	0.052	0.040	0.040

Notes: See table 8.6.

Table 8A.3 **Descriptive statistics for inventors residing in foreign countries and regions**

Summary statistics for full and restricted matching procedures

	Observations	Percentage of region's inventors matched with ethnic database		Percentage of region's inventors assigned ethnicity of their region		Percentage of region's inventors assigned ethnicity of region (partial)	
		Full	Restricted	Full	Restricted	Full	Restricted
United Kingdom	187,266	99	95	85	83	92	91
China, Singapore	167,370	100	98	88	89	91	91
Western Europe	1,210,231	98	79	66	46	73	58
Hispanic nations	27,298	99	74	74	69	93	93
India	13,582	93	76	88	88	90	89
Japan	1,822,253	100	89	100	96	100	96
South Korea	127,975	100	100	84	83	89	88
Russia	33,237	94	78	81	84	93	94
Vietnam	41	100	98	36	43	44	43

Complete ethnic composition of region's inventors (full matching; percentage)

	English	Chinese	European	Hispanic	Indian	Japanese	Korean	Russian	Vietnamese
United Kingdom	85	2	5	3	2	0	0	2	0
China, Singapore	3	88	1	1	1	1	4	1	1
Western Europe	21	1	66	8	1	0	0	3	0
Hispanic nations	11	1	10	74	0	1	0	2	0
India	3	1	1	5	88	0	0	2	0
Japan	0	0	0	0	0	100	0	0	0
South Korea	2	11	0	1	0	1	84	1	0
Russia	5	1	3	9	0	0	0	81	0
Vietnam	17	21	12	0	0	10	2	2	36

Notes: Matching is undertaken at inventor level using the full and restricted matching procedures outlined in the text. The middle columns of the top panel summarize the share of each region's inventors assigned the ethnicity of that region; the complete composition for the full matching procedure is detailed in the bottom panel. The right-hand columns in the top panel document the percentage of the region's inventors assigned at least partially to their region's ethnicity. Greater China includes mainland China, Hong Kong, Macao, and Taiwan. Western Europe includes Austria, Belgium, Denmark, Finland, France, Germany, Italy, Luxembourg, the Netherlands, Norway, Poland, Sweden, and Switzerland. Hispanic nations include Argentina, Belize, Brazil, Chile, Columbia, Costa Rica, Cuba, the Dominican Republic, Ecuador, El Salvador, Guatemala, Honduras, Mexico, Nicaragua, Panama, Paraguay, Peru, the Philippines, Portugal, Spain, Uruguay, and Venezuela. Russia includes former Soviet Union countries.

Table 8A.4 Most common ethnic surnames for inventors residing in the United States

Chinese		English		European		Hispanic/Filipino		Indian/Hindi	
Cai	585	Adams	4,490	Abel	269	Acosta	171	Acharya	338
Cao	657	Allen	5,074	Albrecht	564	Aguilar	138	Agarwal	580
Chan	3,096	Anderson	10,719	Antos	230	Alvarez	446	Aggarwal	282
Chang	3,842	Bailey	2,431	Auerbach	193	Andreas	128	Agrawal	797
Chao	796	Baker	4,671	Baer	422	Ayer	166	Ahmad	355
Chau	486	Bell	2,738	Baerlocher	252	Ayres	180	Ahmed	652
Chen	12,860	Bennett	2,734	Bauer	1,470	Bales	240	Akram	640
Cheng	2,648	Brooks	2,015	Bechtel	179	Blanco	141	Ali	559
Cheung	950	Brown	11,662	Beck	1,712	Bolanos	130	Arimilli	432
Chiang	1,112	Burns	2,098	Bender	650	Boles	118	Arora	214
Chien	429	Campbell	3,959	Berg	1,465	Cabral	154	Ash	290
Chin	423	Carlson	2,745	Berger	1,304	Cabrera	163	Balakrishnan	228
Chiu	924	Carter	2,658	Boehm	256	Calderon	124	Banerjee	371
Chou	1,144	Chang	2,032	Boutaghou	266	Castaneda	116	Basu	233
Chow	1,139	Clark	5,493	Caron	290	Castillo	124	Bhat	224
Chu	2,353	Cohen	2,626	Cerami	172	Castro	119	Bhatia	411
Deng	439	Cole	2,143	Chandraratna	229	Chavez	194	Bhatt	242
Ding	589	Collins	2,992	Chevallier	204	Contreras	137	Bhattacharya	216
Dong	492	Cook	3,556	Dietrich	312	Cruz	319	Bhattacharyya	265
Fan	1,036	Cooper	3,045	Dietz	496	Cuevas	123	Bose	238
Fang	846	Cox	2,407	Eberhardt	192	Das	213	Chandra	221
Feng	658	Davis	8,848	Ehrlich	311	Delgado	216	Chatterjee	647
Fong	727	Edwards	3,375	Errico	190	Dias	174	Daoud	305
Fu	767	Evans	4,082	Farkas	169	Diaz	584	Das	522
Fung	455	Fischer	2,081	Ferrari	177	Dominguez	195	Datta	424
Gao	785	Fisher	2,748	Fischell	280	Duran	142	De	234
Guo	921	Foster	2,616	Fuchs	394	Elias	230	Desai	974
Han	777	Fox	1,990	Gaiser	193	Estrada	142	Dixit	256
He	1,159	Gardner	2,412	Gelardi	176	Fernandes	152	Dutta	338
Ho	1,282	Gordon	2,315	Grilliot	201	Fernandez	546	Gandhi	228
Hsieh	980	Graham	2,042	Guegler	179	Figueroa	146	Garg	345
Hsu	3,034	Gray	2,626	Gunter	177	Flores	191	Ghosh	661
Hu	1,695	Green	3,540	Gunther	247	Freitas	132	Goel	279
Huang	4,605	Hall	4,907	Haas	843	Gagnon	265	Gupta	1,935
Hui	451	Hamilton	1,991	Hampel	187	Garcia	1,310	Hassan	217
Hung	562	Hanson	2,148	Hansen	2,947	Garza	167	Hussain	233
Hwang	800	Harrls	4,793	Hartman	1,214	Gomes	199	Hussaini	299
Jiang	1,399	Hayes	2,031	Hartmann	385	Gomez	413	Islam	266
Kao	714	Hill	3,590	Hause	266	Gonsalves	141	Iyer	601
Kuo	1,157	Hoffman	2,387	Hecht	245	Gonzales	281	Jain	912
Lai	1,134	Howard	2,160	Heinz	168	Gonzalez	1,055	Joshi	886
Lam	1,336	Hughes	2,198	Horodysky	230	Gutierrez	601	Kamath	219
Lau	1,320	Jackson	3,980	Horvath	387	Guzman	139	Kapoor	222
Lee	4,006	Jensen	2,361	Iacovelli	287	Halasa	202	Khanna	378
Leung	1,165	Johnson	17,960	Jacobs	1,962	Hernandez	703	Krishnamurthy	369
Lew	460	Jones	10,630	Karr	196	Herrera	171	Krishnan	512
Li	6,863	Keller	2,041	Kasper	227	Herron	450	Kulkarni	299
Liang	1,173	Kelly	2,775	Kempf	228	Hidalgo	186	Kumar	2,005
Liao	553	Kennedy	2,208	Knapp	833	Jimenez	246	Lal	366
Lim	485	King	4,686	Knifton	206	Lee	237	Malik	532
Lin	5,770	Klein	2,347	Koenig	521	Lopez	738	Mathur	306
Ling	521	Larson	2,537	Kresge	179	Machado	135	Mehrotra	265

(*continued*)

Table 8A.4 (continued)

Chinese		English		European		Hispanic/Filipino		Indian/Hindi	
Liu	6,406	Lee	9,490	Lange	757	Marin	177	Mehta	925
Lo	1,053	Lewis	4,732	Laskaris	192	Marquez	117	Menon	325
Lu	2,289	Long	2,392	Lemelson	324	Martin	183	Mishra	348
Luo	815	Marshall	2,088	Liotta	171	Martinez	1,112	Misra	282
Ma	1,708	Martin	6,773	Lorenz	341	Matis	249	Mookherjee	272
Mao	545	Miller	14,942	Ludwig	500	Medina	192	Mukherjee	327
Ng	1,132	Mitchell	3,075	Lutz	679	Menard	149	Murthy	236
Ong	473	Moore	6,459	Maier	492	Mendoza	173	Nagarajan	270
Pan	1,435	Morgan	2,824	Martin	223	Miranda	140	Nair	560
Peng	530	Morris	3,223	Mayer	1,097	Molina	129	Narasimhan	225
Shen	1,480	Murphy	3,609	Meyer	3,004	Morales	146	Narayan	312
Shi	964	Murray	2,207	Molnar	335	Moreno	128	Narayanan	419
Shih	938	Myers	2,625	Morin	320	Munoz	177	Natarajan	301
Song	636	Nelson	6,444	Mueller	2,242	Nunez	207	Parekh	301
Su	1,025	Olson	3,140	Muller	985	Ortega	206	Parikh	286
Sun	2,521	Parker	3,181	Nagel	383	Ortiz	362	Patel	3,879
Tai	463	Peterson	4,912	Nathan	171	Padilla	116	Patil	352
Tam	589	Phillips	3,875	Nilssen	234	Paz de Araujo	148	Prakash	326
Tan	1,105	Price	2,062	Novak	788	Pereira	280	Prasad	549
Tang	2,277	Reed	2,645	Pagano	177	Perez	675	Puri	233
Teng	437	Richardson	2,114	Palermo	177	Quintana	126	Raghavan	378
Tong	677	Roberts	4,352	Pastor	238	Ramirez	345	Rahman	367
Tsai	1,244	Robinson	3,741	Popp	202	Ramos	226	Rajagopalan	396
Tsang	499	Rogers	2,974	Rao	343	Regnier	137	Ramachandran	388
Tseng	538	Ross	2,377	Reitz	248	Reis	168	Ramakrishnan	270
Tung	565	Russell	2,611	Rohrbach	246	Reyes	150	Raman	222
Wang	11,905	Ryan	2,404	Roman	362	Rivera	489	Ramaswamy	244
Wei	1,317	Scott	3,583	Rostoker	245	Rodrigues	188	Ramesh	364
Wen	455	Shaw	2,369	Schmidt	3,753	Rodriguez	1,314	Rangarajan	244
Wong	4,811	Simpson	2,014	Schneider	2,246	Romero	292	Rao	1,196
Woo	710	Smith	24,173	Schultz	2,273	Ruiz	297	Reddy	459
Wu	5,521	Snyder	2,335	Schulz	921	Salazar	179	Roy	279
Xie	609	Stevens	2,221	Schwartz	2,394	Sanchez	717	Sandhu	878
Xu	2,249	Stewart	2,924	Schwarz	633	Santiago	158	Saxena	213
Yan	826	Sullivan	2,933	Speranza	215	Serrano	172	Shah	2,467
Yang	4,584	Taylor	6,659	Spiegel	177	Silva	457	Sharma	1,249
Yao	699	Thomas	5,312	Straeter	454	Soto	158	Singh	2,412
Ye	525	Thompson	6,424	Theeuwes	247	Souza	145	Singhal	245
Yee	729	Turner	2,855	Trokhan	167	Suarez	150	Sinha	463
Yeh	928	Walker	4,887	Vock	423	Torres	352	Sircar	225
Yen	467	Wallace	1,963	Wachter	199	Valdez	127	Srinivasan	876
Yin	617	Ward	2,913	Wagner	2,499	Varga	130	Srivastava	498
Yu	2,293	Watson	2,139	Weber	3,003	Vasquez	153	Subramanian	702
Yuan	825	White	6,190	Weder	1,067	Vazquez	260	Thakur	381
Zhang	4,532	Williams	10,442	Weiss	1,533	Velazquez	134	Trivedi	383
Zhao	1,337	Wilson	7,677	Wolf	1,604	Vinals	220	Venkatesan	281
Zheng	1,037	Wood	4,525	Wristers	185	Yu	140	Verma	262
Zhou	1,517	Wright	4,521	Zimmerman	1,542	Zamora	120	Viswanathan	218
Zhu	1,749	Young	5,957	Zimmermann	226	Zuniga	128	Vora	223

Table 8A.4 (continued)

Japanese		Korean		Russian		Vietnamese	
Aoki	141	Ahn	610	Aghajanian	77	Abou-Gharbia	22
Aoyama	66	Bae	122	Alperovich	64	Bahn	15
Asato	73	Baek	77	Altshuler	71	Banh	21
Chen	88	Bak	68	Andreev	94	Bi	158
Doi	90	Bang	91	Anscher	95	Bich	18
Fujii	92	Bark	39	Babich	79	Bien	91
Fujimoto	98	Byun	87	Babler	73	Bui	309
Fukuda	84	Cha	45	Barinaga	72	Can	19
Furukawa	218	Chae	33	Barna	96	Cong	41
Hanawa	69	Chang	289	Belopolsky	71	Dang	23
Harada	90	Chin	33	Berchenko	94	Diem	24
Hasegawa	171	Cho	977	Blasko	79	Diep	52
Hashimoto	110	Choe	193	Blonder	82	Dinh	232
Hayashi	148	Choi	1,081	Bonin	97	Dip	11
Hey	75	Chon	33	Codilian	90	Do	13
Higashi	98	Choo	94	Comiskey	74	Doan	616
Higuchi	81	Chun	330	Damadian	118	Dominh	33
Honda	102	Chung	1,499	Danko	69	Donlan	21
Ide	136	Drozd	45	Dayan	143	Dovan	26
Ikeda	98	Eyuboglu	36	Derderian	169	Duan	241
Imai	129	Gang	34	Dombroski	66	Due	20
Inoue	90	Gu	533	Elko	81	Duong	153
Irick	86	Hahm	42	Fetcenko	62	Duong-Van	13
Ishida	93	Hahn	1,016	Fishkin	82	Eskew	12
Ishii	82	Ham	45	Fomenkov	73	Gran	20
Ishikawa	208	Han	145	Frenkel	71	Hac	20
Ito	260	Hansell	39	Fridman	67	Haugan	16
Iwamoto	78	Hogle	43	Frolov	68	Ho	35
Kaneko	157	Hone	78	Garabedian	104	Hoang	277
Kato	113	Hong	907	Gelfand	139	Hopping	15
Kautz	87	Hosking	63	Ginzburg	73	Huynh	317
Kawamura	87	Huh	32	Gitlin	73	Huynh-Ba	19
Kawasaki	104	Hwang	108	Gluschenkov	73	Kha	13
Kaya	78	Hyun	54	Goralski	69	Khaw	20
Kimura	108	Im	80	Gordin	65	Khieu	35
Kino	74	Jang	46	Gorin	99	Khu	13
Kinoshita	93	Jeon	134	Grinberg	104	Khuc	15
Kirihata	107	Jeong	122	Grochowski	77	Lahue	17
Kishi	65	Ji	268	Gurevich	107	Laursen	72
Kiwala	132	Jin	673	Gursky	89	Lavan	18
Kobayashi	296	Jo	41	Guzik	79	Le	1,263
Li	75	Joo	68	Haba	96	Le Roy	29
Liu	84	Ju	55	Hynecek	82	Leen	75
Maki	167	Jung	582	Ibrahim	229	Leminh	17
Matsumoto	147	Kang	809	Ivanov	165	Luong	107
Miyano	70	Kiani	74	Ivers	66	Ly	118
Mizuhara	87	Kim	5,455	Jovanovic	65	Minh	41
Mori	128	Ko	595	Ju	126	Nellums	17
Morita	64	Koo	214	Juhasz	71	Ngo	735
Moslehi	165	Kun	63	Kahle	173	Nguy	12
Motoyama	130	Kwak	96	Kaminski	393	Nguyen	4,720
Murakami	67	Kwon	298	Kaminsky	150	Nho	12

(*continued*)

Table 8A.4 (continued)

Japanese		Korean		Russian		Vietnamese	
Najjar	81	Lee	1,032	Kanevsky	114	Nieh	69
Nakagawa	125	Lim	135	Kaplinsky	69	Nim	14
Nakajima	99	Mennie	96	Kaposi	72	Pham	901
Nakamura	187	Min	242	Khan	104	Phan	27
Nakanishi	64	Na	34	Khandros	161	Phang	11
Nakano	104	Nam	68	Khovaylo	69	Phy	19
Nemoto	70	Nevins	42	Kolmanovsky	70	Postman	12
Nishibori	88	Nyce	56	Korsunsky	153	Quach	95
Nishimura	131	Oh	461	Kowal	74	Qui	11
Noda	107	Paek	41	Lapidus	63	Quy	13
Ogawa	74	Paik	144	Lee	113	Roch	26
Ogura	209	Pak	116	Lopata	113	Ta	91
Ohara	269	Park	2,145	Messing	74	Takach	30
Ohkawa	89	Quay	107	Metlitsky	95	Tau	23
Okada	87	Rhee	191	Mikhail	115	Thach	33
Okamoto	103	Rim	57	Mirkin	66	Thai	86
Ono	148	Ryang	38	Moghadam	72	Thao	21
Ovshinsky	314	Ryu	99	Nadelson	65	Thi	13
Saito	136	Sahm	45	Nazarian	75	Thien	15
Sakai	79	Sahoo	58	Nemirovsky	73	Thut	28
Sasaki	209	Seo	47	Nie	72	Tiedt	14
Sato	231	Shim	162	Ogg	125	Tiep	12
Seto	73	Shin	399	Papadopoulos	132	Tietjen	59
Shimizu	103	Shinn	96	Papathomas	67	To	76
Suzuki	306	Sin	62	Petrov	102	Ton-That	16
Takahashi	245	Sjostrom	39	Pinarbasi	131	Tran	2,050
Takeuchi	242	So	332	Pinchuk	123	Trandai	14
Tamura	83	Sohn	78	Popov	81	Trang	34
Tanaka	328	Son	147	Prokop	86	Trank	11
Thor	66	Song	105	Raber	78	Trieu	49
Tsuji	92	Sue	64	Rabinovich	123	Trong	12
Tsukamoto	89	Suh	311	Robichaux	65	Truc	27
Uchida	72	Suk	75	Rubsamen	69	Tu	545
Ueda	72	Sung	41	Sahatjian	66	Tuten	23
Wada	153	Sur	38	Sarkisian	65	Tuy	16
Wang	81	Toohey	33	Sarraf	82	Ty	27
Watanabe	416	Um	36	Schreier	62	Van	58
Wu	67	Whang	175	Schwan	81	Van Cleve	40
Yamada	180	Won	108	Simko	77	Van Dam	20
Yamaguchi	102	Yi	237	Smetana	69	Van Le	17
Yamamoto	432	Yim	145	Sofranko	66	Van Nguyen	29
Yamasaki	67	Yohn	32	Sokolov	91	Van Phan	26
Yamashita	105	Yoo	290	Sorkin	111	Van Tran	15
Yamazaki	91	Yoon	614	Tabak	85	Viet	11
Yang	65	Youn	38	Tepman	80	Vo	269
Yasuda	75	Yu	198	Terzian	87	Vo-Dinh	32
Yoshida	178	Yuh	96	Vashchenko	96	Vovan	20
Yuan	112	Yum	78	Wasilewski	80	Vu	502
Zhao	81	Yun	222	Zemel	126	Vuong	107

Table 8A.5 **Ethnic inventors and MSA characteristics, including overall ethnic shares**

	English		Chinese		Indian		European		Hispanic	
	(1)	(2)	(3)	(4)	(5)	(6)	(7)	(8)	(9)	(10)
1980 Share of ethnic population in MSA	0.336	0.464	1.126	1.137	0.373	0.498	0.324	0.390	0.105	–0.042
	(0.350)	(0.188)	(0.375)	(0.336)	(0.220)	(0.124)	(0.140)	(0.066)	(0.144)	(0.213)
Log population of MSA	0.473	0.162	–0.374	–0.692	0.315	0.003	0.540	0.266	0.790	0.860
	(0.380)	(0.167)	(0.297)	(0.363)	(0.270)	(0.196)	(0.226)	(0.102)	(0.192)	(0.254)
Log population density of MSA	0.040	0.108	0.108	0.366	0.016	–0.057	0.041	0.193	–0.024	–0.097
	(0.028)	(0.099)	(0.052)	(0.210)	(0.047)	(0.185)	(0.039)	(0.094)	(0.033)	(0.151)
Coastal access of MSA	–0.018	0.098	–0.036	–0.144	0.023	0.335	–0.002	0.105	0.048	0.334
	(0.035)	(0.131)	(0.023)	(0.115)	(0.054)	(0.251)	(0.033)	(0.126)	(0.043)	(0.194)
Share of population with bachelor's education	0.141	0.372	0.082	0.121	0.129	0.428	0.111	0.376	0.089	0.263
	(0.042)	(0.241)	(0.028)	(0.141)	(0.058)	(0.347)	(0.039)	(0.235)	(0.028)	(0.184)
Share of population under 30 in age	–0.138	–0.650	–0.142	–0.518	–0.156	–1.132	–0.110	–0.641	–0.060	–0.509
	(0.072)	(0.537)	(0.066)	(0.247)	(0.116)	(0.913)	(0.068)	(0.555)	(0.045)	(0.430)
Share of population over 60 in age	–0.086	–0.399	–0.110	–0.339	–0.100	–0.693	–0.051	–0.318	–0.016	–0.251
	(0.057)	(0.344)	(0.061)	(0.203)	(0.090)	(0.594)	(0.054)	(0.352)	(0.039)	(0.284)
Share of population female	–0.062	–0.386	–0.038	–0.709	–0.058	–0.328	–0.039	–0.238	–0.038	–0.118
	(0.026)	(0.265)	(0.026)	(0.333)	(0.039)	(0.472)	(0.023)	(0.236)	(0.021)	(0.199)
Weights	No	Yes	No	Yes	No	Yes	No	Yes	No	Yes
R^2	0.79	0.84	0.82	0.84	0.56	0.66	0.81	0.88	0.83	0.90

Notes: See tables 8.3 and 8.4. Estimations incorporate the overall share of each ethnicity in MSAs from the 1990 Census. Dependent variable is share of 1985–2004 ethnic patenting in the MSA.

References

Agrawal, A., D. Kapur, and J. McHale. 2007. Birds of a feather: Better together? Exploring the optimal spatial distribution of ethnic inventors. NBER Working Paper no. 12823. Cambridge, MA: National Bureau of Economic Research, January.

Audretsch, D., and M. Feldman. 1996. R&D spillovers and the geography of innovation and production. *American Economic Review* 86 (3): 630–40.

Borjas, G. 1994. Economics of immigration. *Journal of Economic Literature* 32 (4): 1667–717.

———. 2004. Do foreign students crowd out native students from graduate programs? NBER Working Paper no. 10349. Cambridge, MA: National Bureau of Economic Research, March.

Burton, L., and J. Wang. 1999. How much does the U.S. rely on immigrant engineers? NSF SRS Issue Brief no. 99–327. Arlington, VA: National Science Foundation, Division of Science Resources Statistics.

Card, D. 1990. The impact of the Mariel Boatlift on the Miami labor market. *Industrial and Labor Relations Review* 43 (2): 245–57.

———. 2001. Immigrant inflows, native outflows, and the local labor market impacts of higher immigration. *Journal of Labor Economics* 19 (1): 22–64.

Carlino, G., S. Chatterjee, and R. Hunt. 2007. Urban density and the rate of invention. *Journal of Urban Economics* 61 (3): 389–419.

Duranton, G. 2007. Urban evolutions: The fast, the slow, and the still. *American Economic Review* 97 (1): 197–221.

Duranton, G., and H. Overman. 2005. Testing for localization using micro-geographic data. *Review of Economic Studies* 72 (4): 1077–106.

Duranton, G., and D. Puga. 2001. Nursery cities: Urban diversity, process innovation, and the life cycle of products. *American Economic Review* 91 (5): 1454–77.

Edin, P.-A., P. Fredriksson, and O. Åslund. 2003. Ethnic enclaves and the economic success of immigrants: Evidence from a natural experiment. *Quarterly Journal of Economics* 118 (1): 329–57.

Ellison, G., and E. Glaeser. 1997. Geographic concentration in U.S. manufacturing industries: A dartboard approach. *Journal of Political Economy* 105 (5): 889–927.

Ellison, G., E. Glaeser, and W. Kerr. 2007. What causes industry agglomeration? Evidence from coagglomeration patterns. NBER Working Paper no. 13068. Cambridge, MA: National Bureau of Economic Research, April.

Foley, C. F., and W. Kerr. 2008. US ethnic scientists and foreign direct investment placement. Harvard Business School. Unpublished Manuscript.

Freeman, R. 2005. Does globalization of the scientific/engineering workforce threaten U.S. economic leadership? NBER Working Paper no. 11457. Cambridge, MA: National Bureau of Economic Research, July.

———. 2006. People flows in globalization. *Journal of Economic Perspectives* 20 (2): 145–70.

Friedberg, R., and J. Hunt. 1995. The impact of immigrants on host country wages, employment and growth. *Journal of Economic Perspectives* 9 (2): 23–44.

Furman, J., M. Porter, and S. Stern. 2002. The determinants of national innovative capacity. *Research Policy* 31 (6): 899–933.

Glaeser, E., and M. Kahn. 2001. Decentralized employment and the transformation of the American city. NBER Working Paper no. 8117. Cambridge, MA: National Bureau of Economic Research, February.

Glaeser, E., H. Kallal, J. Scheinkman, and A. Shleifer. 1992. Growth in cities. *Journal of Political Economy* 100 (6): 1126–52.

Glaeser, E., and W. Kerr. 2008. Local industrial conditions and entrepreneurship: How much of the spatial distribution can we explain? NBER Working Paper no. 14407. Cambridge, MA: National Bureau of Economic Research, October.
Graham, S., and D. Mowery. 2004. Software patents: Good news or bad news? Georgia Institute of Technology, College of Management. Manuscript, May.
Griliches, Z. 1990. Patent statistics as economic indicators: A survey. *Journal of Economic Literature* 28 (4): 1661–707.
Hall, B. 2004. Exploring the patent explosion. *Journal of Technology Transfer* 30 (1/2): 35–48.
Hall, B., A. Jaffe, and M. Trajtenberg. 2001. The NBER patent citation data file: Lessons, insights and methodological tools. NBER Working Paper no. 8498. Cambridge, MA: National Bureau of Economic Research, October.
Henderson, J. V. 2003. Marshall's scale economies. *Journal of Urban Economics* 53 (1): 1–28.
Henderson, J. V., A. Kuncoro, and M. Turner. 1995. Industrial development in cities. *Journal of Political Economy* 103 (5): 1067–85.
Hunt, J., and M. Gauthier-Loiselle. 2008. How much does immigration boost innovation? NBER Working Paper no. 14312. Cambridge, MA: National Bureau of Economic Research, September.
Jacobs, J. 1970. *The economy of cities.* New York: Vintage Books.
Jaffe, A., and J. Lerner. 2005. *Innovation and its discontents.* Boston: Harvard Business School Press.
Jaffe, A., M. Trajtenberg, and R. Henderson. 1993. Geographic localization of knowledge spillovers as evidenced by patent citations. *Quarterly Journal of Economics* 108 (3): 577–98.
Johnson, D. 1999. 150 years of American invention: Methodology and a first geographic application. Working Paper no. 99-01. Wellesley College, Department of Economics.
Johnson, J. 1998. Statistical profiles of foreign doctoral recipients in science and engineering: Plans to stay in the United States. NSF SRS Special Report no. 99-304. Arlington, VA: National Science Foundation, Division of Science Resources Statistics.
———. 2001. Human resource contributions to U.S. science and engineering from China. NSF SRS no. 01-311. Arlington, VA: National Science Foundation, Division of Science Resources Statistics.
Kannankutty, N., and R. K. Wilkinson. 1999. SESTAT: A tool for studying scientists and engineers in the United States. NSF SRS Special Report no. 99-337. Arlington, VA: National Science Foundation, Division of Science Resources Statistics.
Keller, W. 2002. Trade and the transmission of technology. *Journal of Economic Growth* 7 (1): 5–24.
Kerr, S. P., and W. Kerr. 2008. Economic impacts of immigration: A survey. HBS Working Paper no. 09-013. Harvard Business School, August.
Kerr, W. 2007. The ethnic composition of US inventors. HBS Working Paper no. 08-006. Harvard Business School, August.
———. 2008a. Ethnic scientific communities and international technology diffusion. *Review of Economics and Statistics* 90 (3): 518–37.
———. 2008b. Heterogeneous technology diffusion and Ricardian trade patterns. Harvard Business School. Unpublished Manuscript.
Kerr, W., and W. Lincoln. 2008. The supply side of innovation: H-1B visa reforms and US ethnic invention. HBS Working Paper no. 09-005. Harvard Business School, December.
Kim, J., and G. Marschke. 2004. Accounting for the recent surge in U.S. patenting:

Changes in R&D expenditures, patent yields, and the high tech sector. *Economics of Innovation and New Technologies* 13 (6): 543–58.
Kortum, S., and J. Lerner. 2000. Assessing the contribution of venture capital to innovation. *RAND Journal of Economics* 31 (4): 674–92.
Lemley, M., and B. Sampat. 2007. Is the Patent Office a rubber stamp? Working Paper no. 999098. Stanford Law School, July.
Lowell, B. L. 2000. H1-B temporary workers: Estimating the population. CCIS Working Paper no. 12. University of California, San Diego, Center for Comparative Immigration Studies.
Mandorff, M. 2007. Social networks, ethnicity, and occupation. University of Chicago, Department of Economics. Unpublished Manuscript.
Marshall, A. 1920. *Principles of economics.* London: MacMillan.
Pedace, R., and S. Rohn. 2008. A warm embrace or the cold shoulder: Wage and employment outcomes in ethnic enclaves. CES Working Paper no. 08-09. Washington, DC: U.S. Census Bureau Center for Economic Studies.
Peri, G. 2007. Higher education, innovation and growth. In *Education and training in Europe,* ed. G. Brunello, P. Garibaldi, and E. Wasmer, 56–70. Oxford: Oxford University Press.
Porter, M. 1990. *The competitive advantage of nations.* New York: Free Press.
Romer, P. 1986. Increasing returns and long-run growth. *Journal of Political Economy* 94 (5): 1002–37.
———. 1990. Endogenous technological change. *Journal of Political Economy* 98 (5): S71–S102.
Rosenthal, S., and W. Strange. 2001. The determinants of agglomeration. *Journal of Urban Economics* 50 (2): 191–229.
———. 2003. Geography, industrial organization, and agglomeration. *Review of Economics and Statistics* 85 (2): 377–93.
Saxenian, A. 1994. *Regional advantage: Culture and competition in Silicon Valley and Route 128.* Cambridge, MA: Harvard University Press.
———. 2002. Silicon Valley's new immigrant high-growth entrepreneurs. *Economic Development Quarterly* 16 (1): 20–31.
Saxenian, A., with Y. Motoyama and X. Quan. 2002. *Local and global networks of immigrant professionals in Silicon Valley.* San Francisco: Public Policy Institute of California.
Scherer, F. 1984. Using linked patent data and R & D data to measure technology flows. In *R & D, patents, and productivity,* ed. Z. Griliches, 417–65. Chicago: University of Chicago Press.
Silverman, B. 1999. Technological resources and the direction of corporate diversification: Toward an integration of the resource-based view and transaction cost economics. *Management Science* 45 (8): 1109–24.
Stephan, P., and S. Levin. 2001. Exceptional contributions to US science by the foreign-born and foreign-educated. *Population Research and Policy Review* 20 (1): 59–79.
Streeter, J. 1997. Major declines in admissions of immigrant scientists and engineers in fiscal year 1994. NSF SRS Issue Brief no. 97-311. Arlington, VA: National Science Foundation, Division of Science Resources Statistics.
Thompson, P., and M. Fox-Kean. 2005. Patent citations and the geography of knowledge spillovers: A reassessment. *American Economic Review* 95 (1): 450–60.
Wadhwa, V., A. Saxenian, B. Rissing, and G. Gereffi. 2007. America's new immigrant entrepreneurs, part 1. Duke University, Pratt School of Engineering. Manuscript, January.

9

Small Establishments/Big Effects Agglomeration, Industrial Organization, and Entrepreneurship

Stuart S. Rosenthal and William C. Strange

> There is more than one way to make the same shoe or dress or toy. One is the way of the New York Metropolitan Region's producers: to accept the handicaps of high labor costs, traffic congestion, urban rents, and urban taxes, while exploiting the advantages of speed, flexibility, and external economies. The other is to shed the New York-type handicaps while accepting the disadvantages of remoteness and inflexibility in a larger and more self-contained plant.
> —Raymond Vernon (1960, 75)

> Large firms . . . are much more fully integrated and therefore depend less on outside suppliers. On the one hand, this means that, dollar for dollar, their business is less of a stimulus to the creation of a community of independent suppliers. On the other hand, the new entrant is not likely to find that the company is anxious to spread its fixed costs by making its services available to outsiders.
> —Benjamin Chinitz (1961, 288)

9.1 Introduction

There is a long history of research on the relationship between agglomeration and productivity; see Rosenthal and Strange (2004) for a review. There is also a long history of urban thinking that has considered the role of the organization of production into firms in the generation of increasing re-

Stuart S. Rosenthal is the Melvin A. Eggers Economics Faculty Scholar and a senior research associate of the Center for Policy Research at Syracuse University. William C. Strange is the

turns. Notable contributions include Vernon (1960) and Chinitz (1961)—as quoted in the epigraph—and also Jacobs (1969), Piore and Sabel (1984), and Saxenian (1994). In particular, there has been much attention paid to the role of small firms in the generation of agglomeration economies. This chapter will carry out an econometric analysis of the organization-agglomeration relationship. It will thus consider the relationship between the corporate organization of production (into establishments) and the spatial organization of production (into cities).

Agglomeration economies are inherently geographic in nature. It does not matter whether the increasing return arises from consumer/supplier linkages (as in the preceding epigraph quotations), from entrepreneurial spillovers (as in Sorenson-Audia [2000] and Klepper [2007]), or from knowledge spillovers or labor market pooling (as in Marshall [1890]). In all cases, the agglomeration economy arises from spatial proximity. We will therefore consider the impact of small establishments on entrepreneurship in an explicitly geographic setting.

To carry out this analysis, we make use of data from the Dun and Bradstreet (D&B) MarketPlace from the first quarter of 2007 and the fourth quarter of 2005. The data are available at the zip code level. We convert zip code data into census tracts in order to make use of Census demographic data. These data allow us to include controls for local socioeconomic characteristics. Next, we compute the levels of activity within one and five miles of the geographic centroid of a given census tract, both total employment and employment at individual two-digit industries. These employment data are disaggregated further by establishment size. Specifically, we break down the employment within a given distance of a Census tract into employment at small establishments (fewer than ten employees), medium-sized establishments (ten to forty-nine employees), and large establishments (fifty or more employees).

Our basic specification will be as in Rosenthal and Strange (2003). This involves estimating arrivals and new establishment employment models with agglomeration variables that account in a flexible way for the size distribution of establishments at a given location. In addition to the socioeconomic controls, the specification includes metropolitan statistical area (MSA) fixed effects to control for a range of MSA-level characteristics that potentially impact entrepreneurship. We also estimate a model with census tract

---

RioCan Real Estate Investment Trust Professor of Real Estate and Urban Economics at the Rotman School of Management, University of Toronto.

We thank Edward Glaeser, Mercedes Delgado, Gregory Lewis, and participants at the NBER conference on the Economics of Agglomeration for their helpful comments. We also thank participants at the North American Regional Science Association meetings. We gratefully acknowledge the financial support of the Ewing Marion Kauffman Foundation, the Center for Policy Research at Syracuse University, and the Social Sciences and Humanities Research Council of Canada. Excellent research assistance has been provided by Michael Eriksen, Sung Hyo Hong, and Shawn Rohlin.

fixed effects to further control for the determinants of entrepreneurial activity.

The results of these models are consistent with the idea that small establishments have big effects. In the arrivals models, our estimates of the marginal effect of employment at large establishments have the wrong sign, are insignificant, or are substantially smaller than the effects of employment at small and middle-sized establishments. The weak effect of employment at large establishments continues to hold in models where new establishment employment is regressed on indicators of local employment. For both arrivals and employment models, the effects tend to be strongest for small establishments. In the cases where the small establishment effect is not the strongest, it is always the case that the medium-sized establishment effect dominates. This pattern of results holds in models where the local environment is defined according to activity within one mile and according to activity within five miles. These results hold for models considering overall activity nearby (urbanization) and activity in an establishment's own two-digit industry (localization). The results persist in the models with tract fixed effects. Taken as a group, these models provide strong evidence of a small establishment effect.

This leads to what is arguably the fundamental question in research on agglomeration: what are the microfoundations of the external increasing returns that give rise to the agglomeration patterns observed in the data? In our case, we are concerned with the microfoundations of the small establishment effect. We began the chapter by discussing the Vernon (1960) and Chinitz (1961) notion that small establishments lead to increasing returns by fostering productive consumer/supplier linkages. There are, of course, other explanations. These include entrepreneurial spin-offs, knowledge spillovers, and labor market economies. We will take several approaches that will allow us to move toward a better understanding of the forces behind the small establishment effect. First, we will consider the implications of the spatial pattern of the small establishment effect for the various microfoundations. Second, we will look directly at the Vernon-Chinitz effect by considering the relationship between key service supplier sectors and the local establishment size distribution. Finally, we will make use of the 1992 Bureau of Economic Analysis (BEA) input-output table to consider further whether the presence of small establishments in linked downstream sectors contributes to new business creation. The results of these approaches are suggestive of the existence of consumer/supplier linkages. The analysis does not allow us to rule out other effects, as will later become clear.

The remainder of the chapter is organized as follows. Section 9.2 reviews the theoretical and empirical literatures on industrial organization and agglomeration. Section 9.3 discusses data and our approach to estimation. Section 9.4 presents the results of the estimation, and section 9.5 concludes.

9.2 Literature

The introduction discussed some of the classic references on the relationship between industrial organization and agglomeration. In order to motivate our empirical work, this section will more completely review this literature. This will both clarify the theoretical foundations of the chapters empirics and also the contribution of the chapter to the empirical literature.

9.2.1 Theory

There is a relatively sparse theoretical literature on organizations and agglomeration. Ota and Fujita (1993) is a salient contribution. It builds on the classic models of interaction and urban structure of Fujita and Ogawa (1982) and Ogawa and Fujita (1980). The model includes three sorts of land use: producers' "front office" activities, producers' "back office" activities, and residential land use by workers. Communication costs determine whether a firm's front office and back office are separated in space. For sufficiently low communication costs, the equilibrium involves a central business district made up of front offices, with back offices at the periphery. This is exactly in the spirit of the quote from Vernon (1960) presented previously. Front office activities benefit from the flexibility made possible by agglomeration, while back office activities are more routine and so better able to operate in a self-contained fashion.

Several recent papers have followed up this line of research. Duranton and Puga (2005) present a model of the spatial disintegration into management and production units in a system of cities rather than taking the within-city approach of Ota and Fujita. The key comparative static is that decreases in communication costs between managers and production workers allow spatial disintegration, with cities specializing in management or production rather than in a particular industry. Rossi-Hansberg, Sarte, and Owens (2009) explain the intracity spatial disintegration of firms into management and production units as a consequence of city growth.[1] These papers focus primarily on the impact of urban fixed factors on corporate organization rather than on the impact of small establishments on entrepreneurship. Helsley and Strange (2007) present a model of vertical disintegration and market thickness. Their paper shows that agglomeration can reduce opportunism, resulting in the more efficient organization of production. There is a coordination issue, however. It is consistent with equilibrium for all firms to choose vertical integration or for all firms to choose disintegration.

The paper that provides the best motivation for our empirical work is

1. Helsley and Strange (2006) present a model of spatial interaction within a city where activities are allocated across space according to differences in values accruing from access to other agents. This can be interpreted in a straightforward way as a within-city model of back office-front office location.

Helsley and Strange (2002). This paper presents a matching model of input sharing. There are two sorts of producers in the model: input suppliers and final goods producers (input demanders). Demanders and suppliers have addresses in a characteristic space, and an adjustment cost is incurred when the addresses of transacting firms are not the same. In keeping with Vernon's notion that physical proximity is most important for "unstable" activities (i.e., ones where the production process is not settled), it is supposed that demander addresses are probabilistic. The birth of new businesses depends, therefore, on expected input matches. In an economy dominated by large firms, the input market will be thinner than in an economy dominated by small establishments.

This is the small establishment effect that we will examine empirically. In Helsley and Strange (2007) and in some of the other models in the theoretical literature, there is a kind of virtuous circle in urban entrepreneurship, where small establishments create a situation that is favorable to the entrepreneurial creation of more small establishments. The theoretical literature is thus consistent with the ideas of Vernon, Chinitz, Jacobs, Piore and Sabel, Saxenian, and others. Our chapter will consider these ideas empirically.

9.2.2 Empirical Research

The empirical literature on the impact of local industrial organization on entrepreneurial growth is somewhat more developed than the theoretical literature. Glaeser et al. (1992) include average establishment size in a regression of city-industry-growth on local characteristics. Henderson (2003) also considers establishment size in a city-level analysis. Both find that activity at small firms contributes more to external economies. Rosenthal and Strange (2003) estimate an alternative model; their paper shows that the agglomeration effect of additional employment is greater for employment at small establishments. This is true even when average size is controlled for. More recently, Faberman (2007) has shown that metropolitan areas with younger firms display higher rates of growth. Delgado, Porter, and Stern (2007) find that the colocation of linked industries in a cluster encourages growth. Further, Glaeser and Kerr (2008) consider the determinants of entrepreneurship at the MSA level. They find a very strong "Chinitz effect" associated with firm size. Finally, Lu and Li (2009) establish a positive relationship between agglomeration and vertical distintegration among Chinese manufacturing firms. Using lagged population as an instrument, they argue for a causal relationship.

A number of other empirical papers examine related issues. Holmes (1999) shows that there is a greater value of purchased input intensity when the activity in an establishment's own industry within fifty miles is larger. This is consistent with establishments being more involved in the local economy in an industry cluster. Holmes and Stevens (2002) consider establishment size directly; looking across the nine Census regions, they find a positive correlation between the location quotient of the location and the size of establishments relative to the industry norm (a different sort of location quotient). This is true regardless of whether the correlation is computed for locations or for establishments. It also holds for the ten largest MSAs. It holds as well when the smallest establishments in an industry (possibly performing different activities) are excluded, although measures of industry concentration do change when the data are cut this way. Holmes and Stevens (2004) present some further results on this issue, showing that unlike the manufacturing sector, in service industries, small establishments are located disproportionately in agglomerations. In a related vein, Garicano and Hubbard (2003) show that the scope of law firms becomes narrower in markets with substantial legal activity.

Our chapter will be closer to Rosenthal and Strange (2003, 2005). Like these papers, the estimation in this chapter will take a geographic approach to characterizing the environment in which entrepreneurship takes place. The specifics of our approach are described next.

9.3 Data and Estimation

9.3.1 Data

Our primary data source is the MarketPlace file from Dun and Bradstreet for the first quarter of 2007 (2007:Q1) and the fourth quarter of 2005 (2005:Q4). These data are used to measure establishment births and the distribution of economic activity. The 2007:Q1 file is used to identify establishments that were created in the twelve months prior to that quarter. Throughout most of the analysis, we focus on arrivals in thirty-five two-digit industries in four one-digit categories: manufacturing, wholesale trade, finance, insurance, and real estate (FIRE), and a select segment of services. The 2005:Q4 file is used to characterize the economic environment that entrepreneurs would have taken as given when deciding whether and where to open a new establishment in the year preceding 2007:Q1. For both quarters, the data are coded to the U.S. postal zip code location of the establishments.

It is important that we control as completely as possible for local characteristics that may affect arrivals of new companies. To do so, we make use of census tract socioeconomic attributes from the 2000 Census. The data were obtained from the Neighborhood Change database of Geolytics, Incorporated, and are coded to the year-2000 census tract boundaries. From these data, we obtain census tract controls for the percent population Hispanic, percent population African American, average age of population, percent population male, average income, average income squared, percent of population with high school degree, percent of population with some college, percent of population with college degree or more, unemployment rate, poverty rate, percent of families that are female headed with children, average age of the housing stock, and percent of the housing stock that is single family.

To match the D&B data geography with the census tract controls, we convert the D&B data from zip code to census tract geography. The U.S. Postal Service zip code boundaries are established "at the convenience of the U.S. Postal Service."[2] They are based on postal logistics rather than on a geographic or socioeconomic concept of a neighborhood, in contrast to census block or tract geography. In response, the U.S. Census Bureau has created a boundary file that approximates the geographic region associated with each U.S. Postal Service zip code based on the associated year-2000 census blocks found in that zip code. The resulting boundary file is referred to as the ZIP Code Tabulation Area (ZCTA) file on the Census Web site and is available for download from the Census Bureau. We augmented the ZCTA boundary file with a 1999 file available on the U.S. Census Web site that reports the latitude and longitude of the U.S. postal zip codes in the United States in 1999.[3] Using this augmented ZCTA boundary file and also the year-2000 census tract boundary file (available from the Census Bureau on the Web), we calculated the correspondence between ZCTA geographic units and census tracts. Those correspondence weights were used to calculate the number of establishments and employees present in each census tract, given the original U.S. postal zip code-level data from D&B. Having converted all of the employment data to census tract geography allows us to match the D&B data with year-2000 tract-level socioeconomic attributes of the local population.

Our primary objective is to see how the local environment is related to the births of new establishments and the scale at which they operate. Our data allow us to take a geographic approach rather than assuming that the MSA or country is the level at which agglomeration economies operate. Prior empirical work strongly suggests that agglomeration effects are localized geographically (i.e., Rosenthal and Strange 2003, 2005). In the present chapter, we will define the environment as comprising the activity that takes place within one mile of the geographic centroid of a census tract. We will also consider the activity that takes place within five miles. In order to ensure that our geographic treatment of the data produces a reliable estimate of local activity, we will estimate using a sample of MSAs, each of which is large enough to contain at least 250 census tracts, a number that corresponds roughly to a population of 1 million people.

Our estimation will relate the creation of new establishments and their employment to the levels of activity within one and five miles of the cen-

2. See http://www.census.gov/epcd/www/zipstats.html.

3. After merging those coordinates into the year-2000 ZCTA file, we were able to geocode all but a very small number of the year-2001 zip codes obtained from D&B.

troid of a given census tract. When measuring existing activity, we take into account both total employment and employment in an arriving establishment's own two-digit industry. These employment data are disaggregated further by establishment size. Specifically, we break down the employment within a given distance of a census tract into employment at small establishments (fewer than ten employees), medium-sized establishments (ten to forty-nine employees), and large establishments (fifty or more employees). Newly created establishments are defined as those created in the last twelve months. This window is wide enough to allow for many new establishments in the data. It is also narrow enough to at least partially mitigate concerns about newly created companies that fail prior to 2007:Q1 and do not appear in the data.

9.3.2 Estimation

The key hypothesis with which we are concerned is that an increase in activity at small establishments will have a larger effect on entrepreneurship than will an equivalent increase in activity at large establishments. We will measure entrepreneurship in two ways: the births of small establishments and the scale or level of employment at which these new establishments operate.

To motivate the empirical specification, we make use of a model adapted from Rosenthal and Strange (2003, 2005). Suppose that the price of output is normalized to 1. In this case, an establishment generates profit equal to $\pi(y) = a(y)f(x) - c(x)$, where $a(y)$ shifts the production function $f(x)$, y is a vector of local characteristics, the components of which will be clarified next, and x is a vector of factor inputs that cost $c(x)$. Input quantities will be chosen to maximize profits by satisfying the usual first-order conditions. Employment (n), for example, is chosen, such that $a(y)\partial f(x)/\partial n - \partial c(x)/\partial n = 0$.

Establishment births occur if an establishment can earn positive profits, with all inputs chosen at their profit-maximizing levels. Establishments are heterogeneous in their potential profitability. This is captured by rewriting the profit function as $\pi(y,\varepsilon) = \max_x a(y)f(x)(1 + \varepsilon) - c(x)$. We suppose that ε is independent and identically distributed across establishments according to the cumulative distribution function $\Phi(\varepsilon)$. For any y, there is a critical level $\varepsilon^*(y)$, such that $\pi(y, \varepsilon^*[y]) = 0$, and $\pi(y, \varepsilon) > (<) 0$, as $\varepsilon > (<) \varepsilon^*(y)$. In this case, the probability that an establishment is created is $\Phi(\varepsilon^*[y])$.

We assume that new establishments are opened at locations chosen from among all of the census tracts in the cities that contain them. We also assume that location and employment decisions are made taking the prior economic environment (2005:Q4) as given. Let the vector y_j describe the local characteristics of each tract. Aggregating over establishments in a given tract gives the number of births (B) and total new establishment employment (N) in industry i and tract j. In the empirical work to follow, we express these as follows:

$$B_{ij} = by_{ij} + b_m + b_i + \varepsilon_{b,ij}, \quad (1)$$

$$N_{ij} = ny_{ij} + n_m + n_i + \varepsilon_{n,ij}, \quad (2)$$

where ε_b and ε_n are error terms, b and n are vectors of slope coefficients, b_m and n_m are MSA fixed effects, and b_i and n_i are industry fixed effects. We estimate equations (1) and (2) using a Tobit specification to account for the censoring of both kinds of entrepreneurial activity at zero.[4]

As previously discussed, local variation in agglomeration that affects productivity will affect births and employment at the new establishments. Thus, the vector y_{ij} includes variables characterizing the spatial distribution of employment as perceived by industry i in tract j. Specifically, y_{ij} includes the level of employment within and outside of industry i. These measures are referred to as localization and urbanization, respectively. These variables are measured separately for establishments of various sizes. This allows us to examine the impact of proximity to small establishments. In addition, y_{ij} also includes the long list of tract-level socioeconomic characteristics already presented.

The city and industry fixed effects in equations (1) and (2) control for a number of unobserved determinants of entrepreneurship that might vary geographically. For example, Blanchflower, Oswald, and Stutzer (2001) report that "latent entrepreneurship," the unfulfilled desire for self-employment, varies substantially across countries. It is reasonable to suspect that it might also vary between cities. Black, De Meza, and Jeffries (1996) show the availability of collateral to be an important determinant of new enterprise creation in the United Kingdom. The entrepreneur's own housing is shown to be the single most important source of such collateral. Since housing markets in larger cities are different than in smaller cities, this may be another metropolitan-wide effect captured in the model fixed effects. Furthermore, there is a well-documented correlation between entry and failure. See Caves (1998) for a review of this literature. This correlation implies that resources that can be used by new establishments may be more plentiful where there has been activity of a similar sort previously. Carlton (1983) includes this in his concept of the "birth potential" of an area. This is clearly an important issue in estimation where identification is based on intercity variation in the data. In our case, however, the identification comes from intracity variation. As long as establishments that fail were free to have

4. An alternative would have been to estimate a count model of the number of new establishments while estimating new establishment employment by Tobit. We chose to estimate both by Tobit to facilitate comparison of results across models. Note also that estimating the Tobit models with fixed effects raises a potential econometric issue. Noisy estimates of the fixed effects in nonlinear models typically lead to inconsistent estimates of the slope coefficients (e.g., Chamberlain 1980, 1985; Hsiao (1986)). However, such bias goes toward zero as the number of observations per fixed effect becomes large. In our sample, the number of observations per fixed effect is in fact quite large. In the first model presented in table 9.3, for instance, there are 632,180 observations and seventy-six fixed effects.

chosen any location within their MSAs, this effect will be captured by the fixed effects. This is obviously an important advantage of estimating below the MSA level of geography.

To further address the issue of unobserved determinants of entrepreneurship, we also estimate models with tract fixed effects. The functional forms are:

$$B_{ij} = by_{ij} + b_j + b_i + \varepsilon_{b,ij}, \quad (3)$$

$$N_{ij} = ny_{ij} + n_j + n_i + \varepsilon_{n,ij}, \quad (4)$$

where B_{ij} and N_{ij} are, respectively, births and new establishment employment in tract j. The key difference with equations (1) and (2) is that MSA fixed effects are replaced with tract fixed effects, b_j and n_j. As a result, all tract-specific variables drop out of the model, including local socioeconomic attributes and measures of the total amount of employment in the census tract.

9.3.3 Brief Data Description

The data are described in tables 9.1 and 9.2, which report the census tract values for various sorts of activity. In every case, we restrict attention to cities large enough to have 250 census tracts. Table 9.1 reports establishment and employment counts computed at the two-digit level and then aggregated to one-digit industry groups. Each observation is a census tract two-digit industry pair. The number of observations, therefore, is equal to the number of census tracts covered in the sample multiplied by the number of two-digit industries.

The first panel reports arrival data. There are 16,616 new establishments employing 36,256 workers in manufacturing industries. The number is similar for wholesale trade. Not surprisingly, the numbers are larger in FIRE and the portion of service industries included in our sample. Looking at the bottom of the first panel shows that a large fraction of census tract/two-digit industry pairs experienced positive arrivals for the one-digit industry groups—wholesale trade, FIRE, and service. There are more zero observations in manufacturing, but even for this one-digit grouping, there are arrivals in more than one-quarter of the census tract/industry pairs.

The rest of table 9.1 breaks down the employment within one mile of the centroid of a given census tract into employment in the establishment's own industry (localization) and employment in all industries (urbanization). The data are broken down further into employment at small establishments (fewer than ten workers), medium-sized establishments (ten to forty-nine workers), and large establishments (fifty or more workers). In every instance, there is more employment at large establishments than in any other category.

Table 9.2 repeats this exercise for select two-digit industries: business services (Standard Industrial Classification [SIC] 73), legal services (SIC 81),

Table 9.1 One-digit industry establishment and employment counts, in MSAs with 250 or more census tracts

	Manufacturing SIC 20–39	Wholesale trade SIC 50, 51	FIRE SIC 60–65, 67	Services SIC 73, 80, 81, 86, 87, 89
Arrivals in census tract in the last 12 months for establishments with < 10 workers (2007:Q1)				
Total new establishments	16,616	18,914	38,836	96,861
Total workers at new establishments	36,256	42,928	88,385	179,472
Number of census tract/industry pairs with > 0 arrivals	149,692	55,998	139,823	158,141
Number of census tract/industry pairs with 0 arrivals	488,468	7,818	83,533	33,307
Average employees in OWN industry within 1 mile of arriving company's census tract centroid (2005:Q4)				
All size establishments	309	692	479	1,480
Small establishments (< 10 workers)	28	178	82	248
Medium establishments (10 to 49 workers)	65	246	107	342
Large establishments (≥ 50 workers)	217	268	290	891
Average employees in ALL industries within 1 mile of arriving company's census tract centroid (2005:Q4)				
All size establishments	18,096	18,410	16,243	18,448
Small establishments (< 10 workers)	2,726	2,838	2,395	2,727
Medium establishments (10 to 49 workers)	3,969	4,076	3,453	3,944
Large establishments (≥ 50 workers)	11,401	11,496	10,395	11,777

and engineering-accounting-research-management-related services (SIC 87). These are all activities for which a firm might be expected to choose between internal and external sourcing. We will therefore be interested in how these specific sectors are related to the local organization of production. In table 9.2, we see that the pattern from table 9.1 continues to hold. While there are some tracts that have no arrivals, a large fraction of tracts have positive arrivals. Furthermore, large establishments in aggregate tend to employ larger fractions of neighboring employment than small or middle-sized establishments in aggregate.

9.4 Empirical Results

This section presents the results of our estimation. We will control for the local environment in two ways. First, we control for urbanization, the total activity nearby. Second, we control for activity in the own industry, localiza-

Table 9.2 Selected two-digit industry establishment and employment counts, in MSAs with 250 or more census tracts

	Business services SIC 73	Legal services SIC 81	Engineering, accounting, research, management, and related services SIC 87
Arrivals in census tract in the last 12 months for establishments with < 10 workers (2007:Q1)			
Total new establishments	46,209	2,403	26,581
Total workers at new establishments	77,833	5,867	49,093
Number of census tracts with > 0 arrivals	31,687	14,954	30,821
Number of census tracts with 0 arrivals	221	16,954	1,087
Average employees in OWN industry within 1 mile of arriving company's census tract centroid (2005:Q4)			
All size establishments	1,646	2,824	1,681
Small establishments (< 10 workers)	271	522	261
Medium establishments (10 to 49 workers)	394	606	412
Large establishments (≥ 50 workers)	981	1,695	1,008
Average employees in ALL industries within 1 mile of arriving company's census tract centroid (2005:Q4)			
All size establishments	16,972	49,321	21,022
Small establishments (< 10 workers)	2,545	6,277	3,039
Medium establishments (10 to 49 workers)	3,665	9,958	4,466
Large establishments (≥ 50 workers)	10,761	33,087	13,516

tion. For both, we disaggregate by establishment size, breaking down the employment within a given distance of a census tract into employment at small establishments (fewer than ten employees), medium-sized establishments (ten to forty-nine employees), and large establishments (fifty or more employees). Some establishments in the D&B data have missing values for employment. It is possible that these might be small establishments, and this has the potential of biasing our estimates. To address this, we include in the regressions the number of establishments for which D&B does not report employment.

9.4.1 Small Establishment Effects: Tobit Models

Table 9.3 reports results for Tobit models estimated separately for one-digit industries. In these models, all of the own-industry variables are measured at the two-digit level. For each industry group, there are two

Table 9.3 **Tobit models for the number of arrivals and employment for new (< twelve months old) small (< ten workers) establishments by one-digit industry category (robust standard errors in parentheses)**

	Manufacturing SIC 20–39		Wholesale trade SIC 50, 51		FIRE SIC 60–65, 67		Services SIC 73, 80, 81, 86, 87, 89	
	Arrivals	Employment	Arrivals	Employment	Arrivals	Employment	Arrivals	Employment
ALL industries within 1 mile of census tract centroid (all controls in 1,000s)								
Establishments with size unknown	–0.2072	–0.6069	–0.2963	–0.8977	–0.4405	–0.9936	–1.9500	–4.4170
	(0.0425)	(0.1158)	(0.2934)	(0.8236)	(0.1669)	(0.4123)	(0.5052)	(1.0542)
Employees at establishments with < 10 workers	0.0142	0.0370	0.0309	0.0984	0.0165	0.0301	0.1093	0.2183
	(0.0029)	(0.0078)	(0.0232)	(0.0643)	(0.0108)	(0.0269)	(0.0334)	(0.0693)
Employees at establishments with 10 to 49 workers	–0.0002	0.0013	–0.0272	–0.0844	0.0060	0.0176	–0.0136	–0.0154
	(0.0009)	(0.0024)	(0.0088)	(0.0251)	(0.0028)	(0.0070)	(0.0086)	(0.0179)
Employees at establishments with ≥ 50 workers	–0.0002	–0.0004	0.0013	0.0042	0.0003	0.0006	0.0022	0.0055
	(0.0001)	(0.0003)	(0.0008)	(0.0024)	(0.0004)	(0.0011)	(0.0013)	(0.0027)
OWN industry within 1 mile of census tract centroid (all controls in 1,000s)								
Establishments with size unknown	7.1420	26.2700	–68.6100	–170.6000	–10.4100	–28.8600	3.3490	8.4460
	(2.3649)	(6.6675)	(16.9407)	(45.8602)	(1.0866)	(2.8184)	(1.3237)	(3.9102)
Employees at establishments with < 10 workers	0.0245	–0.3390	0.8419	1.5850	0.5602	1.4060	0.1888	0.4994
	(0.1441)	(0.3942)	(0.1900)	(0.4818)	(0.0905)	(0.2264)	(0.0444)	(0.1051)
Employees at establishments with 10 to 49 workers	0.1597	0.6065	0.3007	1.2120	–0.0237	0.0601	0.2710	0.5707
	(0.0626)	(0.1758)	(0.1489)	(0.4081)	(0.0550)	(0.1397)	(0.0299)	(0.0687)
Employees at establishments with ≥ 50 workers	–0.0121	–0.0435	0.2232	0.6056	0.0184	0.0420	–0.0195	–0.0581
	(0.0049)	(0.0156)	(0.0603)	(0.1628)	(0.0048)	(0.0124)	(0.0075)	(0.0174)
Two-digit SIC fixed effects	20	20	2	2	7	7	6	6
MSA fixed effects	56	56	56	56	56	56	56	56
P-value on 14 year-2000 socioeconomic status tract controls	0.00	0.00	0.00	0.00	0.00	0.00	0.00	0.00
Observations	632,180	632,180	63,218	63,218	221,263	221,263	189,654	189,654
Censored observations	483,717	483,717	7,701	7,701	82,589	82,589	32,911	32,911
Uncensored observations	148,463	148,463	55,517	55,517	138,674	138,674	156,743	156,743
Log-*L*	–137,226.94	–275,614.82	–55,246.96	–107,748.80	–140,201.70	–260,451.85	–254,359.05	–360,088.72

columns—the first reporting the arrivals model and the second reporting the new establishment employment model. To facilitate review of the results, we scale the right-hand-side control variables by 1,000. This allows us to avoid scientific notation in the regression tables. In both the arrival and new establishment employment models, the coefficients thus measure the effect of adding 1,000 additional workers to the local environment at establishments of given size (or 1,000 additional companies among those for which size is not known). We are interested here in the impact of industrial organization on agglomeration economies, so we do not report coefficient estimates for our socioeconomic controls. It is worth pointing out, though, that in this model and in all models that follow, the socioeconomic variables are highly significant. This is evidenced by the extremely low *p*-values reported at the bottom of the table for the various models that we estimate.

The upper rows of table 9.3 report coefficients associated with urbanization (aggregate activity). For manufacturing, the only significant urbanization coefficients are associated with employment at small establishments. An increase in aggregate activity in small establishments is associated with an increase in both arrivals and the total scale of arrivals. The effects of increases in medium-sized or large establishment employment are insignificant. For wholesale trade, the small establishment coefficients are the largest but are insignificant. The large establishment coefficients for wholesale trade are an order of magnitude smaller and are also insignificant. For FIRE, the medium-sized establishment coefficients are significant in both the arrivals and new establishment employment models. The small establishment coefficients are larger but are insignificant. The large establishment effects are much smaller and are clearly insignificant. Finally, for services, the small establishment coefficients are again largest. They are also significant. While the large establishment coefficients are significant, they are nearly two orders of magnitude smaller than the small establishment coefficients.

The pattern of urbanization coefficients in table 9.3 is thus quite clear. The large establishment coefficients are either of the wrong sign, are insignificant, or are much smaller than coefficients for smaller establishment sizes. The small or medium-sized establishment coefficient is always significant and is largest for all four industry groups.

The bottom rows of table 9.3 report localization effects (own two-digit industry employment). For manufacturing, the medium-sized establishment employment coefficients are significant in both the arrivals and employment models. The other localization coefficients are either insignificant (small establishment) or have the wrong sign (large establishment). For wholesale trade, all sizes of establishment are associated with significant increases in entrepreneurship, whether measured as arrivals or as new establishment employment. However, the small and medium-sized establishment coefficients are largest. For FIRE, the small establishment coefficients are both the largest and significant. For services, the largest coefficients are associated with employment in medium-sized establishments, but the small establishment coefficients are of similar magnitude. The results hold for both the arrivals and employment models.

This pattern of results is obtained in models that estimate the arrival and scale of small establishments as functions of the activity that takes place within one mile. The result is robust. We have estimated models using a five-mile geography, and we have found the same pattern of results. We have also estimated models for the arrival of all establishments, not just small ones. Again, the pattern of results does not change. Finally, we have also estimated this relationship separately for various individual two-digit SIC industries: apparel (SIC 23), printing and publishing (SIC 27), machinery and equipment (SIC 35), wholesale trade (SIC 50), brokerage and exchanges (SIC 62), business services (SIC 73), legal services (SIC 81), and engineering-accounting-research-management-related services (SIC 87).[5] While the pattern varies slightly among industries, employment at smaller establishments is consistently more important in these models.

The basic pattern is now in place: an increase in employment at a small establishment is associated with a larger increase in entrepreneurial activity than is an increase in employment at large establishments. Put bluntly, the 1960 analysis of Vernon and Chinitz about urban development generally applies in the new century to urban entrepreneurship.

It is important for us to be clear that our identification of these effects is based on within-MSA variation in an establishment's local business environment. Any effects that operate at the MSA level are captured by MSA fixed effects. It is also important to observe that the models have been estimated with controls for a range of tract-level socioeconomic characteristics that proxy for other characteristics of the local business environment.[6] This will control for at least some of the local variation of the business environment within cities. These socioeconomic variables are highly significant in every model presented in tables 9.3 to 9.6.

Despite these extensive controls, the possibility remains that unmeasured characteristics could be responsible for both the prior level of small business activity and also contemporaneous small business activity. However, such factors must (a) not operate at the MSA level, (b) not be captured by the range of extensive and highly significant socioeconomic variables, (c) be associated with the presence of small and medium-sized establishments but not large establishments, and (d) be broadly consistent across a range of manufacturing and service sectors and industries.

5. Results for the three service industries are presented shortly. Results for the other two-digit industries noted are not reported to avoid proliferation of tables.

6. As noted previously, these controls include census tract racial composition (percent Hispanic, percent African American), average age of population, percent male, average income and its square, percent high school degree, percent with some college, percent with college degree or more, unemployment rate, poverty rate, percent of families that are female headed with children, average age of the housing stock, and percent of the housing stock that is single family.

9.4.2 Census Tract Fixed Effect Models

To further assess the robustness of the small establishment effect that we have found, we also estimate models that employ census tract fixed effects. These obviously control for an even greater range of local factors that might impact entrepreneurial activity. In these models, identification comes from within-tract variation, so it is not possible to estimate urbanization effects. Tract-specific socioeconomic control variables also drop out of the model. Given the very large number of fixed effects (nearly 32,000), we estimated these models by ordinary least squares. As before, we estimate models for both arrivals and for new establishment employment. In addition, estimates are presented for two samples: first, for a sample in which we pool data across all thirty-five two-digit industries used in the previous analysis, and then again pooling just the twenty two-digit industries in manufacturing. In all cases, we control for two-digit industry fixed effects. We also continue to use one-mile controls as our preferred geography in measuring the agglomeration variables. In some models, we augment this specification by including additional controls for agglomeration within five miles. This allows us to highlight the degree to which the small establishment effects are highly spatially localized.

Table 9.4 reports the results. Consider first the models that control for just the one-mile agglomeration measures and for the sample with all thirty-five two-digit industries. For these specifications, we again have a pattern where the effects of own two-digit industry employment are much stronger for employment at small and medium-sized establishments than for employment at large establishments. The small establishment coefficients are all significant. The medium-sized establishment coefficients are roughly three times as large. The large establishment coefficients are negative and insignificant in both the arrivals and employment models. A similar pattern is evident for the manufacturing industries. For arrivals, the small establishment effect is bigger than the medium-sized establishment effect by roughly an order of magnitude. The large establishment effect is negative and insignificant. For employment, the small and medium-sized establishment coefficients are similar in magnitude, but only the latter is significant. The large establishment coefficient is negative and marginally significant. The small establishment effect result from the Tobit models is thus quite robust. It persists even in models that make great demands on the data, such as these tract fixed effect specifications.

Consider next those models in table 9.4 that include agglomeration controls for activity between zero and one mile and also activity between zero and five miles. Specified in this manner, the 1-mile variables are interactive terms; their coefficients reflect the degree to which effects differ when employment is located within one mile as compared to one to five miles. The five-mile variable coefficients, in contrast, reflect the influence of employment

Table 9.4 **Linear tract fixed effect models for the number of arrivals and employment for new (< twelve months old) small (< ten workers) establishments, controlling for local employment within one and five miles (robust standard errors in parentheses)**

	All 35 two-digit industries				Manufacturing SIC 20–39			
	One-mile controls only		One- and five-mile controls		One-mile controls only		One- and five-mile controls	
	Arrivals	Employment	Arrivals	Employment	Arrivals	Employment	Arrivals	Employment
	Local activity within 1 mile (in 1,000s)							
OWN industry establishments with size unknown	–5.6000	–10.5000	–4.8500	–7.4800	4.2700	18.2200	4.7800	20.1800
	(0.7407)	(1.8261)	(0.8802)	(2.1808)	(1.5641)	(4.4657)	(1.7836)	(5.1349)
OWN industry employees at establishments with < 10 workers	0.1000	0.2300	0.2400	0.5400	0.2900	0.3500	0.4500	0.8200
	(0.0254)	(0.0644)	(0.0363)	(0.0853)	(0.0983)	(0.2734)	(0.1148)	(0.3118)
OWN industry employees at establishments with 10 to 49 workers	0.3000	0.7000	0.2500	0.5700	0.0200	0.2500	–0.0400	0.0600
	(0.0217)	(0.0552)	(0.0260)	(0.0642)	(0.0333)	(0.1168)	(0.0500)	(0.1200)
OWN industry employees at establishments with ≥ 50 workers	–0.0015	–0.0094	0.0069	0.0100	–0.0025	–0.0200	–0.0003	–0.0100
	(0.0031)	(0.0085)	(0.0037)	(0.0085)	(0.0028)	(0.0104)	(0.0029)	(0.0072)
	Local activity within 5 miles (in 1,000s)							
OWN industry establishments with size unknown	—	—	–0.0500	–0.4200	—	—	–0.1300	–0.5000
			(0.0658)	(0.1479)			(0.0872)	(0.2688)
OWN industry employees at establishments with < 10 workers	—	—	–0.0094	–0.0200	—	—	–0.0300	–0.1100
			(0.0022)	(0.0044)			(0.0062)	(0.0205)
OWN industry employees at establishments with 10 to 49 workers	—	—	–0.0041	–0.0039	—	—	0.0100	0.0400
			(0.0017)	(0.0035)			(0.0025)	(0.0084)
OWN industry employees at establishments with ≥ 50 workers	—	—	–0.0020	–0.0050	—	—	–0.0004	–0.0005
			(0.0002)	(0.0005)			(0.0001)	(0.0004)
Census tract fixed effects	31,908	31,908	31,908	31,908	31,908	31,908	31,908	31,908
Observations	1,116,780	1,116,780	1,116,780	1,116,780	638,160	638,160	638,160	638,160
R^2 within	0.2945	0.2484	0.2962	0.2505	0.1049	0.0681	0.1055	0.0688
R^2 between	0.0274	0.0350	0.0367	0.0446	0.0300	0.0406	0.0323	0.0433
R^2 overall	0.2564	0.2138	0.2593	0.2172	0.0919	0.0637	0.0927	0.0647

situated at companies one to five miles away.[7] These models allow us to test whether the marginal impact of employment at a given size category of establishment differs depending on whether that establishment is within one mile or one to five miles.

The attenuation patterns revealed by the one-mile coefficients are noteworthy. For both the aggregate thirty-five industry and manufacturing samples and for both the arrival and employment specifications, the coefficients on the small establishment one-mile variables are significant and positive. This is consistent with geographic attenuation. We also find significant one-mile effects of similar magnitude for the medium-sized establishments in the thirty-five industry models but not for manufacturing. For large establishments, the one-mile coefficients are either negative or insignificant or much smaller than the coefficients for small establishments. Once again, we continue to observe small establishment patterns. In this instance, the evidence indicates that small establishment effects attenuate with distance.

The persistence of the small establishment effect pushes us inexorably to ask, why? We now turn to this question.

9.4.3 Identifying the Sources of the Small Establishment Effect

As discussed in section 9.2, there are a number of potential explanations for the small establishment effect. The emphasis in Chinitz and Vernon is given to consumer/supplier linkages. In a market dominated by small establishments, a thick input supplier market will arise. This will further support the entrepreneurial creation of additional small establishments. However, as previously noted, there are other standard explanations for agglomeration, and it makes sense to consider these as possible explanations for small establishment effects. It is at least possible that some sorts of labor market pooling might take place more readily in a small establishment-dominated environment, that knowledge spillovers might be greater from small establishments, and that entrepreneurial spin-offs might occur more frequently from small establishments. With regard to knowledge spillovers, however, the work on "anchor tenants" and innovation (Agrawal and Cockburn 2003; Feldman 2005) reaches the conclusion that larger innovators exert stronger effects on neighbors. With regard to entrepreneurial spin-offs, Klepper (2007) finds that entrepreneurs who have worked previously at successful firms are more likely to themselves be successful. These studies have found what amounts to large establishment effects. Thus, we may need to look beyond knowledge spillovers or entrepreneurial spin-offs for explanations of small establishment effects.

We will take several approaches to shed light on the sources of the small establishment effect. It is important for us to be clear at this point that

7. Note that the effect of employment within one mile is given by the sum of the one- and five-mile coefficients.

none of the approaches will provide a definitive answer. This should not be surprising. Our task is parallel to identifying the microfoundations of agglomeration economies, an undertaking that continues to resist definitive solutions, despite the considerable intellectual energies that have been devoted to it. Since this issue is so important and so resistant to definitive resolution, we believe that even the modest results that we will present are useful additions to knowledge.

Our first approach is to consider more carefully the geographic pattern of the small establishment effect that was reported in table 9.4. Recall that the small establishment effect clearly attenuates with distance. The conclusion is clear: the small establishment effect is highly localized. This suggests that at least one of the underlying mechanisms that drives the small establishment effect must operate primarily at the very local level.

We discussed several mechanisms earlier in the chapter. These were labor market effects, entrepreneurial spin-offs, knowledge spillovers, and the Chinitz-Vernon consumer/supplier linkages explanation. Labor market effects are likely to operate at the scale at which workers commute. This is essentially how the MSA definition of a city is constructed. These effects are likely to operate at a large geographic range and would be at least partly swept out by our location fixed effects. In contrast, knowledge spillovers are likely to have a local element for a range of activities, as noted by Rosenthal and Strange (2003, 2005, 2008), and for advertising, as noted by Arzaghi and Henderson (2008). In addition, the geographic range at which entrepreneurial spin-offs might operate is unclear. The spin-off process might operate at the MSA level because entrepreneurs are fixed to a particular city. Or, the entrepreneur might be fixed to a neighborhood by highly specialized local knowledge. Similarly, customer/supplier effects could operate at a highly local level (the level of New York's garment district for some of the effects discussed by Vernon) or at the MSA level (which is implied by the two quotes at the beginning of the chapter.) On balance, our geographic results are suggestive that knowledge spillovers, entrepreneurial spin-offs, or customer/supplier effects could all potentially lie behind the local nature of the small establishment effect. Labor pooling seemingly does not. Since the anchor tenant and entrepreneurial spin-off work discussed previously seems to suggest that large firms have larger effects, we are left with customer/supplier linkages as the most appealing explanation of our small establishment effects.

To investigate the microfoundations issue further, it would be desirable to look for direct evidence that would be consistent with various mechanisms. The D&B data that we use does not contain information that allows us to directly address either knowledge spillovers, entrepreneurial spinoffs, or labor market pooling. It does, however, contain information that speaks directly to the presence of consumer/supplier linkages.

The heart of the linkages hypothesis is that the presence of many small downstream establishments encourages upstream activity. Since large establishments tend to internally source to a greater degree, employment at large establishments does not encourage upstream activity to the same degree that employment at small establishments does. In order to assess the consumer/supplier linkages hypothesis, we will therefore look for direct evidence that the presence of small downstream firms encourages the growth of upstream sectors.

To do this, we will begin by focusing on three industries whose services are sometimes contracted out, but at other times provided internally. These industries are business services (SIC 73), legal services (SIC 81), and engineering-accounting-research-management-related services (SIC 87). We then consider whether an increase in aggregate economic activity (urbanization) in smaller establishments is associated with an increase in the supplier industry's scale. This involves estimation parallel to the Tobit models in table 9.3, where we separately regress arrivals and new establishment employment on urbanization variables disaggregated by establishment size. We include localization variables as controls, and we also include both MSA fixed effects and socioeconomic controls, as in table 9.3.

The results are presented in table 9.5. Since any establishment could potentially be a customer of these sectors, we are particularly interested in the urbanization coefficients (based on employment across all industries). These coefficients exhibit a clear and familiar pattern. For business services, in both the arrivals and employment models, the small and medium-sized establishment coefficients are of similar magnitude, positive, and significant. The large establishment coefficients are insignificant. For legal services, it is the small establishment coefficients that are positive and significant. For engineering-accounting-research-management-related services, the small and medium-sized coefficients are again positive and of quite similar magnitude for both the arrivals and employment models. All have coefficients significant at least at the 10 percent level.

These results indicate that when a local environment has many small establishments, there is much more activity in these three key service input sectors. When the environment is instead dominated by large establishments but is otherwise identical in overall scale, there is less activity in the three sectors. This is obviously consistent with the Chinitz-Vernon customer/supplier linkages hypothesis.

In fact, we see a similar pattern when we revisit the urbanization coefficients in table 9.3. For manufacturing and services, the coefficients on small establishment urbanization employment are positive, significant, and larger in magnitude than the other urbanization variables. For FIRE, the middle-sized coefficients are largest. For wholesale trade, the small establishment coefficients are again largest, but they are only marginally significant, or they are insignificant. To the extent that the entire local economy comprises potential customers for a given industry sector, these patterns are suggestive

Table 9.5 Tobit models for select service industries of the number of arrivals and employment for new (< twelve months old) small (< ten workers) establishments (robust standard errors in parentheses)

	Business services SIC 73		Legal services SIC 81		Engineering, accounting, research, management, and related services SIC 87	
	Arrivals	Employment	Arrivals	Employment	Arrivals	Employment
ALL industries within 1 mile of census tract centroid (all controls in 1,000s)						
Establishments with size unknown	–4.5910	–9.7430	–1.0730	–2.5020	–2.6830	–6.2180
	(2.5648)	(5.1279)	(0.1717)	(0.4802)	(1.2899)	(2.8787)
Employees at establishments with $<$ 10 workers	0.1992	0.3137	0.0527	0.1212	0.0890	0.1972
	(0.1119)	(0.2241)	(0.0111)	(0.0308)	(0.0514)	(0.1078)
Employees at establishments with 10 to 49 workers	0.1488	0.3343	–0.0106	–0.0289	0.0878	0.1753
	(0.0295)	(0.0624)	(0.0054)	(0.0159)	(0.0412)	(0.0985)
Employees at establishments with $\geq$ 50 workers	0.0032	0.0068	0.0012	0.0040	0.0068	0.0153
	(0.0077)	(0.0161)	(0.0010)	(0.0036)	(0.0044)	(0.0096)
OWN industry within 1 mile of census tract centroid (all controls in 1,000s)						
Establishments with size unknown	–158.50	–318.90	–42.380	–135.00	–62.560	–141.80
	(68.6147)	(141.1062)	(17.6583)	(49.0909)	(33.2766)	(74.2408)
Employees at establishments with $<$ 10 workers	–0.2469	0.0898	0.6249	1.5210	–0.2009	–0.6157
	(0.5742)	(1.1220)	(0.1570)	(0.4422)	(0.4367)	(1.0616)
Employees at establishments with 10 to 49 workers	0.6067	1.0910	0.3180	1.0320	0.2129	0.7640
	(0.2696)	(0.5538)	(0.1747)	(0.4914)	(0.2839)	(0.6761)
Employees at establishments with $\geq$ 50 workers	0.0223	0.0652	–0.0559	–0.1506	–0.0453	–0.0725
	(0.0421)	(0.0905)	(0.0174)	(0.0477)	(0.0220)	(0.0465)
MSA fixed effects	56	56	56	56	56	56
P-value on 14 year-2000 socioeconomic status tract controls	0.00	0.00	0.00	0.00	0.00	0.00
Observations	31,609	31,609	31,609	31,609	31,609	31,609
Censored observations	210	210	16,803	16,803	1,063	1,063
Uncensored observations	31,399	31,399	14,806	14,806	30,546	30,546
Log-*L*	–63,870.71	–83,290.28	–13,645.92	–28,009.61	–49,140.04	–70,689.49

that the presence of small establishment customer companies enhances new business creation among suppliers. Of course, our filter used here to identify the customer base is rather crude compared to the three-sector analysis discussed previously.

Our final approach to identifying direct evidence of customer/supplier linkages makes use of the 1992 Bureau of Economic Analysis input-output table. We first calculate the percentage of a given industry's total sales to each two-digit industry throughout the economy. We do this for thirty of our thirty-five two-digit industries, including all industries in manufacturing, wholesale trade, FIRE, and also business services.[8] For each of these industries, we then calculate a weighted sum of downstream employment. The weights used for these calculations are the percentages obtained in the first step; these are multiplied by the corresponding industry employment levels in the local economy.[9] We then estimate linear tract fixed effect models, as in table 9.4. These models now include both the localization measures (own-industry employment) and also the downstream employment measures. Both are broken down by establishment size.

Results are presented in table 9.6. The first point to make about these results concerns the own-industry coefficients. We continue to find greater effects for small and medium-sized establishments, even controlling for downstream activity. This is true for both the thirty-industry sample and for manufacturing. This underlines the robustness of the chapter's main finding.

There is also an interesting pattern to the downstream employment coefficients. In the thirty-industry sample, results are mixed and inconclusive when comparing estimates between the arrivals and employment models. This finding could be interpreted as being inconsistent with Chinitz. However, an alternate plausible explanation is that the cross-industry coefficient restrictions implicit in the thirty-industry model obscure customer/supplier effects that differ across industries. Partly for that reason, we also estimate the model for just the manufacturing sector.

In table 9.6, for the manufacturing sample, the presence of downstream employment at small establishments is always positively associated with a greater degree of new entrepreneurial activity. In two of four models, these effects are clearly significant. This finding is similar to that found for the three service industries highlighted in table 9.5. The result is also consistent with the urbanization coefficient patterns from table 9.3. Together, these

8. Five additional service industries were not represented in the 1992 BEA input-output files and are dropped from this portion of the analysis for that reason. These include SIC industries 80, 81, 86, 87, and 89—health, legal, membership, engineering, and services not classified elsewhere, respectively.

9. It is worth noting that this weighted sum of downstream employment is identical in form to the urbanization employment variables included in tables 9.2 and 9.4. The difference arises with the weights. In tables 9.2 and 9.4, the urbanization variables attach equal weight to employment at all local industries.

Table 9.6 **Linear tract fixed effect models of the number of arrivals and employment for new (< twelve months old) small (< ten workers) establishments with downstream controls (robust standard errors in parentheses)**

	30 two-digit industries				Manufacturing SIC 20–39			
	Local activity within 1 mile		Local activity within 5 miles		Local activity within 1 mile		Local activity within 5 miles	
Local activity (in 1,000s)	Arrivals	Employment	Arrivals	Employment	Arrivals	Employment	Arrivals	Employment
OWN industry establishments with size	–5.7500	–12.6900	–0.2800	–0.8200	4.1800	17.6300	0.1700	0.7400
unknown	(1.1454)	(2.5636)	(0.0735)	(0.1701)	(1.5200)	(4.3000)	(0.0720)	(0.2085)
OWN industry employees at establishments with	0.2400	0.4400	–0.0300	–0.0700	0.2800	0.3600	–0.0063	–0.0500
< 10 workers	(0.1048)	(0.2178)	(0.0037)	(0.0106)	(0.1007)	(0.2769)	(0.0063)	(0.0189)
OWN industry employees at establishments with	0.1600	0.4700	0.0300	0.0600	0.0400	0.2600	0.0200	0.0500
10 to 49 workers	(0.0653)	(0.1511)	(0.0039)	(0.0091)	(0.0421)	(0.1209)	(0.0037)	(0.0079)
OWN industry employees at establishments with	0.0084	–0.0057	0.0015	0.0054	–0.0051	–0.0200	–0.0014	–0.0028
≥ 50 workers	(0.0089)	(0.0218)	(0.0005)	(0.0013)	(0.0036)	(0.0114)	(0.0002)	(0.0007)
Downstream industry establishments with size	–2.5200	–4.2100	–0.0500	–0.1200	0.1500	0.8100	0.0028	0.0085
unknown	(0.4444)	(1.0795)	(0.0291)	(0.0609)	(0.1064)	(0.3632)	(0.0054)	(0.0166)
Downstream industry employees at	–0.1000	–0.3000	0.0100	0.0100	0.0300	0.0400	0.0029	0.0040
establishments with < 10 workers	(0.0465)	(0.1167)	(0.0023)	(0.0041)	(0.0121)	(0.0348)	(0.0009)	(0.0026)
Downstream industry employees at	0.1200	0.3100	0.0042	0.0200	–0.0200	–0.0200	–0.0046	–0.0073
establishments with 10 to 49 workers	(0.0350)	(0.0957)	(0.0025)	(0.0060)	(0.0082)	(0.0238)	(0.0008)	(0.0021)
Downstream industry employees at	–0.0034	0.0053	–0.0033	–0.0087	0.0026	0.0035	0.0012	0.0023
establishments with ≥ 50 workers	(0.0067)	(0.0172)	(0.0004)	(0.0011)	(0.0017)	(0.0051)	(0.0001)	(0.0004)
Census tract fixed effects	31,908	31,908	31,908	31,908	31,908	31,908	31,908	31,908
Observations	957,240	957,240	957,240	957,240	638,160	638,160	638,160	638,160
R^2 within	0.3033	0.2545	0.2887	0.2349	0.1050	0.0682	0.0908	0.0496
R^2 between	0.0285	0.0357	0.0000	0.0003	0.0276	0.0371	0.0002	0.0011
R^2 overall	0.2720	0.2247	0.2556	0.2027	0.0914	0.0629	0.0736	0.0406

results are suggestive of Chinitz-type effects: nearby downstream employment housed in small companies contributes to business creation in supplier industries.

9.5 Conclusion

This chapter has considered the relationship between local industrial organization and entrepreneurship. We estimate models of the birth of small establishments and the magnitude of their operations. This estimation is carried out at the census tract level, using within-MSA variation in local industrial organization to estimate the models. By estimating at below the MSA level, we are able to employ MSA and in some instances census tract-level fixed effects. These fixed effects control for a range of unobserved characteristics that might impact entrepreneurship. In addition, our MSA fixed effects models include a long list of tract-level socioeconomic controls to further reduce unobserved heterogeneity.

A very clear pattern emerges from this estimation. Additional employment at large establishments has an effect on births and on new establishment employment that is insignificant, of the wrong sign, or much smaller than the effects for small or medium-sized establishments. In contrast, for nearly every one-digit industry group or two-digit industry that we estimate models for, there are positive and significant effects associated with employment at small and/or medium-sized establishments. The results prove to be very robust. These results are very much in the spirit of the more particular and less econometric analysis of Vernon (1960), Chinitz (1961), and others.

A further implication of this pattern is that the small establishment effect will reinforce other tendencies in the system of cities toward a core-periphery type of outcome. In part, this is because small companies benefit and rely more on shared infrastructure and related agglomeration economies characteristic of central cities (e.g., Holmes 1999). As a result, those cities with vibrant small business sectors will tend to continue to have vibrant small business sectors. Those without much small business will have difficulty achieving takeoff.

The chapter also provides some evidence regarding the mechanisms responsible for this small establishment effect. We find suggestive evidence that the sort of customer-supplier linkages considered by Chinitz and Vernon are at work.

References

Agrawal, A., and I. Cockburn. 2003. The anchor tenant hypothesis: Exploring the role of large, local, R&D-intensive firms in regional innovation systems. *International Journal of Industrial Organization* 21 (9): 1227–53.

Arzaghi, M., and J. V. Henderson. 2008. Networking off Madison Avenue. *Review of Economic Studies* 75 (4): 1011–38.
Black, J., D. de Meza, and D. Jeffries. 1996. House prices, the supply of collateral, and the enterprise economy. *Economic Journal* 106 (434): 60–75.
Blanchflower, D. G., A. Oswald, and A. Stutzer. 2001. Latent entrepreneurship across nations. *European Economic Review* 45 (4–6): 680–91.
Carlton, D. W. 1983. The location and employment choices of new firms: An econometric model with discrete and continuous endogenous variables. *Review of Economics and Statistics* 65 (3): 440–9.
Caves, R. 1998. Industrial organization and new findings on the turnover and mobility of firms. *Journal of Economic Literature* 36 (4): 1947–82.
Chamberlain, G. 1980. Analysis of covariance with qualitative data. *Review of Economic Studies* 47 (1): 225–38.
———. 1984. Panel data. In *Handbook of econometrics,* vol. 2, ed. Z. Griliches and M. Intriligator, 1247–318. New York: Elsevier.
Chinitz, B. 1961. Contrasts in agglomeration: New York and Pittsburgh. *American Economic Review: Papers and Proceedings* 51 (2): 279–89.
Delgado, M., M. E. Porter, and S. Stern. 2007. Convergence, clusters, and economic performance. Harvard Business School. Manuscript, December.
Duranton, G., and D. Puga. 2005. From sectoral to functional urban specialisation. *Journal of Urban Economics* 57 (2): 343–70.
Faberman, R. J. 2007. The relationship between the establishment age distribution and urban growth. Working Paper no. 07-18. Federal Reserve Bank of Philadelphia, July.
Feldman, M. P. 2005. The locational dynamics of the US biotech industry: Knowledge externalities and the anchor hypothesis. In *Research and technological innovation,* ed. A. Q. Curzio and M. Fortis, 201–25. Heidelberg: Physica-Verlag.
Fujita, M., and H. Ogawa. 1982. Multiple equilibria and structural transition of non-monocentric urban configurations. *Regional Science and Urban Economics* 12 (2): 161–96.
Garicano, L., and T. N. Hubbard. 2003. Specialization, firms, and markets: The division of labor within and between law firms. NBER Working Paper no. 9719. Cambridge, MA: National Bureau of Economic Research, May.
Glaeser, E. L., H. D. Kallal, J. A. Scheinkman, and A. Shleifer. 1992. Growth in cities. *Journal of Political Economy* 100 (6): 1126–52.
Glaeser, E. L., and W. R. Kerr. 2008. Local industrial conditions and entrepreneurship: How much of the spatial distribution can we explain? NBER Working Paper no. 14407. Cambridge, MA: National Bureau of Economic Research, October.
Helsley, R. W., and W. C. Strange. 2002. Innovation and input sharing. *Journal of Urban Economics* 51 (1): 25–45.
———. 2006. Urban interactions and spatial structure. *Journal of Economic Geography* 7 (2): 119–38.
———. 2007. Agglomeration, opportunism, and the organization of production. *Journal of Urban Economics* 62 (1): 55–75.
Henderson, J. V. 2003. Marshall's scale economies. *Journal of Urban Economics* 53 (1): 1–28.
Holmes, T. J. 1999. Localization of industry and vertical disintegration. *Review of Economics and Statistics* 81 (2): 314–25.
Holmes, T. J., and J. J. Stevens. 2002. Geographic concentration and establishment scale. *Review of Economics and Statistics* 84 (4): 682–90.
———. 2004. Geographic concentration and establishment size: Analysis in an alternative economic geography model. *Journal of Economic Geography* 4 (4): 227–50.

Hsiao, C. 1986. *Analysis of panel data.* New York: Cambridge University Press.
Jacobs, J. 1969. *The economy of cities.* New York: Vintage.
Klepper, S. 2007. Disagreements, spinoffs, and the evolution of Detroit as the capital of the U.S. automobile industry. *Management Science* 53 (4): 616–31.
Lu, Y., and B. Li. 2009. Geographic concentration and vertical disintegration: Evidence from China. *Journal of Urban Economics* 65 (3): 294–304.
Marshall, A. 1980. *Principles of economics.* London: MacMillan.
Ogawa, H., and M. Fujita. 1980. Equilibrium land use patterns in a nonmonocentric city. *Journal of Regional Science* 20 (4): 455–75.
Ota, M., and M. Fujita. 1993. Communication technologies and spatial organization of multi-unit firms in metropolitan areas. *Regional Science and Urban Economics* 23 (6): 695–729.
Piore, M. J., and C. F. Sabel. 1984. *The second industrial divide: Possibilities for prosperity.* New York: Basic Books.
Rosenthal, S. S., and W. C. Strange. 2003. Geography, industrial organization, and agglomeration. *Review of Economics and Statistics* 85 (2): 377–93.
———. 2004. Evidence on the nature and sources of agglomeration economies. In *Handbook of urban and regional economics,* vol. 4, ed. J. V. Henderson and J.-F. Thisse, 2119–72. Amsterdam: Elsevier.
———. 2005. The geography of entrepreneurship in the New York metropolitan area. *Economic Policy Review* 11 (2): 29–54.
———. 2008. The attenuation of human capital spillovers. *Journal of Urban Economics* 64 (2): 373–89.
Rossi-Hansberg, E., P.-D. G. Sarte, and R. E. Owens. 2009. Firm fragmentation and urban patterns. *International Economic Review* 50 (1): 143–86.
Saxenian, A. 1994. *Regional advantage: Culture and competition in Silicon Valley and Route 128.* Cambridge, MA: Harvard University Press.
Sorenson, O., and P. G. Audia. 2000. The social structure of entrepreneurial activity: Geographic concentration of footwear production in the United States, 1940–1989. *American Journal of Sociology* 106 (2): 424–62.
Vernon, R. 1960. *Metropolis 1985.* Cambridge, MA: Harvard University Press.

10

Did the Death of Distance Hurt Detroit and Help New York?

Edward L. Glaeser and Giacomo A. M. Ponzetto

10.1 Introduction

Thirty years ago, every major northeastern and midwestern city looked troubled. America had twenty cities with more than 450,000 people in 1950. Every one of them lost population between 1950 and 1980, except for Los Angeles, Houston, and Seattle. The primary source of economic decline for these places was a decline of manufacturing, which first suburbanized, as in the case of Henry Ford's River Rouge Plant, and then left metropolitan areas altogether. Improvements in information technology had made it quite easy for corporate leaders, who often remained in the older cities, to manage production in cheaper locales.

But since 1980, a number of older cities, which had been declining, started once again to grow, both in population, and often more strikingly, in incomes. Places like New York, San Francisco, Boston, and Minneapolis have all thrived since the 1970s, generally in idea-intensive industries like finance, professional services, and new technology. Urban density that once served to connect manufacturers with railroads and boats now serves to facilitate contact of smart people in idea-producing sectors. The idea-producing

Edward L. Glaeser is the Fred and Eleanor Glimp Professor of Economics at Harvard University, and a research associate and director of the Urban Economics working group at the National Bureau of Economic Research. Giacomo A. M. Ponzetto is a researcher at the Centre de Recerca en Economia Internacional, and assistant professor of economics at Universitat Pompeu Fabra.

We are grateful to Diego Puga and participants at the NBER Economics of Agglomeration conference for helpful comments. Glaeser thanks the Taubman Center for State and Local Government, and Ponzetto thanks the Institute for Humane Studies for financial assistance. Kristina Tobio and Scott Kominers provided superb research assistance. E-mail: eglaeser@harvard.edu, gponzetto@crei.cat.

advantages of geographic concentration are not a new phenomenon. After all, Alfred Marshall wrote in 1890 (225) that in dense agglomerations, "the mysteries of the trade become no mystery, but are, as it were, in the air." However, these idea-producing advantages appear to be more and more critical to the success of older, high-density cities.

This chapter advances the hypothesis that improvements in transportation and communication technology can explain both the decline of Detroit and the reinvigoration of Manhattan. While we present some suggestive evidence, the main contribution of this chapter is a model that illustrates how reductions in the costs of communication can cause manufacturing cities to decline and innovative cities to grow. Reductions in transport costs reduce the advantages associated with making goods in the Midwest, but they increase the returns to producing new ideas in New York.

In the model, individuals choose between three activities: (a) innovating, which creates more varieties of advanced products; (b) manufacturing those advanced goods; and (c) producing in a traditional sector, which we think of as agriculture. Firms can also choose whether to locate in a city or in the hinterland. Urban location is associated with the scarcity of real estate but also with the availability of shared infrastructure and with knowledge spillovers that depend on the direct interaction between individuals and therefore thrive on density.

We assume that the traditional sector needs land the most and suffers the least from poor communication, while the innovative sector needs land the least and loses the most from communication difficulties. Since the city has a comparative advantage in speeding communication and has limited—and hence expensive—land, the traditional sector locates entirely in the hinterland, while the innovative sector locates entirely in the city. The manufacturing sector is generally split between the city and the hinterland. These predictions of the model roughly describe modern America, where high human capital industries tend to be centralized within metropolitan areas, manufacturing is in medium-density areas, and natural resource-based industries are generally nonurban (Glaeser and Kahn 2001).

All individuals have the same level of productivity in the manufacturing or traditional sectors, but we assume that there is heterogeneous ability to innovate. As a result, the most able people end up in the innovative sector. Heterogeneity of ability determines decreasing returns to the size of the innovative sector, and it also predicts that the economy will become more unequal if it becomes more innovative.

The model allows us to consider the impact of improvements in information technology. We model these improvements as a reduction in the disadvantage that people working in the hinterland suffer due to the local nature of knowledge spillovers and the inability to share urban infrastructure. This may affect both the manufacturing and innovative sectors; however, as long as the innovative sector stays entirely in the city, what matters at the margin is the cost associated with advanced manufacturing in the hinterland. In our view, the comparative statics are meant to reflect the increasing ability of corporate leaders or idea producers, who remain in urban areas, to communicate with far-flung production facilities.

When the costs of distance fall, manufacturing firms leave the city, which causes a decline in urban income and property values. The economy as a whole is getting more productive as the city's advantage in production is disappearing. This effect captures the decline in erstwhile manufacturing powerhouses like Cleveland and Detroit.

But the decline in communication costs also has two other impacts, which are more benign for the city. Most importantly, reducing these communication costs increases the returns to innovation. Since the city has a comparative advantage in producing new ideas, this effect increases incomes in the urban area. The exodus of manufacturing and the decline in the costs of urban land also increase the total size of the innovative sector in the city, which in turn further bolsters urban success through the increasing returns to new idea production that are a key element in models like ours (Grossman and Helpman 1991; Romer 1990).

As communication costs decline and the size of the innovative sector increases, within-city inequality increases. This increase in inequality does not represent a welfare loss, for improvements in communication technology improve the real wages for all workers, even though nominal wages for workers in the city decline. City population will rise as city manufacturing declines, because the innovative sector is less land intensive than the manufacturing sector.

As long as manufacturing is the industry on the margin between the city and the hinterland, decreasing the productivity costs of locating in the hinterland will reduce city property values. However, once all manufacturing has left the city, further decreases in communication costs impact the city mainly by increasing the returns to innovation through a reduction of the costs of production. In this case, further improvement in information technology causes urban land values to rise. We think of the first case as capturing cities like New York and Boston in the 1970s, when the exodus of manufacturing first caused property values to plummet, while the extension reflects these cities in more recent years, when booming innovative sectors have been associated with rising real estate costs.

We also extend the model to consider a second city. The agglomeration externality implied by local knowledge spillovers makes it efficient for the innovative sector to cluster completely in one of the two cities. Manufacturing instead locates in both. In this case, an improvement in communication technology causes the more innovative city to increase its population and real income relative to the manufacturing city. When improvements in transportation technology reduce manufacturers' dependence on urban infrastructure, property values in the two cities also diverge. This model is meant to show how technological progress can strengthen idea-oriented cities and hurt production-oriented cities.

After discussing the model, we turn to a little suggestive evidence. First, we document the connection between urban success and specialization in innovation, measured, as the model suggests, by employment in primarily nongovernmental occupations that are high education. Specialization in these high-education and presumably more innovative sectors is positively correlated with income growth between 1980 and 2000 and with employment growth over the same time period in the Northeast and Midwest. We also find that successful places increased their specialization in these activities, just as the model suggests.

Second, we turn to the model's predictions about urban inequality. We find that inequality within cities rose more in cities that had faster income growth and in cities with more initial specialization in skilled occupations initially. These effects, however, are modest.

10.2 Urban Diversity and Improvements in Communication Technology

Before proceeding to the model, we first review four facts that motivate the model: (a) the past forty years have seen spectacular improvements in communication and transportation technology; (b) those improvements have made separation between idea producers and manufacturers increasingly common; (c) there has been a remarkable heterogeneity in the growth of both income and population among many older cities since 1980; and (d) while all of the older cities suffered a significant decline in manufacturing jobs, the successful older cities have increasingly specialized in idea-intensive sectors.

Thousands of pages have been written about the improvements in transportation and telecommunication that have made it easier to ship goods and communicate ideas over long distances. Glaeser and Kohlhase (2004) summarize some of the evidence on the decline in moving goods over space; the real cost of moving a ton one mile by rail has declined by more than 90 percent over the last 120 years. The improvements in other transport modes have been at least as striking, and the improvements in communications technology are, if anything, even more miraculous. Figure 10.1 shows the decline in the real cost of a three-minute phone call between New York and London from 1930 to 2000. The decline has been more than 99 percent.

The substantial improvement in information and transportation technology has at least two separate sources. First, there has been a proliferation of new technologies that facilitate communication across space. Among the communication technologies that were not generally available in 1975 but are commonplace today are fax machines, cellular phones, e-mail, the Internet, Wi-Fi, and personal digital assistants. Many of these technologies, such as cellular phones, existed before 1975, but they only became widely affordable after that date.

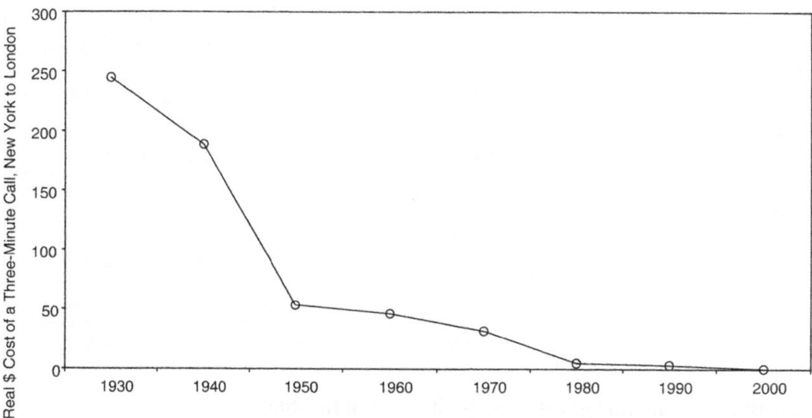

Fig. 10.1 Secular decline in communication costs
Source: International Monetary Fund *World Economic Outlook* (1997).

Increased competition in key communication sectors like telephones, air travel, and cargo shipping has also improved the ability to exchange information, goods, and services over long distances. For example, in 1973, Federal Express began challenging the U.S. Postal Service in providing speedy delivery of packages. In 1982, as part of a settlement of an antitrust case, AT&T divested its local exchanges. After this divestment, there was a considerable increase in long-distance phone companies, such as MCI and Sprint, that made long-distance communication cheaper. In the late 1970s, the airline industry was also deregulated, which increased competition and reduced prices in that sector.

These technological improvements have been accompanied by an "increasing separation of the management and production facilities of individual firms" (Duranton and Puga 2005). Duranton and Puga (2005) connect this separation to the increasing specialization of cities on the basis of function (i.e., management or production) rather than industrial sector. Kim (1999) is among the empirical sources cited by those authors, and he found that the share of manufacturing workers in the United States working in multiunit firms increased from 51 percent in 1937 to 73 percent in 1977. There is also an increase in the number of corporate headquarters that are separate from their production facilities (Kim 1999), which is also seen in the work of Henderson and Ono (2008). The rise in multinational firms, which has been extensively documented and discussed (Markusen 1995), represents a particularly extreme example of increasing geographic distance between firm leadership and production.

Our third motivating fact concerns the heterogeneity in urban success

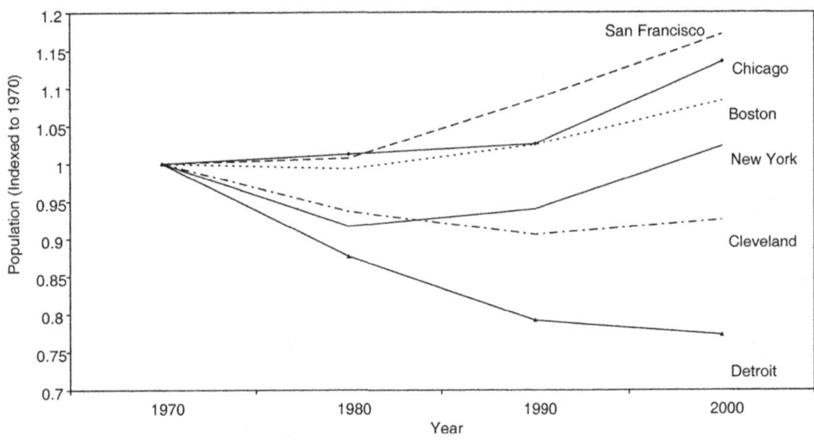

Fig. 10.2 Population growth across cities, 1970 to 2000
Source: U.S. Census Bureau.

within the United States over the last forty years. Population and income give us two alternative measures of urban growth, and figure 10.2 shows the path of population for six major metropolitan areas. Since 1970, San Francisco has grown by more than 17 percent. Chicago has grown by 13 percent, while Detroit has lost more than 20 percent of its population. New York and Boston lost population in the 1970s but have gained since then. Over the third decade, the population of New York increased by 2 percent, while the population of Boston rose by 8 percent. Cleveland has steadily lost population.

There has also been substantial divergence in income levels across metropolitan areas. Figure 10.3 shows the time path of earnings per worker in the largest county of each of these metropolitan areas. Since the U.S. Census Bureau County Business Patterns is the natural source of firm-level data, this pushes us to look at the counties that surround the areas' economic centers. The earnings of New York and San Francisco soar over this time period. Wayne county (Detroit) begins with the highest payroll per worker and declines over the time period, starting out quite prosperous but losing substantially relative to the other two areas. In 1977, Wayne's payroll per worker was slightly higher than that of New York, and today it is less than 60 percent of income in New York.

Figure 10.4 shows the distribution of median family income across metropolitan areas in 1980 and 2000. As the figure shows, the variance of incomes across metropolitan areas increased substantially over this twenty year period. Almost all of the increase occurred in the 1980s.

Our final motivating fact is that the successful cities are specialized in idea-producing industries, while the less successful cities are in social ser-

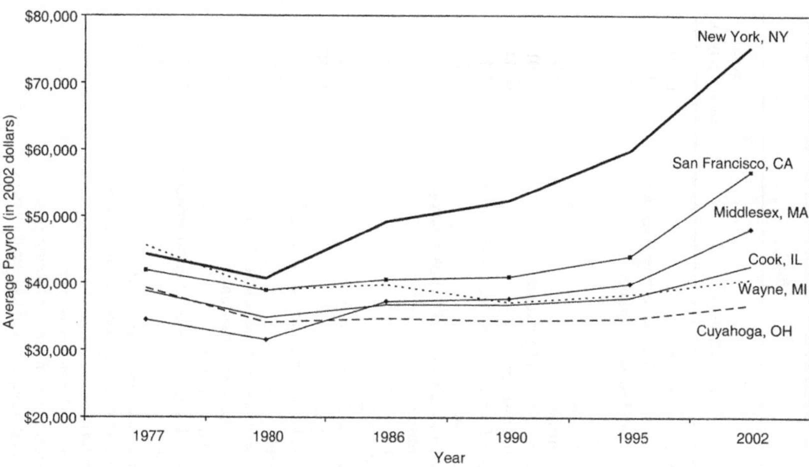

Fig. 10.3 Trends in earnings per worker across cities, 1977 to 2002 (by country)
Source: U.S. Census Bureau *County Business Patterns.*

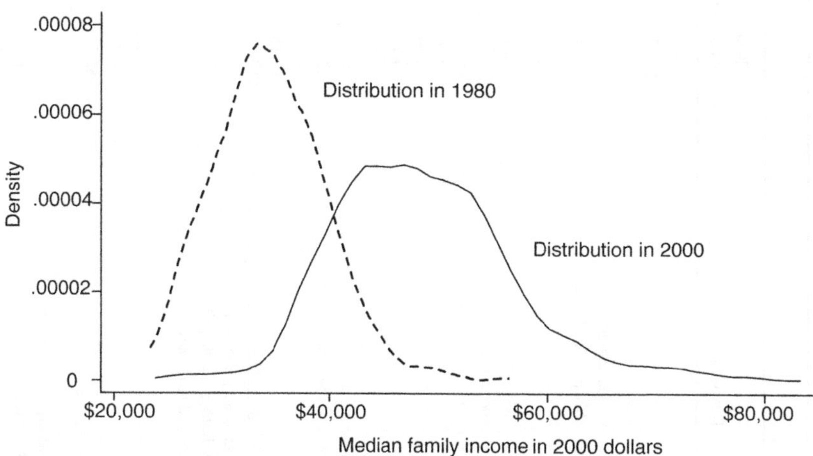

Fig. 10.4 Change in the distribution of median family income across cities, 1980 to 2000
Source: U.S. Census Bureau.

vices with some remaining manufacturing. Table 10.1 shows the top five industry groups measured by total payroll in the largest counties of the six metropolitan areas shown in 1977 and 2002. In 1977, manufacturing dominates four of the six cities, sometimes by a very substantial margin. In 1977, more than one-half of Wayne county's payroll was in manufacturing. Even in New York, the payroll in finance and insurance only slightly nudged out manufacturing.

Table 10.1 **Main industry groups by share of total city payroll, 1977 and 2002 (by county)**

	1977		2002	
	Top industries	% Total annual payroll	Top industries	% Total annual payroll
Chicago	Manufacturing	36.03	Finance and insurance	14.00
(Cook county)	Retail trade	10.62	Professional, scientific, and technical services	12.72
	Wholesale trade	10.35	Health care and social assistance	11.03
	Finance, insurance, and real estate	9.37	Manufacturing	11.01
	Transportation and other public utilities	8.41	Wholesale trade	6.77
Cleveland	Manufacturing	44.07	Manufacturing	15.94
(Cuyahoga county)	Wholesale trade	9.92	Health care and social assistance	15.01
	Retail trade	9.52	Finance and insurance	10.44
	Transportation and other public utilities	8.77	Professional, scientific, and technical services	9.40
	Health and social services	6.70	Wholesale trade	8.27
Boston	Manufacturing	39.26	Professional, scientific, and technical services	18.85
(Middlesex county)	Retail trade	10.89	Manufacturing	12.92
	Wholesale trade	9.31	Information	8.91
	Educational services	7.24	Wholesale trade	8.30
	Health and social services	6.77	Health care and social assistance	8.23
New York	Finance, insurance, and real estate	22.96	Finance and insurance	39.50
(New York county)	Manufacturing	19.85	Professional, scientific, and technical services	14.25
	Wholesale trade	11.18	Information	7.91
	Business services, including legal and computer services	10.68	Management of companies and enterprises	6.70
	Transportation and other public utilities	9.77	Health care and social assistance	5.91
San Francisco	Transportation and other public utilities	23.37	Finance and insurance	23.07
(San Francisco county)	Finance, insurance, and real estate	17.14	Professional, scientific, and technical services	21.26
	Manufacturing	11.85	Information	8.40
	Construction	10.16	Health care and social assistance	7.89
	Retail trade	8.27	Management of companies and enterprises	4.86
Detroit	Manufacturing	55.22	Manufacturing	20.46
(Wayne county)	Retail trade	8.83	Health care and social assistance	11.66
	Transportation and other public utilities	7.17	Management of companies and enterprises	8.56
	Health and social services	6.86	Professional, scientific, and technical services	6.17
	Wholesale trade	6.61	Transportation and warehousing	6.01

Source: U.S. Census Bureau *County Business Patterns.*

By 2002, manufacturing remains the dominant sector in Detroit and Cleveland, but it is now a much smaller share of the total payroll. In 2002, more than 53 percent of the payroll in New York is in finance and insurance and professional, scientific, and technical services. More than 40 percent of the payroll of San Francisco lies in these two areas. Chicago and Boston are more mixed, and they do both idea-oriented production and manufacturing. In the next section, we present a model that attempts to explain the divergence of city economies as a result of improvements in the ability to communicate across space.

10.3 The Model

10.3.1 Basic Setup

This model attempts to describe innovation and production in a closed economy where labor is mobile across space. We will address interurban inequalities in an extension that allows for a second city, but we begin with two locations: a city and the hinterland. Workers choose between three occupations: working in the traditional sector, working in the advanced sector, and innovating in a way that produces more varieties of differentiated goods for the advanced sector.

Individual utility is defined over the traditional good Z and measure n of advanced goods that are aggregated into a composite commodity Y in the manner of Dixit and Stiglitz (1977):

$$(1) \qquad Y = \left[\int_0^n x(j)^\alpha dj\right]^{1/\alpha}, \text{ with } \alpha \in (0, 1).$$

The traditional good Z is produced with a fixed technology that has constant returns to scale. The market for Z is perfectly competitive, so its price equals unit cost: $p_Z = c_Z$. We treat Z as the numeraire so that p_Z equals 1.

Our focus is on demand for the advanced goods, and we will characterize aggregate demand by the homothetic preferences of a representative household, whose budget share for Y is

$$(2) \qquad \beta(p_Y) = \frac{p_Y Y}{p_Y Y + Z}.$$

For example, if the utility function has constant elasticity of substitution σ so that $U(Y, Z) = (1 - \zeta)^{1/\sigma} Y^{(\sigma-1)/\sigma} + \zeta^{1/\sigma} Z^{(\sigma-1)/\sigma}$, then the budget share is $\beta(p_Y) = [p_Y^{\sigma-1}\zeta/(1 - \zeta) + 1]^{-1}$. We will assume that elasticity of substitution is never below 1; equivalently, that demand for the advanced good has no less than unitary own-price elasticity; hence, that $\beta'(p_Y) \leq 0$. Individuals will also need to consume exactly one unit of location-specific capital as a residence.

Each differentiated advanced good is produced by a monopolistic competitor at a constant unit cost of c_x. As in Dixit and Stiglitz (1977), monopolistic competition with constant elasticity of substitution implies markup pricing, so the price of each differentiated good, p_x, satisfies

$$p_x = \frac{1}{\alpha} c_x, \tag{3}$$

and monopoly profits are

$$\pi = (1 - \alpha) p_x \frac{X}{n}, \tag{4}$$

where X is the total output of differentiated varieties by identical producers. This implies the price index for the composite commodity Y:

$$p_Y = n^{-(1-\alpha)/\alpha} p_x. \tag{5}$$

Thus, greater variety is equivalent to higher efficiency. As in Ethier (1982), we could interpret the invention of new goods as an increase in specialization, associated with productivity gains arising from the division of labor.

10.3.2 The Innovation Sector

Each worker requires κ_n units of location-specific capital (i.e., land) to produce innovation and one unit of location-specific capital for a residence.

Advanced goods are invented by an innovative sector that thrives on proximity. The urban advantage in producing new ideas is a reflection of knowledge spillovers that depend on the face-to-face interactions of researchers and are therefore local. Each innovator's productivity depends on the external effect S of aggregate human capital. In the manner of Fujita and Thisse (2003), we assume that the innovation knowledge spillovers in the city are a function of the number of innovators in the city L_n^U and of the number of innovators outside of the city L_n^R:

$$S_U = \left[\int_0^{L_n^U} h(j)dj + \eta \int_0^{L_n^R} h(j)dj \right]^\delta, \tag{6}$$

where $\delta > 0$ measures the returns to scale in knowledge externalities, and $\eta \in (0,1)$ is an inverse measure of the difficulty of achieving profitable spillovers by means of occasional long-distance communication rather than day-to-day proximity. For innovators who locate outside of the city, low density implies that all interactions are sporadic, yielding spillovers

$$S_R = \left[\eta \int_0^{L_n^U + L_n^R} h(j)dj \right]^\delta. \tag{7}$$

Each worker's knowledge stock is assumed for simplicity to be identical, depending on worldwide scientific progress. With a convenient normalization, $h(j) = 1$ for all j. Hence,

$$S_U = (L_n^U + \eta L_n^R)^\delta > S_R = \eta\,(L_n^U + L_n^R)^\delta \text{ for all } L_n^U, L_n^R, \tag{8}$$

implying that it is efficient for all knowledge workers to congregate in the city.

Workers are heterogeneously endowed with creativity, according to a Pareto distribution (cf. Helpman, Melitz, and Yeaple 2004) with minimum $\underline{a} > 0$ and shape $\theta > 1$ so that

$$F(a) = 1 - \left(\frac{a}{\underline{a}}\right)^{-\theta} \text{ and } f(a) = \theta \underline{a}^\theta a^{-\theta-1}, \tag{9}$$

and each urban innovator's output is aS_U. We assume that all individuals have the same output in manufacturing both the differentiated goods and the numeraire and that all heterogeneity is in creativity. As a result, creative people sort perfectly into the innovative sector, and employment in this sector is characterized by a marginal worker with creativity t. Heterogeneity in the ability to innovate both acts as a check on the amount of innovation—because eventually, the marginal innovator is not very good at innovating—and as a predictor of more inequality in the innovative sector.

When all innovation occurs in the city, total employment in innovation is

$$L_n = L_n^U = L[1 - F(t)] = L\underline{a}^\theta t^{-\theta}, \tag{10}$$

and therefore knowledge spillovers are

$$S_U = L_n^\delta = L^\delta \underline{a}^{\delta\theta} t^{-\delta\theta}, \tag{11}$$

and the total amount of innovation is

$$n = LS_U \int_t^\infty af(a)da = L^{1+\delta} \underline{a}^{(1+\delta)\theta} \frac{\theta}{\theta - 1} t^{1-(1+\delta)\theta}. \tag{12}$$

For notational convenience, define the inverse measure of productivity

$$\psi_n \equiv L^{-1/[(1+\delta)\theta-1]} \left(\frac{\underline{a}\theta}{\theta-1}\right)^{-\theta/[(1+\theta)\theta-1]}, \tag{13}$$

which is decreasing in the mean of the skill distribution $\underline{a}\theta/(\theta - 1)$ and in the size of the pool of workers L, because a larger pool means that more able people will be available to this sector.

Then, as a function of the amount of innovation, employment equals

$$L_n = \psi_n n^{\theta/[(1+\theta)\theta-1]}, \tag{14}$$

and the output of the marginal innovator equals

$$tS_U = \frac{\theta-1}{\theta\psi_n} n^{(\delta\theta-1)/[(1+\delta)\theta-1]}. \tag{15}$$

Free entry into this sector means that $\pi t S_U$ must equal the opportunity cost of labor for this marginal worker plus the cost of κ_n units of location-specific capital.

10.3.3 The Spatial Equilibrium

Production of manufacturing goods occurs with a Leontief technology, with κ_x unit of location-specific capital per worker employed in production, in addition to one unit of capital as a residence. Output per worker depends on local knowledge spillovers S^{μ}, with $\mu \in [0,1]$ measuring the importance of knowledge spillovers for manufacturing relative to innovation. It is also a function of the availability of labor-saving urban infrastructure. Producing one unit of advanced goods in the city requires $\psi_x S_U^{-\mu}$ units of labor, and producing it in the hinterland requires $\psi_x(1 + \tau_x)S_R^{-\mu}$.

This setup enables us to nest two extreme versions of the model. In the first version, there are no knowledge spillovers, which requires $\delta = 0$, but cities have innate productivity advantages due to transportation and other infrastructure. We assume that this infrastructure costs a fixed amount $F \leq K[(1 + \tau_x)\eta^{-\delta\mu} - 1]/(1 + \kappa_x)$ that is defrayed by real estate taxation. In the second version, cities have no innate productivity advantages, but there are spillovers.

Production of the traditional good is unaffected by knowledge spillovers, requiring ψ_z unit of labor in the city and $\psi_z (1 + \tau_z)$ in the hinterland, as well as κ_Z units of location-specific capital per unit of labor in production, plus one unit in consumption. We normalize the units of labor so that $\psi_Z(1 + \tau_z)$ equals 1.

We also allow innovators to derive a productivity benefit from the presence of urban infrastructure, so a rural innovator's output is $aS_R/(1 + \tau_n)$ for some parameter τ_n capturing the substitution of labor for infrastructure.

We assume that the traditional sector is quite capital intensive, which is meant to reflect the heavy use of land in agriculture. The advanced production sector uses an intermediate level of capital, and innovation requires the least amount of capital, because that sector is in the business of producing ideas. As such,

$$\kappa_Z > \kappa_x > \kappa_n \geq 0. \tag{16}$$

We also assume that the value of urban infrastructure has the reverse ranking across sectors, so

$$\tau_n \geq \tau_x \geq \tau_Z \geq 0. \tag{17}$$

The city is endowed with K units of location-specific capital, and the hinterland is endowed with K_R units of this same capital. We assume that rural capital is not a scarce resource, because $K_R > (1 + \kappa_Z)L$, so there would be excess land, even if everyone lived in the hinterland and worked in the most land-intensive sector. As a result, the price of rural capital will equal zero.

On the other hand, urban capital is scarce, so not all the population can be productively employed in the city, even in the least land-intensive sector: $K < (1 + \kappa_n)L$.

We are interested in the case where there is some advanced manufacturing in both the rural and urban areas. If the advanced producers are indifferent between these two locations, which is necessary for production to occur in both places, then the traditional producers, who have greater land requirements and less productivity losses due to distance from the city, will all prefer to locate in the hinterland. Since both the price of the traditional output and the labor requirement $\psi_z\,(1 + \tau_z)$ are normalized to 1 the wage in the hinterland also equals 1.

Workers must pay for their one unit of residential capital. Since they could earn a wage of 1 in the hinterland, they must then be paid a wage

$$w_U = 1 + w_K \tag{18}$$

in the city, where w_K is the price of location-specific capital in the urban area. This implies that the cost of producing one unit of each advanced good in the urban area equals $\psi_x[1 + (1 + \kappa_x)w_K]S_U^{-\mu}$, and the cost of producing the same good in the hinterland equals $\psi_x(1 + \tau_x)S_R^{-\mu}$.

When advanced manufacturing takes place in both the city and the rural area, then the price of urban capital must make advanced producers indifferent between the two locations, which requires that

$$w_K = \frac{1}{1 + \kappa_x}\left[(1 + \tau_x)\left(\frac{S_U}{S_R}\right)^{\mu} - 1\right]. \tag{19}$$

Indifference for the marginal worker between the urban innovation sector and the two manufacturing sectors implies that the value of research output for the marginal researcher, net of capital costs, must equal the wage that could be earned in urban manufacturing:

$$\pi t S_U - w_K \kappa_n = w_U. \tag{20}$$

As long as there is urban manufacturing, no innovators choose to locate out of the city. The latter would be the most profitable choice for an individual with creativity a if and only if

$$\frac{1}{S_R} < \frac{\pi a}{1 + \tau_n} < \frac{(1 + \kappa_n)w_K}{(1 + \tau_n)\,S_U - S_R}, \tag{21}$$

and this is impossible when equation (19) holds, because then, equations (8), (16), and (17) imply

$$w_K = \frac{1}{1 + \kappa_x}\left[(1 + \tau_x)\left(\frac{S_U}{S_R}\right)^{\mu} - 1\right] \leq \frac{1}{1 + \kappa_n}\left[(1 + \tau_n)\frac{S_U}{S_R} - 1\right]. \tag{22}$$

To complete the equilibrium, we note that the total production of advanced goods combines rural and urban production, or

(23) $$X = \frac{L_n^{\delta\mu}}{\psi_x}\left(L_U + \frac{\eta^{\delta\mu}}{1+\tau_x}L_R\right),$$

where L_U and L_R denote, respectively, urban and rural employment in advanced manufacturing. The total amount of labor used in the three sectors must sum to the total amount of labor in the economy, which implies:

(24) $$L = L_n + L_U + L_R + Z.$$

We are interested in the case where capital is scarce in the city and is completely used up by residential and production uses associated with the innovative sector and the production of differentiated goods:

(25) $$K = (1+\kappa_n)L_n + (1+\kappa_x)L_U.$$

10.3.4 Comparative Statics

The primary value of this model is to examine the impact that an improvement in communication technology would have on the success of the city. The state of transport and information technology can be summarized by the single parameter

(26) $$\Delta \equiv (1+\tau_x)\eta^{-\delta\mu} - 1 > 0,$$

which captures the productivity gain that manufacturers derive from locating in the city. The urban advantage includes two different components. For $\tau_x > 0$, manufacturers benefit from the value of urban infrastructure—for example, as a transport hub. For $\eta < 1$ and $\mu > 0$, they also profit from knowledge spillovers by colocating with urban innovators.

As we show in the appendix, the equilibrium of this model is defined by urban employment in innovation

(27) $$L_n = \frac{(\theta-1)(1-\alpha)\beta(p_Y)}{\theta-(1-\alpha)\beta(p_Y)}\,\frac{(1+\kappa_x)L+\Delta K}{1+\kappa_x+(1+\kappa_n)\Delta}.$$

Innovation reduces the cost of producing advanced goods and therefore the Dixit-Stiglitz price index p_Y. This decrease in price may then increase the share of the budget spent on advanced goods if demand is sufficiently elastic: then, the increase in demand for the advanced sector in turn drives innovation up further. To guarantee a stable equilibrium, we must assume that the budget share does not increase too much as price declines:

(28) $$\frac{\alpha[\theta-(1-\alpha)\beta(p_Y)]}{(1-\alpha)[(1+\delta)\theta-1]+\alpha\delta\theta\mu} > -\frac{p_Y\beta'(p_Y)}{\beta(p_Y)}.$$

The right-hand side of this equation is the own-price elasticity of the budget share of Y, which can identically be expressed as $\varepsilon - 1$, where ε is the (absolute value of) own-price elasticity of demand for Y. The left-hand side captures the extent to which heterogeneous ability creates decreasing returns in the innovative sector (low θ). The decreasing returns that come from drawing less and less able people into the innovative sector must offset the increasing returns that come from greater variety (low α), as well as those deriving from knowledge spillovers (high δ and μ).

In a stable equilibrium where manufacturing locates in both the city and the hinterland, improvements in transportation and communication technology are described by a reduction in Δ. A decrease in the cost of distance may also reduce the value of urban infrastructure for innovators τ_n, and any decrease in η reduces the value of proximity for innovation, as well as for manufacturing. However, as long as the innovative sector is not so large that the city is completely specialized, manufacturing rather than innovation is on the spatial margin; therefore, changes in the productivity of innovation in the hinterland do not impact equilibrium quantities.

A decline in Δ causes urban property values to decline. As it becomes easier to produce differentiated goods in the hinterland, the price of urban capital declines, since the value of being in the city for advanced manufacturers declines. This effect captures the decline of old manufacturing cities in the first twenty-five years after World War II, when manufacturing suburbanized and then went to lower-density areas within the United States. The wages for production workers in the city also fall, since they need to be paid less to be compensated for having to buy urban residential capital.

The reduction in the cost of urban capital, however, is a boon to the innovative sector, because that capital is an input into production that has decreased in price. As the price of urban capital falls, the amount of urban innovation rises, because it has become cheaper to produce. This is one reason why decreasing communication costs increases the amount of innovation.

A second reason is that improvements in communication technology cause the cost of producing the advanced good to fall. As this price falls, the budget share of Y increases if demand is elastic—or in other words, if the elasticity of substitution between the two goods Y and Z in the utility function (σ) is above unity.[1] Then, the market for the advanced sector expands, making innovation more profitable, thereby attracting previously extramarginal innovators.

Proposition 1. *As Δ declines because of an improvement in information and transportation technology, the price of advanced goods falls, and all real incomes rise. Output of advanced manufacturing increases, while output of the traditional good and employment in its production contract. Innovation and employment in innovation increase.*

1. Furthermore, if advanced goods were a luxury, their budget share would increase with real income and therefore decrease with p_Y. However, we retain the conventional assumption of homothetic preferences.

Improvements in transportation technology are essentially reductions in the cost of producing the advanced goods. We should therefore not be surprised that their price declines. Those declining goods prices then drive real incomes up. As the advanced sector gains a cost advantage, it expands, and the traditional sector contracts.

The improvement in communication technology also increases the amount of innovation for two reasons, as previously discussed. The returns to innovation rise as communication costs fall, and the cost of urban capital declines, as we discuss in the next proposition.

PROPOSITION 2. *As Δ declines, the price of urban capital falls. The output and employment levels in urban manufacturing decline, and wages for production workers in the city fall. But innovation and employment in its production increase, and the total production of the city increases.*

This proposition suggests how we might expect changes in communication technology to impact various measures of urban success. The price of land, which is one widely used metric for the demand for a place, must fall, since the urban advantage that accrues to the sector that is on the margin between urbanizing and not declines. Urban manufacturing employment also declines, because the urban edge in manufacturing falls. As the price of urban real estate falls, nominal wages in the city also fall, since those wages are set to keep real incomes for production workers equal between the city and the hinterland.

On the other hand, population in the city increases, because urban capital is fixed, and manufacturing is such a heavy user of capital relative to innovation. For this process to work, we must have conversion of old manufacturing space to new residential space for innovators, and we have certainly seen much of that in old manufacturing areas such as lower Manhattan. Warehouses converted into lofts are a prime example of this process in action. The rise of the innovative sector in the city is another more positive sign of urban promise.

For the next proposition, we assume that $\kappa_n = 0$ so that the distribution of innovators' income is Pareto like the distribution of ability. In this case, proposition 3 follows.

PROPOSITION 3. *If $\kappa_n = 0$, the ratio of the income of the worker who earns more than $\overline{P}$ percent of the urban workforce to the income of the worker who earns more than $\underline{P}$ percent of the urban workforce rises as Δ declines, whenever the first worker is in the innovative sector and the second worker is in manufacturing.*

This proposition shows that at least some measures of inequality will be increasing in the city as technology improves. Decreasing communication costs increase the share of the population working in the highly unequal innovative sector. The real-world analogy to this is that as New Yorkers moved from working in highly equal unionized jobs in the textile industry to working in financial services, where the returns to ability (or luck) are immense, we witnessed a sizable increase in inequality.

10.3.5 A Purely Innovative City

So far, we have considered an equilibrium with some manufacturing both inside and outside of the city. We now consider the case where communication technology has improved to the point that goods production in the city entirely disappears, and the city comes to specialize in innovation. To keep things simple, we continue to assume that the information costs associated with innovators leaving the city are such that innovation only occurs in the city. In this case, the city is entirely innovative, and all innovation is in the city. The total amount of innovation in the city is limited by the amount of urban capital so that the maximum city population is

$$\overline{L}_n = \frac{K}{1 + \kappa_n}. \tag{29}$$

Employment in innovation equals this upper limit for a positive value of Δ and thus with a positive price of urban capital w_K if and only if urban capital is sufficiently scarce:

$$\frac{K}{(1 + \kappa_n)L} < \frac{(\theta - 1)(1 - \alpha)\beta(\hat{p}_Y)}{\theta - (1 - \alpha)\beta(\hat{p}_Y)}, \tag{30}$$

$$\text{with } \hat{p}_Y = \frac{1}{\alpha}\psi_x\psi_n^{(1-\alpha)[(1+\delta)\theta-1]/(\alpha\theta)}\left(\frac{K}{1 + \kappa_n}\right)^{-\{(1-\alpha)[(1+\delta)\theta-1]+\alpha\delta\theta\mu\}/(\alpha\theta)}.$$

If this condition holds, then there is a threshold $\underline{\Delta} > 0$ such that if the cost of distance falls below $\underline{\Delta}$, innovation rises to the maximum level possible in the city.[2] In that case, proposition 4 follows.

PROPOSITION 4. *If Δ declines below $\underline{\Delta}$, the amount of innovation, innovative employment, and city population remain constant; output of advanced manufacturing increases; the price of advanced goods declines; and all real incomes increase.*

If and only if $\beta'(p_Y) < 0$, as Δ declines below $\underline{\Delta}$ the price of urban capital increases, employment in the advanced sector increases, and output and employment in the traditional sector contract.

2. Symmetrically, there is also a minimum level of innovation, below which all advanced manufacturing, and possibly some traditional production, would occur in the city:

$$\underline{L}_n(\Delta) = \frac{K}{1 + \kappa_n}\left[1 + \frac{\alpha\theta}{(1-\alpha)(\theta-1)}\frac{(1 + \kappa_x)/(1 + \kappa_n) + \Delta}{1 + \Delta}\right]^{-1} < \overline{L}_n.$$

Although this corner solution is reached for a finite value of Δ, it does not seem to be relevant for a modern economy, and we simply assume that Δ is always sufficiently small for manufacturing to be profitable outside of the city.

Once the city has completely specialized in innovation, further improvement in communication technology will not impact city population any more. They may instead start to increase the value of urban property if demand for the advanced good is sufficiently elastic. The elasticity of demand for the composite advanced good is important, because it ensures that the falling production costs will make innovation more profitable. In that case, further improvements in communication technology increase the amount spent on advanced goods, which boosts demand for the ideas produced in the city. The model seems to suggest that during an earlier period, when manufacturing was still leaving cities like New York and Boston, improving communication technologies were associated with declining urban property values. However, in the post-1980 world, when these places have specialized highly in idea production, the rise in real estate costs may reflect the continuing improvement in the ability of communicating ideas, which has acted to increase the returns to innovation.

10.3.6 Two Cities

Finally, we consider an extension of the model that is intended to capture the heterogeneous experiences of different older cities since 1970, and in particular, the diverging fates of innovating and manufacturing cities. Divergence occurs in our model, because manufacturing cities are merely hit by the declining value of their infrastructure, such as a port or a rail hub; while this is true also of innovating cities, they enjoy the counterbalancing positive effect of an increase in innovation and therefore in local knowledge spillovers.

Suppose that city $i \in \{1, 2\}$ host L_n^i innovators, with $L_n^1 > L_n^2 \geq 0$, while $L_n^R \geq 0$ are employed in innovation outside of both cities. Then, knowledge spillovers are

$$(31) \qquad S_1 = [L_n^1 + \eta(L_n^2 + L_n^R)]^\delta > S_2 = [L_n^2 + \eta\,(L_n^1 + L_n^R)]^\delta \\ \geq S_R = [\eta(L_n^1 + L_n^2 + L_n^R)]^\delta,$$

implying that it is naturally efficient for all knowledge workers to congregate in the same location. While an unstable equilibrium where innovators split equally between the two cities is a possibility, we assume that the innovators, either through coordination or decentralized location choices, have succeeded in reaping the advantages of locating in a single place, and we will refer to the city where innovators cluster as the innovative city. The cities are otherwise assumed to be identical: in particular, $K_1 = K_2 = K < (1 + \kappa_n)L/2$, the last inequality ensuring again that not all the population can be urbanized, given the scarcity of urban capital.

When the innovative city hosts both innovation and manufacturing, while the manufacturing city is entirely specialized in manufacturing, proposition 5 follows.

PROPOSITION 5. *As Δ declines, relative to the manufacturing city, the innovative city will see the size of its innovative sector grow, the size of its manufacturing sector shrink, its population grow, and its average real income increase.*

When the value of urban infrastructure τ_x falls, property values in the manufacturing city fall relative to the innovative city.

This proposition emphasizes that declining communication costs increase the degree of inequality across cities, as we saw in the previous section. As those costs decline, the innovative city sees its population and income grow more quickly than the income and population of the manufacturing city.

The second part of the proposition is meant to capture the increasing divergence of housing values in New York and Detroit. Older cities were built on their physical advantages as transportation hubs, whose importance has been steadily diminishing; those that did not find a new source of comparative advantage in the agglomeration of innovative individuals are bound to decline as their geographic edge is blunted.

10.4 Evidence on Urban Growth

In this section, we turn to the empirical implications of the model about disparity between areas. The model predicted that cities that specialized in innovation would benefit from declining communication costs, while cities that specialized in production would be hurt by those costs. The model also predicts that urban success will be accompanied by increasing specialization in innovative activities.

We start with the awkward task of defining specialization in innovation. We mean to define innovation broadly, and we certainly believe that the financiers of Wall Street and the management consultants of Chicago are no less innovative than the software engineers of Silicon Valley. The finance sector in New York, for example, is clearly enormously innovative in ways that can and do reduce the costs of producing final goods. As such, to define innovation, we followed the prediction of the model that high human capital people will specialize in innovation. The prediction pushed us to use skilled occupations as a proxy for specialization in innovation. Specifically, we defined innovative occupations as those that were among the top 20 percent of occupations on the basis of education, where the share of workers with college degrees in 1970 is our measure of education. However, since our model is really about the private sector, we excluded those occupations that had more than one-half of their employees working for the government.

Table 10.2 gives a list of the twenty largest occupations ranked by education in 1970. While doctors and lawyers rank high on the list, perhaps justifiably so, the list of skilled occupations includes many different types of engineers. While there are many reasons to be skeptical about this method of

Table 10.2 **Main occupations of skilled workers, 1970**

1	Physicians
2	Dentists
3	Lawyers
4	Physicists and astronomers
5	Veterinarians
6	Geologists
7	Chemical engineers
8	Optometrists
9	Petroleum, mining, and geological engineers
10	Other health and therapy occupations
11	Chemists
12	Architects
13	Economists, market researchers, and survey researchers
14	Pharmacists
15	Clergy and religious workers
16	Metallurgical and materials engineers, variously phrased
17	Aerospace engineers
18	Electrical engineers
19	Civil engineers
20	Mechanical engineers

Source: Integrated Public Use Microdata Series (Ruggles et al. 2004).

measuring innovative activity, we think it provides a measure that is at least correlated with the level of innovation in the local economy. Moreover, at the very least, this measure enables us to test the predictions of the model about the correlation between specialization in the high-skill sector and urban success.

In figure 10.5, we show the correlation between this measure of innovative occupations and the metropolitan-area fixed effect in a wage regression based on year-2000 Census Individual Public Use Micro Sample data. The wage regression has controlled for individual human capital measures like years of schooling and age. The correlation between the wage residual and the measure of skilled occupations reminds us that in places with more skilled occupations, the wages of everyone appear to be higher, perhaps because of human capital spillovers (as in Rauch [1993]).

The model predicts that those cities that specialized in innovation were more likely to benefit from the improvements in information technology that have occurred over the last twenty-five years. We test this hypothesis by looking at specialization in skilled occupations in 1980 and city growth since then. Figure 10.6 shows the 26 percent correlation between income growth at the metropolitan-area level and the initial share of employment in the more skilled occupations. A 1 percent increase in skilled occupations in 1980 is associated with an approximately 4 percent increase in income growth since then.

Table 10.3 considers in a multivariate regression the relationship between

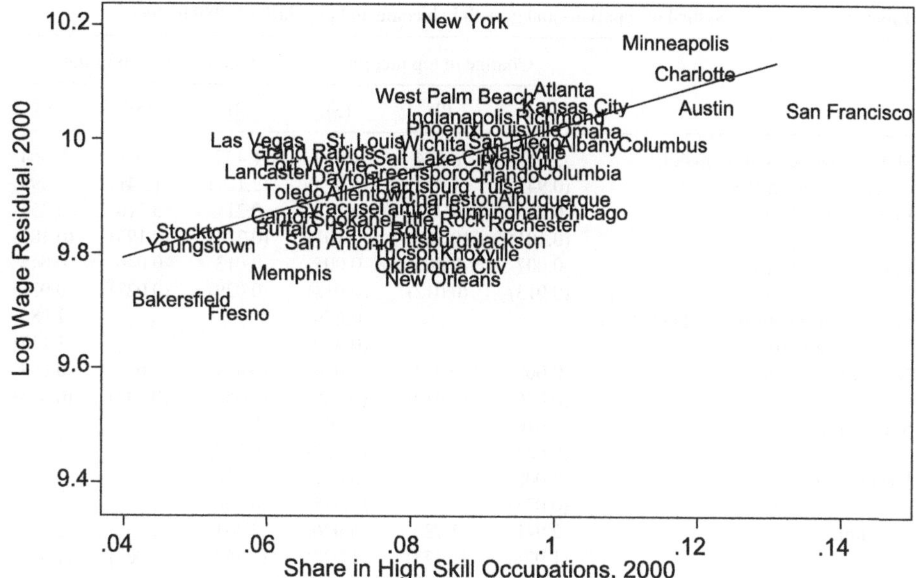

Fig. 10.5 Employment in skilled occupations and knowledge spillovers, 2000
Source: U.S. Census Bureau and Integrated Public Use Microdata Series (Ruggles et al. 2004).

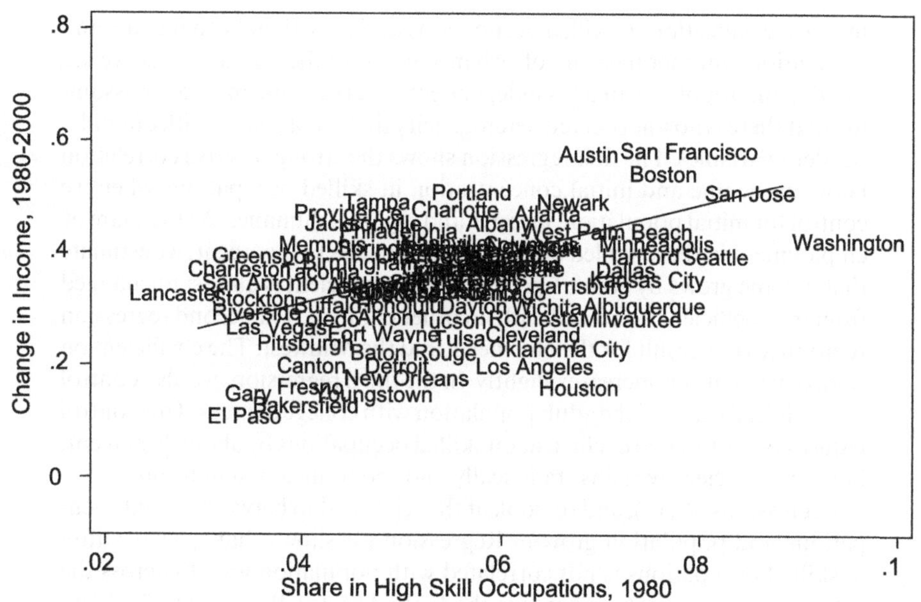

Fig. 10.6 Skilled occupations and income growth, 1980 to 2000
Source: U.S. Census Bureau and Integrated Public Use Microdata Series (Ruggles et al. 2004).

Table 10.3 Skilled occupations and growth in income and population, 1980 to 2000

	Change in log income			Change in log population		
	(1)	(2)	(3)	(4)	(5)	(6)
Share of workers in high-skill occupations in 1980	5.757	6.684	3.839	1.437	6.071	0.564
	(0.943)	(1.076)	(1.698)	(2.129)	(1.941)	(3.494)
Log income 1980	–0.266	–0.351	–0.278	–0.21	–0.216	–0.254
	(0.101)	(0.108)	(0.101)	(0.228)	(0.195)	(0.189)
Log population 1980	–0.007	–0.003	–0.005	–0.013	–0.046	–0.044
	(0.013)	(0.012)	(0.013)	(0.029)	(0.022)	(0.021)
Share of population with bachelor's degree in 1980			0.676			2.084
			(0.499)			(1.117)
Northeast dummy	0.062	0.054	0.054	–0.029	–0.04	–0.063
	(0.026)	(0.019)	(0.026)	(0.058)	(0.033)	(0.035)
South dummy	0.016		0.006	0.203		
	(0.026)		(0.027)	(0.059)		
West dummy	0.008		–0.011	0.316		
	(0.025)		(0.028)	(0.056)		
Constant	2.941	3.729	3.026	2.431	2.73	3.045
	(1.031)	(1.123)	(1.027)	(2.327)	(2.027)	(1.96)
Observations	85	37	85	37	37	37
R^2	0.4173	0.6999	0.4309	0.4425	0.2631	0.338

Source: U.S. Census Bureau and Integrated Public Use Microdata Series (Ruggles et al. 2004).

initial specialization in skilled occupations and growth in both income and population, another measure of urban success. In these regressions, we are treating metropolitan areas as independent observations, and we are assuming that there is no unobserved heterogeneity that is correlated with our independent variables. The first regression shows the strong positive correlation between income and initial concentration in skilled occupations when we control for initial population, income, and regional dummies. As the share of employment in these skilled occupations increases by 1 percent, we estimate that income grows by about 5 percent. This coefficient is almost unchanged from the coefficient estimated with no other controls. The second regression reproduces this result for the Northeast and the Midwest. The coefficient on skilled occupations increases slightly. In the third regression, we also control for the initial share of the adult population with college degrees. This control reduces our estimated coefficient on skilled occupations by about 40 percent, but the coefficient remains statistically and economically significant.

Regressions (4), (5), and (6) look at the relationship between skilled occupations and population growth. Regression (4) shows that specialization in skilled occupations is not correlated with population growth across the entire set of metropolitan areas in the United States. Regression (5) shows that the correlation is significantly positive in the set of older metropolitan areas in the Northeast and Midwest. Regression (6) shows that in this case, controlling for initial skills does make the skill occupation coefficient insignificant. As such, specialization in innovation does not seem to be important in the growing areas of the Sun Belt, but it does seem to be related to the success of older places (as in Glaeser and Saiz [2004]). One interpretation of the greater importance of innovation in the Rust Belt than in the Sun Belt is that the cities in the Sun Belt do not have the same high costs of production that limit urban manufacturing in the older areas. Later development of these places means that land is more readily available and accessible by highways. An alternative interpretation emphasizes the role of skilled people in opposing new housing in California.

We now turn to the model's predicted correlations about increasing innovation. Figure 10.7 shows that places that began within a higher concentration of workers in skilled industries increased the degree of that concentration between 1980 and 2000. An increase in the initial share of skilled occupations of 10 percent is associated with a growth in the share of skilled occupations of 5.6 percent. Just as skilled places became more skilled over the period (Berry and Glaeser 2005), places that started in more skilled occupations increased their concentration in those occupations. This supports the predictions of the model that decreasing communication costs increase the differences in specialization between cities.

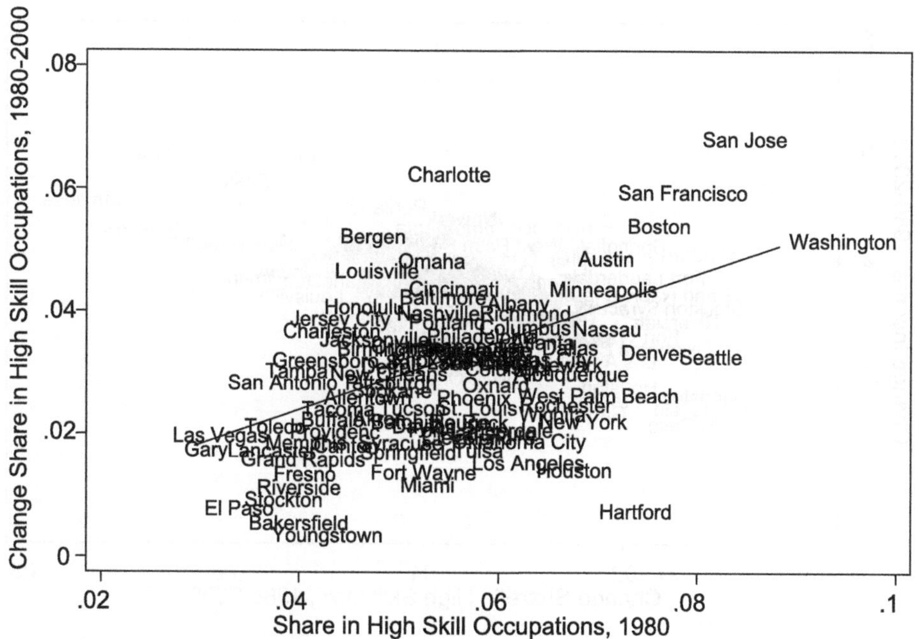

Fig. 10.7 Increasing employment in skilled occupations, 1980 to 2000
Source: U.S. Census Bureau and Integrated Public Use Microdata Series (Ruggles et al. 2004).

The model also predicts that there will be a positive correlation between places that specialized further in idea production and income growth. The extremely strong link between changes in income and changes in the share of workers in skilled occupations is borne out by the data, as shown in figure 10.8. The correlation is 46 percent, and from 1980 to 2000, an increase in the specialization in skilled sectors by 1 percentage point is associated with a 5 percent increase in income. Places that specialized further in skilled occupations became richer.

While patents are only one form of innovation, they do at least represent a hard measure of innovative activity. As such, we can look at whether our measure of high human capital occupations is correlated with patenting and whether we see a correlation between increases in patenting and increases in income at the metropolitan-area level. Our patent data come from the U.S. Patent and Trademark Office. The correlation between our measure of skilled occupations and the logarithm of the number of patents at the metropolitan level is 57 percent. The 18 percent correlation between increases in patenting and increases in income between 1990 and 2000 is also significant, with a regression coefficient of 0.066 and a standard error of 0.015. None of these correlations are overwhelming. Certainly, patented innovations reflect many local idiosyncrasies and do not fully capture the full range of relevant

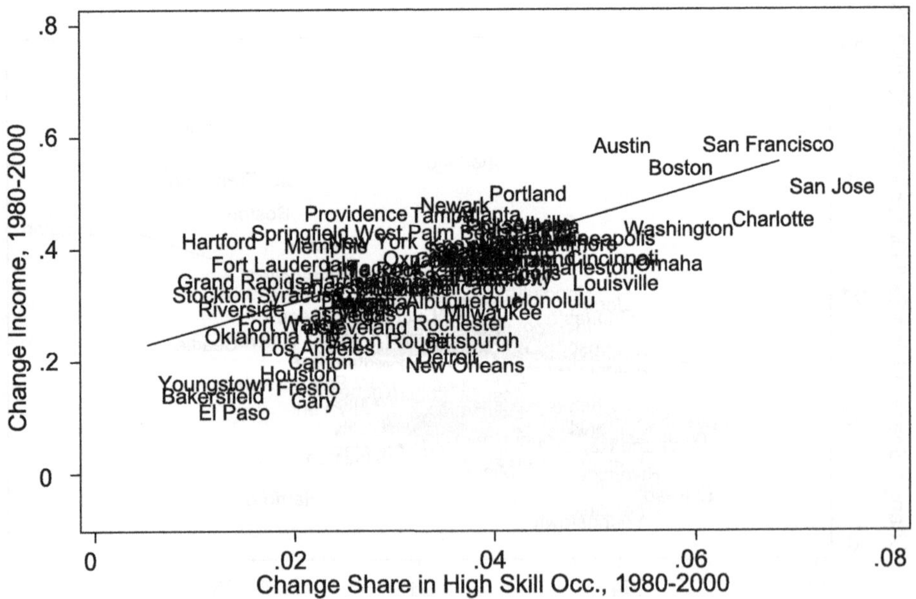

Fig. 10.8 Increasing employment in skilled occupations and income growth, 1980 to 2000

Source: U.S. Census Bureau and Integrated Public Use Microdata Series (Ruggles et al. 2004).

breakthroughs. Yet, there is certainly a pattern where skilled occupations and patents move together and both correlate with rising income levels.

10.4.1 Inequality within Cities

A second implication of the model is that declining communication costs will increase the returns to innovative people and that urban inequality will rise. The model can also predict that inequality will rise faster in cities that are specialized in innovation and more successful.

Figure 10.9 shows the 16 percent correlation between the increase in the variance of log incomes within metropolitan areas and the initial specialization of the metropolitan area in skilled occupations. Places that had more skilled occupations became more unequal. The correlation is weaker, but still significant, if we measure inequality by the difference between the log wage at the ninetieth percentile of the income distribution and the log wage at the tenth percentile of the income distribution.

Table 10.4 examines whether these regressions hold up in a multivariate setting. Regression (1) shows that there is a positive correlation between initial specialization in skilled occupations and increases in the variance of log income, even controlling for initial income, income variance, population, and region dummies. Regression (2) shows that this relationship becomes statistically insignificant once we control for the share of the population with

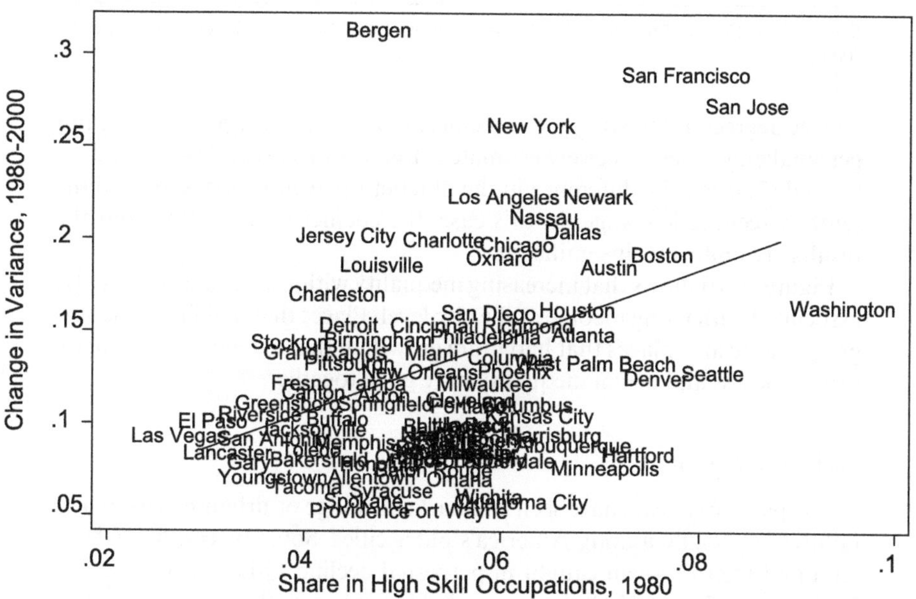

Fig. 10.9 Skilled occupations and increasing income inequality, 1980 to 2000
Source: U.S. Census Bureau and Integrated Public Use Microdata Series (Ruggles et al. 2004).

Table 10.4 **Skilled occupations and increasing income inequality, 1980 to 2000**

	Change in variance of log income		Change in 90/10 income ratio	
	(1)	(2)	(3)	(4)
Share of workers in high-skill occupations in 1980	1.158	1.224	1.088	1.351
	(0.516)	(0.941)	(0.947)	(1.729)
Variance of log income 1980 or 90/10 income ratio 1980	–0.139	–0.14	–0.455	–0.458
	(0.206)	(0.207)	(0.157)	(0.159)
Log income 1980	0.05	0.051	0.077	0.079
	(0.055)	(0.056)	(0.101)	(0.103)
Log population 1980	0.03	0.03	0.054	0.053
	(0.008)	(0.008)	(0.013)	(0.014)
Share of population with bachelor's degree in 1980		–0.023		–0.093
		(0.276)		(0.509)
Northeast dummy	0.015	0.015	0.01	0.011
	(0.014)	(0.014)	(0.025)	(0.026)
South dummy	0.033	0.033	0.069	0.07
	(0.016)	(0.017)	(0.030)	(0.032)
West dummy	0.039	0.038	0.098	0.01
	(0.015)	(0.017)	(0.028)	(0.032)
Constant	–0.859	–0.862	–0.842	–0.852
	(0.564)	(0.569)	(1.04)	(1.05)
Observations	85	85	85	85
R^2	0.412	0.412	0.346	0.347

Source: U.S. Census Bureau and Integrated Public Use Microdata Series (Ruggles et al. 2004).

college degrees. Interestingly, the coefficient on skilled occupations does not get smaller, just less precisely estimated. Regressions (3) and (4) reproduce (1) and (2) using the difference in the ninetieth-percentile log wage and the tenth-percentile log wage. In this case, the coefficient is positive, but the results are uniformly insignificant.

Figure 10.10 shows that increasing inequality within cities is also (weakly) associated with rising income at the city level. Places that had faster income growth were also places that had more growth in the variance of log wages: urban success and urban inequality have gone together.

10.5 Conclusion

The past forty years have seen a remarkable range of urban successes and failures, especially among America's older cities. Some places, like Cleveland and Detroit, seem caught in perpetual decline. Other areas, like San Francisco and New York, had remarkable success as they became centers of idea-based industries.

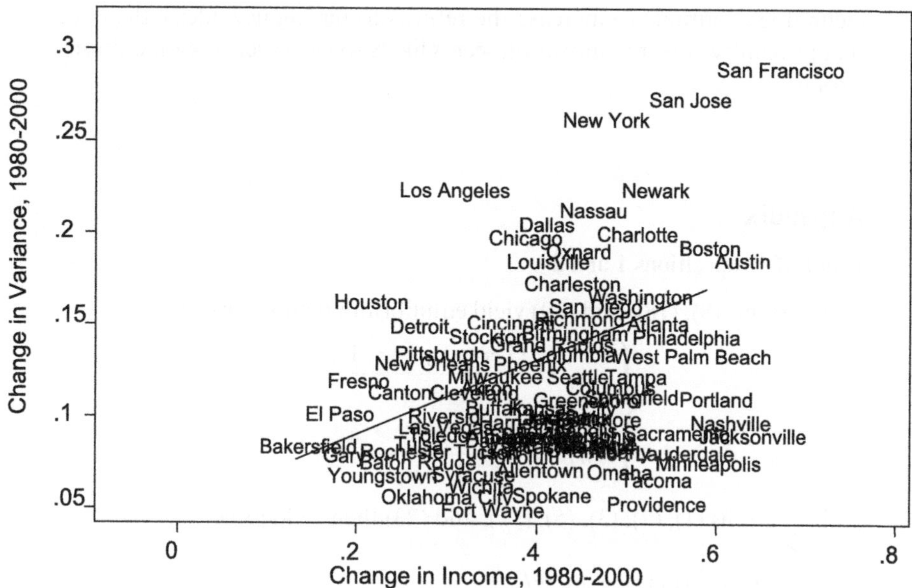

Fig. 10.10 Income growth and increasing income inequality, 1980 to 2000
Source: U.S. Census Bureau and Integrated Public Use Microdata Series (Ruggles et al. 2004).

In this chapter, we suggested that these urban successes and urban failures might reflect the same underlying technological change: a vast improvement in communication technology. As communication technology improved, it enabled manufacturing firms to leave cities, causing the urban distress of Detroit or Manhattan in 1975. However, declining communication costs also increased the returns to new innovations, and since cities specialize in idea production, this helped invigorate some cities.

The model suggests that future improvements in information technology will continue to strengthen cities that are centers of innovation but continue to hurt cities that remain oriented toward manufacturing. Certainly, there is every reason to think that the free flow of people and capital across space will only continue to increase the returns to new ideas. The important question for the future of cities is whether urban areas will continue to have a comparative advantage in producing ideas.

The great challenge to urban areas therefore comes from the possibility that innovation will also leave dense agglomerations. While this is possible, there is a remarkable continuing tendency of innovative people to locate near other innovative people. Silicon Valley, for example, is built at lower densities than New York, because it is built for drivers, not pedestrians, but it is certainly a dense agglomeration. As long as improvements in information technology continue to increase the returns to having new ideas, the edge that proximity gives to innovation seems likely to keep such agglomerations strong.

Appendix

Proof of Propositions 1 and 2

Equations (8), (18), and (19) yield equilibrium factor rewards

$$\begin{cases} w_K = \dfrac{(1+\tau_x)\eta^{-\delta\mu} - 1}{1+\kappa_x} \\ w_U = \dfrac{(1+\tau_x)\eta^{-\delta\mu} + \kappa_x}{1+\kappa_x}, \end{cases}$$

and equations (1), (2), (3), (5), (14), and (23) then yield prices

$$\begin{cases} p_x = \dfrac{1}{\alpha}\psi_x(1+\tau_x)\eta^{-\delta\mu}L_n^{-\delta\mu} \\ p_Y = \dfrac{1}{\alpha}\psi_x(1+\tau_x)\eta^{-\delta\mu}\psi_n^{(1-\alpha)[(1+\delta)\theta-1]/(\alpha\theta)}L_n^{-\{(1-\alpha)[(1+\delta)\theta-1]+\alpha\delta\theta\mu\}/(\alpha\theta)} \end{cases}$$

and quantities

$$\begin{cases} n = \psi_n^{-[(1+\delta)\theta-1]/\theta}L_n^{[(1+\delta)\theta-1]/\theta} \\ X = \dfrac{1}{\psi_x}\left(L_U + \dfrac{\eta^{\delta\mu}}{1+\tau_x}L_R\right)L_n^{\delta\mu} \\ Y = \dfrac{1}{\psi x}\psi_n^{-(1-\alpha)[(1+\delta)\theta-1]/(\alpha\theta)}\left(L_U + \dfrac{\eta^{\delta\mu}}{1+\tau_x}L_R\right)L_n^{\{(1-\alpha)[(1+\delta)\theta-1]+\alpha\delta\theta\mu\}/(\alpha\theta)} \\ Z = \dfrac{1-\beta(p_Y)}{\alpha\beta(p_Y)}[(1+\tau_x)\eta^{-\delta\mu}L_U + L_R]. \end{cases}$$

The factor market-clearing conditions in equations (24) and (25) yield

$$\begin{cases} L_U = \dfrac{K}{1+\kappa_x} - \dfrac{1+\kappa_n}{1+\kappa_x}L_n \\ L_R = \dfrac{\alpha\beta(p_Y)}{1-(1-\alpha)\beta(p_Y)}L \\ \qquad - \left[\alpha\beta(p_Y) + \dfrac{1-\beta(p_Y)}{1-(1-\alpha)\beta(p_Y)}(1+\tau_x)\eta^{-\delta\mu}\right]\dfrac{K}{1+\kappa_x} \\ \qquad - \left[(\kappa_x-\kappa_n)\alpha\beta(p_Y) - \dfrac{1-\beta(p_Y)}{1-(1-\alpha)\beta(p_Y)}(1+\kappa_n)(1+\tau_x)\eta^{-\delta\mu}\right]\dfrac{L_n}{1+\kappa_x}. \end{cases}$$

Finally, considering also equations (4) and (15), the free-entry condition in equation (20) becomes the equilibrium condition

$$L_n = \frac{(\theta - 1)(1 - \alpha)\beta(p_Y)}{\theta - (1 - \alpha)\beta(p_Y)} \frac{(1 + \kappa_x)L + [(1 + \tau_x)\eta^{-\delta\mu} - 1]K}{\kappa_x - \kappa_n + (1 + \kappa_n)(1 + \tau_x)\eta^{-\delta\mu}},$$

which defines a unique and stable equilibrium, provided that

$$\frac{\alpha[\theta - (1 - \alpha)\beta(p_Y)]}{(1 - \alpha)[(1 + \delta)\theta - 1] + \alpha\delta\theta\mu} > -\frac{p_Y\beta'(p_Y)}{\beta(p_Y)}.$$

In an interior equilibrium (i.e., for $L_U \geq 0$ and $L_R \geq 0$), as Δ declines:

1. Factor rewards in the city decline, since

$$w_K = \frac{\Delta}{1 + \kappa_x} \Rightarrow \frac{\partial \log w_K}{\partial \log \Delta} = 1,$$

and

$$w_U = 1 + w_K \Rightarrow \frac{\partial w_K}{\partial w_U} = 1.$$

2. Employment in innovation increases, because for $\beta'(p_Y) \leq 0$, the equilibrium system

$$\begin{cases} L_n = \dfrac{(\theta - 1)(1 - \alpha)\beta(p_Y)}{\theta - (1 - \alpha)\beta(p_Y)} \dfrac{(1 + \kappa_x)L + \Delta K}{1 + \kappa_x + (1 + \kappa_n)\Delta} \\ p_Y = \dfrac{1}{\alpha}\psi_x(1 + \Delta)\psi_n^{(1-\alpha)[(1+\delta)\theta - 1]/(\alpha\theta)} L_n^{-\{(1-\alpha)[(1+\delta)\theta - 1] + \alpha\delta\theta\mu\}/(\alpha\theta)} \end{cases}$$

implies

$$\begin{cases} \dfrac{dL_n}{L_n} = -\dfrac{(1 + \kappa_x)[(1 + \kappa_n)L - K]}{[1 + \kappa_x + (1 + \kappa_n)\Delta][(1 + \kappa_x)L + \Delta K]} d\Delta + \theta \dfrac{p_Y\beta'(p_Y)}{\beta(p_Y)} \dfrac{dp_Y}{p_Y} \\ \dfrac{dp_Y}{p_Y} = \dfrac{1}{1 + \Delta} d\Delta - \dfrac{(1 - \alpha)[(1 + \delta)\theta - 1] + \alpha\delta\theta\mu}{\alpha\theta} \dfrac{dL_n}{L_n} \end{cases}$$

and therefore

$$\frac{\partial L_n}{\partial \Delta} = \frac{\dfrac{(1+\kappa_x)[(1+\kappa_n)L - K]}{[1+\kappa_x + (1+\kappa_n)\Delta][(1+\kappa_x)L + \Delta K]} + \dfrac{\theta}{1+\Delta}\left|\dfrac{p_Y\beta'(p_Y)}{\beta(p_Y)}\right|}{1 - \left|\dfrac{p_Y\beta'(p_Y)}{\beta(p_Y)}\right| \dfrac{(1-\alpha)[(1+\delta)\theta - 1] + \alpha\delta\theta\mu}{\alpha}} L_n < 0$$

by the stability condition in equation (28). As the technology of production does not change, this implies that the amount of innovation increases.

3. The prices of advanced goods and the relative price index decline, since

$$p_x = \frac{1}{\alpha}\psi_x(1+\Delta)L_n^{-\delta\mu} \Rightarrow \frac{\partial p_x}{\partial \Delta} = p_x\left(\frac{1}{1+\Delta} - \frac{\delta\mu}{L_n}\frac{\partial L_n}{\partial \Delta}\right) > 0,$$

and

$$\frac{\partial p_Y}{\partial \Delta} = p_Y\left\{\frac{1}{1+\Delta} - \frac{(1-\alpha)[(1+\delta)\theta - 1] + \alpha\delta\theta\mu}{\alpha\theta L_n}\frac{\partial L_n}{\partial \Delta}\right\} > 0.$$

It follows that the real income of all agents increases.

4. Employment in urban manufacturing contracts, since

$$L_U = \frac{K}{1+\kappa_x} - \frac{1+\kappa_n}{1+\kappa_x}L_n \Rightarrow \frac{\partial L_U}{\partial \Delta} = -\frac{1+\kappa_n}{1+\kappa_x}\frac{\partial L_n}{\partial \Delta} > 0.$$

As the technology of production does not change, this implies that the output of urban manufacturing declines.

5. Urban population increases, since

$$\frac{\partial L_n}{\partial \Delta} + \frac{\partial L_U}{\partial \Delta} = \frac{\kappa_x - \kappa_n}{1+\kappa_x}\frac{\partial L_n}{\partial \Delta} < 0.$$

6. Total output of advanced goods expands, because

$$X = \frac{\alpha\theta}{(1-\alpha)(\theta-1)\psi_x}\frac{1 + [(1+\kappa_n)/(1+\kappa_x)]\Delta}{1+\Delta}L_n^{1+\delta\mu}$$

$$\Rightarrow \frac{\partial X}{\partial \Delta} = -X\left\{\frac{\kappa_x - \kappa_n}{(1+\Delta)[1+\kappa_x + (1+\kappa_n)\Delta]} - \frac{1+\delta\mu}{L_n}\frac{\partial L_n}{\partial \Delta}\right\} < 0.$$

A fortiori, output of advanced manufacturing outside of the city expands, and output of the Dixit-Stiglitz aggregate expands, because

$$Y = X\left(\frac{L_n}{\psi_n}\right)^{(1-\alpha)[(1+\delta)\theta-1]/(\alpha\theta)}$$

$$\Rightarrow \frac{\partial \log Y}{\partial \Delta} = \frac{\partial \log X}{\partial \Delta} + \frac{(1-\alpha)[(1+\delta)\theta - 1]}{\alpha\theta}\frac{\partial \log L_n}{\partial \Delta} < 0.$$

7. Output of the traditional good contracts, because

$$Z = \frac{\theta[1-\beta(p_Y)]}{\theta - (1-\alpha)\beta(p_Y)}\left(L + \frac{\Delta K}{1+\kappa_x}\right)$$

$$\Rightarrow \frac{\partial Z}{\partial \Delta} = Z\left\{\frac{K}{(1+\kappa_x)L + \Delta K} + \frac{(\theta+\alpha-1)|\beta'(p_Y)|}{[\theta-(1-\alpha)\beta(p_Y)][1-\beta(p_Y)]}\frac{\partial p_Y}{\partial \Delta}\right\} > 0.$$

Proof of Proposition 3

The income of an urban innovator with productivity a is

$$y(a) = a\pi S_U - w_K\kappa_n.$$

Thus, for $\kappa_n = 0$, the income distribution of innovators follows a Pareto distribution, with shape θ and minimum $1 + w_K$ dictated by the indifference condition of the marginal innovator. Recalling equation (9), the value of percentile p in a Pareto distribution with minimum $1 + w_K$ is $(1 + w_K)(1 - p)^{-1/\theta}$.

If fraction λ of the city population is employed in manufacturing and $1 - \lambda$ in innovation, the value of percentile $\underline{P} \leq \lambda$ of the urban income distribution is the homogeneous income of manufacturing workers $1 + w_K$, while percentile $\overline{P} > \lambda$ corresponds to percentile $p = (\overline{P} - \lambda)/(1 - \lambda)$ of the income distribution of innovators. Thus, their ratio is

$$R = \left(\frac{1-\lambda}{1-\overline{P}}\right)^{1/\theta} \Rightarrow \frac{\partial R}{\partial \Delta} = -\frac{1}{\theta}\frac{1}{1-\lambda}R\frac{\partial \lambda}{\partial \Delta} < 0.$$

Proof of Proposition 4

When the city is completely specialized and all innovation occurs in the city, equation (29) denotes total employment in innovation, while $L_U = 0$. Then, prices are

$$\begin{cases} p_x = \dfrac{1}{\alpha}\psi_x(1+\Delta)\overline{L}_n^{-\delta\mu} \\ p_Y = \dfrac{1}{\alpha}\psi_x(1+\Delta)\psi_n^{(1-\alpha)[(1+\delta)\theta-1]/(\alpha\theta)}\overline{L}_n^{-\{(1-\alpha)[(1+\delta)\theta-1]+\alpha\delta\theta\mu\}/(\alpha\theta)}, \end{cases}$$

and quantities are

$$\begin{cases} n = \psi_n^{-[(1+\delta)\theta-1]/\theta}\overline{L}_n^{[(1+\delta)\theta-1]/\theta} \\ X = \dfrac{1}{(1+\Delta)\psi_x}L_R\overline{L}_n^{\delta\mu} \\ Y = \dfrac{1}{(1+\Delta)\psi_x}\psi_n^{-(1-\alpha)[(1+\delta)\theta-1]/(\alpha\theta)}L_R\overline{L}_n^{-\{(1-\alpha)[(1+\delta)\theta-1]+\alpha\delta\theta\mu\}/(\alpha\theta)} \\ Z = \dfrac{1-\beta(p_Y)}{\alpha\beta(p_Y)}L_R, \end{cases}$$

and by the labor market-clearing condition in equation (24),

$$\begin{cases} n = \psi_n^{-[(1+\delta)\theta-1]/\theta}\overline{L}_n^{[(1+\delta)\theta-1]/\theta} \\ X = \dfrac{\alpha\beta(p_Y)}{1-(1-\alpha)\beta(p_Y)}\dfrac{1}{(1+\Delta)\psi_x}(L-\overline{L}_n)\overline{L}_n^{\delta\mu} \\ Y = \dfrac{\alpha\beta(p_Y)}{1-(1-\alpha)\beta(p_Y)}\dfrac{1}{(1+\Delta)\psi_x}\psi_n^{-(1-\alpha)[(1+\delta)\theta-1]/(\alpha\theta)} \\ \quad \times (L-\overline{L}_n)\overline{L}_n^{\{(1-\alpha)[(1+\delta)\theta-1]+\alpha\delta\theta\mu\}/(\alpha\theta)} \\ Z = \dfrac{1-\beta(p_Y)}{1-(1-\alpha)\beta(p_Y)}(L-\overline{L}_n). \end{cases}$$

Finally, the free-entry condition in equation (20) yields the equilibrium price of urban capital

$$w_K = \frac{(\theta - 1)(1 - \alpha)\beta(p_Y)}{\theta[1 - (1 - \alpha)\beta(p_Y)]} \frac{1}{1 + \kappa_n} \left[\frac{L}{\overline{L}_n} - \frac{\theta - (1 - \alpha)\beta(p_Y)}{(\theta - 1)(1 - \alpha)\beta(p_Y)} \right],$$

which is positive by the condition in equation (30).

Innovation does not expand out of the city, as long as

$$(1 + \tau_n)\eta^{-\delta} \geq 1 + (1 + \kappa_n)w_K = \frac{(\theta - 1)(1 - \alpha)\beta(p_Y)}{\theta[1 - (1 - \alpha)\beta(p_Y)]} \left(\frac{L}{\overline{L}_n} - 1 \right).$$

Then, as Δ declines below $\underline{\Delta}$, it is straightforward that:

1. The amount of innovation is fixed at $\overline{n}$ by the urban capacity constraint; employment in the innovative sector and city population are likewise constrained.
2. The relative price of differentiated goods p_x declines. The price index for the advanced sector p_Y declines, and therefore the real income of all agents increases.
3. Output of the differentiated goods X and of their aggregate Y increases.

If and only if $\beta'(p_Y) < 0$, as Δ declines below $\underline{\Delta}$:

1. The relative price of urban capital increases, since

$$\frac{\partial w_K}{\partial \Delta} = 0 \text{ and } \frac{\partial w_K}{\partial p_Y} = \frac{[1 + (1 + \kappa_n)w_K]}{(1 + \kappa_n)[1 - (1 - \alpha)\beta]} \frac{\beta'(p_Y)}{\beta(p_Y)}.$$

2. The traditional sector contracts, because

$$\frac{\partial Z}{\partial \Delta} = 0 \text{ and } \frac{\partial Z}{\partial p_Y} = -\frac{\alpha(L - \overline{L}_n)}{[1 - (1 - \alpha)\beta(p_Y)]^2} \beta'(p_Y).$$

Thus, employment in the traditional sector contracts, and conversely, employment in the advanced sector expands.

Proof of Proposition 5

Equilibrium factor rewards are

$$\begin{cases} w_K^1 = \dfrac{(1 + \tau_x)\eta^{-\delta\mu} - 1}{1 + \kappa_x} \\ w_U^1 = \dfrac{(1 + \tau_x)\eta^{-\delta\mu} + \kappa_x}{1 + \kappa_x} \\ w_K^2 = \dfrac{\tau_x}{1 + \kappa_x} \\ w_U^2 = 1 + \dfrac{\tau_x}{1 + \kappa_x}, \end{cases}$$

prices are

$$\begin{cases} p_x = \dfrac{1}{\alpha}\psi_x(1+\tau_x)\eta^{-\delta\mu}L_n^{-\delta\mu} \\ p_Y = \dfrac{1}{\alpha}\psi_x(1+\tau_x)\eta^{-\delta\mu}\psi_n^{(1-\alpha)[(1+\delta)\theta-1]/(\alpha\theta)}L_n^{-\{(1-\alpha)[(1+\delta)\theta-1]+\alpha\delta\theta\mu\}/(\alpha\theta)}, \end{cases}$$

and letting L_1 and L_2 denote employment in manufacturing in the two cities, quantities are

$$\begin{cases} n = \psi_n^{[(1+\delta)\theta-1]/\theta}L_n^{[(1+\delta)\theta-1]/\theta} \\ X = \dfrac{1}{\psi_x}\left(L_1 + \eta^{\delta\mu}L_2 + \dfrac{\eta^{\delta\mu}}{1+\tau_x}L_R\right)L_n^{\delta\mu} \\ Y = \dfrac{1}{\psi_x}\psi_n^{-(1-\alpha)[(1+\delta)\theta-1]/(\alpha\theta)}\left(L_U + \eta^{\delta\mu}L_2 + \dfrac{\eta^{\delta\mu}}{1+\tau_x}L_R\right)L_n^{\{(1-\alpha)[(1+\delta)\theta-1]+\alpha\delta\theta\mu\}/(\alpha\theta)} \\ Z = \dfrac{1-\beta(p_Y)}{\alpha\beta(p_Y)}(1+\tau_x)\eta^{-\delta\mu}\left(L_1 + \eta^{\delta\mu}L_2 + \dfrac{\eta^{\delta\mu}}{1+\tau_x}L_R\right). \end{cases}$$

Factor market-clearing implies

$$\begin{cases} L_1 = \dfrac{K}{1+\kappa_x} - \dfrac{1+\kappa_n}{1+\kappa_x}L_n \\ L_2 = \dfrac{K}{1+\kappa_x} \\ L = L_n + L_1 + L_2 + L_R + Z, \end{cases}$$

so the free-entry condition becomes the equilibrium condition

$$L_n = \frac{(\theta-1)(1-\alpha)\beta(p_Y)}{\theta-(1-\alpha)\beta(p_Y)}\,\frac{(1+\kappa_x)L + [(1+\tau_x)\eta^{-\delta\mu}+\tau_x-1]K}{\kappa_x-\kappa_n+(1+\kappa_n)(1+\tau_x)\eta^{-\delta\mu}}.$$

The comparative statics are analogous to those in propositions 1 and 2, even if τ_x and $\eta^{-\delta\mu}$ now appear independently and not only combined in the single parameter Δ. The equilibrium system

$$\begin{cases} L_n = \dfrac{(\theta-1)(1-\alpha)\beta(p_Y)}{\theta-(1-\alpha)\beta(p_Y)}\,\dfrac{(1+\kappa_x)L + [(1+\tau_x)\eta^{-\delta\mu}+\tau_x-1]K}{\kappa_x-\kappa_n+(1+\kappa_n)(1+\tau_x)\eta^{-\delta\mu}} \\ p_Y = \dfrac{1}{\alpha}\psi_x(1+\tau_x)\eta^{-\delta\mu}\psi_n^{(1-\alpha)[(1+\delta)\theta-1]/(\alpha\theta)}L_n^{-\{(1-\alpha)[(1+\delta)\theta-1]+\alpha\delta\theta\mu\}/(\alpha\theta)} \end{cases}$$

implies

$$\begin{cases} \dfrac{dL_n}{L_n} = -\dfrac{\{(1+\kappa_n)(1+\kappa_x)\eta^{-\delta\mu}L - [\kappa_x - \kappa_n + (2+\kappa_n+\kappa_x)\eta^{-\delta\mu}]K\}}{[\kappa_x - \kappa_n + (1+\kappa_n)(1+\tau_x)\eta^{-\delta\mu}]\{(1+\kappa_x)L + [(1+\tau_x)\eta^{-\delta\mu} + \tau_x - 1]K\}} d\tau_x \\ \quad - \dfrac{(1+\tau_x)\{(1+\kappa_x)(1+\kappa_n)L - [1+\kappa_x - (1+\kappa_n)\tau_x]K\}}{[\kappa_x - \kappa_n + (1+\kappa_n)(1+\tau_x)\eta^{-\delta\mu}]\{(1+\kappa_x)L + [(1+\tau_x)\eta^{-\delta\mu} + \tau_x - 1]K\}} d(\eta^{-\delta\mu}) \\ \quad + \theta \dfrac{p_Y \beta'(p_Y)}{\beta(p_Y)} \dfrac{dp_Y}{p_Y} \\ \dfrac{dp_Y}{p_Y} = \dfrac{1}{1+\tau_x} d\tau_x + \dfrac{1}{\eta^{-\delta\mu}} d(\eta^{-\delta\mu}) - \dfrac{(1-\alpha)[(1+\delta)\theta - 1] + \alpha\delta\theta\mu}{\alpha\theta} \dfrac{dL_n}{L_n}, \end{cases}$$

and therefore, for all $\beta'(p_Y) \leq 0$,

$$\frac{dL_n}{d\tau_x} = -\frac{\dfrac{(1+\kappa_n)(1+\kappa_x)\eta^{-\delta\mu}L - [\kappa_x - \kappa_n + (2+\kappa_n+\kappa_x)\eta^{-\delta\mu}]K}{[\kappa_x - \kappa_n + (1+\kappa_n)(1+\tau_x)\eta^{-\delta\mu}]\{(1+\kappa_x)L + [(1+\tau_x)\eta^{-\delta\mu} + \tau_x - 1]K\}} + \dfrac{\theta}{1+\tau_x}\left|\dfrac{p_Y\beta'(p_Y)}{\beta(p_Y)}\right|}{1 - \left|\dfrac{p_Y\beta'(p_Y)}{\beta(p_Y)}\right| \dfrac{(1-\alpha)[(1+\delta)\theta - 1] + \alpha\delta\theta\mu}{\alpha}} L_n < 0,$$

and

$$\frac{dL_n}{d(\eta^{-\delta\mu})} = -\frac{\dfrac{(1+\tau_x)\{(1+\kappa_x)(1+\kappa_n)L - [1+\kappa_x - (1+\kappa_n)\tau_x]K\}}{[\kappa_x - \kappa_n + (1+\kappa_n)(1+\tau_x)\eta^{-\delta\mu}]\{(1+\kappa_x)L + [(1+\tau_x)\eta^{-\delta\mu} + \tau_x - 1]K\}} + \dfrac{\theta}{\eta^{-\delta\mu}}\left|\dfrac{p_Y\beta'(p_Y)}{\beta(p_Y)}\right|}{1 - \left|\dfrac{p_Y\beta'(p_Y)}{\beta(p_Y)}\right| \dfrac{(1-\alpha)[(1+\delta)\theta - 1] + \alpha\delta\theta\mu}{\alpha}} L_n < 0,$$

recalling the scarcity assumption $(1 + \kappa_n) L > 2K$ and the stability condition in equation (28).

As Δ falls, because of a decline in any combination of τ_x and $\eta^{-\delta\mu}$, L_n increases: this implies that in the first city, the innovative sector grows, the manufacturing sector contracts, and population grows—none of which happens in the second city. Relative real income grows with L_n, because all inframarginal innovators are earning a positive profit from their creativity.

Moreover, the relative value of urban capital in the innovative city increases when urban infrastructure becomes less valuable, because

$$\frac{w_K^1}{w_K^2} = \frac{(1+\tau_x)\eta^{-\delta\mu} - 1}{\tau_x} \Rightarrow \frac{\partial(w_K^1/w_K^2)}{\partial\tau_x} = -\frac{\eta^{-\delta\mu} - 1}{\tau_x^2} < 0.$$

References

Berry, C., and E. L. Glaeser. 2005. The divergence of human capital levels across cities. *Papers in Regional Science* 84 (3): 407–44.

Dixit, A., and J. E. Stiglitz. 1977. Monopolistic competition and optimal product diversity. *American Economic Review* 67 (3): 297–308.

Duranton, G., and D. Puga. 2005. From sectoral to functional urban specialization. *Journal of Urban Economics* 57 (2): 343–70.

Ethier, W. J. 1982. National and international returns to scale in the modern theory of international trade. *American Economic Review* 72 (3): 389–405.

Fujita, M., and J.-F. Thisse. 2003. Does geographical agglomeration foster economic growth? And who gains and loses from it? *Japanese Economic Review* 54 (2): 121–45.

Glaeser, E. L., and M. E. Kahn. 2001. Decentralized employment and the transformation of the American city. In *Brookings-Wharton papers on urban affairs,* vol. 2, ed. J. R. Pack and W. G. Gale, 1–63. Washington, DC: Brookings Institution Press.

Glaeser, E. L., and J. E. Kohlhase. 2004. Cities, regions and the decline of transport costs. *Papers in Regional Science* 83 (1): 197–228.

Glaeser, E. L., and A. Saiz. 2004. The rise of the skilled city. In *Brookings-Wharton papers on urban affairs,* vol. 5, ed. W. G. Gale and J. R. Pack, 47–94. Washington, DC: Brookings Institution Press.

Grossman, G. M., and E. Helpman. 1991. *Innovation and growth in the global economy.* Cambridge, MA: MIT Press.

Helpman, E., M. Melitz, and S. Yeaple. 2004. Export versus FDI with heterogeneous firms. *American Economic Review* 94 (1): 300–16.

Henderson, J. V., and Y. Ono. 2008. Where do manufacturing firms locate their headquarters? *Journal of Urban Economics* 63 (2): 431–50.

International Monetary Fund (IMF). 1997. *World economic outlook.* Washington, DC: IMF.

Kim, S. 1999. The rise of multiunit firms in U.S. manufacturing. *Explorations in Economic History* 36 (4): 360–86.

Markusen, J. R. 1995. The boundaries of multinational enterprises and the theory of international trade. *Journal of Economic Perspectives* 9 (2): 169–89.

Marshall, A. 1890. *Principles of economics.* London: Macmillan.

Rauch, J. E. 1993. Productivity gains from geographic concentration of human capital: Evidence from the cities. *Journal of Urban Economics* 34 (3): 380–400.

Romer, P. M. 1990. Endogenous technological change. *Journal of Political Economy* 98 (S5): S71–S102.

Ruggles, S., M. Sobek, T. Alexander, C. A. Fitch, R. Goeken, P. K. Hall, M. King, and C. Ronnander. 2004. *Integrated Public Use Microdata Series: Version 3.0.* Minneapolis, MN: Minnesota Population Center.

11

New Evidence on Trends in the Cost of Urban Agglomeration

Matthew E. Kahn

11.1 Introduction

The benefits of urban agglomeration cannot take place if city living exposes the population to deadly levels of ambient air pollution and raises the risk of experiencing infectious diseases such as cholera, diarrhea, and dysentery (Melosi 2000). At the turn of the twentieth century, the average white urbanite in the United States paid a ten-year "mortality penalty" for not living in the countryside (Haines 2001). By 1940, big-city investments in water treatment and sanitation significantly reduced the threat of water pollution (Cutler and Miller 2004; Haines 2001).

Over the twentieth century, U.S. big cities have experienced rising and then declining levels of crime and pollution. Ambient air pollution grew sharply over the twentieth century, peaking in the early 1970s and declining over the last thirty years. Urban crime rates have been documented to have risen during the 1970s and 1980s and to have declined sharply since the early 1990s (Levitt 2004; Reyes 2007).

At this point in time, big cities feature more congestion, pollution, and crime than smaller cities (Glaeser 1998; Glaeser and Sacerdote 1999). These nonmarket local public bads can significantly reduce big-city quality of life (Tolley 1974; Blomquist, Berger, and Hoehn 1988; Gyourko and Tracy 1991). In contrast, larger cities offer greater cultural amenities and a better variety of shopping and cuisine options than smaller cities (Waldfogel 2008). Big cities also offer greater possibilities for good matches in the marriage and

Matthew E. Kahn is professor of economics and of public policy at the University of California, Los Angeles, and a research associate of the National Bureau of Economic Research.

This research was supported by the Richard S. Ziman Center for Real Estate at UCLA. I thank Ed Glaeser, Joe Gyourko, Jed Kolko, and two reviewers for useful comments.

labor markets. This suggests that big cities offer a quality-of-life trade-off: they offer a greater variety of market goods than small cities but suffer from worse levels of nonmarket local public goods.

This chapter examines how the population elasticity of producing local public bads such as crime, pollution, and commute times has changed over time and how it varies across U.S. census regions. In a nutshell, I find that the commute time/population elasticity is relatively small but stable over time. I document sharp, negative time trends in ambient pollution and violent crime in big cities.

In addition to exploring time trends in key determinants of quality of life, this chapter also documents significant geographical variation in the relationship between ambient air pollution and population size and between crime and population size at a point in time. Relative to cities in other regions, the metropolitan areas in the Northeast suffer the highest "big-city premium" with respect to pollution and crime. This chapter also documents that employment suburbanization in major cities has sharply reduced suburban commute times.

Big-city quality-of-life progress along the crime and pollution dimensions means that these cities will have an easier time attracting and retaining the skilled to live there (Glaeser, Kolko, and Saiz 2001). This in turn raises their prospects for future growth.

11.2 Urban Quality-of-Life Dynamics

The cross-city quality-of-life literature has used hedonic techniques to compare city quality of life at certain points in time. Leading studies such as Blomquist, Berger, and Hoehn (1988) and Gyourko and Tracy (1991) have estimated cross-city wage and rental hedonic regressions to parse out how much of the cross-city differences in quality standardized wages and rents is due to tied locational amenities such as climate, street safety, and so forth.

While climate is a crucial nonmarket public good, in this chapter, I focus on city attributes that evolve over time. New York City today bears little resemblance to the bankrupt, unsafe New York City of the 1970s. Similar urban rejuvenations can be found in a range of cities, such as Boston, Los Angeles, and San Francisco.

Recent cross-city hedonic wage and real estate research documents overall recent quality-of-life progress in big cities relative to small cities (Glaeser and Gottlieb 2006). They contrast the 1970 and 2000 wage and rent premium data in big and small cities. In 1970, workers with observationally identical demographics were paid higher wages in big cities relative to small cities, but by the year 2000, this cross-city pattern had reversed, such that quality adjusted wages were *lower* in big cities relative to small cities. Between 1970 and 2000, home prices increased more in big cities relative to smaller cities. These findings are consistent with the claim that big-city quality of life has improved.

While metropolitan areas differ along several dimensions, in this chapter, I focus on three major disamenities: namely, commute times, urban air pollution, and crime. Throughout this chapter, I will present new estimates of the cross-sectional relationship between these city attributes and city population size.

Estimates of the relationship between commute times, pollution, crime, and city population size represent important inputs in determining whether the observed dynamics in big city/small overall compensating differentials (as documented by Glaeser and Gottlieb [2006]) can be explained by big-city progress with respect to three classic challenges that these cities face.

To link this chapter's empirical work to the hedonic quality-of-life dynamics literature, suppose that we know the marginal willingness to pay to avoid a small change in commute time, pollution, and crime, and we make the strong assumption that utility is linear in these nonmarket public bads. Define these valuation weights as b_{commute}, $b_{\text{pollution}}$, and b_{crime}, respectively. At a point in time t, the marginal quality-of-life damage caused by living in a bigger city relative to a smaller city equals $b_{\text{commute}} \times \partial \text{ Commute}_t/\partial \text{ Pop}_t + b_{\text{pollution}} \times \partial \text{ Pollution}_t/\partial \text{ Pop}_t + b_{\text{crime}} \times \partial \text{ Crime}_t/\partial \text{ Pop}_t$. While the estimates of these valuation weights remain contentious, this simple equation highlights this chapter's key empirical goals. I will provide new estimates of these marginal effects at several points in time, and I will estimate how these marginal effects vary across regions.

11.3 The Commute Time versus City-Size Relationship Over Time

To document the commute time/city-size relationship and how it has changed over time, I use the Integrated Public Use Microdata Series (IPUMS) Census microdata from the 1 percent 1980, 1990, and 2000 samples. For person i living in city j at time t, I estimate:

$$(1) \quad \text{Log(Commute Time}_{jit}) = c_t + b_t \times \log(\text{Pop}_{jt}) + b_t \times X_{jit} + U_{jit}.$$

The regression results are reported in table 11.1. In this regression, I control for a vector of household-level demographic variables, including the head's age, sex, and socioeconomic status. My sample includes all workers who report positive commute times and who live in a metropolitan area that I could identify in all three of these Census data sets. I am able to identify one hundred metropolitan statistical areas (MSAs) that are geocoded in each of these census years. This sample includes all of the major metropolitan areas. The five smallest metropolitan areas in this sample include Boise City, Idaho; Sarasota, Florida; Modesto, California; Melbourne, Florida; and Pensacola, Florida. Table 11.1 presents two ordinary least squares (OLS) estimates of this pooled cross-sectional regression, and two key findings emerge. In 1980, the elasticity of commute time with respect to metropolitan-area population size was 0.13. In 1990 and 2000, this elasticity did not change. In the right column of table 11.1, I report the same regres-

Table 11.1 **One-way commute time elasticities by city size**

	All		Private vehicle	
	Beta	Standard error	Beta	Standard error
Log(MSA population)	0.1379	0.0271	0.0906	0.0087
Log(MSA population) × 1990 dummy	–0.0018	0.0059	0.0071	0.0051
Log(MSA population) × 2000 dummy	–0.0052	0.0064	0.0120	0.0048
Age	0.0018	0.0001	0.0018	0.0001
Male	0.1239	0.0092	0.1503	0.0080
Duncan socioeconomic index	0.0014	0.0002	0.0013	0.0001
Constant	0.8081	0.3348	1.2950	0.1363
Observations	1,400,363		1,197,907	
R^2	0.038		0.032	
Year dummies	Yes		Yes	

Note: The dependent variable is the log of the one-way commute time. The data set is the 1 percent IPUMS sample from the 1980, 1990, and 2000 Censuses. The sample includes all workers who live in one of the one hundred metropolitan areas that are identified in the 1980, 1990, and 2000 Census 1 percent samples. The omitted category is a female worker in the year 1980.

sion, but this time it is for the subset of workers who commute by private vehicle. In this case, the city-size elasticity shrinks to 0.09.

Public transit is a relatively slow commuting mode, and it is more likely to be used in major cities.[1] In 1980, the average worker in New York City, Chicago, and Los Angeles had a one-way commute time that was 5.9 minutes longer than the average commute time of the one hundred MSAs (29.9 minutes to 24 minutes). In 2000, this differential had not changed, with an average commute time of 32.3 minutes in these three major cities relative to a national average of 26.4 minutes for the sample of one hundred MSAs. It is important to note that across this sample of one hundred metropolitan areas in the year 2000, the average one-way commute time using public transit was forty-four minutes, while the average one-way commute time by private vehicle was twenty-five minutes. In addition, in New York City, Chicago, and Los Angeles, public transit usage is much higher. In the year 2000, 4.1 percent of workers in the one hundred MSAs commuted by public transit, while 20 percent of workers in New York City, Chicago, and Los Angeles commuted by public transit.

To provide some evidence on how commute speeds are affected by city size, public transit use, and location within the metropolitan area, I use microdata from the 2001 National Household Transportation Survey (NHTS). An attractive feature of this data is that it is possible to obtain residential zip

1. These results are roughly in line with cross-city estimates reported in Glaeser (1998). Using 1990 city-level data for the fifty largest cities, he estimates that a doubling of a city's population size is associated with a 1.9 minute increase in the one-way commute.

code identifiers. I use this information to calculate each metropolitan-area resident's distance to the central business district (CBD). Using information on each respondent's distance to work and commute time allows me to estimate the speed at which they commute to work. Table 11.2 reports three regressions based on equation (2). The dependent variable is the speed at which workers commute as measured in miles per hour. The unit of analysis is person i in metropolitan area j in 2001.

$$(2)\quad \text{Speed}_{ij} = \text{constant} + b \times \log(\text{MSA Population}_j) + b \times (\text{Distance to CBD}_{ij}) + b \times 1(\text{Commute using Public Transit}_{ij}) + U_{ij}.$$

The standard errors are clustered by metro area. In column (1), I only include the metropolitan area's population as the explanatory variable. A doubling of a metro area's population is associated with a reduction in speed of 1.6 miles per hour. In column (2), I control for a worker's residential distance to the CBD. For every extra mile that a household lives from the CBD, its commuting speed increases by 0.45 miles per hour. The third specification reported in table 11.2 demonstrates how slow public transit is. People in big cities are more likely to commute using public transit, and this increases their commute times. All else equal, a worker who commutes using public transit travels 10.5 miles per hour slower than a worker who commutes by car. Note that controlling for whether a worker commutes using public transit shrinks the city-size coefficient from –2.46 to –1.81. Public transit use in big cities is an important explanation for long commute times.

Population suburbanization and reduced use of public transit in big cities have both helped to increase urbanites' commute speeds. Based on census tract-level data, the average person living in a metropolitan area in 1970 lived

Table 11.2 Commuting speeds in cities based on 2001 NHTS microdata

	Speed measured in miles per hour					
	(1)		(2)		(3)	
Column	Beta	Standard error	Beta	Standard error	Beta	Standard error
Log(metropolitan-area population size)	–2.2870	0.4227	–2.4625	0.2774	–1.8149	0.2067
Distance to CBD			0.4472	0.0363	0.3847	0.0306
Commute using public transit					–10.5490	0.7344
Constant	62.5491	6.1644	59.9064	3.8177	51.6993	2.9003
Observations	25,778		25,778		25,778	
R^2	0.023		0.0680		0.1010	

Note: This table reports three OLS regressions. The unit of observation is a commuter. Standard errors are clustered by metropolitan area. In column (3), the omitted category is a worker who commutes by private vehicle.

8.72 miles from the CBD, while the average person living in a metropolitan area in the year 2000 lived 11.44 miles from the CBD. Over this same time period, the share of urbanites who commuted using public transit decreased by 10 percentage points. Based on the estimate reported in column (3) of table 11.2, these two trends would increase commute speeds by $(11.44 - 8.72) \times 0.3847 - 10.55 \times (0.059 - 0.121)$, or 1.7 miles per hour.

11.4 Within Major City Commute Time Differentials

In the past, when metropolitan-area employment was concentrated in the central business district, urban growth would translate into rising commute times, both because the marginal growth took place at the urban fringe and because the commuters would exacerbate congestion bottlenecks as they sought to get downtown. The ongoing decentralization of employment has helped to alleviate some of these congestion effects (Glaeser and Kahn 2001).

To study within-city trends over time in commuting, I use census tract data from 1980 and 2000 (for details on the data, see Baum-Snow and Kahn [2005]). Figure 11.1 presents results from 1980 and 2000. For all people who live within thirty miles of a CBD, I calculate the share of workers who have

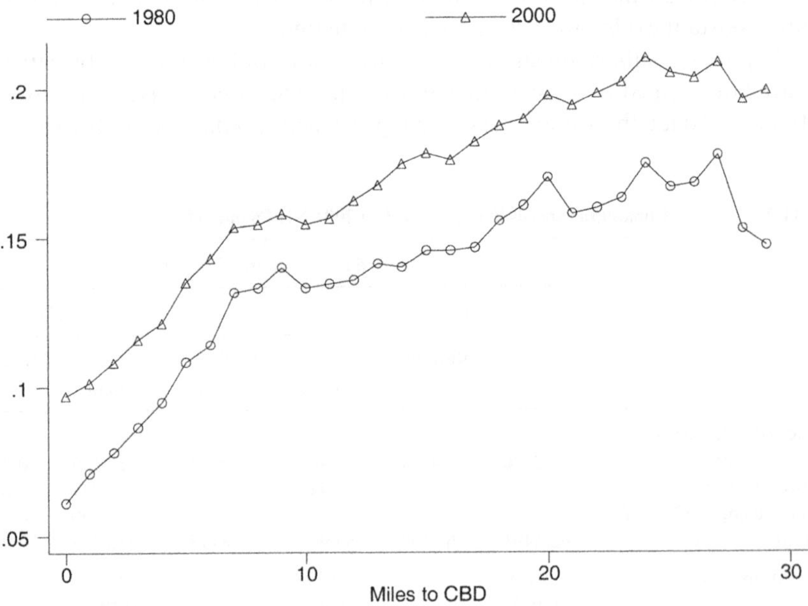

Fig. 11.1 Share of workers whose one-way commute time is over forty-five minutes: All metro areas

a commute over forty-five minutes long by mileage distance to the CBD of the metro area they live in. The figure's lines are roughly parallel. Very few commuters living close to a CBD have a long commute in 1980 or 2000. The share with long commutes increases out to about ten miles from the CBD, and then in both years, the slope flattens. It is important to note that in the year 2000, a larger share of commuters do have long commutes relative to the year 1980. This gap roughly equals 2 percentage points.

Figure 11.2 is identical to figure 11.1, but now I focus only on Chicago, Los Angeles, and New York City. This cut of the data allows me to investigate changes in commuting patterns in the very biggest cities. The first point to note is that the figure does not look like figure 11.1. From zero miles to eight miles from the CBD, the share with a long commute increases, but in the eight-to-twenty-mile range, it declines sharply. In these major cities, these commute times reject the claim that these are monocentric cities.

Figure 11.3 examines the share of workers whose commute is less than twenty-five minutes long in the year 2000 by distance from the CBD. The facts for the major metropolitan areas of Chicago, Los Angeles, and New York City echo those presented in figure 11.2. Starting at zero miles from the CBD, the share of workers with a short commute declines sharply with distance, but at roughly eight miles out, this function reaches its minimum

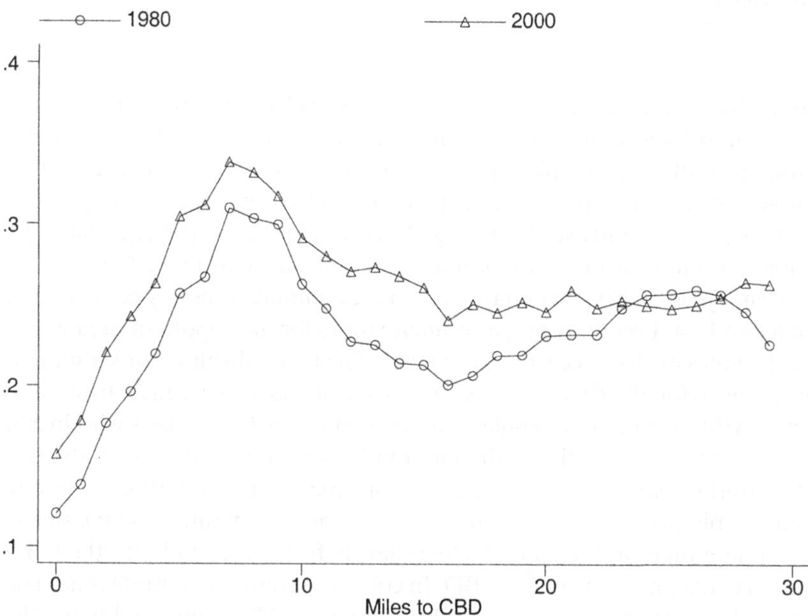

Fig. 11.2 Share of workers whose one-way commute time is over forty-five minutes: Sample includes Chicago, Los Angeles, and New York City

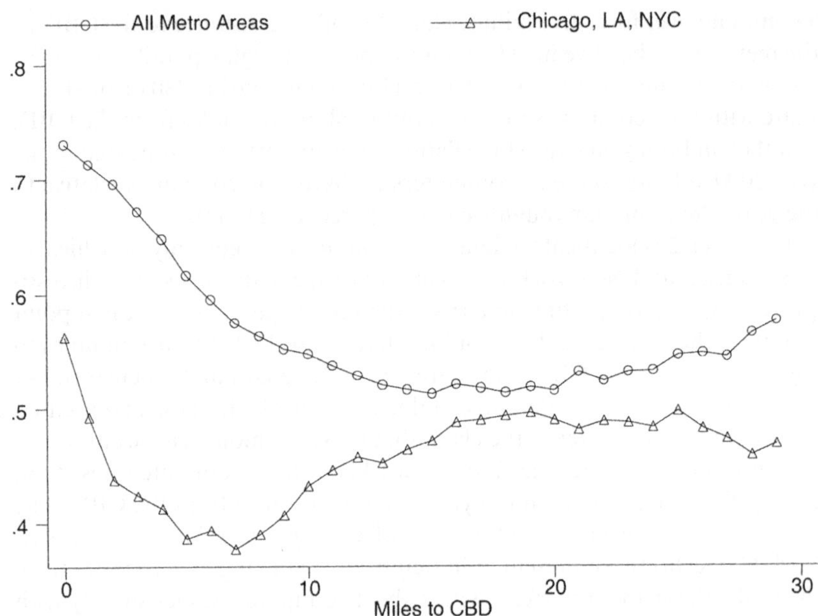

Fig. 11.3 Year-2000 share of commuters with one-way commute less than twenty-five minutes

and turns around, such that workers who live twelve miles from the CBD are much more likely to have a short commute than workers who live eight miles from the CBD. One simple explanation for this pattern is that in these cities, suburban residents work at suburban jobs and are avoiding big-city urban bottlenecks. In contrast, the average MSA worker's probability of having a short commute declines monotonically with distance from the CBD.

Using year-2000 Census data on average commute times by census tract, in figure 11.4, I report average commute times for metropolitan-area workers by miles of distance from their CBD. The figure displays three different lines: one is for all urban workers, one is for workers who live in metropolitan areas with four million people or more, and one is for workers who live in metropolitan areas with less than four million people. The figure highlights that average commute times rise with distance from the CBD. Commute times in big cities take longer on average, but note the nonmonotonic shape. Commute times in big cities decline sharply from seven miles to the CBD out to twenty miles from the CBD. In contrast, average commute times rise in smaller cities over this same mileage interval. This figure highlights the role that employment decentralization in major cities has played in helping suburbanites to enjoy shorter commutes.

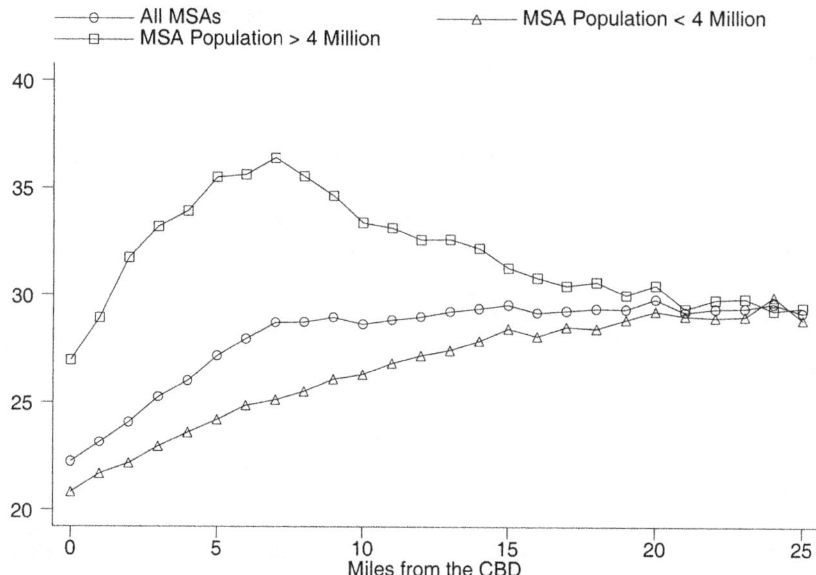

Fig. 11.4 Average commute time in the year 2000 by city size

11.5 Urban Pollution Progress

Today, major cities such as Los Angeles and New York City compete to be "green cities".[2] Such cities seek to enhance their environmental quality to improve public health and to retain the footloose skilled.

A city's pollution level at a point in time is a function of scale, composition, and technique effects. Scale represents a city's population size. While urban economists have emphasized the role of the sheer scale of activity in imposing social costs, environmental economists have countered that composition and technique effects can offset the externality costs of population growth (Kahn and Schwartz 2008). Composition effects focus on the major industries that are clustered in a city at a point in time. Technique effects are defined as the emissions per unit of activity from various forms of capital, such as cars, power plants, and factories. A city could have many steel mills (a brown composition), but if the steel mills released few emissions per dollar of output (a green technique), then the city may not be polluted.

Composition effects have played an important role in "greening" U.S. cities. The rise and decline of urban manufacturing was an important factor driving urban pollution levels in the twentieth century. In the twentieth cen-

2. For example, see New York City's plan, available at: http://www.nyc.gov/html/planyc2030/html/greenyc/greenyc.shtml, and Los Angeles's plan, available at http://www.lacity.org/ead/EADWeb-AQD/GreenLA_CAP_2007.pdf.

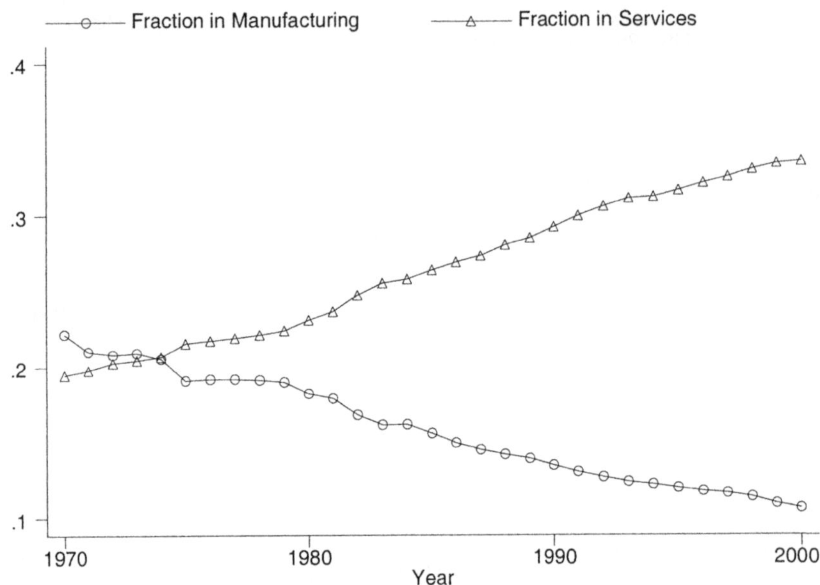

Fig. 11.5 Employment trends in U.S. metropolitan areas

tury, the rise of Pittsburgh as a steel capital had the unintended consequence of sharply increasing particulate levels. An unintended silver lining of the U.S. Rust Belt's decline in the 1960s and 1970s has been to sharply improve environmental quality in heavily industrial cities such as Pittsburgh, Pennsylvania, and Gary, Indiana (Kahn 1999). Between 1969 and 2000, the number of manufacturing jobs in New York county (Manhattan) declined from 451,330 to 146,291. Similar declines in manufacturing have taken place in London, England. There are large public health gains from removing older, polluting manufacturing plants from heavily populated areas. As shown in figure 11.5, metropolitan areas in the United States have experienced a composition shift as the share of workers in urban manufacturing has declined and as the service sector's share has grown.

Technique is the final key determinant of urban pollution levels. Technique refers to the emissions rates of different technologies used within the cities. Electric utilities are more likely to be located in counties with a larger population (Kahn 2009). Coal-fired power plants are major polluters. Many of these are located in the Midwest in states such as Ohio. Newer cohorts of electric utilities feature emissions factors (emissions per unit of power generation) that are 50 percent lower than older power plants (Burtraw and Evans 2003).

Vehicle emissions progress offers another example of the greening of urban technique. Cars cluster where people cluster, and the rise of private vehicle use contributed to rising levels of ambient smog in cities. Under the Clean Air Act, new vehicles only faced stringent emissions standards starting in the early 1970s. As vehicles built before 1975 have been scrapped, the average vehicle on the roads has become so much cleaner that many major cities, such as Los Angeles, have experienced significant smog progress, despite ongoing growth in population and miles driven (Kahn and Schwartz 2008). Between 1980 and 2000, Los Angeles county's population grew by 29 percent, while total automobile mileage grew by 70 percent. Yet, the number of days per year exceeding the federal one-hour ozone standard declined from about 150 days per year at the worst monitoring stations in this metropolitan area during the early 1980s down to twenty to thirty days per year today (Kahn and Schwartz 2008).

I now present some new estimates of the time trend in urban ambient pollution levels. Using county/year-level data, in table 11.3, I estimate five pollution-production regressions. I use the U.S. Environmental Protection Agency's Annual Summary Table Query database to examine the relationship between urban population size and ambient pollution levels between 1973 and 2000.[3] The sample includes counties in metropolitan areas that have at least one monitoring station operating. The estimation equation for county j in year t is:

$$\text{(3)}\quad \text{Log(Ambient Pollutant}_{jt}) = c + b_1 \times \log(\text{Population}_{jt}) + b_2 \times \log(\text{Population}_{jt}) \times \text{Region}_j + b_3 \times \text{Trend}_t + U_{jt}.$$

The time trend results document the overall progress. Ambient carbon monoxide has declined by 4.2 percent per year. Particulate matter has improved by over 2.1 percent per year, and ambient urban PM10 (particulate matter of ten microns or smaller in diameter) levels have fallen by 3.2 percent. I find no evidence supporting the claim that bigger cities have experienced a more differential time trend than smaller counties. For carbon monoxide, total suspended particulates (TSP), and smaller particulate matter (PM10), I find the largest county population-elasticity effects. The regressions indicate that the pollution/population elasticity is consistently largest in the Northeast relative to other regions.

11.6 Urban Crime Progress

Crime is a key urban disamenity. Big-city crime rates are higher than smaller cities (Glaeser and Sacerdote 1999), but crime has been declining in big cities since in the early 1990s. An empirical literature continues to debate

3. See U.S. Environmental Protection Agency, "Monitor Data Queries: Annual Summary Table Query," available at: www.epa.gov/aqspubl1/annual_summary.html.

Table 11.3 **Time trends in U.S. ambient pollution levels in metropolitan areas**

	Log(carbon monoxide)		Log(ozone)		Log(nitrogen oxide)		Log(TSP)		Log(PM10)	
	Beta	Standard error	Beta	Standard error	Beta	Standard error	Beta	Standard error	Beta	Standard error
Time trend	–0.0424	0.0007	0.0024	0.0003	–0.0206	0.0006	–0.0206	0.0004	–0.0315	0.0007
Log(county population)	0.2547	0.0152	–0.0138	0.0052	0.3272	0.0133	0.1142	0.0064	0.1245	0.0088
Log(county population) × Midwest dummy	–0.2072	0.0200	–0.0242	0.0067	–0.0623	0.0166	–0.0476	0.0082	–0.0681	0.0114
Log(county population) × South dummy	–0.1460	0.0192	–0.0128	0.0061	–0.1960	0.0152	–0.0928	0.0076	–0.1126	0.0103
Log(county population) × West dummy	–0.1684	0.0188	0.0330	0.0074	–0.0609	0.0171	0.0128	0.0086	–0.0049	0.0112
Constant	–0.8979	0.0815	4.0750	0.0274	0.2322	0.0630	3.4027	0.0318	3.0604	0.0456
Fixed effects	Region		Region		Region		Region		Region	
Observations	6,366		9,695		6,540		10,709		5,653	
R^2	0.4160		0.0630		0.3720		0.2770		0.3220	

Note: The unit of analysis is a county/year for counties that are part of a metropolitan statistical area. The dependent variable is the log of a specific ambient pollutant. The data are from the years 1973 to 2000. The omitted category is a county in the Northeast.

what role abortion, lead, crack cocaine, police hires, and incapacitation has played in explaining this trend (Levitt 2004; Reyes 2007).

In this section, I present new estimates of crime trend rates over the time period from 1994 to 2002 for counties located in metropolitan areas. I report results on the murder count and the violent crime count. The unit of analysis is county j in year t. I estimate equation (4):

$$(4)\quad \text{Crime Per-Capita}_{jt} = c + b_1 \times \log(\text{Pop}_{jt}) + b_2 \times \log(\text{Pop}_{jt}) \times \text{Region}_j + b_3 \times \text{trend}_t \times \log(\text{Pop}_{jt}) \times \text{Region}_j + U_{jt}.$$

The data source is the Federal Bureau of Investigation county crime database (http://fisher.lib.virginia.edu/collections/stats/crime/). The results reconfirm the well-known fact that per capita crime victimization is higher in more populated areas. In terms of quality of life in big cities, the good news is that this effect is sharply declining over time. The Northeast is the region with the steepest crime/population relationship.

The estimates reported in table 11.4 provide insights into big city/small city quality-of-life convergence. I use the OLS estimates reported in column (1) to conduct a difference-in-difference thought experiment. Consider two different counties that are located in a metropolitan area. The first has a population of 200,000, and the second has a population of 1 million. Based on the estimates reported in column (1) of table 11.4, between 1994 and 2002, the murder rate per 1,000 people between these two counties declined by 0.018 [$0.0148 \times \log(5) - (0.0148 - 0.0014 \times 8) \times \log(5)$]. Given the standard estimate of a \$6 million value of a statistical life, each person in the million-person county would be willing to pay \$108 for this reduction in risk, and family of four would be willing to pay \$432 in after-tax income for this reduction in risk. While sizable, this calculation reveals that even crime reductions by themselves cannot explain the large overall convergence in wages and divergence in home prices that Glaeser and Gottlieb (2006) document to have taken place over the last thirty years. In table 11.3, I documented significant negative time trends in urban air pollution. While households certainly value such reductions, the overall gains in big cities versus small cities in pollution are unlikely to exceed the total willingness to pay for the crime risk reduction.

11.7 Conclusion

Congestion, pollution, and crime represent three important factors that discourage urban agglomeration. Unlike other spatial amenities such as climate, these local public bads change over time, and this chapter has used a variety of data sets to examine their time trends in major cities in the United States. This chapter has used a production function approach to estimate how city size is associated with local public bads at different points in time and across U.S. regions.

Table 11.4 **Metropolitan-area crime trends from 1994 to 2002**

	Murders per 1,000 people				Violent crime per 1,000 people			
	Beta	Standard error	Beta	Standard error	Beta	Standard error	Beta	Standard error
Log(population)	0.0148	0.0029	0.0212	0.0039	0.4862	0.0582	0.8585	0.1365
Log(population) × Midwest			0.0070	0.0075			–0.2354	0.1564
Log(population) × South			–0.0057	0.0050			–0.5379	0.1468
Log(population) × West			–0.0045	0.0048			–0.1387	0.1966
Log(population) × time trend	–0.0014	0.0004	–0.0015	0.0004	–0.0280	0.0056	–0.0305	0.0056
Constant	–0.0614	0.0250	–0.1605	0.0417	–2.5825	0.5445	–7.3409	1.5321
Observations	6,338		6,338		6,338		6,338	
R^2	.043		.108		.097		.183	
Year fixed effects	Yes		Yes		Yes		Yes	
Region fixed effects	No		Yes		No		Yes	

Note: The sample includes all counties that are located in a metropolitan area. In columns (2) and (4), the omitted category is a county in the Northeast. Murders per 1,000 people has a mean and standard deviation of 0.047 and 0.071. Violent crimes per 1,000 people has a mean and standard deviation of 1.86 and 1.63.

Big cities have enjoyed sharp, recent reductions in ambient pollution and crime. This chapter has documented that the commute time/city-size relationship is small (an elasticity of 0.13) and stable over time.

This chapter's results complement a recently revealed preference literature that has used cross-city hedonic approaches to infer city quality of life (Glaeser and Gottlieb [2006] and Albouy [2008]). While I have documented crime and pollution progress, it is not clear whether these gains are large enough to fully explain the big-city quality-of-life progress documented by these other authors.

One possible reconciliation of these findings is that a social multiplier effect is at work. Consider New York City during the 1990s. As crime fell, the city made a sharp comeback. Street safety and rising incomes may work synergistically to encourage more upscale stores, restaurants, and nightlife to open. Put simply, market goods and city quality of life are complements in providing consumer utility. A hedonic approach that solely focuses on conducting a separable decomposition by teasing out each of these effects individually is likely to underestimate the overall impact of these factors on urban quality of life. The net effect of crime and pollution reductions is stronger cities. This reduction in the cost of "city bigness" means that cities can grow and enjoy the beneficial effects of agglomeration.

This study has focused solely on U.S. cities. In developing countries where government regulation may be ineffective, is the marginal social cost of megacity-size growth at a point in time much larger?

References

Albouy, D. 2008. Are big cities really bad places to live? Improving quality-of-life estimates across cities. NBER Working Paper no. 14472. Cambridge, MA: National Bureau of Economic Research, November.

Baum-Snow, N., and M. E. Kahn. 2005. Effects of urban rail transit expansions: Evidence from sixteen cities from 1970–2000. *Brookings-Wharton papers on urban affairs,* vol. 6, ed. G. Burtless and J. R. Pack, 147–206. Washington, DC: Brookings Institution Press.

Blomquist, G., M. Berger, and J. Hoen. 1988. New estimates of quality of life in urban areas. *American Economic Review* 78 (1): 89–107.

Burtraw, D., and D. Evans. 2003. The evolution of NOx control policy for coal-fired power plants in the United States. RFF Working Paper no. 03-23. Washington, DC: Resources for the Future.

Cutler, D. M., and G. Miller. 2004. The role of public health improvements in health advances: The 20th century United States. NBER Working Paper no. 10511. Cambridge, MA: National Bureau of Economic Research, May.

Glaeser, E. L. 1998. Are cities dying? *Journal of Economic Perspectives* 12 (2): 139–60.

Glaeser, E. L., and J. Gottlieb. 2006. Urban resurgence and the consumer city. *Urban Studies* 43 (8): 1275–99.

Glaeser, E., and M. E. Kahn. 2001. Decentralized employment and the transformation of the American city. In *Brookings-Wharton papers on urban affairs,* vol. 2, ed. W. G. Gale and J. R. Pack, 1–63. Washington, DC: Brookings Institution Press.

Glaeser, E., J. Kolko, and A. Saiz. 2001. Consumer city. *Journal of Economic Geography* 1 (1): 27–50.

Glaeser, E., and B. Sacerdote. 1999. Why is there more crime in cities? *Journal of Political Economy* 107 (S6): S225–S229.

Gyourko, J., and J. Tracy. 1991. The structure of local public finance and the quality of life. *Journal of Political Economy* 91 (4): 774–806.

Haines, M. 2001. The urban mortality transition in the United States, 1800–1940. NBER Historical Working Paper no. 134. Cambridge, MA: National Bureau of Economic Research, July.

Kahn, M. E. 1999. The silver lining of Rust Belt manufacturing decline. *Journal of Urban Economics* 46 (3): 360–76.

———. 2009. Regional growth and exposure to nearby coal fired power plant emissions. *Regional Science and Urban Economics* 39 (1): 15–22.

Kahn, M. E., and J. Schwartz. 2008. Urban air pollution progress despite sprawl: The "greening" of the vehicle fleet. *Journal of Urban Economics* 63 (3): 775–87.

Levitt, S. D. 2004. Understanding why crime fell in the 1990s: Four factors that explain the decline and six that do not. *Journal of Economic Perspectives* 18 (1): 163–90.

Melosi, M. V. 2000. *The sanitary city: Urban infrastructure in America from colonial times to the present.* Baltimore: Johns Hopkins University Press.

Reyes, J. W. 2007. Environmental policy as social policy? The impact of childhood lead exposure on crime. *B. E. Journal of Economic Analysis and Policy* 7 (1): 1796.

Tolley, G. S. 1974. The welfare economics of city bigness. *Journal of Urban Economics* 1 (3): 324–45.

Waldfogel, J. 2008. The median voter and the median consumer: Local *private* goods and population composition. *Journal of Urban Economics* 63 (2): 567–82.

Contributors

Katherine Baicker
Department of Health Policy and Management
Harvard School of Public Health
677 Huntington Avenue
Kresge, Fourth floor
Boston, MA 02115

Amitabh Chandra
John F. Kennedy School of Government
Harvard University
Mailbox 104
79 JFK Street
Cambridge, MA 02138

Pierre-Philippe Combes
Groupement de Recherche en Economie Quantitative d'Aix Marseille (GREQAM)
2 Rue de la Charité
13236 Marseille cedex 02 France

Gilles Duranton
Department of Economics
University of Toronto
150 Saint George Street
Toronto, Ontario M5S 3G7 Canada

Edward L. Glaeser
Department of Economics
Littauer Center 315A
Harvard University
Cambridge, MA 02138

Laurent Gobillon
Institut National d'Études Démographiques
133 Boulevard Davout
75980 Paris cedex 20 France

Joseph Gyourko
Wharton School
University of Pennsylvania
1480 Steinberg Hall-Dietrich Hall
3620 Locust Walk
Philadelphia, PA 19104-6302

Thomas J. Holmes
Department of Economics
University of Minnesota
4-101 Hanson Hall
1925 Fourth Street South
Minneapolis, MN 55455

Matthew E. Kahn
Institute of the Environment
La Kretz Hall, Suite 300
University of California, Los Angeles
619 Charles E. Young Drive, East
Los Angeles, CA 90095

William R. Kerr
Entrepreneurial Management Unit
Harvard Business School
Soldiers Field Road
Boston, MA 02163

Jed Kolko
Public Policy Institute of California
500 Washington Street, Suite 600
San Francisco, CA 94111

Sanghoon Lee
Sauder School of Business
University of British Columbia
2053 Main Mall
Vancouver, British Columbia V6T 1Z2 Canada

Christopher Mayer
Graduate School of Business
Columbia University
Uris Hall 808
3022 Broadway
New York, NY 10027

Henry G. Overman
Department of Geography and Environment
London School of Economics
Houghton Street
London WC2A 2AE United Kingdom

Giacomo A. M. Ponzetto
Centre de Recerca en Economia Internacional
Universitat Pompeu Fabra
Carrer de Ramon Trias Fargas, 25–27
08005 Barcelona, Spain

Diego Puga
Madrid Institute for Advanced Studies (IMDEA) Social Sciences
Isaac Newton 2, 1ª planta
28760 Tres Cantos (Madrid)
Spain

Stuart S. Rosenthal
Department of Economics and Center for Policy Research
426 Eggers Hall
Syracuse University
Syracuse, NY 13244-1020

Sébastien Roux
Centre de Recherche en Économie et Statistique (CREST)
15 Boulevard Gabriel Péri
92245 Malakoff cedex France

Todd Sinai
Wharton School
University of Pennsylvania
1465 Steinberg Hall-Dietrich Hall
3620 Locust Walk
Philadelphia, PA 19104-6302

William C. Strange
Rotman School of Management
University of Toronto
105 Saint George Street
Toronto, Ontario M5S 3E6 Canada

Joel Waldfogel
Public Policy and Management
Wharton School
1403 Steinberg Hall-Dietrich Hall
University of Pennsylvania
Philadelphia, PA 19104-6372

Author Index

Subject Index

Page numbers followed by "f" *or* "t" *refer to figures or tables, respectively.*

Printed and bound by CPI Group (UK) Ltd, Croydon, CR0 4YY

23/04/2025

14661003-0003